MOBILE CITIZENS

NIAS – Nordic Institute of Asian Studies
New and recent Monographs

109. Anders Poulsen: *Childbirth and Tradition in Northeast Thailand*
110. R. A. Cramb: *Land and Longhouse*
111. Deborah Sutton: *Other Landscapes*
112. Søren Ivarsson: *Creating Laos*
113. Johan Fischer: *Proper Islamic Consumption*
114. Sean Turnell: *Fiery Dragons*
115. Are Knudsen: *Violence and Belonging*
116. Noboru Ishikawa: *Between Frontiers*
117. Jan Ovesen and Ing-Britt Trankell: *Cambodians and Their Doctors*
118. Kirsten Endres: *Performing the Divine*
119. Gerhard Hoffstaedter: *Modern Muslim Identities*
120. Malcolm McKinnon: *Asian Cities*
121. David I. Steinberg and Hongwei Fan: *Modern China–Myanmar Relations*
122. Vibeke Børdahl: *Wu Song Fights the Tiger*
123. Hiromi Sasamoto-Collins: *Power and Dissent in Imperial Japan*
124. Eren Zink: *Hot Science, High Water*
125. Monica Janowski: *Tuked Rini, Cosmic Traveller*
126. Martin Platt: *Isan Writers, Thai Literature*
127. John Becker: *Pattern and Loom*
128. Ziayan Zhang: *Coping with Calamity*
129. Natasha Pairaudeau: *Mobile Citizens*
130. Halfdan Siiger: *The Bodo of Assam*
131. Andrew Cock: *Governing Cambodia's Forests*
132. John Coast: *Recruit to Revolution*
133. Souchou Yao: *The Malayan Emergency*
134. Megha Amrith: *Caring for Strangers*
135. Sophorntavy Vorng: *A Meeting of Masks*

NIAS Press is the autonomous publishing arm of NIAS – Nordic Institute of Asian Studies, a research institute located at the University of Copenhagen. NIAS is partially funded by the governments of Denmark, Finland, Iceland, Norway and Sweden via the Nordic Council of Ministers, and works to encourage and support Asian studies in the Nordic countries. In so doing, NIAS has been publishing books since 1969, with more than two hundred titles produced in the past few years.

UNIVERSITY OF COPENHAGEN

Nordic Council of Ministers

MOBILE CITIZENS

French Indians in Indochina, 1858–1954

NATASHA PAIRAUDEAU

Mobile Citizens: French Indians in Indochina, 1858–1954
by Natasha Pairaudeau
Nordic Institute of Asian Studies
Monograph series, no. 129

First published in 2016 by NIAS Press
NIAS – Nordic Institute of Asian Studies
Øster Farimagsgade 5, 1353 Copenhagen K, Denmark
Tel: +45 3532 9501 • Fax: +45 3532 9549
E-mail: books@nias.ku.dk • Online: www.niaspress.dk

© Natasha Pairaudeau 2016

A CIP catalogue record for this book is available from the British Library

ISBN: 978-87-7694-158-1 (hbk)
ISBN: 978-87-7694-159-8 (pbk)

Typeset in Arno Pro 12/14.4
Typesetting by Lene Jakobsen

Printed and bound in Great Britain
by Marston Book Services Limited, Oxfordshire

Cover illustration: 'Types of the Far East: Annamite, Chinese and Malabar', early 19th century postcard, Mottet and Company, Saigon.

CONTENTS

Acknowledgements	*vii*
Note on Terms and Spellings	*xii*
Acronyms and Abbreviations	*xiv*
Glossary	*xvi*
Maps	*xviii*
1. Introduction	1
2. Shaping legal status in India and Indochina	34
3. At work in Indochina: Indian French citizens and Tamil spheres of activity	71
4. The Indian vote in Cochinchina	119
5. Colonial citizenship and contractual privileges	153
6. Vietnamese engagement with Indian migrants	191
7. Raising the Indian public profile	231
8. Diasporic dilemmas	273
Afterword	322
Appendix: Text of the 'Decree relative to personal status', 21 September 1881	335
Bibliography	338
Index	353

Maps

1. The French Establishments in India	xviii
2. Pondicherry and Environs, circa 1870	xix
3. French Indochina	xx

Plates

1. Plaque outside Pounnoutamby Laporte's Pondicherry villa	44
2. An Indian functionary and his family, Hanoi circa 1920	81
3. Indian magistrate and his wife in Cochinchina, 1925	87
4. Tamil Muslim merchants in Cochinchina	89
5. Map of Central Saigon, 1928	93
6. 'Chetty types', Saigon	95
7. Tamil carters, Cochinchina	100
8. Tamil milkman admonished by a Vietnamese servant	102
9. Tamil sesame press, Cochinchina	112
10. Public bill printed in Saigon by 'a group of Indian voters'	135
11. Voting card of an Indian, Virassamipoullé, Cochinchina legislative election 1888	135
12. The 'Villa Ernest Outrey', Pondicherry	151
13. Recipients of the 'Bronze Medal for Mutuality', Symphorien Lami and Lourdes Nadin	237
14. Advertisement for the Indian supplier 'Au Comptoir Hindou'	243
15. Announcement of a Tamil film screening in Saigon	244
16. Monsieur Appapoulé, banker, promoting the 1933 'Clothing Crusade'	267
17. Hanoi's Indian community posed with Nehru, August 1939	274
18. Vietnamese army parading through Hanoi following their victory at Dien Bien Phu	310

Tables

1. Population in Cochinchina of residents of Indian origin, 1888–1936	53
2. Population and distribution of South Indian Muslims in Cochinchina, 1926	90

ACKNOWLEDGEMENTS

I am very grateful for the financial assistance I received that allowed me to undertake the doctoral research upon which this book is based. This includes a Doctoral Fellowship from the Social Sciences and Humanities Research Council of Canada (2003–2007), and awards from the UK Overseas Research Students Scheme, the University of London's Central Research Fund, and the School of Oriental and African Studies (SOAS) Fieldwork Awards. William Gervase Clarence-Smith supervised this research from my arrival at SOAS to undertake a research degree through to its completion. I am indebted as much for his calculated silences as I struggled at the outset with the numerous directions the thesis could have taken, as I am for the depth of his knowledge and his infectious interest in the fine but nevertheless consequential details of history. Not least, he was as supportive and patient a supervisor as anyone could hope for, and I am deeply appreciative of this.

Had I not met Dr. Susan Bayly in Hanoi in 1997 I may never have undertaken this project. I am grateful to her for encouraging me to develop the bundle of notes I then held into an extended piece of research. I am equally grateful for the many fruitful conversations we have had since then, and especially for her invaluable help in navigating through the Indian scholarship.

Just as my aim has been to understand social and political relationships developed over long distances, so these relationships have been pieced together from sources in numerous localities, emphasising the geographic discontinuity in the lives of Indochina-connected Indians which continues up to the present day. I am indebted to the staff of archives and libraries in five countries for assisting me to access their holdings. In Vietnam these include the Vietnamese National Archives Number Two (*Trung Tâm Lưu Trữ Quốc Gia II*) in Ho Chi Minh City, where former Director Dr. Phan Đình Nham offered astute words of advice at the very outset. At the General Sciences Library, Ho Chi Minh City (*Thư Viện Khoa Học Tổng Hợp*) I am indebted in particular to Ms.

Lê Thị Thanh Thuý (former Deputy Head of Professional Research and Guidance) both for her friendship and for facilitating my work there. I also thank staff at the National Archive Number One in Hanoi (*Trung Tâm Lưu Trữ Quốc Gia I*), at the newspapers section of the Hanoi National Library (*Thư Viện Quốc Gia Việt Nam*), and at the Hanoi Institute of Social Sciences Library (*Thư Viện Khoa Học Xã Hội*). At the French colonial archives at Aix-en-Provence (*Archives nationales d'outre mer*), Mme. Lucette Vachier's intimate knowledge of the Indochinese papers and her keen interest in the Indian question were invaluable. In Paris, members of staff at the archives of the French Foreign Ministry (*Archives du Ministère des Affaires Etrangères*), the French National Archives (*Centre d'accueil et de recherche des Archives nationales*), at the *Documentation Française* library, at the library of the *Institut National des Langues et Civilisations Orientales* (INALCO), and at the archive of the League of Human Rights at Nanterre (*Ligue des Droits de l'Homme*) all deserve my sincere thanks. In Pondicherry, my research relied on the National Archives of India Record Centre and libraries at the *Institut Français* and the *École Française d'Extrême Orient*. I am grateful for the access gained to all three of these institutions and in particular to guidance from Dominic Goodhall at the EFEO. Elsewhere, the National Archives of Cambodia, Phnom Penh, the India Office Library within the British Library in London and the British National Archives at Kew all proved very amiable places to work, and each revealed unanticipated holdings.

Many scholars and other individuals have helped me, in ways both large and small, to carry out this research. I would like to thank Dr. Tôn Nữ Quỳnh Trân, of the Centre for Urbanisation and Development (*Trung Tâm Nghiên Cứu Đô Thị và Phát Triển*) for her long-standing friendship and for her help in organising my research in Ho Chi Minh City; Dr. Nguyễn Mạnh Hùng, president of Hồng Bàng University, also in Ho Chi Minh City, for sponsoring my research stay there; and Professor Trịnh Văn Thảo, formerly of the Department of Sociology, Université de Provence, Aix-Marseille, for his early support for the idea.

Numerous people aided me, too, with valuable leads either to relevant sources of documentation, individuals to interview, hidden sites of overseas Indian interest, or engaging anecdotes. Philippe Peycam was an early champion of this cause and I have him to thank for several contacts who proved crucial to this study. It was not until I reached Pondicherry that I understood how far Yann Martel had pedalled on my behalf, and I now have the chance to fulsomely thank him for it. Christopher Goscha's invitation to speak at the EHESS seminar in Paris helped to take my work forward, and I am deeply appreciative of his continued support. Brij V. Lal, Peter Reeves, and Rajesh Rai gave me the opportunity to contribute to the *Encyclopedia of the Indian Diaspora* and thereby think through the thesis at a crucial stage. I am grateful to Vasoodevan Vuddamalay for his keen interest in my research, and to the editors at *Hommes et Migrations* for a similar opportunity to think things through. Both Professor Nguyễn Đình Đầu in Ho Chi Minh City and the late Professor Đào Hùng in Hanoi were supportive and generous in sharing their knowledge and reminiscences about the Indian presence. Ann Marie Leshkowitz generously shared her knowledge of the comings-and-goings at Saigon's Mariamman temple with me. A number of scholars who participate in the on-line Vietnamese Studies Group (VSG) offered me valuable leads; I have thanked them individually within the text but will mention here Tài Văn Tạ who very kindly arranged for me to meet the Indian side of his family, and was generous with his time and his own insights. I presented an earlier version of Chapter Six to the Berkeley Graduate Student Conference in 2007, and a re-working of that chapter later appeared in the *Journal of Vietnamese Studies*. I am grateful to Peter Zinoman for his clear-headed comments on that paper, as well as the equally helpful observations of Nguyễn Nguyệt Cầm. I would also like to acknowledge Frederick Cooper for his careful reading and insightful remarks on the framing chapters of the manuscript.

A special word of thanks is due to the community of *bon viveurs* who constituted the *Câu Lạc Bộ* (*CLB* or 'club') of Yên Phụ village. The CLB was both a source of great fun and of serious scholarly insight during the years I lived in Hanoi. My greatest debt is owed to the late Professor Đặng Phong at whose table I learned much about Vietnam, its history and its people. Professor Phong aided my research by directing me to several Indian sites in Hanoi, through his generous introductions to numerous Vietnamese and Indo-Vietnamese with memories of the Indian presence, and with his own characteristically irreverent reminiscences. I also enjoyed, over the years, the friendship and support of several other CLB members, both *à table* and during the CLB's many expeditions to places near and far. They include the late Melanie Beresford, Đào Thị Kim Lan, Lê Thị

Mai, the late Lê Xuân Tú, and Kirsten Endres. I thank Andrew Hardy, too, especially for sesame presses and pigs' ears. Other friends and scholars who have assisted this project in diverse ways include Nguyễn Thị Nguyệt Minh, Dương Bích Hạnh, Vũ Hồng Liên, Julie Phạm, Claire Burkert, Drew Smith, Meagan Enticknap, Barley Norton, Pascal Bourdeaux, and François Tainturier. Ravi Kumar of the Tandoor Restaurant, Hanoi and HCMC, gave me advice and assistance for which I am greatly appreciative. I offer my sincerest thanks to Nguyễn Tạo Ngô, for his decoding of southern Vietnamese slang, for his lengthy transcription and for keeping my growing family in shoes. Erich DeWald kept his eyes peeled for me during his own stay in the archives and libraries. I am grateful to him for several documents he unearthed on my behalf, for lakeside coffees and for his help in bridging the distance between Hanoi and the SOAS examinations office.

My greatest debt is reserved for the many Indians and Indo-Vietnamese who gave generously of their time to recount for me their family histories and their own memories of life in pre- as well as post-colonial Vietnam. Their own thinking and reflections on the Indian presence have been invaluable, whether or not they are respected scholars in their own right (as several of them are). My experience would have been less rich, and far less enjoyable, without their input. I trust I have done credit to the histories they have recounted, and that they might also find new discoveries and new connections here. Any errors of fact are entirely my own, while on points of interpretation I can only hope this work will provide plentiful avenues for further discussion and debate.

I am lucky to have met Dr. Joseph Antoine in Saigon in 1996, while he was in search of the childhood tree house his father had built in the garden of the family villa. His story intrigued me and got me started. In this early period Bà Alam also generously traced for me the contours of Indian (and particularly Muslim) Saigon, past and present. In Saigon, Kemal Nguyễn kindly recounted his family's fascinating and complex history. There are other Vietnam-based Indians whom I will not name but to whom I am very grateful for the time they spent to relate their experiences to me.

In India and Paris I am indebted to more people than I can mention here who described their connections to Indochina with enthusiasm, patience and good humour. I am no less appreciative for not being able to name each of these individuals personally, but there are a few people to whom I owe a special thanks. They include Claude Marius and his wife

ACKNOWLEDGEMENTS

Rita for many engaging conversations and for their hospitality; Maurice Sinnas and his family for their generous welcome and all of their help; and JBP More for gripping stories and many email exchanges since. The story Pichaya Manet recounted for me at his guesthouse in 2002 first convinced me of the great scope that lay in re-connecting Pondicherry to Saigon; I thank him too for his friendship and his infectious enthusiasm. Mrs. Amélie Marius Le Prince was particularly generous with her time and her memories, and was great company over two long rainy Pondicherry afternoons. I was fortunate to meet Meenakshi Meyyappan who shared her deep knowledge of the Chettiar presence in Indochina. She and her brother, journalist S. Muthiah were generous with their help in arranging interviews in Tiruchirrapalli (Trichinopoly) and Chettinad. I am grateful to the late Atmenadene Michel Audemar and his mother, Bà Saú, for extending their welcome in Paris, Pondicherry and Saigon. Among the ongoing 'translocal' friendships I have formed in the course of this research, Michel Audemar's as well as that of Tony Bui deserve a special mention. I owe thanks too to Abdoul Gaffour and to the Said family who graciously welcomed me during my stay in Pondicherry, and to Douglas Gressieux of the Paris-based association *Les Comptoirs de l'Inde*.

I am immensely grateful for a Newton Postdoctoral Fellowship awarded through the Cambridge Centre for History and Economics and the Cambridge Faculty of History (2012–14), which enabled me to revise this manuscript for publication. At the Centre I owe thanks in particular to Tim Harper, Sunil Amrith and Inga Huld Markan for their encouragement and support. I would like to acknowledge financial assistance provided by the same centre to prepare the maps for this book. These maps were drawn by Philip Stickler at the Cartographic Unit of the Cambridge University Department of Geography, whom I thank for his careful and patient work. Finally, many thanks to Gerald Jackson at NIAS Press for his guidance, patience and good cheer, and to the three anonymous readers at NIAS whose careful reviews were vital to the final revision of this manuscript.

My parents guided this project more than they realise, by their own unflagging interest in the wider world and its unexpected connections. My sister too deserves a word of thanks. William Smith has been endlessly supportive as husband and informal research assistant. Our two children have made the journey much longer than it should have been, but have always been willing to come along for the ride.

NOTE ON TERMS AND SPELLINGS

Nearly every term available to describe the group of people to whom this book refers is problematic in one way or another. I refer to the central subjects of this study at different points in their history as 'renouncers' (a term pointing to the means by which they obtained their citizenship), 'Indian French citizens', the 'French of India', 'Franco-Indians', 'Franco-Pondicherrians', or 'Pondicherrians'. I tend to use 'renouncers' when referring to them in the period when their citizenship was still contested, and 'Indian French Citizens' once their legal status was more firmly established. The term *Français de l'Inde* or the 'French of India' was already in use in Indochina from the late nineteenth century, but became more standard in the interwar years when the interests of renouncers (Indians claiming French citizenship) and Indo-Europeans (those of mixed Indian and European heritage) began to converge. By then, *'Français de l'Inde'* sometimes referred strictly to those Indians with French nationality, but usually indicated a broader category which included both renouncers and the small number of Indo-Europeans residing in Indochina. When France made changes to its citizenship laws in its overseas territories shortly after the Second World War, and again in the process of decolonisation, the term 'Pondicherrian' or 'Franco-Pondicherrian' came to signify those Indians who had become French citizens either through their own acts of 'renunciation' or earlier acts of 'renunciation' on the part of their ancestors.

The French word *hindou* (or *indou*), as the English *Hindu*, referred until the mid-twentieth century to a quasi-national group rather than followers of the Hindu religion. To add to the confusion, the French often called the Hindu religion '*brahmanism*'. I have marked these antiquated usages in italics.

The term 'Malabar' is found in some citations from French in this text, and I have kept this term in translation. 'Malabars' meant Indians in colonial Indochina, but just which Indians is not always clear. Population figures in some early colonial yearbooks include two separate catego-

NOTE ON TERMS AND SPELLINGS

ries, 'Malabars' and 'Indians'.[1] Some commentators used the misnomer strictly for people of ethnic Tamil origin (similar to its misappropriation in the French possessions of the Indian Ocean), while for others it referred to overseas Indians more generally.[2] Vietnamese terms for Indians (*Chà Và, Bảy, Tây đen*) are explained within the text.

For Vietnamese place names and proper names, English-language spellings are used when these are well-known and standardised in English. I use the Vietnamese spelling, including diacritical marks, for terms in Vietnamese, and where proper names or place names are less well-known in English. The term itself, 'Vietnamese', is employed here as an adjective, to refer to the language, and with reference to the ethnic majority within the modern state of Vietnam. Another term, *Annamite*, was widely used in French colonial documents to describe the ethnic Vietnamese. I have retained *Annamite* where it appeared in discussions of the time, but its use is now considered derogatory.

Indian place names have undergone reform in recent years. Although Chennai (formerly Madras) has become commonplace, Puducheri (for Pondicherry) may not be familiar to most readers. For that reason, I have kept the more familiar English forms, which were also in use during the period under study. I have included modern transliterations for some Tamil terms but have not done the same for proper names in Tamil. This is in the interest of retaining the sense of transformation brought about both by renunciation of personal status and by migration to foreign territory. Indians often translated their names to French when they 'renounced' (for example 'Pushpanadin' became 'De la Flore'), or chose French transliterations of their Tamil names ('Prouchandy' for 'Purushanti'). In official documents some Indian names appear in their Vietnamese transcription: thus Yakum Sahib went by the name of Yaccoumsah in local circles in Cantho. I have kept the spelling of all names as they were presented in the original documents. All foreign language terms are written in italics.

---

1. *Annuaire de la Cochinchine Française* [hereafter ACCH] *pour l'année 1867*, Saigon: Imprimerie Impériale, pp. 50–51.
2. See Hugh Tinker, 'Between Africa, Asia and Europe: Mauritius: Cultural Marginalism and Political Control', *African Affairs*, 76, 304, 1977, 321–337, p. 324; Marina Carter, 'Mauritius' and 'The Mascarenes, Seychelles and Chagos Islands', in *Encyclopedia of the Indian Diaspora*, pp. 264, 273.

ACRONYMS AND ABBREVIATIONS

ACCH	*Annuaire de la Cochinchine Française*
AF	*Anciens fonds*
AGI	*Annuaire Générale de l'Indochine*
AMAE	*Archives du Ministère des Affaires Etrangères (Paris)*
ANOM	*Archives Nationales d'Outre Mer* (Aix-en-Provence, France)
BL	British Library (London)
CARAN	*Le Centre d'accueil et de recherche des Archives nationales* (Paris)
CP	*Conseil Privé*
DM	*Dépêches Ministérielles* (Ministerial Despatches)
EFEO	*École Française d'Extrême Orient*
EFI	*Établissements français dans l'Inde*
Eng.	English
FO	Foreign Office Records
Fr.	French
Goucoch	Governor of Cochinchina
GD	*Goucoch divers*
GCCH	*Gouverneur de la Cochinchine*
GGI	*Gouvernement Général de l'Indochine*
GEFI	*Gouverneur des Établissements français dans l'Inde*
IOR	India Office Records

ACRONYMS AND ABBREVIATIONS

JOEFI	*Journal Officiel des Établissements Français dans l'Inde*
LTTV	*Lục Tỉnh Tân Văn*
MOEFI	*Moniteur Officiel des Établissements Français dans l'Inde*
MMC	*Ministère de la Marine et des Colonies*
NAC	National Archives of Cambodia
NAIP	National Archives of India Record Centre, Pondicherry
NF	*Nouveau fonds*
RST	*Résidence Supérieure du Tonkin*
SLOTFOM	*Fonds du Service de liaison des originaires des territoires français d'outre mer*
Tm.	Tamil
TNA	The National Archives (British National Archives, London)
Vn.	Vietnamese
VNA1	Vietnamese National Archives Number One (*Lưu Trữ Quốc Gia I*) Hanoi
VNA2	Vietnamese National Archives Number Two (*Lưu Trữ Quốc Gia II*), Ho Chi Minh City
WO	War Office Records

GLOSSARY

Annamite	(Fr.) ethnic Vietnamese (colonial usage)
Bảy	(Vn.) literally 'seven'; person of Indian origin, especially Muslim
chattiram	(Tm.) dormitory, guesthouse
Chà Và	(Vn.) literally 'Java'; originally Javanese trader in Cochinchina; later came to include Indians, Malays, Bawean, and any darker-skinned Asian migrant to Cochinchina
Chệc (Chệt)	(Vn.) derogatory term for overseas Chinese (literally 'chink')
Chetty (Chetti)	person of the Nattukottai Chettiar banking caste; more generally, as used in Indochina, any Indian or any moneylender
congaie	(Fr.) from Vietnamese *con gái* ('girl' or 'daughter'); native concubine
hindou (indou)	(Fr.) person from the Indian subcontinent
indigène	(Fr.) 'native'; an original inhabitant of a country or territory, usually as regarded by European colonists
Khmer	ethnic Cambodian
kitangi	(Tm.) Nattukottai Chettiar bank office, also serving as a place of residence for the bankers
Malabar	(Fr.) (as used in Indochina), Tamil or Indian
pariah	(Fr.) title of person of 'impure' or 'unclean' status in Hindu social order (nineteenth-century usage)

GLOSSARY

quốc ngữ	(Vn.) romanised Vietnamese script
Tây đen	(Vn.) literally 'Black Westerner'; Indian or other dark-skinned colonial intermediary
Vellala	(Eng.) (Tm. veḷḷālar, *vellaja* in French sources) high-status Tamil caste title (traditionally agriculturalists, landowners)
Viet Minh	(Vn.) *Việt Nam Độc Lập Đồng Minh Hội*, 'League for the Independence of Vietnam'; communist-led national coalition for independence, formed by Ho Chi Minh in 1941

Map 1: The French Establishments in India

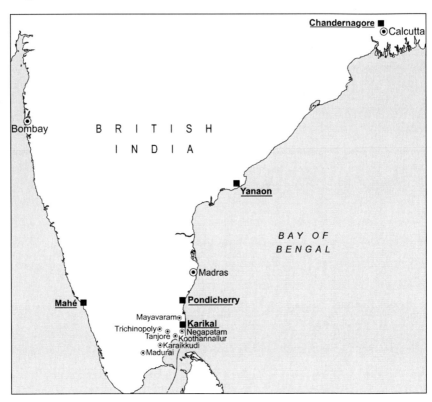

Source: Based on Government of India, *The Imperial Gazetteer of India, Volume XXVI, Atlas*, Oxford: Clarendon Press, 1931, p. 21.

Map 2: Pondicherry and Environs, circa 1870

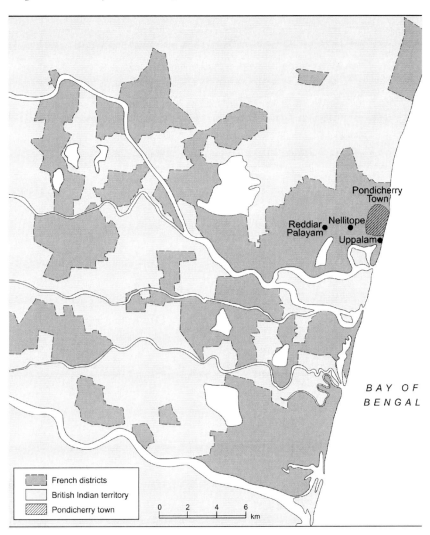

Source: French National Library, 'Carte du territoire de Pondichéry', signed by colonial engineer C. Carriol, 10 December 1871.

Map 3: French Indochina

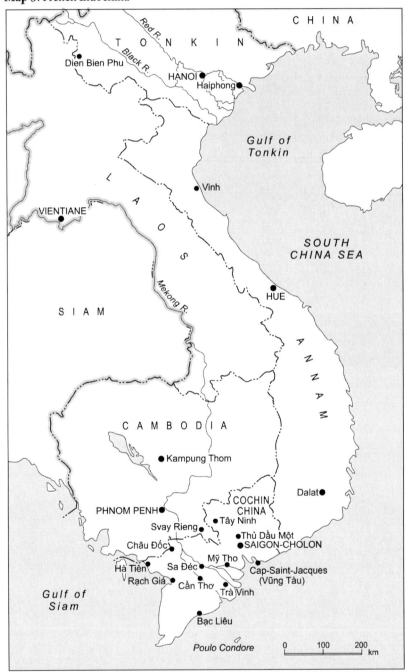

Source: Derived from 'India East, including Burma, Siam and French Indo-China', in *The Century Atlas of the World*, The Century Company: New York, 1913, p. 38.

CHAPTER ONE

INTRODUCTION

By the latter half of the nineteenth century, France's struggle with Britain for supremacy in India was long lost, and its dream of an expansive French Empire in the sub-continent had collapsed. It was left with little more than a handful of coastal trading posts or *comptoirs*. The 'French possessions', or as they were formally known the 'French Establishments in India' comprised Pondicherry, Karikal, Chandernagore, Yanaon and Mahé. They were tiny, had little internal coherence, and were separated from one another by great expanses of territory under British control.[1] The largest of them, and French India's administrative seat, was Pondicherry. Covering an area of less than three hundred square kilometres, with a population of 150,000 in 1880, it comprised twelve isolated tracts of land which could be reached only by passing through British territory. Karikal was the only other French possession with substantial ties to Pondicherry; its Tamil inhabitants shared a language, ethnicity and culture with its sister port to the north. It nonetheless lay a full 130 kilometres down the Coromandel Coast and was even smaller. Its population (92,000 in 1880) occupied a total area of only 160 square kilometres. Like Pondicherry, Karikal was made up of fragmented tracts of land.[2]

These conditions limited the development of the French *comptoirs*. They frustrated the growth of an official economy based primarily on the production and export of indigo and cotton. The real economy relied heavily on smuggling across the *comptoirs'* porous borders.[3] Agreements

---

1. French India also included twelve subsidiary trading posts, the main ones being Masulipatam, Kozhikode, and Surat. French sovereignty over these 'lodges' or *loges* remained ambiguous. William F. S. Miles, *Imperial Burdens: Countercolonialism in Former French India*, Boulder: Lynne Rienner, 1994, p. 3.
2. The total area of the other three possessions was a mere forty-seven square kilometres. Statistics are from Raymond Delval, *Musulmans français d'origine indienne*, Paris: Centre des Hautes Etudes sur l'Afrique et l'Asie Modernes, 1987, p. 141, and Miles, *Imperial Burdens*, p. 5.
3. Robert Aldrich, *Greater France: A History of French Overseas Expansion*, Basingstoke: Palgrave, 1996, p. 23.

with Britain which forbade the construction of military fortifications in French India and severely limited the number of troops that France could retain on its soil in India further restricted the utility of these sites to France.[4]

Within their restricted and discontiguous boundaries though, Pondicherry and Karikal both held growing populations whose ideas, ambitions and abilities were nurtured by two centuries of French influence. Among them were traders and service people whose forebears' had interacted, as interpreters and intermediaries, with men of the French East India Company. In the late nineteenth century, when education at Pondicherry's French *lycée* became accessible to them, a generation of Francophone and Francophile graduates emerged from this group. They were keen to advance within the French colonial system, but the limits of French India circumscribed their opportunities.

France's imperial ambitions further east however, soon began to give new purpose to its 'lost empire' in India. New opportunities arose for this constrained, French-educated elite, but also for men of more humble stock. French ships embarked from Pondicherry to launch attacks against the Nguyễn dynasty at Danang and Saigon (1858 and 1859). These ventures were financed by Pondicherry-based merchants. The seizure of Saigon was France's first claim on the territories it would gradually accrue and bring together as 'French Indochina'. When French troop ships sailed from Pondicherry, Indians joined them aboard their ships. Drawn from both the upper and lower levels of French Indian society, they included literate *magasiniers* (storemen managing military supplies) and men from further down the social scale who served as soldiers in the French conquest, or as carters and cattle herders providing transport and fresh milk to French troops.[5] In 1868, when France established the colony of Cochinchina in the southern part of the Nguyễn rulers' beleaguered kingdom of Đại Nam, the newly appointed

---

4. As stipulated in the (second) Treaty of Paris, signed with Britain in 1815. Arthur Annasse, *Les comptoirs français dans l'Inde (Trois siècles de présence française)*, Paris: La Pensée Universelle, 1975, pp. 107–108; Miles, *Imperial Burdens*, p. 5.

5. Claude Marius, 'Les Pondichériens dans l'administration coloniale de l'Indochine', in J. Weber (ed.), *Les relations entre la France et l'Inde de 1673 à nos jours*, Paris: Les Indes Savantes, 2002, 391–398, 392; Vietnamese National Archive Number Two (hereafter VNA2) IA.12/149(11) Tân An demande de dégrèvement d'impôt demandé par le sieur Mamoucani (Indien) 1902; *ACCH pour l'année 1865*, Saigon: Imprimerie Impériale, p. 68.

INTRODUCTION

French Lieutenant General in Saigon requested 'young recruits from Pondicherry' to serve as writers in the fledgling administration.[6]

Cochinchina was vast in comparison to France's modest patchwork of territories in India. Once the French had completed their conquest of its several provinces, it covered an area of 60,000 square kilometres. In 1884 the colony's population was 1.6 million. By the start of the twentieth century, France had extended its influence in the region much further. The political entity it created, 'French Indochina', included the colony of Cochinchina as well as four protectorates. Cambodia and Laos were created by incorporating the neighbouring kingdoms to the west. Annam and Tonkin both came into existence as France claimed first the central, and later the northern regions of the former Nguyễn polity. Hanoi, in Tonkin, served as the capital of French Indochina.[7]

The first Indian recruits called to serve in the early French administration came to Cochinchina's capital, Saigon. Cochinchina maintained a more extensive administration than the protectorates, due to its status as a colony; it was also the centre of French commercial interests in Indochina. Thus French Indians who followed seeking opportunities in France's expanding empire continued to be drawn to Cochinchina for the jobs on offer there both in the public service and with private French interests. They lived in Saigon, in its ethnic Chinese 'sister' city Cholon, and in the towns of the Mekong Delta.[8] There were small but significant communities of like-minded French Indians in Cambodia and Tonkin. They resided in Phnom Penh, in Hanoi (the centre of government for the Indochinese Union as a whole), and in the port city of Haiphong. In Laos and Annam their numbers were negligible. With frequent transfers within Indochina and the presence of relatives and friends elsewhere on the peninsula, a web of connections was created, linking together Indochina's urban nodes with Saigon at their centre. Thus while Saigon and Cochinchina were the central foci of this group of French Indians, their lives and experiences reached into other regions of French Indochina. Yet as most members of their community resided

---

6. Archives Nationales d'Outre Mer (hereafter ANOM), GGI 10410 Personnel recruté aux Indes françaises 1868: GEFI to Lt-GGCCH, 6 May 1868 and 5 October 1868.
7. A. Bouinais and A. Paulus, *Indo-Chine française contemporaine*, Paris: Challamel Aîné, 1885, pp. 32, 224.
8. Saigon and Cholon were together renamed Ho Chi Minh City following the victory of communist forces in South Vietnam in 1975.

in Cochinchina they engaged more with the Vietnamese, and to a lesser extent with the Khmer and Cham populations of the Mekong Delta, than they did with the other peoples of Indochina.

According to one estimate, there were close to 3,000 persons residing in all of French Indochina who originated from French India on the eve of the Second World War. Among them were approximately 2,000 Indians who were legally recognised by that time as French citizens.[9] They had become citizens through 'renunciation'; I shall return to this process and its meaning shortly. This small community of citizens is the main subject of this book. It was made up of people who were mostly, but not exclusively, Catholic and were the descendants of many of the first Indians who came to Cochinchina with the French conquest in search of opportunities to advance themselves within the expanding French Empire. The size of this community belies the remarkably powerful ways in which its members secured their rights to French citizenship on Cochinchinese soil. This modest group reveals the surprising ways in which, in particular contexts, colonised people could seize upon the power of French citizenship. In turn its scale is out of keeping with the role it played in shaping colonial Indochina's political and social order and the impact it had on Vietnamese struggles. The case of Indochina's Indian French citizens emphasises crucial differences in how citizenship for colonised people functioned at the beginning of the nineteenth century, and how it was understood in new colonial contexts at the end of that century. Increased migration created inter-colonial linkages which, for the French Empire, revived flagging bits of its old empire while helping to build the new. This situation was on the one hand of mutual benefit to the two French colonial centres. On the other hand it created social and political frictions (but also occasional sympathies) between colonised Indians and Vietnamese, which undermined French control.

A LOST EMPIRE AND A SECOND METROPOLE

For nearly two decades after the establishment of French rule in Cochinchina, the young, *lycée*-educated writers first called over in 1868, and others like them in the middle levels of Cochinchina's administration enjoyed the privileges and salaries of Europeans working at the same grades. In the

---

9. P. Huard, 'Chinois, Japonais et Hindous en Indochine', *Bulletin Économique Indochinois*, 3, 1939, 467–486, p. 485.

same early period, all Indians were able to participate freely in local elections in Cochinchina as long as they could demonstrate they originated from French India (and sometimes when they couldn't). This included a wide range of individuals, from wealthy Muslim traders from Karikal, to relatively humble but enterprising milkmen, to men of 'pariah' (untouchable) backgrounds who had obtained sufficient French in mission schools to allow them to read the addresses on the envelopes passing through Cochinchina's nascent postal service.

The contractual and electoral privileges French Indians enjoyed in early Cochinchina were those normally reserved for French citizens. By extending these privileges, officials in early French Cochinchina were acknowledging the ambiguous forms of citizenship status that Indians from the French Establishments and peoples of France's other 'old colonies' had gained when the fervour generated by the French Revolution touched France's overseas territories. Citizenship in France's enclave colonies – Senegal's *Quatre Communes* and France's possessions in India – was underwritten by an official eagerness to nurture the loyalty of small trading communities who had long attachments to France. French efforts to willingly create citizens ran into difficulties in both places though. By metropolitan definitions citizenship was enshrined in two fundamental and inseparable rights: electoral franchise and civil equality. The latter in legal terms meant the individual's right to have all civil matters including marriage, paternity, and inheritance regulated by the French Civil Code. In both enclave colonies, local populations happily accepted electoral franchise; French notions of civil equality, though, could not be introduced with the same ease. Senegal's largely Muslim population refused to forfeit its indigenous civil practices which it held to as fundamental expressions of Islamic faith. In French India, on the other hand, it was French authorities who held back. There, in the interest of preventing social unrest, they maintained a policy of non-interference in religious, caste, and other social complexities which regulated the private lives of those they governed. In both places, France had produced men who were '*électeurs*', but it had not clearly established them as '*citoyens*'.

In 1870s Pondicherry, a group of Indians stepped in to solve this problem of colonial not-quite-citizenship for themselves. They referred to legal precedents to claim that while France had granted them the right to maintain their indigenous civil practices, they were free if they so desired to willingly renounce these practices and adopt the French Civil Code. On this basis they launched a movement for equality; they publicly renounced their indigenous civil practices and claimed that by accepting the French Civil Code their status was now equal to that of French citizens. The group was headed by elites but consciously drew in followers from the lowest, 'untouchable', end of the social scale. It was made up primarily of Catholics but also attracted, to a more limited extent, people of other faiths. This group came to be known as 'renouncers' *(renonçants)*, the term emphasising the process of 'renunciation' by which they claimed their citizenship. In time the label 'renouncer' helped to distinguish them too from those Indians from the French possessions who had not claimed citizenship (the non-renouncers, or *non-renonçants*).[10]

'Renunciation' here is a specifically French colonial concept distinct from the sense of religious renunciation more familiar to scholars of South Asian society. French India's renouncers were not gurus and ascetics who had 'renounced' worldly life.[11] Rather, they were giving up their indigenous civil practices in order to be governed by the French Civil Code. These practices consisted of the habits and customs regulating family life and inheritance. They were shaped by religion and caste, though not entirely determined by them; many civil practices were highly localised. As with British practice in India, French colonial legislators adhered to the principle of not interfering in the civil practices of the peoples they governed. French authorities also sought to regulate civil practice in India in ways similar to those employed in British India. Both imperial powers defined standardised indigenous 'personal laws' (personal status or *statut personnel* in French colonial contexts) for use in colonial courts through the translation and interpretation of indigenous legal texts. Historians of British India have argued that in doing so the colonial legal system transformed the civil practices themselves.[12] While a similar argument can be made for French India, of more immediate relevance in relation to

---

10. Huard, 'Chinois, Japonais et Hindous en Indochine', p. 485.
11. The classic treatment of religious renunciation is found in Louis Dumont, *Homo Hierarchicus: The Caste System and its Implications*, Chicago: University of Chicago Press, 1970.
12. See Eleanor Newbigin, 'The codification of personal law and secular citizenship; revisiting the history of law reform in late colonial India', *Indian Economic and Social History Review*, 46, 2009, 83–114, p. 86.

the formation of colonial citizenships is the way in which, throughout its overseas empire, France came to regard indigenous civil practices as the differing moral codes of the people whom it governed.

In Cochinchina, Indians' political franchise and their right to European contractual privileges came under official attack from 1881. The Cochinchinese authorities' mood shifted; they became intolerant of Indian privilege even as Pondicherry's colonial government moved to endorse the claims of Pondicherry-based Indians seeking legal equality through 'renunciation'. The new uncertainties for Indians in Cochinchina were more immediately linked with developments within that colony than with debates in French India. Indian privileges in Cochinchina fell foul of regulations issued on the heels of a decree permitting the indigenous peoples of Cochinchina to become French citizens through naturalisation.[13]

With the rise of the Third Republic in France in 1870 came a reassertion of republican ideals, including the notion of a Greater France made up of citizens of all colours. The extension of citizenship to the inhabitants of Cochinchina has tended to be understood as yet another indication of republican values restored to the French Empire. Yet colonised people in France's older overseas territories acquired the rights of citizenship in ways fundamentally different from the new and restrictive process of naturalisation. In practice, because acquiring citizenship through naturalisation required the applicant to meet stringent criteria as well as the approval of French authority, it severely restricted the number of Cochinchinese who could become French. Naturalisation was less a mark of the triumph and renewal of republican values in France's overseas empire than a symptom of a new colonial order adopted by France, and shared with other European colonial powers of the time; as they expanded their overseas realms in the late nineteenth century into larger, more heavily administered territorial empires, all of the European powers sought to establish more distant relationships between the 'natives' and their colonial masters.

In reaction to restrictions on their privileges in Cochinchina, French Indian residents of Saigon wrote forceful petitions and staged lively pub-

---

13. The proper term for this process, because the Cochinchinese were already French subjects and thus French 'nationals', was 'accession to the quality of citizen' (*l'accession à la qualité de citoyen*). The legal effect, however, was the same, and the term 'naturalisation' was more commonly used. See Arthur Girault, *Principes de colonisation et de législation coloniale*, Paris: Recueil-Sirey, 1927, p. 467.

lic protests in defence of their own rights. They seized the initiative in ways that allowed them to make particularly powerful claims to French citizenship. French Indians were remarkably effective at persuading their superiors of their right to equal treatment with their European colleagues in the administration; the limits of their power were evident at the point where the demands of Indians working alongside Vietnamese at subordinate levels threatened the local-level colonial order. The powerful defence the 'renouncers' mounted of their right to remain within the French electorate of Cochinchina prompted the French Supreme Court to confirm that Indians who renounced their indigenous personal status and accepted the French Civil Code were to be legally recognised as full French citizens.

Indians employed in the lower levels of the colonial administration in Cochinchina never managed to secure contractual terms which properly reflected their rights as citizens. Nevertheless, Indians with French citizenship in Indochina enjoyed electoral privileges which were better than the rights they could exercise as voters back in French India. Such were their levels of privilege and comfort by the early 1920s that Saigon's prominent Pondicherry journalist Édouard Marquis was prompted to declare:

> There is no one at this time who contests the role of Indochina as a 'Second Metropole' … . Powerful and rich in activities of all sorts, brimming with life and seductive in its beauty and resources, Indochina appears … as the centre of a new world where [colonial peoples] must henceforth expend their energy and their vitality.[14]

French Indians took pleasure, like their Vietnamese hosts, in Saigon's interwar mood of cosmopolitan and modernist enquiry. They contributed with enthusiasm to the city's lively press scene and its thriving forms of associational life. Other realities soon began to intrude, though, upon the dream of a colonial 'new world'. Indians with French citizenship now became a problem in the eyes of politically moderate Vietnamese reformers. These reformers felt the Indians stood in the way of their own participation in political and public life; in their calls for reform they made stern critiques of Indian privileges. Anti-Indian feeling grew more widespread in Cochinchina from the late 1920s, with the rise of

---

14. Édouard Marquis, 'Indochine, Métropole seconde', *Réveil Saigonnais*, 21 September 1923.

radicalised forms of Vietnamese anti-colonialism and the collapse of the global economy.

Indian French citizens responded to these pressures by aiming to justify their presence and raise their profile in the colony. They presented themselves as modern men striving for advancement. They embraced the notion of 'Greater India' developed by French and Indian scholars of Southeast Asia, an interpretation of India's ancient influences in the region that attributed to the subcontinent a legacy of benevolent colonialism and an unparalleled flowering of art and civilisation. Saigon's French Indians inscribed themselves into this history as torchbearers carrying the legacy into a bright future, a future which in their vision remained firmly French. They tried to improve the standing of the wider Indian migrant community in Indochina. Through the 1930s they sometimes monitored and at other times defended the behaviour of other overseas Indians whose fate they now saw as tied to their own. These public relations exercises exposed internal differences but they also pressed the French Indians to engage more thoughtfully with questions of social and political change taking place both in India and in Vietnamese Indochina. The concerns which preoccupied Indian French citizens in the interwar years bought to the fore other forms of belonging and placed new importance on identities and attachments beyond their French citizenship.

From the outbreak of the Second World War until Vietnam gained its independence from France in 1954, French Indians in Indochina were forced to negotiate a complex set of conflicting allegiances. Throughout much of the war they were held in a political tension between Vichy Indochina, Gaullist French India, Japan's wartime programme of Pan-Asian solidarity, and the militarised Southeast Asia-based campaign of Indian nationalist leader Subash Chandra Bose. The end of the Second World War brought no peace to Indochina. British India's freedom from colonial rule briefly brought Indochina's migrant Indians into favour with the Viet Minh (*Việt Nam Độc Lập Đồng Minh Hội*, or 'League for the Independence of Vietnam'), the communist-led coalition for national independence formed in 1941. Yet it remained far from clear whether French Indians had a future in Indochina, and with India's independence from British rule the cession of French Indian territories to the newly independent state became a political *fait accompli*. With their own futures compromised by the prospect of decolonisation in both India and Indochina, Indian French citizens stepped in to play a part in negotiations over the post-colonial status of French India's mobile population. They aimed to ensure that the advantages of French citizenship would continue to be available to them within the nationalist frameworks taking shape. These negotiations allowed them to remain mobile citizens, attached to the ideal of the French Republic rather than its soil, and to 'Second Metropoles' rather than to France itself.

CONNECTED MIGRANT FLOWS

The Indian French citizens, or renouncers, were by no means the only people who came to Indochina from the Indian subcontinent in the French colonial period. Indo-French *créoles*, and a wider group of Indian migrants from both British and French India also lived and worked there. Their lives were in many ways inseparable from those of Indian French citizens, and the distinctions between these groups sometimes blurred.

A small group of Indo-French *créoles*, of mixed French (or more often Portuguese) and Indian parentage, worked alongside renouncers in the French colonial service. The Indo-French were also French citizens; most had gained this status through a father or forefather's recognition of paternity, but in the absence of paternal recognition others may have become citizens through the process of renunciation. By the 1920s, the renouncers and Indo-French had developed stronger shared interests. The term the 'French of India' (*Français de l'Inde*) came into use to refer to both groups, but it also becomes difficult by this period to distinguish between those *Français de l'Inde* who were Indian and those who were Eurasian.

Créole is another fuzzy term. Within the French Empire a *créole* could refer to an individual of mixed parentage, but the word was also used in the French Antilles and French India with reference to long-standing or locally-born residents who claimed pure European stock. In Indochina, French Indian *créoles* of European origin stood apart socially from the *Français de l'Inde*. Yet while this group identified itself with the Europeans, it included people who passed as European or, for reasons of status and dignity in the social world they inhabited, simply denied their Indian heritage.[15]

---

15. See for example Denise Affonço's description of her father, employed by the Cambodian Ministry of Culture in the 1920s, and his attitude towards his mixed Portuguese and Indian

There were far fewer French Indian *créoles* (mixed or otherwise) than renouncers in Cochinchina. Cochinchina's census-takers were diligent in ensuring people with French citizenship were absorbed into the legal category of 'citizen', making it now difficult to establish a reliable breakdown of figures for French citizens who were not of metropolitan origin. Other sources, though, give a rough indication; a 1937 list of persons 'originating from French India' and employed in the Cochinchinese administration reveals that only a small proportion, eight out of sixty-three such employees, was a *créole* ('mixed blood or otherwise'), all others being 'renounced' French citizens.[16]

Indochina also supported a larger and more diverse Indian migrant population, occupied primarily as merchants, petty traders, and tradespeople. Over half of all migrants who came to Indochina from the Indian subcontinent were from parts of India under British rule or influence. They came primarily from the Tamil region and thus shared a language, culture, and ties of religious faith and practice with Indians from Pondicherry and Karikal. Among Indian migrants from the French possessions, some had chosen to remain French subjects. These 'non-renouncers' worked alongside British Indians in many of the same occupations. In late 1930s Indochina there were 3,000 British Indians against 800 Indians who were French subjects, in addition to the approximately 2,000 Indian French citizens across Indochina at the time.[17]

The boundaries within the larger group of Tamil migrants were blurred in two ways. Firstly, although they were exceptions to a general rule, Indians who were French citizens could be found among the community of Tamil traders and service people. Secondly, the highly porous borders between British India and the fragmented tracts of French India favoured the relatively free movement of people across these boundaries.[18] Thus those who presented themselves as 'French' when they went to work and live in Indochina may have had any number of ties with British India, and their 'Frenchness' may well have been of very recent date.

---

origins. Denise Affonço, *To the End of Hell: One woman's struggle to survive the Khmer Rouge*, London: Reportage Press, 2009.

16. Vietnamese National Archives Number One (hereafter VNA1) GD 1812 Listes des fonctionnaires originaires de l'Inde française 1983: GEFI to GGI, 21 September 1937.
17. Huard, 'Chinois, Japonais et Hindous en Indochine', p. 485.
18. Miles, *Imperial Burdens*, p. 5.

Indochina's Indians can equally be viewed as one flow in the mass movement of migrants from India to Southeast Asia which took off in the latter half of the nineteenth century as European empires expanded in the region. There are similarities as well as substantive connections between Indian migrant groups in Indochina and migrants from the subcontinent situated in other parts of Southeast Asia. As elsewhere in the region, the majority of Indochina's Indians were ethnic Tamils. Merchants and tradespeople seized the opportunities that arose as port cities developed and agricultural frontiers and plantation zones expanded. Indochina attracted many of the same mobile merchant and banking groups – Chettiar moneylenders, *Marakkayar* (Tamil Muslim) traders, Sindhi merchants – whose activities elsewhere in the region have been well-documented. These long-distance trading and banking groups had ties throughout the region and beyond. Indians residing in Indochina were also connected to multiple localities in Southeast Asia through networks of kinship and by a Tamil press which (operating both in India and in Southeast Asia) circulated print media throughout the region.[19]

One feature which set Indochina's Indian migrant flow apart from those of other countries in Southeast Asia was the lack of large numbers of contract labourers. Unlike Malaya, Burma, or Sumatra, where Indian workers were brought in to work in the rubber plantations, oilfields, and industries, French Indochina did not import large numbers of Indian (or for that matter Chinese) labourers. Its labour needs were filled instead by a cheap and ample supply of men from impoverished and overcrowded areas of Tonkin and Annam. Indochina's Indian population was thereby smaller than comparative migrant populations in British and Dutch colonies in Southeast Asia. Its structure differed too, favouring the middle and upper ends of the socio-economic scale over those at the lower end. These factors helped shape the character of Vietnamese reform and anti-colonial unrest; as this book later demonstrates, Indian commercial interests, like Chinese ones, threatened an aspiring entrepreneurial class in early twentieth-century Cochinchina, and Indian French citizens stood in the way of a moderate bourgeois class of men seeking political

---

19. On the Tamil press in Southeast Asia see Sunil S. Amrith, 'Tamil diasporas across the Bay of Bengal', *The American Historical Review*, 114, 3, 2009, 547–572; also Khoo Salma Nasution, *The Chulias in Penang: Patronage and Place-Making around the Kapitan Kling Mosque 1786–1957*, Penang: Areca Books, 2014, ch. 20.

reforms in the interwar years. But Indian migrants did not pose a threat to the interests of Indochina's labouring classes to the same degree as in British Burma for example, where large-scale working-class Indian migration produced forceful dockside riots in the 1930s.[20]

The other distinguishing feature of Indian migration to Indochina was the presence there of Indians whose life circumstances had been shaped by French rather than British colonial rule. There are superficial similarities between men who served in intermediary roles in say British Burma or Malaya and those in Indochina. In all cases Indians were employed by the colonial state in similar positions: as civil servants, policemen, and soldiers. The similarities in patterns of employment mask fundamental differences in the ways in which France as opposed to Britain intervened in India's indigenous social orders.

In British India and among its Indian administrative intermediaries overseas, Brahmins dominated the colonial civil service, while Sikhs, Gurkhas, and others labelled 'martial races' were channelled into the police forces and the army on the basis of their supposedly innate 'warrior stock' (as well as their perceived loyalty). Historians of British India have argued that instruments employed for the purposes of 'knowing and ordering' the peoples of the subcontinent were important tools in the exercise of colonial power. Colonial ethnography emphasised the immutable characteristics of ethnic 'types', while the colonial census enumerated India's peoples and created systematic caste, ethnic, and religious categories. These were no mere descriptive exercises. On the basis of this body of knowledge, political franchise was granted or denied to specific sectors of Indian society; groups were classified as deserving of special treatment or as criminals; the 'innate' characteristics of India's peoples became the basis for hire in the public service and the

---

20. The French government proposed the import of British Indian workers to Indochina in the late 1920s, but it never took place; see British Library (hereafter BL) IOR/L/E/7/1530 (554/1928) Request from French government to send British Indian workers to Madagascar and Indo-China, 8 February 1928. Another short-lived attempt at introducing export labour into Indochina involved a small group of Javanese labourers brought in from the Dutch East Indies. See M. Stokhof, 'Javanese in Hồ Chí Minh City today: an Aftermath of Coolie Migration in French Colonial Vietnam', unpublished Master's thesis, University of Amsterdam, 2002; on the Chinese working class, or lack thereof, in Indochina, see Li Tana, 'Vietnam' in *Encyclopedia of the Chinese Overseas*, Lynn Pan (ed.), Richmond: Curzon, 1999, p. 231; on Indian migrant labour and labour unrest in British Burma see Ian Brown, *Burma's Economy in the Twentieth Century*, Cambridge: Cambridge University Press, 2013, pp. 60–71.

British Indian Army, both in India and abroad. A further consequence of the British generation of knowledge about India was the self-conscious deployment of this knowledge by Indians themselves. By the late nineteenth century caste-based movements and other social organisations were striving to receive official sanction for favourable depictions of their castes in order to press for political concessions or preferment in employment.[21]

The religious and caste affiliations of French Indians employed in the colonial service go against British colonial expectations. In Pondicherry as in Saigon, *Vellala* and other agricultural castes secured higher-placed administrative positions, while men of untouchable backgrounds could often be found in subordinate positions (the latter simply did not feature in British India's public service). In both cases the majority of these Indian employees were Catholic converts. The population of French India was primarily Tamil and thus it was Tamils who were recruited for the French Army; within British 'martial races' theory, Tamils were classed as effeminate and weak, and not of warrior stock.

France did not refrain from counting, categorising, and studying the customs and habits of the peoples it colonised. Indeed, some of India's most prominent colonial ethnographers were French.[22] Yet the shaping of assimilationist policies in France's old colonies meant that is was French citizenship rather than categories of caste or creed which became the basis for French Indian social and political advancement. Politics in French India, since the introduction of universal franchise, was similarly not a struggle between people of different castes and creeds but between the 'Indian' party, representing 'indigenous' values, and the 'French' party, which included Indians who had chosen French

---

21. This is a vast and contentious area of scholarship. For central arguments see Bernard S. Cohn, *Colonialism and its Forms of Knowledge: The British in India*, Princeton: Princeton University Press, 1996 and Nicholas B. Dirks, *Castes of Mind, Colonialism and the Making of Modern India*, Delhi: Permanent Black, 2003. Challenges to the more radical view that India's social categories were 'invented' under British rule can be found in Susan Bayly, *Caste, Society and Politics in India from the Eighteenth Century to the Modern Age*, Cambridge: Cambridge University Press, 2001, and Sumit Guha, 'The Politics of Identity and Enumeration in India, c. 1600–1990', *Comparative Studies in Society and History*, 20, 2003, 148–167. On martial races see David Omissi, *The Sepoy and the Raj*, Basingstoke: Macmillan, 1994, ch. 1, esp. pp. 23–35; also Thomas R. Metcalf, *Imperial Connections: India in the Indian Ocean Arena, 1860–1920*, Berkeley: University of California Press, 2007, pp. 71–78.
22. Jyoti Mohan, 'British and French Ethnographies of India: Dubois and his English Commentators', *French Colonial History*, 5, 1, 2004, 229–246.

citizenship.²³ French modes of intervention in Indian society are at the heart of what makes the migration of French Indians to Indochina so distinctive from migrant flows from British India.

TROUBLESOME MIGRANT FLOWS

The largest Asian migrant group in French Indochina, the Chinese, was a longer-standing one, and one whose history is much better documented than that of the Indians. It was also a considerably larger group. Some 156,000 Chinese merchants, traders, and artisans inhabited Cochinchina in the 1920s (and 293,000 in all of Indochina).²⁴ Despite the difference in scale of these migrant flows, most migrants involved in commerce, be they Chinese or Indian, created similar kinds of tensions due to their economic activities. The political problems they posed, however, were each of a different order.

Chinese commercial interests were managed by the colonial state in many of the same ways as the (mainly British-) Indian business interests. Both were given access to the colonial economy in ways the Vietnamese (and Cambodians, and Lao, and other indigenous peoples) were not, in the form of trading concessions, and special tax regimes. Yet both were also feared by the French for the economic power they could wield, even if not in equal measure. French business was protected against competition from foreign Asians by regulations which saw Chinese and Indian trading licences cost double those for Frenchmen. Subsidies were available only to French entrepreneurs, and Chinese and British-Indian goods were heavily taxed. Chinese merchants complained that their trading and tax arrangements were unfair in comparison to those of their French competitors; they also had a reputation for evading the regulations applying to them.²⁵ Meanwhile, the Vietnamese in Cochinchina deeply resented both Chinese and Indian migrant businesspeople.²⁶

---

23. N. Gupta, 'The Citizens of French India: the Issue of Cultural Identity in Pondicherry in the XIXth Century', *Association historique internationale de l'Océan Indien, Les relations historiques et culturelles entre la France et l'Inde XVIIe-XXe siècles, Actes de conférence internationales France-Inde, 21–28 juillet 1986*, 161–173, pp. 166, 170–171.
24. *Annuaire Statistique de l'Indochine: Vol. 1, Recueil des statistiques relatives aux années 1913–1922*, Hanoi: IDEO, 1927, p. 33.
25. Li Tana, 'Vietnam', p. 231; Charles Robequain, *The Economic Development of Viet-Nam and Indo-China*, London: Oxford University Press, 1944, p. 39.
26. See Chapter Six.

Comparing the status of Chinese and *French* Indians in Cochinchina the two groups presented quite different challenges to the colonial social and political order. The substantial Chinese population, particularly in the Mekong Delta, had pre-dated the arrival of the French and were being gradually assimilated; this process was assisted by a long history of Chinese political influence over Vietnamese lands, which for Vietnamese created cultural affinities with the Chinese which they did not share with the Indian migrants.²⁷ French regulation of Chinese immigrants relied on maintaining the system of congregations – the self-run institutions which managed immigration and collected tax on behalf of the French government, while guaranteeing the good conduct of their members. By maintaining these organisations the French colonial government gave Chinese migrants autonomy to manage their own affairs, afforded them a level of security as important economic intermediaries, and recognised their status as foreigners. The congregations also served as a means for France to prevent successive Chinese governments from gaining unwanted influence over settlers' affairs.²⁸ Local people in Indochina, however, came to view the congregations as a key part of the 'Chinese problem'. Vietnamese commentators in the interwar period judged that the congregation system gave Chinese migrants undue power and autonomy, allowing them to behave like a 'state within a state'. In 1919 and through the early 1920s, Vietnamese moderate reformers mounted protests insisting that the Chinese should be managed under the same rules as the Vietnamese, according to the *status quo* for French subjects, and should not enjoy special privileges.²⁹

Unlike the Chinese migrants, but akin to their Indochinese hosts, French Indians were people colonised by France, and had shared stakes in how the French Empire was to rule over them. The Chinese presence challenged the colonial authorities' ability to manage different peoples within the Indochinese framework; by 1919 Vietnamese moderates in the south were demanding that the Chinese be treated equally to any

---

27. Pierre Brocheux, *The Mekong Delta: Ecology, Economy and Revolution, 1860–1960*, Madison: University of Wisconsin-Madison Centre for Southeast Asian Studies, 1995, pp. 102–103.
28. Alain G. Marsot, *The Chinese Community in Vietnam under the French*, Lewiston, N.Y.: Edwin Mellen Press, 1993, p. 114; see also Tracy Barrett, *The Chinese Diaspora in South-East Asia: The Overseas Chinese in Indochina*, London: I.B. Tauris, 2013, p. 203.
29. Christopher Goscha, 'Widening the Colonial Encounter: Asian Connections inside French Indochina during the Interwar Period', *Modern Asian Studies*, 43, 5, 2009, 1189–1228, pp. 1200–1208.

colonial subjects. The French Indians' presence in Cochinchina was arguably more politically dangerous. By the 1920s (as described in Chapter Six) the same Vietnamese reformers were asking to be treated on a par with French citizens in political and public life, and were holding up the Indian French citizens' free enjoyment of such rights to justify their own demands. The Indians' electoral rights exposed the contradictions within the French Empire as a whole, prompting the peoples of Cochinchina to begin questioning the empire's very legitimacy.

CITIZENSHIP, MIGRATION, AND COLONIAL SOCIETY

One feature distinguishing the French Empire from other modern European imperial projects was the explicit way it purported to assimilate colonised people and make them into equal citizens. Theorists of citizenship have long held that the French Revolution heralded the return of a 'nobler' form of citizenship understood primarily as a political commitment tying the individual to the state.[30] French citizenship in this conception was a political contract with the state, which transcended racial and cultural distinctions of origin. From this conception has followed the notion that French colonialism in turn created colour-blind societies of equal citizens. Yet close scrutiny of the processes by which specific groups of people acceded to citizenship – or didn't – in France's overseas territories shows this assumption to be too comfortable. Such studies demonstrate that colonial citizenship did not follow a uniform regime handed down from the Metropole. Colonial citizenship regimes were often far removed from the republican principles upon which they were supposedly based. Some colonised peoples became citizens only in part, holding some but not all of the rights or obligations normally associated with citizenship. In other colonial settings race and acculturation were freely used as criteria to determine who qualified for citizenship and who did not. And republican values were compromised when colonial decision-makers felt they hampered imperial designs.[31] French

---

30. Rogers Brubaker, *Citizenship and Nationhood in France and Germany*, Cambridge, Mass.: Harvard University Press, 1992, p. 34; Michael Walzer, 'Citizenship', in Terence Ball, James Farr, and Russell L. Hanson (eds), *Political innovation and conceptual change*, Cambridge: Cambridge University Press, 1995, 211–219, p. 211.
31. These studies are numerous, although earlier works tend to reveal rather than explicitly remark upon the gap between the principles and practices of citizenship. See H. Oludare Idowu, 'Assimilation in 19th Century Senegal', *Cahiers d'Etudes Africaines*, 9, 34, 1969, 194–218; Michael Brett, 'Legislating for Inequality in Algeria: The *Senatus-Consulte* of

citizenship in its colonial forms was no pure, noble egalitarian concept based solely on political commitment, but was conditioned by ethnic, racial, and cultural criteria. Far from a model received fully-formed from the Metropole, it was constructed *in situ* in the political and social contexts of France's various overseas possessions.[32]

Yet the reconfiguration of citizenship regimes in colonial contexts cannot be taken to mean that colonial governments and the imperial centre were at all times motivated to block citizenship and to prevent the 'natives' from becoming Frenchmen. Nor should it imply that colonised peoples themselves played no role in shaping the terms of their citizenship. The work of a new wave of scholars of French colonial citizenship is valuable for the light it casts on how colonial citizenship was actually shaped and experienced. However, in their eagerness to take a firm political stance against the errors and exclusions of colonialism, these studies have been prone to overlook the changes of regimes of citizenship across time and locale. More specifically, this scholarship tends to pass over the more open ways in which citizenship was interpreted and re-shaped by the peoples of France's old colonies, and can thereby obscure our understanding of an important shift in the French management of indigenous colonial social orders. There was a sharp distinction between citizenship regimes in the 'old' colonies, the older French-ruled islands and ports with circumscribed slave and trading populations, and France's 'new' colonies. As France expanded along with other European powers to involve itself in greater direct administration over larger territories and larger populations, its colonial citizenship regimes underwent a significant change. In the old colonies, French India among

---

14 July 1865', *Bulletin of the School of Oriental and African Studies, University of London*, 51, 3, 1988, 440–461; Michael C. Lambert, 'From Citizenship to Negritude: "Making a Difference" in Elite Ideologies of Colonized Francophone West Africa', *Comparative Studies in Society and History*, 35, 2, 1993, 239–262; Mamadou Diouf, 'The French Colonial Policy of Assimilation and the Civility of the *originaires* of the Four Communes (Senegal): A Nineteenth Century Globalisation Project', *Development and Change*, 29, 1998, 671–696; Damien Deschamps, 'Une citoyenneté différée: cens civique et assimilation des indigènes dans les Établissements français de l'Inde', *Revue française de science politique*, 47, 1, 1997, 49–69; Emmanuelle Saada, *Les enfants de la colonie: les métis de l'Empire français entre sujétion et citoyenneté*, Paris, La Découverte, 2007; Joshua Schreier, *Arabs of the Jewish Faith: The Civilising Mission in Colonial Algeria*, New Brunswick: Rutgers University Press, 2010.

32. This is not meant to imply that citizenship in France itself operated as a fixed model. The struggle for women's electoral franchise is one example of how metropolitan citizenships were not all equal and were themselves a source debate. See Pierre Rosanvallon, *Le sacré du citoyen: le suffrage universel en France*, Paris: Gallimard, 1992.

them, there were high levels of French official will to create loyal citizens among small groups of colonised peoples. This led to high degrees of local involvement in deciding whether citizenship was desirable and what shape it might take. In France's newer colonial territories, with much larger colonised populations, very low levels of official will existed with regard to extending citizenship rights to the colonised. In these new colonies, French Indochina included, local people had very little if any influence on the terms upon which their citizenship was granted, and very few were allowed to accede to the status of citizens.

The distinction between regimes of French citizenship in France's old colonies and its newer ones is seldom noticed or remarked upon. The idea that citizenship became much more difficult for colonised people to obtain from the late nineteenth century contradicts the received knowledge that the rise of the Third French Republic from 1870 reinvigorated the process of assimilation in the colonies.[33] Yet this assertion has begun to be questioned, notably in the work of historians Emmanuelle Saada and Alice Conklin, both of whom demonstrate that Republican ideals of democracy and equality were compromised under the Third Republic in order for France to attend to the harsher and more pragmatic realities of exerting its control over the foreign lands it claimed.[34] The change in citizenship regimes is consistent with this shift, and indeed constitutes its most significant manifestation.

The sharp difference between an older, more liberal context in which citizens could be created, and a newer more restrictive one was exposed and became problematic when connections were established between French India and French Indochina. When Indians from the French possessions came to Indochina not only did one group of French colonised people come into contact with another; an older mode of managing the French colonial social order confronted a newer mode. Renouncers initiated their move to improve their status in French India, but their status was ultimately a product of the confrontation between two modes

---

33. Martin Deming Lewis, 'One Hundred Million Frenchmen: The Assimilation Theory in French Colonial Policy', *Comparative Studies in Society and History*, 4, 1962, 129–153, p. 135.
34. Emmanuelle Saada, 'Citoyens et sujets de l'Empire Français: Les usages du droit dans la situation coloniale', *Genèses*, 53, 2003, 4–24, p. 13; Alice Conklin, *A Mission to Civilise: The Republican Idea of Empire in France and West Africa, 1895–1930*, Stanford: Stanford University Press, 1997.

of colonial rule, and was formed not within a single colonised space but across two such spaces.

The confrontation between citizenship regimes was itself a product of an age of mass migration unprecedented in human history. Fuelled by the rising demands of industrialisation and imperial expansion, and facilitated by improvements in transportation and communications, people across the globe were on the move from the mid-nineteenth century. Settlers traversed the Atlantic to the New World; others flowed from the Russian and Qing empires into the frontier lands of Manchuria, Siberia, and Central Asia, while contract labourers, merchants, and colonial auxiliaries were drawn from India and China to expanding European empires in Southeast Asia.[35]

South Asian and Chinese movements to Southeast Asia have been the subject of extensive research, but more recently scholars have expressed their dissatisfaction with a standard approach many of these studies take to their subject. A tendency to treat migrants as minorities, as bounded entities within their host societies, has prompted the charge that such approaches fail to take seriously the roles migrants played in the making of colonial societies.[36] In this case it would be difficult to do justice to the story of Indian French citizens and the shaping of their citizenship without reference to events and circumstances both in French India and in Indochina, and without nods to the Metropole and other corners of the French Empire. Their mobility was integral to forcing old and new approaches to citizenship into the same imperial frame. The contradictions produced, the efforts to manage them, and the migrant and local responses to them were all forces shaping colonial Indochina and post-colonial Vietnam. It is because Indochina's Indian communities

---

35. Adam McKeown, 'Global Migration, 1846–1940,' *Journal of World History*, 15, 2, 2004, 155–189.
36. For illustrations of the methods under scrutiny, see Ravindra K. Jain, *Indian Communities Abroad: Themes and Literature*, New Delhi: Manohar, 1993, and Colin Clarke, Ceri Peach and Steven Vertovec, 'Introduction: themes in the study of the South Asian diaspora', in Clarke et al. (eds), *South Asians Overseas, Migration and Ethnicity*, Cambridge: Cambridge University Press, 1990. Claudine Salmon critiques such approaches with regard to the Chinese diaspora in 'The Contribution of the Chinese to the Development of Southeast Asia: A New Appraisal', in *Journal of South East Asian Studies*, 12, 1, 1981, 260–275, p. 260. For critical analyses of similar approaches to South Asian migrant history, see Mark-Anthony Falzon, *The Sindhi Diaspora 1860–2000*, New Delhi: Oxford University Press, 2005, p. 12; also Sunil Amrith, *Migration and Diaspora in Modern Asia*, Cambridge: Cambridge University Press, 2011, p. 5.

have so far been viewed as a side-show, as marginalised, self-contained communities, that the role of Indian French citizens in driving demands for social, political, and legal recognition in Cochinchina has gone unacknowledged.

Asian migrants carried to Southeast Asia on the great wave of late nineteenth and early twentieth century mobility played a role in shaping not only the economies but also the modern politics and societies of the region. When migrants made cross-colonial journeys within a single imperial space – within the British or French Empires for example – more specific effects were produced. These connections strengthened and reinforced the empire as a whole, but served in other ways to weaken and undermine imperial power. Two influential pieces of writing have addressed in turn these two sides of the imperial coin with regard to movements out of British India. Thomas Metcalf has identified a spider's web of British imperial linkages criss-crossing the Indian Ocean region from the late nineteenth century, with India at its centre serving as the locus from which ideas and expertise about British colonial rule were disseminated. British India became a 'centre of British imperial authority', a 'reservoir of expertise' used to 'extend and secure the British Empire', and an imperial possession whose scale was so vast that it began to have colonial ambitions of its own.[37] Sugata Bose's *Hundred Horizons* is equally important for the way it offsets the centrality of imperial power in Metcalf's conception. The traffic which criss-crossed the Indian Ocean arena, he insists, was not all produced by imperial imperative, but included universalist, anti-colonial and nationalist ideas, and movements which displayed continuities with pre-colonial legacies of trade and religious pilgrimage.[38]

French imperial linkages within the region are a foil to the grandeur and scale of the British narrative. The French Empire did not have a resource comparable to British India from which to draw its colonial expertise. Instead much of this expertise came from marginal parts of France (Corsica, Alsace-Lorraine) and from small bounded islands and enclaves, including the French Antilles, the Mascarenes, and French India. French India did become, like its British counterpart, a source of

---

37. Metcalf, *Imperial Connections*, pp. 68, 103, 122.
38. Sugata Bose, *A Hundred Horizons: The Indian Ocean in the Age of Global Empire*, Cambridge, Mass.: Harvard University Press, 2006.

colonial expertise and knowledge and a strategic supply station for imperial possessions further east. Yet this connection grew from France's imperial weaknesses in India, rather than its strengths. Indochina provided an outlet for Indians whose hopes of advancement in French India were limited by the modest scale of France's hold there. French Indian soldiers were sent to Indochina to secure the empire there; but this arrangement also allowed France to circumvent an agreement imposed by Britain which prevented France from retaining any significant military presence in India.

It was beneficial to the French colonial project in Indochina that French India was nearby and had people with suitable skills who were eager to leave the confines of the French *comptoirs* to better themselves elsewhere. The French Indians' citizenship rights were less helpful to the smooth implementation of French colonial designs in Cochinchina. French Indians arrived there with electoral rights and ambiguous forms of European status just as official colonial opinion was beginning to assert that these were privileges which should not be made so freely available in the new imperial possessions. In their claims to equality in French India and their struggle to secure the rights of French citizenship in Cochinchina, renouncers were striving for rights within the French imperial system, rather than seeking to overturn the system itself.[39] Thus the nature of these inter-colonial connections was neither pro-imperial in the manner of Metcalf's spider-webs, nor was it of the explicitly anti-colonial type which Bose identifies. Yet renouncers' success in securing their citizenship rights in Cochinchina spurred later Vietnamese reformist demands for the same rights, and subsequently helped to nurture more radical anti-colonial Vietnamese demands. Migration generally, and the inter-colonial linkages it established specifically, mattered as a convenience and a necessity from a French imperial point of view, to sustain older isolated colonial tracts and to help to develop new ones. But they mattered too because these movements carried unintended social and political consequences which reached far beyond imperial designs. Migration helped to build empire but also to undo it.

---

39. Conklin, *A Mission to Civilise*, pp. 4–5; also see Frederick Cooper, *Colonialism in Question: Theory, Knowledge, History*, Berkeley: University of California Press, 2005, p. 22; Lambert, 'From Citizenship to Negritude', p. 240.

Scholars tend to discuss the structuring of colonial societies within one of two dominant analytic frames. The notion of a 'plural society', on the one hand, is routinely employed to describe the interactions, or lack thereof, between indigenous peoples and non-European migrant diasporas. Racial discourse, on the other hand, is used to explain the positioning of European populations vis-à-vis the 'natives' within the same societies. A major drawback of these two approaches taken together is the way they herd discussion about the interactions in colonial societies into two separate camps. The plural society discussion has come to serve relations between 'them' (to adopt the imperialist's perspective), while ideas of racial hierarchy cover interactions between 'us and them'. This has held back more comprehensive analyses of colonial society which might consider all of these interactions within the same framework. Indochina's Indian migrants, and Indian French citizens specifically, helped to shape a particular kind of Cochinchinese colonial society that was more complex than either of these approaches would allow. There were dense interactions between the different Asian, as well as European, communities. The Indian presence shaped a colonial hierarchy which was partly racial, but also partly legal, and alongside it existed a counter-colonial hierarchy based on local Vietnamese understandings of society's 'proper' racial order.

The notion of the 'plural society', first proposed by the Burma-based British civil servant John Furnivall, rests on the tenet that European colonialism produced highly stratified, migration-dependent societies whose 'medley of peoples' met only in the context of economic exchange. It has provided an influential framework to describe the ordering of colonial societies ever since, despite on-going objections that the notion needed more thorough and critical examination to separate myth from reality.[40] Some of the boldest challenges to the 'plural society' have emerged only in recent years, in the form of studies which set out to recover interactions across ethnic, cultural, and racial boundaries. Evidence that the 'plural' societies of Southeast Asia were deeply compartmentalised is

---

40. J.S. Furnivall, *Colonial Policy and Practice: A Comparative Study of Burma and Netherlands India*, New York: New York University Press, 1956, p. 301; cf. H. S. Morris, 'The Plural Society', *Man*, 57, 1957, 124–125; Maurice Freedman, 'The Growth of a Plural Society in Malaya', *Pacific Affairs*, 33, 2, Jun, 1960, 158–168, p. 168; Harry J. Benda, 'The Structure of Southeast Asian History: Some Preliminary Observations', *Journal of Southeast Asian History*, 3, 1, 1962, 106–138, p. 133.

sometimes compelling, but these interactions, it turns out, were also plentiful and powerful. The most vibrant of these exchanges were in the form of modernist, revivalist, and nationalist debates which took place between the wars. Those participating in the urban public spheres which took shape were properly cosmopolitan in their awareness of, and connections to, other parts of the world.[41] Indian French citizens, this study shows, interacted in Indochina with Europeans, Vietnamese, other Asians both indigenous to Indochina and foreign, and a vibrant Tamil community in Saigon in relations which went far beyond purely economic prescriptions. Saigon's interwar public culture, moreover, was shaped not only by a Vietnamese engagement with the modern western world, but by multiple Asian interactions.

Europe's convictions of its own superiority made racial discourse pervasive across its colonial societies. Analyses of the concept of race have served usefully to inform how colonial societies were constructed and to shed light on the development of modern imperial statecraft. There is a lack of agreement across this literature as to whether European forms of discrimination which reach back farther than the mid-nineteenth century can be considered 'racial' in the same sense as the idea of 'race' emerging from Social-Darwinist thinking. Nor do scholars agree whether this 'modern' concept of race was spurred on by imperial conquests or used only after the fact to justify them. Whether or not it had older antecedents, the development in the latter half of the nineteenth century of techniques which defined and sharpened racial categories (among them census-taking, anthropometry, climatology, and practices associated with 'racial hygiene') provided racial thinking with a powerful scientific – or pseudo-scientific – foundation that empires harnessed to reinforce their rule.[42]

---

41. For convincing statements of this approach and case studies, see T. N. Harper, 'Globalism and the Pursuit of Authenticity: The Making of a Diasporic Public Sphere in Singapore', *Sojourn: Journal of Social Issues in Southeast Asia*, 12, 2, 1997, 261–292; and special issues of the following journals: Tim Harper and Sunil S. Amrith (eds), 'Sites of Asian Interaction', *Modern Asian Studies*, Special Issue, 46, 2, 2012; Isabel Hofmeyr, Preben Kaarsholm and Bodil Folke Frederiksen (eds), 'Print cultures, nationalism, and publics of the Indian Ocean', *Africa*, Special Issue 1, 81, 2011; Andrew Arsan, Su Lin Lewis and Anne-Isabelle Richard (eds), 'The roots of global civil society and the interwar moment', *Journal of Global History*, Special Issue, 7, 2, 2012.

42. For useful overviews of these approaches see Jane Samson, *Race and Empire*, Harlow: Pearson, 2005, and Damon Salesa, 'Race', in Philippa Levine and John Marriott (eds), *The*

Racial thinking in the twentieth century became a powerful and destructive ideology, but it has grown in our time into an emotive and repellent one. Few regret that racist understandings of the world are no longer the norm, and fewer still would argue with complacency that they are entirely a thing of the past. The strength with which racism is rightly condemned, though, makes it more, rather than less, difficult to distinguish forms of discrimination which were racial from those that were not. Within French colonial contexts, policies of legal assimilation often presented themselves as colour-blind when effectively they were not. It is therefore particularly important to locate those points where racial justifications fed directly into the denial or granting of privilege, where other factors be they fiscal threats or political concerns brought out racial thinking to justify social inequalities, and other points where legal rights could be brought to the fore (as the renouncers managed to do in late nineteenth-century Saigon), to invalidate racial rationales for inequality.

Scholars of race and empire do not always examine how racial inequalities existed in conjunction with other types of inequality. They have seldom considered either the ways in which colonised peoples themselves embraced racial thinking. Capturing trends in global history, Christopher Bayly has noted that: 'the 1880s and 1890s seem to have been a period when racial awareness and segregation on the grounds of race became more obtrusive in almost all societies ... [it became] a global phenomenon with local variants'.[43] In interwar Saigon, modernist ideas of progress and reform were often expressed by Vietnamese, Indians, and other communities using the language and logic of racial discourse. The contradictory nature of Indochina's social order – it accepted that those who had gained citizenship were legally equal to Frenchmen regardless of their race, while using racial arguments to justify a more privileged position for those of European stock – was also fuel for local re-interpretation by Vietnamese who incorporated indigenous understandings of physical difference and an engagement with the new 'science' of race into a counter-interpretation of the colonial social and racial hierarchy.

Ashgate Research Companion to Modern Imperial History, Farnham: Ashgate, 2012, 429–448. For the French Empire, see Aldrich, *Greater France*, ch. 6.
43. C. A. Bayly, *The Birth of the Modern World 1780–1914*, Oxford: Blackwell 2004, p. 190.

Major transformations took place through the Indian Ocean and Asia Pacific region from the late 1920s, with the global economic collapse, the convergence of regional and international politics within the region during the Second World War, and the unravelling of Europe's Asian empires in the war's aftermath. Great pressures were put on migrants in this period of upheaval, which concluded with the exclusion or marginalisation of migrants from national narratives in their Southeast Asian host countries and their homelands alike.[44] From this later exclusion we should not be led to understand though that the migrants laid down no stones to line paths to national independence. An assumption that migrants were apolitical derives from the notion that the sole aim of merchant diasporas was economic success; they therefore sought to maintain stable relationships with host authorities by never seeking to challenge the political *status quo*. In one sense this was never entirely true. In the context of colonial Indochina, migrants – and not only merchants – regularly put forward bids to the state, for preferential treatment, for tax concessions, or as the case of the renouncers demonstrates for recognition of their legal status. These were 'political' actions even if they were demands made from within the system.[45] Studies that have begun to take more seriously migrants' interactions within their host societies and the connections they maintained with their homelands have revealed, too, the existence of very active transnational forms of anti-colonialism and nationalist politics.[46] The majority of Indian French citizens remained loyal to the colonial state. Yet their efforts to reposition themselves within French Indochina and to align themselves with other Indian migrants in order to guard themselves against the threats that internal reformist and nationalist movements posed to their continued stay in Indochina, played a role in creating a sense of proto-national Indian identity among migrants in Indochina. The Viet

---

44. Amrith, *Migration and Diaspora in Modern Asia*, Chapters 3 and 4; Robert Cribb and Li Narangoa, 'Orphans of Empire: Divided Peoples, Dilemmas of Identity, and Old Imperial Borders in East and Southeast Asia', *Comparative Studies in Society and History*, 2004, 46, 1, 164–187; Engseng Ho, *The Graves of Tarim, Genealogy and Mobility Across the Indian Ocean*, Berkeley: University of California Press, 2006, Chapter 10.
45. See Claude Markovits, *The Global World of Indian Merchants 1750–1947, Traders of Sind from Bukhara to Panama*, Cambridge: Cambridge University Press, 2000, Chapter 7.
46. See for example Sugata Bose and Kris Manjapra, (eds), *Cosmopolitan Thought Zones: South Asia and the Global Circulation of Ideas*, London: Palgrave Macmillan, 2010; Sana Aiyer, 'Anticolonial Homelands across the Indian Ocean: The Politics of the Indian Diaspora in Kenya, ca. 1930–1950', *American Historical Review*, 116, 4, 2011, 987–1013.

Minh's attempts to make flag-waving 'Indian' and 'Pakistani' patriots of Indian merchants (and one particularly resistant Indian French citizen) held for several months in its liberated zones in the late 1940s in turn illustrates how migrants could become written into national politics not just as figures on the margins. They could become powerful emblems of transnational anti-colonial solidarity even if they were not always active participants or even supporters of the actual fights for freedom.

While few, if any, Indian renouncers became nationals within an independent Vietnam, and although the new India was not necessarily a natural homeland for them, they found a unique solution which prevented them from being immobilised within the new nationally-bounded geography. Indian French citizens managed to use their long legacy of citizenship, their loyalty to the French Empire, and their mobility within it to insist upon a novel form of post-colonial French citizenship. It provided them with an association with the new Indian state, secured their relationship with the old Metropole, and allowed them to embark on new circuits of mobility. They did not become 'orphans of empire' in post-colonial times, but very mobile French citizens.

Historical blind spots

France's Coromandel ports, which now form part of the Union Territory of Pondicherry, and the modern state of Vietnam are two parts of the former French Empire which became disassociated from one another with the falling way of imperial frameworks and the construction of new national ones. Political change brought new views of the past, with independent nations now placed at the centre of historical narratives. National histories tended to depict the period of colonial rule as a two-sided affair of imperial control and national resistance. Blind spots formed around other parties present in colonial societies and around more ambiguous and complex colonial relationships; these were relationships which complicated otherwise clear visions of anti-colonial struggles for national independence. Practices of writing history in the immediate post-colonial period became so 'nationally bound', as Frederick Cooper has put it, as to 'blind us to the circuits of knowledge and communication that took routes other than those shaped by the Metropole–colony axis alone'.[47] This 'nationalising' of the history of

---

47. Cooper, *Colonialism in Question*, p. 22.

empire explains why neither Indochina's importance to French India, nor the impact of the Indian presence on Indochina's colonial societies, is seriously acknowledged in histories written about either place.

Like other post-colonial nation-states, Vietnam was prone in the years following national independence to deny the role played by other peoples in the country's past and in its development. Vietnamese historians emphasised national unity in the fight against French colonial repression, while downplaying both the ways in which colonialism was organised on the ground and ethnic, religious, and regional differences within the country.[48] The interests of Western historians too in the post-colonial period have until recently concentrated on imperial power and national struggle rather than colonial practice. The Indian presence in the country has constituted one of the blind spots in these narratives. Modern historians of Vietnam have taken little interest in the economic impact of Indian business in colonial Vietnam, or the political and social implications of the presence in French Indochina of Indians who held French citizenship.[49]

When France ceded its possessions in India to independent India in 1956 the histories of these places were subsumed within a much larger national narrative. Visions of the colonial past similarly became focused within the boundaries of the nation rather than reaching beyond them. The relationship between the former Coromandel coast *comptoirs* and Indochina holds a peculiar position in histories of French India; it looms large but never pulls into focus. Authoritative works on French India refer to a French Indian presence in Indochina, but only ever in passing.[50]

---

48. On this point see Brocheux, *Mekong Delta*, p. xvii; also Patricia M. Pelley, *Postcolonial Vietnam: new histories of the national past*, Durham NC: Duke University Press, 2002.
49. Pierre Brocheux's work is the most attentive to Indian communities. See Brocheux, *The Mekong Delta*, pp. 70, 72–74, 77, 80, 87–88, 103, 114, 156–157, 210. To capture the scope of the Indian presence in historical accounts of Vietnam, see for example Ngô Vinh Long, *Before the Revolution: The Vietnamese Peasants Under the French*, New York: Columbia University Press, 1991 [1973], pp. 88–89; Martin Murray, *The Development of Capitalism in Colonial Indochina (1870–1940)*, Berkeley: University of California Press, 1980, pp. 454–455; David Marr, *Vietnamese Tradition on Trial, 1920–1945*, Berkeley: University of California Press, 1981, p. 24.
50. Jacques Weber, *Pondichéry et les comptoirs de l'Inde après Dupleix: La démocratie au pays des castes*, Paris: Denoel, 1996, pp. 331, 344, 349. See also Paul Michalon, 'Des Indes françaises aux Indiens français ou Comment peut-on être Franco-Pondichérien?', unpublished DEA thesis, Université Aix-Marseille, Aix-en-Provence, 1990, pp. 39, 46. On Weber's omission of migration to Indochina see Claude Marius, 'Les Pondichériens dans l'administration coloniale de l'Indochine' p. 391.

Similarly, analyses of the renunciation movement miss, or brush over, its extraterritorial dimensions.[51] As for the genre of historical memoirs, which blend personal anecdote with wider historical events, their authors often mention that they lived in Indochina, but oddly they never connect their presence there to the history they are writing. Thus Arthur Annasse, who followed a long legal career in Indochina before taking up his pen, mentions his time in Indochina with sentiment and great pride, but his presence there never becomes part of his analysis of French India during the Second World War.[52] The idea that Indochina was too obvious a part of their everyday lives to warrant explicit mention is a trait carried over from colonial times. Mathias Clairon, a Pondicherry lawyer based in Saigon, wrote a legal study in 1926 whose main purpose was to establish beyond a doubt that the act of renunciation conferred French citizenship. The legal cases he cited to that end were overwhelmingly brought by renouncers residing in Cochinchina. Astonishingly, he did not remark upon the fact.[53]

It is a symptom of how bounded post-colonial histories became that mention of the Indian presence in Indochina is hard to come by in the literature on Vietnam or French India but appears quite readily in studies of immigrants from the colonies who settled in France. Anthropological research in refugee camps in rural France in the 1970s revealed that the French citizens of Indochina who had been 'repatriated' there included Indian French citizens and people of mixed Indian and Indochinese heritage alongside naturalised Vietnamese, Lao, and Cambodians. A study of Indian Muslims in France in the late 1980s noted that many of those Muslims who hailed from French India arrived in France directly from Indochina, and this community too included Indo-Vietnamese. Other studies of *Pondichériens* residing in the Paris region today similarly show that many of them did not move to France directly but came via Indochina.[54]

---

51. Jacques Weber, 'Accumulation et assimilation dans les Établissements de l'Inde: la caste et les valeurs de l'occident', conference proceedings, CRASOM XXXVIII – 2–3 February 1978, pp. 190, 209; Michalon, 'Des Indes françaises', pp. 102–103. Also Annasse, *Les comptoirs français dans l'Inde*, pp. 122–124; Miles, *Imperial Burdens*, pp. 40–41.
52. Annasse, *Les comptoirs français dans l'Inde*, pp. 141–144. In the same vein see Evariste Dessama, *Tribulations de l'Inde française*, Saigon: France Asie, 1950.
53. M. Clairon, *La renonciation au statut personnel dans l'Inde Française*, Montpellier: Causse, Graille et Castelnau, 1926, p. 81.
54. Pierre-Jean Simon, *Rapatriés d'Indochine: Un village franco-indochinois en Bourbonnais*, Paris: Éditions l'Harmattan, 1981, pp. 324–337; Raymond Delval, *Musulmans français d'origine*

Recent historical studies have begun to recover the ethnic and cultural heterogeneity which was a long-standing characteristic of the Mekong Delta. These works draw attention to the complex relationships and diversity of players within French Indochina, in particular within what is now the southern part of Vietnam. This scholarship helps to correct the view that the actual work of colonisation was carried out strictly by Frenchmen from the Metropole, with Chinese traders constituting the only intermediaries of any sort or any consequence in the relationship between coloniser and colonised.[55]

Collective changes in scholarly thinking are attributed within the academe to 'turns', with one of the latest such turns being the 'transnational' one. Yet Vietnam's own recent history has been just as instrumental in stirring renewed interest in the ethnic diversity of the Lower Mekong, and drawing new attention to the roles of different peoples in shaping the colonial experience and the path to independence. By the early 1990s, there were to my knowledge no *Franco-Pondichériens* (as the descendants of Indians who obtained their French citizenship through 'renunciation' are referred to today) still remaining in Vietnam. A very small community of Indians, or Indo-Vietnamese, stayed behind after the departure of the French in 1954 and the subsequent communist victory over the south in 1975. These individuals were twice ostracised by national projects, firstly as colonial collaborators by the Republic of Vietnam (South Vietnam) from 1954, and then as capitalists under

---

indienne, Paris: Centre des Hautes Etudes sur l'Afrique et l'Asie Modernes, 1987; Brigitte Sébastia, 'Les Pondichérriens de l'Ile de France. Étude des pratiques sociales et religieuses', unpublished DEA thesis, Université Toulouse, 1999. Also see my article, 'Via l'Indochine: trajectoires coloniales de l'immigration sud-indienne', *Hommes et Migrations*, 1268–1269, 2007, 24–33.

55. Important recent scholarship has drawn attention to the precolonial heterogeneity of the Mekong Delta (Cooke and Tana eds 2004), and to historical interactions between ethnic groups in the Delta which constitute the basis of contemporary practice or politics (Taylor 2004, McHale 2013). Recent decades have seen the publication of new works on the ethnic Chinese presence in colonial Indochina and Vietnam (Engelbert 2008, Barrett 2013, also Goscha 2009), on gender and mixed-race populations (Edwards 1998, Stoler 2002, Saada 2007, Firpo 2010), on the Corsican community (Pretini 1992, also Aldrich 2009), and on the positioning in the Lower Mekong of the ethnic Cham (Taylor 2007) and Khmer (Englebert 1993, McHale 2013). Inter-Indochinese relationships are addressed by Goscha (2009, 2012), including Vietnamese as colonial intermediaries in Laos and Cambodia. The force of capricious individuals in shaping or mis-shaping the colonial endeavour comes across in Zinoman (2001) and also in Muller (2006). Full references may be found in the bibliography.

the Socialist Republic of Vietnam after 1975.[56] When Vietnam began to open its doors to foreign investment from the late 1980s under its programme of economic renovation, it also saw an increase in other movements across its borders. These included visits from former Indian residents returning to reconnect with their childhood pasts and in some cases with Indo-Vietnamese relatives who had remained behind. While Indo-Vietnamese living in Vietnam remained reticent at that time to identify their origins as such, this was beginning to change. Cafes selling *cà ri Ấn Độ* (Indian curry) could be spotted among the new burgeoning street-side private enterprises. Ho Chi Minh City's Indian religious sites, temples and mosques, closed or put to other purposes through the 1980s, began to reopen, even though the majority of their eager worshippers were (and still are) respectively Cham or Vietnamese.

Vietnam's new accessibility has spurred some valuable studies of the Indian presence by French Indian scholars, some of them both personal and historical accounts, as well as a number of historical overviews of the Indian migrant population as a whole.[57] Meanwhile within Vietnam itself political and social transformations continue to make the region's ethnic diversity and cultural complexity more acceptable subjects of discussion and study. The re-printing of the more 'heterogeneous' histories of some southern writers is an indication that views of history which are ethnically and culturally more complex are slowly becoming more acceptable in the new political climate.[58] Where ten years ago the suggestion of studying the Indian presence in Indochina drew puzzled looks from Vietnamese academics, in the last decade scholars in Vietnamese

---

56. Nayan Chanda, 'Indians in Indochina', in K.S. Sandhu and A. Mani (eds), *Indian Communities in Southeast Asia*, Singapore: Times Academic Press, ISEAS, 1993, 31–45, p. 33.
57. See articles by Marius and More in the bibliography. Two DEA theses on Indians in Cochinchina (renouncers and Chettiars respectively) were produced in the noughties (Leconte 2001, Brun 2003). For brief overviews of the Indian presence see Vidy (1949), Reddi (1982), Abdoule-Carime (2003), Pairaudeau (2006). See also Chanda (1993) for a valuable account from first-hand sources of the fate of Indian communities post-1975. The present work is the first extended study of Indians in Indochina using primary sources, but a PhD thesis currently in preparation (Pham Phương Chi, 'Who killed Ganesh Sang: Nationalism and Survival of the Indian Diaspora in Vietnam') promises to complement this study by examining the Indian presence, and Indo-Vietnamese communities in Vietnam from the post-independence period to the present. All references are listed in the bibliography.
58. Sơn Nam (2003, 2004) and Vương Hồng Sển (2003). These were works originally published either in the 1960s and 1970s under the relatively more accepting government of South Vietnam, or under strained circumstances in the 1980s and 1990s.

universities have begun to research the Indian community and its places of worship in Ho Chi Minh City.[59] This new interest is driven by a more open climate within the academe in Vietnam; it is also framed by a new geopolitics in the region. The two ancient civilisations, Chinese and Indian, which Europeans have long used as their main references to understand the region, are now both world economic superpowers. As Vietnamese hostility to the former grows over territorial claims and fears of economic dominance, India emerges as an appealing new regional partner for Vietnam. As a subject of study, Indian connections reaching back into Vietnam's past now carry new appeal.

Mobile citizens

The chapters that follow unfold around questions central to the themes of colonial citizenship, inter-imperial connections, the colonial social order, and post-colonial belonging.

Chapter Two ('Shaping legal status in India and Indochina') traces the beginnings of the 'renunciation movement' as an Indian struggle for equality in late nineteenth-century Pondicherry, and the many ways in which the movement was associated with Indochina at its inception. The chapter examines forms of legal status available to renouncers and other foreign and indigenous residents of Indochina, comparing in particular the French Indians' entitlement to citizenship by means of voluntary 'renunciation' with the Cochinchinese population's right to apply for French citizenship through naturalisation. The third chapter ('At work in Indochina: Indian French citizens and Tamil spheres of activity') explores the range of occupations and activities undertaken by Indian French citizens and other Indian migrants in Indochina, and the interconnections within a larger Indian community. The chapter analyses the extent to which Indochina's renouncers, while striving for equality as Frenchmen, also continued to participate in an overlapping Tamil expatriate world.

Chapters Four and Five examine how French Indians challenged colonial authorities to lay claim to 'European' privileges in Cochinchina. Their debates confirm that colonies were complex contexts in which colonial boundaries of rule and hierarchies of race could be negoti-

---

59. Huỳnh Văn Út (2011) and Phan Thị Hồng Xuân (2013).

ated; they were not simply 'outposts for policies formulated at home'.[60] French Indian campaigns in Indochina in the late nineteenth century to retain the right to vote in Cochinchina, and the subsequent Indian role in electoral politics in Cochinchina are analysed in Chapter Four ('The Indian vote in Cochinchina'). Chapter Five ('Colonial citizenship and contractual privileges') examines the substance of debates between Indians employed by the Cochinchinese colonial administration and their French superiors, and their outcome.

Despite a prolonged silence on the part of local people while Indians debated with French authorities to secure their rights in Cochinchina, Vietnamese commentators were later very vocal in their criticism both of the economic dominance of Indians more generally and of the privileges of Indian renouncers specifically. Chapter Six ('Vietnamese engagement with Indian migrants') investigates the complex catalogue of Vietnamese responses to the Indian presence. These include the reactions of the Cochinchinese elite to Indian business from the 1900s onwards, the views of non-communist Southern Vietnamese reformers who specifically attacked the privileges of Indian French citizens in the 1920s, and popular responses, which could be hostile and racialised but also reveal more sympathetic understandings and forms of cooperation. Chapter Seven ('Raising the Indian public profile') demonstrates how political stresses from within Indochina and calls for social and political reform at home prompted Indian French citizens to reorganise and raise their profile, for the benefit of the wider Indian community as well as the Indochinese public. Finally, Chapter Eight ('Diasporic dilemmas') examines how Indian French citizens experienced the pull of their allegiances in all directions as Europe's colonial empires began to unravel from World War Two, and how they negotiated the closely-linked processes of decolonisation in Indochina and French India.

---

60. Conklin, *A Mission to Civilise*, p. 4.

CHAPTER TWO

SHAPING LEGAL STATUS IN INDIA AND INDOCHINA

Indian French citizens obtained their citizenship by 'renouncing' their indigenous personal status. The idea of renunciation grew out of post-revolutionary French enthusiasm for the legal and social assimilation of its colonised peoples. But Indian reasons for embracing renunciation and French reasons for legally endorsing it were both firmly rooted in local-level society and politics. Renunciation was very different from processes of naturalisation which have now become commonplace. It relied on individual choice, rather than the discretion of any state authority. It was up to the individual to give up his (or her) customary civil practices, and thus attain a status equal to French citizenship, or to retain these civil practices and remain a French subject. The promise of the equality it held made renunciation appeal to the leaders of Pondicherry's 'Renunciation Movement' and their followers. For others however, the disadvantages of renunciation firmly outweighed its benefits.

Indian renunciation was linked to Indochina in a number of ways. Those Indians who chose to renounce tended to come from the same ambitious group who sought opportunities in Indochina. Others renounced once they reached Cochinchina, and did so for the practical advantages it lent them. The decree on renunciation of 21 September 1881 in French India was remarkably similar in its wording to a decree introduced just months earlier extending the right to naturalisation to people native to French Cochinchina. Yet while the first document freely extended legal equality to Indians, the second, for the Cochinchinese, severely limited it. Viewed side-by-side, the two legal documents demonstrate how official French thinking about the possibilities of assimilation in its overseas possessions narrowed in the late nineteenth century. This created a legal gulf across which the indigenous Cochinchinese and the more privileged expatriate Indian French citizens saw each other. In turn the legal status of renouncers was in some respects distinct from and in other ways overlapped with the status in Cochinchina of other categories of expatriate Indian.

Colonial manifestations of citizenship

Contestations over French Indians' citizenship are one knot in a string of debates produced in the wake of the French Revolution over whether and how far 'the rights of man and of the citizen would extend to different categories of people in the Empire'.[1] Studies of assimilation and association in French colonialism from the 1960s, which have now become standard texts, tended to view the granting of French citizenship to colonised peoples as the outcome of theoretical debates taking place among metropolitan authorities.[2] In contrast, detailed studies of the ways in which the rights of citizens were introduced into France's old colonies show there was much debate produced from within the colonies, and by colonised peoples themselves. Citizenship, they show, was not sent down fully formed from the metropole. The demands, reactions, and assertions of local peoples, and within local contexts, fed into shaping the status of colonised people in France's post-revolutionary overseas possessions.

In the Caribbean sugar colony of St Domingue (modern Haiti), different sectors of plantation society made demands to be considered as French citizens almost immediately following the 1789 Declaration of the Rights of Man and the Citizen in Paris. The island's white planters, its propertied mixed-race *gens de couleur*, and subsequently its slaves (who rose in revolt in 1791) each pressed to be extended the rights of French citizenship. Political pragmatism as much as revolutionary ideals led the revolutionary government to accede to these various demands.[3] France abolished slavery in its remaining slave colonies (Guadeloupe, Martinique, French Guyana, and Réunion) in 1848, where abolitionist arguments won over in determining the status of former slaves.

---

1. Jane Burbank and Frederick Cooper, *Empires in World History: Power and the Politics of Difference,* Princeton and Oxford: Princeton University Press, 2010, p. 221.
2. Raymond F. Betts, *Assimilation and Association in French Colonial Theory: 1890–1914,* Lincoln: University of Nebraska Press, 2005 [1962]; Deming Lewis, 'One Hundred Million Frenchmen'.
3. C.L.R. James, *The Black Jacobins: Toussaint L'Ouverture and the San Domingo Revolution,* London: Allison and Busby, 1989 [1938]; Frederick Cooper, *Citizenship between Nation and Empire: Remaking France and West Africa, 1945–1960,* Princeton: Princeton University Press, 2014, p. 14.

France granted blanket citizenship to its freed slaves on the basis that their moral development necessitated their full political participation and their regulation by the French Civil Code.[4] French citizenship was shaped along different lines again in Senegal's *Quatre Communes* and in French India. Neither of these parts of France's early nineteenth-century empire had been subject to slavery, but both were trading posts with long-standing connections to France. The imperial centre actively sought to encourage citizenship as a means of nurturing the loyalty of its small enclave populations. Yet in these 'enclave colonies' local people and colonial governments alike stalled over the acceptance of the French Civil Code (and the changes it brought to the regulation of family matters and other social practices) as a prerequisite for French citizenship. As a consequence, it became difficult to establish whether colonised people qualified as citizens or not.

Citizenship in post-revolutionary France was a relationship to the state which sought to render each citizen a free and equal member of the political community. One radical change brought by the revolution was the expression of this relationship as a set of legal rights.[5] Citizens enjoyed electoral franchise, the right to elect members to an assembly that would represent the will of the people, and civil equality, the right to be formally equal before the law.[6] Civil equality was assured in France in the common application of the French Civil Code to all citizens. In the metropolitan context it was one of the most deeply-valued notions produced by the Revolution.[7]

In France's overseas empire, the project of creating 'little overseas Frances' whose inhabitants would become 'French men and women of a different colour' entailed the removal of legal differences between the Metropole and the colonies.[8] The sticking point for France's projects of assimilation in its non-slave colonies in the nineteenth century proved to be civil equality. Considered a virtue in the post-revolutionary metropolitan

---

4. Saada, 'Citoyens et Sujets de l'Empire Français', p. 16.
5. Cooper, *Citizenship between Nation and Empire*, p. 13.
6. Yet women in metropolitan France, while recognised as citizens, did not obtain the vote until 1944. Full citizenship was withheld in France itself, and was not a problem confined to its overseas possessions. See Rosanvallon, *Le sacré du citoyen*.
7. Brubaker, *Citizenship and Nationhood in France and Germany*, ; see also Saada, 'Citoyens et sujets de l'Empire Français', p. 18.
8. Aldrich, *Greater France*, p. 110; Saada, 'Citoyens et Sujets de l'Empire Français', p. 13.

context, the application of the Civil Code became an unwanted or politically risky intrusion into the prevailing social order in France's overseas possessions, where different cultural practices and values held sway.

Assimilation policies in the enclave colonies became shaped either by local resistance to France's imposition of the French Civil Code, or by French caution at imposing its will over private matters in its colonial possessions. The *originaires* of the *Quatre Communes*, the residents of its four trading enclaves in Senegal, were granted full citizenship in 1848, including political participation and the right to be judged by the French Civil Code. They embraced the political rights they had been granted, but objected to French efforts to replace their indigenous personal status (practices related to marriage, inheritance, and family life and shaped in Senegal by Islamic law) with the French Civil Code. At their own insistence, they secured the formation of Muslim tribunals. For a time they enjoyed the right to exercise their political franchise while retaining their indigenous personal status, a legal condition known as 'status naturalisation' (*naturalisation dans le statut*).[9]

The *indigènes* ('natives') of the French Establishments in India were also granted political franchise for the first time in 1848. Unlike the *originaires*, however, they were not made subject to the French Civil Code. French authorities in India were conscious, from experience, that their interference in the ordering of local societies along complex religious and caste lines was liable to instigate social unrest. They thus maintained a policy of non-interference, one similar to that prevailing in British India, allowing Indians to continue to be judged according to personal laws determined by their 'caste and creed'.[10]

Whether the imperial state imposed civic equality and the people rejected it, or the imperial state refrained from interference, both approaches compromised the idea of citizenship as a unified whole binding together electoral and civil rights. Neither the Senegalese *originaires* nor the French Indians clearly met the conditions of full citizenship. Yet France continued to favour the creation of small loyal populations of ambiguously labelled *citoyens* in both places. It conceded to Senegalese pressure for 'status naturalisation', but France readily endorsed the ac-

---

9. Lambert, 'From Citizenship to Negritude', pp. 241–242.
10. France first recognised the right of Indians in the French Establishments to be judged by their own personal laws in 1819. See Arthur Girault, *Principes*, p. 410; also H. Ternisien, 'La Question Électorale en Cochinchine', Supplement of *Journal d'Outre Mer*, 21 February 1888.

tions of a small elite of French Indians when in the 1870s they sought to improve their social and political standing by publicly 'renouncing' their indigenous personal status and voluntarily adopting the French Civil Code. Revolutionary France conceived of citizenship as a commitment which was fundamentally political; this group effectively appropriated the powerful link that nonetheless existed in French thought between citizenship and cultural practice, and used it to their own ends.

France encouraged the extension of citizenship to former slave colonies and to small circumscribed enclave colonies. But when it extended its influence into Algeria it found itself in a larger and more populous landscape. Scale mattered, and it now sought to extend citizenship to some while seeking to restrict it to others. During its early involvement in Algeria, France had seized upon the Jewish trading community as a small and potentially loyal ally in furthering French interests in Algeria. When the Second Republic granted political rights in 1848 in Senegal and French India, it also gave political franchise to Jews in Algeria. Here too, citizenship was directed towards a small, circumscribed group, although with a greater level of French official involvement in shaping citizenship as a cultural project. French authorities attempted, through the establishment of Jewish 'consistories', to reform Jewish personal laws, seeking in particular to do away with polygamy and divorce, to bring these into line with the French Civil Code.[11]

French law in 1848 had been silent on the question of citizenship for Algeria's much larger Muslim population. Through the middle of the nineteenth century Algerian Muslims began to demand the right to political franchise, while over the same period, French attempts to reform the personal status of the small Jewish population proceeded at a slow pace. The *Senatus-Consulte* of 1865 can be viewed as a legal effort to solve both problems, by encouraging the creation of a small loyal group of citizens and keeping citizenship away from those in whose hands it was considered a political threat. This legal act extended French citizenship to Muslims and Jews (as well as foreigners) in Algeria, but only on condition that they renounced their personal status and accepted the French Civil Code.[12] The law was marginally successful at persuading

---

11. Schreier, *Arabs of the Jewish Faith*, p. 23.
12. Michael Brett, 'Legislating for Inequality in Algeria', pp. 440–461.

the Jews to become French.¹³ It was very effective however, at preventing Algerian Muslims from obtaining French citizenship. As they considered their indigenous personal status to be inseparable from their religion, very few Muslims were willing to give it up in order to become French citizens. They continued instead to press, right through to the late 1930s, for the 'status naturalisation' enjoyed by Senegal's *originaires*, but with little success.¹⁴

Deming Lewis has portrayed native assimilation in French colonial policy as a cyclical phenomenon linked to political upheavals in France through the nineteenth century: 'assimilative measures became associated with republican governments, their abolition with the overthrow of these governments'.¹⁵ Yet although France once again began to speak the language of assimilation to its colonies with the rise of the Third Republic, it also embarked upon a much more controlled programme of colonial citizenship as it extended its reach, beginning with Algeria, to territories which were more vast. Until the later part of the nineteenth century France encouraged colonised peoples in its small enclave colonies to adopt the French Civil Code and become citizens – and often tacitly accepted them as citizens even when they didn't accept the Code. Algeria marks an interim period where France used renunciation as a tool to nudge a group it perceived as potentially desirable citizens, and to repel a group it viewed as a political threat. With the conquest of French Cochinchina, France made its citizenship accessible only through naturalisation. This required individuals to apply to French authorities and be judged by them to be worthy of the privilege. It was a fundamental change in the French handling of colonial citizenship, and one which is seldom remarked upon, perhaps because it is masked both by the liberal rhetoric of the Third Republic and by the persistence of the old modes of assimilation even as a new mode was being introduced. As I explain later in this chapter, French Cochinchina's decree on naturalisation was approved some months before French Indians formally gained the right

---

13. The *Crémieux* Law of 1870 forced the issue for Algerian Jews by granting them blanket citizenship. It was issued, according to political theorist Hannah Arendt, at a time of crisis 'when the Jews were regarded as the only trustworthy part of the Algerian population'. Hannah Arendt, 'Why the Cremieux Law was abrogated', in Hannah Arendt, *The Jewish Writings*, New York: Random House, 2007 [1943], 244–253, p. 245.
14. Saada, 'Citoyens et Sujets de l'Empire Français', p. 18.
15. Deming Lewis, 'One Hundred Million Frenchmen', p. 135.

to renounce their personal status. Saada describes this shift in official French assimilationist thinking in the following terms:

> Towards the end of the nineteenth century, the aim of 'assimilation', understood as the adoption of French legal institutions by the 'natives' – an ideal raised at the time of the Revolution and which remained dominant to the end of the nineteenth century – was definitively abandoned in face of the reality of colonial practice.[16]

The reality of colonial practice was France's recognition that despite its newly reinvigorated republican ideology, a more expansive empire could not stand up to the creation of so many citizens.

THE 'RENUNCIATION' MOVEMENT IN FRENCH INDIA

From the late eighteenth century, a French policy in India of non-interference in local custom established that the 'laws, usages, and customs of [each] caste and creed' should continue to regulate marriage, inheritance, and family matters. Local practices pertaining to these matters were then incorporated into a French legal framework and defined as 'indigenous personal law'. The sources of this legislation were Islamic and Hindu law, as interpreted by an advisory board of representatives of Pondicherry's several creeds and various castes. Christians, who to the dismay of the Catholic Church did not put aside many of their 'usages and customs' upon conversion, continued to be governed by Hindu law. While non-interference in indigenous matters was the French intention, it was nonetheless through French civil courts that legal decisions based on indigenous personal law were enacted.[17]

Nor did upholding indigenous personal laws imply that indigenous people were held fast to them. A French Supreme Court order of 1852 made this clear. The ruling was brought in the case of an Indian labourer and his family returning from work abroad, and revealed how migration could confound colonial efforts to regulate civil status. The labourer Ramastrapoullé had registered his marriage in Mauritius with the French *état civil*, but then returned to Pondicherry (with his Indian wife and children) to find his marriage considered nul and his children

---

16. Saada, 'Citoyens et Sujets de l'Empire Français', p. 13; See also Conklin, *A Mission to Civilize*, p. 105.
17. Girault, *Principes*, pp. 409–410; Weber, *Pondichéry*, pp. 45–46; M. B. Hooker, *Legal Pluralism. An Introduction to Colonial and Neo-Colonial Laws*, Oxford: Clarendon Press, 1975, pp. 216–218.

illegitimate because the couple had not married according to their Hindu custom. The Court declared his union legitimate, recognising that certain acts, such as marriage in accordance with the French Civil Code, could constitute a tacit renunciation of indigenous personal laws by the parties involved, and thus the acquisition of French citizenship.[18] The ruling recognised that:

> Although the decree of 6 January 1819, promulgating several French codes in the French Establishments in India, declared...that the Indians, be they Christian, Moor or Gentile, would be judged as in the past according to the laws and customs of their castes, this disposition...is purely optional [*facultatif*] and in no way prevents Indians who are French subjects from freely and voluntarily submitting to the empire of French laws.[19]

Some twenty years later, certain sectors of Indian society actively seized upon the notion that Indians in the French Establishments were not obliged to retain their indigenous 'usages and customs' but could voluntarily choose to live by the French Civil Code. This came about as a result of debates between two opposing factions of the powerful *Vellala* caste. In status terms, this caste comprised a landed 'aristocracy' in Pondicherry in the late nineteenth century because of the virtual absence of other castes considered to rank higher in the ritual hierarchy. At root, the factional disputes were differences over how to respond to French colonial rule. Some *Vellalas* were Catholic converts who had long benefited from the French presence, in roles as middlemen in French trade and in administrative posts. Catholic *Vellalas* were content to continue to work, and rise, within the French colonial system and were receptive to French cultural influences. Pondicherry's Hindu *Vellalas*, by contrast, were opposed to French interference in the Indian social order. In their view Catholic *Vellalas*' susceptibility to French ideas threatened the caste structure from which they drew much of their own power.[20]

One of two opposing figures in this drama was Chanemougan, a Hindu who was elected to Pondicherry's first municipal council in 1872. He served as Mayor of Pondicherry from 1880 to 1908. Chanemougan made use of the French introduction of universal suffrage to oppose

---

18. See Girault, *Principes*, p. 419.
19. 'Bulletin des arrêts de la cour de cassation rendus en matière civile', Imprimerie Nationale, août 1852, p. 157.
20. This account follows Weber, 'Accumulation et assimilation'. See also A. Esquer, *Essai sur les Castes dans l'Inde*, Pondicherry: A. Saligny, 1870, p. 103.

'progressive' social policies, and to block French interference in caste matters and the free exercise of other indigenous customs and practices. He called renunciation a 'sacrilege' committed against the caste system; the renouncers were 'worse than the pariahs'.[21] In pro-Catholic readings of Chanemougan's 'reign', he held his position for four long decades not because of widespread opposition in Pondicherry to French attempts to interfere in the social order, but because of his flair for electoral fraud and manipulation.[22]

Chanemougan's opponent was Pounnoutamby (later Pounnoutamby Laporte), a Catholic lawyer and a Pondicherry municipal councillor alongside Chanemougan. Pounnoutamby may be considered the founder of a 'movement' of renunciation. At its beginning this movement sought to promote equality between Indians as much as it did their equality with their French rulers. It began in 1873 when Pounnoutamby was expelled from court for wearing European-style shoes rather than the slippers deemed appropriate to his caste. In keeping with the legal procedure in rulings related to indigenous personal law, a French court sanctioned him for wearing shoes which degraded his caste position. European footwear had been adopted only among *pariahs*, the 'untouchables' who were deemed impure and existed on the lowest end of the status hierarchy, but who were also employed as servants in Pondicherry's European houses.

Pounnoutamby took his case to France. There he successfully argued that while Indians in the French Establishments had the right to be judged by their own 'usages and customs' this did not withhold from them the right, should they so choose, to accept French civil law. Pounnoutamby's public declaration of his desire to renounce his indigenous personal status led to similar informal renunciations. Most early renunciations occurred among individuals who were, like Pounnoutamby, *Vellala* and Catholic. The growing movement among the 'small liberal Francophile minority' emboldened Pounnoutamby to call for the abolishment of caste privileges in the French colony. He and other like-minded *Vellalas* began to cross caste lines in church, taking their place among *pariahs*. Catholics of caste had previously insisted upon caste segregation at

---

21. E. Divien, quoted in Michalon, 'Des Indes françaises', p. 47.
22. On Chanemougan's term in power, see Weber, *Pondichéry*, pp. 237–269. A more favourable view of him is found in Felix Falk, 'Situation Politique de l'Inde Française', pamphlet published for private circulation, no publisher, no date (circa 1880).

church services and in cemeteries. They hosted banquets, too, at which they broke taboos about inter-caste dining by sharing meals with their 'untouchable' compatriots.[23]

'Renunciation of personal status', as the cases of Algeria and Senegal show, was by no means a notion unique to French India. Its novelty in India was the way in which it was actively promoted by colonised people themselves. The historical record cannot confirm how well-informed were Pounnoutamby and his followers of the progress of assimilation in France's other colonies. They appear nonetheless to have known of the importance French authorities attached to civil equality as an integral dimension of citizenship. It was a door, they seemed to sense, that would open with relatively little resistance if pushed.

Laporte's renunciation movement was given official recognition with a decree enacted in 1881 (September 21) inviting Indians from the French Establishments in India to voluntarily renounce their personal status (*renonciation du statut personnel*). Renunciation was a formal declaration, made in the presence of a magistrate. The declarant voiced his desire to no longer adhere to indigenous regulations pertaining to his personal status and to consent instead to be judged by the French Civil Code. The declaration was applicable to the declarant, his spouse, and any children who were still minors. Those who had undergone renunciation were referred to as 'renouncers' (*renonçants*). Although the faculty of renunciation was open equally to both sexes, in practice most acts of renunciation were made by men (with women included as spouses).

As a sign of their changed status, renouncers were obliged to adopt a surname. This was a departure from general Tamil practice, where the use of a single name was the norm. The adoption of surnames by renouncers publicly marked their change in legal status. The identifiable patterns which renouncers followed in coining new names for themselves makes it possible today to identify Indians of French origin as the descendants of those who chose in the past to 'renounce'.[24]

This reading of the rise of renunciation in French India depicts a local movement driven by the wish for colonial assimilation and indigenous social reform. It emphasises local agency and suggests that the ability

---

23. The account in this and the previous paragraph draws from Weber, *Pondichéry*, pp. 227–236, and Michalon, 'Des Indes françaises', p. 47.
24. The text of the renunciation decree can be found in the Appendix. On renouncer names see Michalon, 'Des Indes françaises', p. 43.

Plate 1: Plaque outside Pounnoutamby Laporte's Pondicherry villa. Photograph by N. Pairaudeau, 2005.

to renounce was formally decreed because it drew strong support from colonial officials frustrated by their own inability to handle caste matters with a sure hand. Pounnoutamby Laporte is firmly placed in a leadership role, a position which descendants of renouncers in Pondicherry maintain for him to this day. A street in Pondicherry bears his name, and a plaque outside his house commemorates his role as the first renouncer, who took the name of 'Laporte' because renunciation had 'opened the door for Indians to the West'.[25]

---

25. See Weber, *Pondichéry*, p. 235.

Other readings help to further explain why French authorities accepted and endorsed this arrangement. In one view, Pondicherry's small group of progressive Francophile Indians were granted a status equal to Europeans so that their votes could carry the same weight as those of French voters in French India's electoral system. All Indians in nineteenth-century French India had the right to vote, but a system of electoral colleges gave vastly disproportionate weight to the votes of French citizens from the Metropole (see Chapter Four). Despite the controls France placed on its 'democratic' system in French India, and despite his own apparent disdain for French liberal values, Chanemougan was nonetheless elected Mayor in 1880. Colonial authorities hoped, to follow the logic of this argument, that if Indians who were loyal to the French cause had equal status to French citizens they could now be included in the European electoral college. This would allow France to rein in the electoral influence of less cooperative Indians, and thus regain control of its beleaguered democracy. The British Consular agent at Karikal certainly saw electoral politics as a motive driving official French support for renunciation. He was eager to point out the foolishness of French colonial practice to his superiors in Delhi. 'The decree,' he claimed, 'originated in the ambition of a perfervid, noisy and not very scrupulous group of "politicians" … who were anxious to work the administration of these settlements according to their own – more or less, sincere ideas.'[26]

Yet if political ambitions played a role in prompting the French authorities to endorse the process of renunciation, so too did French hopes of creating a corps of indigenous public servants in whom they felt they could put their trust. 'Renunciation of personal status' was promoted in late 1870s French India to enable Indians to take up posts within the French colonial administration requiring proofs of 'moral responsibility'. French anxieties over culture and moral behaviour, voiced elsewhere in the French Empire in discussions of assimilation, are reiterated here in the context of employment. The appointment in 1879 of the first Indian Justice of the Peace in the French Establishments prompted concerns that Indians in public posts might have beliefs and customs out of keeping with the French civil (and moral) code they were appointed to pro-

---

26. British Library (hereafter BL) BL IOR/L/PJ/6/84 Naturalisation of Indian Coolies, etc, (1833) [sic]: British Consular Agent Karikal to Chief Secretary to Government, 4 July 1882.

tect and uphold. The Minister of Colonies in Paris raised the question of whether a 'native' holding moral values incompatible with those dear to the Republic (polygamy was the example sited) was able to make judgements founded on values entrenched in the French Civil Code. The Minister took comfort from the news that the man whose moral fibre was in question, Cannoussamy, was a Catholic and therefore must have already made some progress towards embracing French values. As long as Indians renounced their personal status and agree to be ruled by the French Civil Code, this discussion concluded, they were eligible to apply for high-level posts.[27]

The text of the 1881 decree on the renunciation of personal status reads: 'By this act of renunciation, which will be definitive and irrevocable, [the person or persons renouncing] will be ruled ... by the civil and political laws applicable to the French in the colony.'[28] Sympathetic readers of this decree understood that renunciation conferred citizenship upon its bearers. In Cochinchina, however, where many renouncers resided by the late nineteenth century, colonial administrators disagreed. It was through protests mounted by Indian renouncers based in Cochinchina, described in Chapter Four, that renouncers' status came to be legally recognised as French citizenship and thus valid throughout the French Empire.

The Extent and Appeal of Renunciation, at Home and Abroad

Figures vary as to how many Indians had renounced by the turn of the twentieth century. One source claims there were 3,700 by 1883, another that in 1900 there were 3,000 renouncers.[29] It is likely that the lower figure is a count only of acts registered. If family members named under a single act and descendants of renouncers were included, the figure at a modest estimate would increase at least five-fold. Weber and Michalon concur that renunciations peaked in the initial year or so after the decree was put in place, and then dropped off sharply. Michalon used the legal registers of acts of renunciation still kept at Pondicherry's Municipal

---

27. National Archive of India at Pondicherry (hereafter NAIP), DM 1879: correspondence MMC and GEFI, June–November 1879.
28. 'Decret relatif au statut personnel, 21 septembre 1881', *Annuaire des Établissements français dans l'Inde 1881*, pp. 472–473 (and see Appendix).
29. Morrachini and Divien, both cited in Michalon, 'Des Indes françaises', p. 45.

Building to chart trends in the incidence of renunciation over time. According to these records, which begin in 1882, some 1,000 acts of renunciation were registered in the first year. This fell to 295 in 1883. In subsequent years anywhere from 20 to 100 acts were registered, right through until 1963, the last year in which renunciations were possible.[30]

The great majority of renouncers were Catholic. Indeed, it was rare for Catholics not to renounce. As one author observed, 'the native Christian [in French India] almost always renounces his personal status'.[31] Hindu renouncers were fewer, relative to the much larger Hindu population overall, and Muslim renunciations were fewer still. In caste terms renouncers were either from high-status groups or, at the opposite extreme, from the ranks of the ritually impure (*pariahs*). The vast majority of renunciations took place among people from Pondicherry and Karikal, with very few renunciations registered among people from France's other colonial possessions in India.[32]

Lists of renunciations registered at local offices of the *état civil* were published periodically in the *Moniteur Officiel* (and subsequently the *Journal Officiel*) of French India. These first appeared in 1882, but from the late 1890s until 1937 they included information about the religion and professed caste of every renouncer listed.[33] Confirming the general observations above, these lists show the number of Catholic renunciations was high in proportion to the total indigenous Catholic population of Pondicherry and Karikal.[34] The number of renunciations recorded

---

30. Weber, 'Accumulation et assimilation', p. 209; Michalon, 'Des Indes françaises', p. 45; also interview with Annoussamy David, Pondicherry, August 2004.
31. Philippe Herchenroder, *Étude sur le statut juridique des indigènes chrétiens*, Paris: Domat Montchrestien, 1935, p. 10.
32. Annasse, *Les comptoirs français dans l'Inde*, p. 123; Michalon, 'Des Indes françaises', p. 45; Weber, 'Accumulation et assimilation', p. 209.
33. In an effort to diminish the prejudicial effects of caste on sectors of French Indian society, the government of the French Establishments imposed a ban in 1937 on the use of caste names in civil and notary acts. Caste information disappears from the lists after this date. 'État civil des natifs dans les Établissements français dans l'Inde et suppression dans les actes publics de la mention de la caste des intéressés', *Journal Officiel des Établissements français dans l'Inde (JOEFI)*, June 1937, pp. 916–919. A full series of the official journals was not available to me; thus my observations are drawn from selected years for which full series were available: 'Relevé hebdomadaire des actes de renonciation au statut personnel', *Moniteur Officiel des Établissements français dans l'Inde (MOEFI)*, 1898, and 'Relevé mensuelle des acts de renonciation', *JOEFI*, 1916 and 1928.
34. In 1880, 86 percent of Pondicherry's population was Hindu, 12 percent Catholic, and 2 percent Muslim. Karikal's Muslim population was larger in comparison, at 16 percent, while Hindus represented 69 percent of the population there and Catholics 15 percent. These

in a given year was more or less equally divided between two groups: Catholics *Vellalas* and people of the lowest status on the caste hierarchy (Catholic or Hindu and with '*pariah*' or '*Valangamougattar*' recorded as their caste).[35] Muslim renouncers were very few, but nonetheless represented two to three percent of all persons who renounced in any given year.[36]

Renouncers were also drawn from specific localities within Pondicherry and Karikal. Catholic *Vellalas* from the village of Reddiar Palayam appear repeatedly on the lists of renunciations in the official journals. So too do *Vannias* from Nellitope. Both villages belonged to French Pondicherry, and both were associated not only with renunciation, but with Indochina. Reddiar Palayam is to this day dubbed 'Little Saigon'. Tombs in the Catholic cemeteries of both Reddiar Palayam and Nellitope, as well as the larger cemetery at Uppalam to the south of Pondicherry, bear epitaphs describing careers pursued in Indochina. Indochina connections are also evident in the published lists of renunciations in entries which indicate that the person or family in question was domiciled in Indochina at the time of their renunciation. The father and son Bavazy and Pakiry, Muslims from Karikal, were described in 1898 as milk vendors 'resident in Phnom Penh, Cambodia'.[37] Two Catholic *Vellalas* who renounced in August of 1912, Teivassayagayam and Mariassouce were 'residing in Tonkin' at the time of their renunciation. The common surname they chose, Sinnou suggests they were probably related. In the same year Andonissamy, a Catholic *Vellala* from Reddiar Palayam who chose the surname Derock, was described as 'currently in Saigon'.[38]

There is very little evidence of renunciations taking place in French possessions other than Pondicherry and Karikal. One renunciation was

---

proportions had not changed greatly by the interwar years. Delval, *Musulmans français*, pp. 141–142.

35. 'Valangamouggatar' translates as 'people of the right hand division' and was assumed as a caste name by some groups in Pondicherry, probably in an effort to escape social (and caste) disenfranchisement. The distinction between 'right hand' (*valangai*) and 'left hand' (*idangai*) castes was an important one in South India in the nineteenth century. According to the French ethnographer Esquer, *Vellalas* were allied with *Valangamougattars* as the respective leaders and servants of the right-hand division. Esquer, *Essai sur les Castes*, p. 95. See also E. Thurston, *Castes and Tribes of South India*, Madras: Government Press, 1909, p. 80.

36. The few Muslim renunciations listed either did not mention caste, or the persons registered were described as 'of Muslim caste' (*de caste musulmane*).

37. *MOEFI*, 1898.

38. *JOEFI*, 1912.

recorded for Chandernagore in 1898. Another man renounced in Mahé in 1928.[39] Over many years there are no renunciations recorded in these *comptoirs* at all. This suggests that Pounnoutamby Laporte's movement was very localised, spilling over from Pondicherry only to nearby Karikal where many ties, familial and educational, were already established.

The reasons why some people native to French India chose to 'renounce' their personal status are complex, as are the reasons why others rejected the offer. They encompass the question of what renouncers thought they were doing by declaring their rejection of their indigenous civil practices, thought of the ideas and principles embedded in the French Civil Code, and thought they might gain (or lose) in material or status terms by undergoing this legal transformation of their identities.

When Pounnoutamby Laporte wore European shoes in court in 1873, his action was a declaration of equality in two senses. The footwear he sported was worn routinely by his colonial masters and superiors. Thus his gesture 'reached up' in their direction. Yet in Indian terms the shoes he wore were also considered to have been sullied through their adoption by the lowest, 'untouchable' ranks of Indian society; his act simultaneously 'reached down' in solidarity. Laporte stood equal, his action said, to Europeans, but also to all other Indians regardless of their caste status. Like Laporte, the vanguard of Catholic *Vellala* renouncers appear to have understood by their renunciation that they were declaring this double commitment, to seek equality with the French and to avowedly reject the caste system.

The main appeal of renunciation for *pariahs* was no doubt the promise of escape from the social stigma of their lowly position on the caste ladder. Certainly conversion to Catholicism, a tactic previously employed by them to evade Hindu society's stigmatising value system, had not entirely succeeded. Despite the church's disapproval, Indian converts of higher castes had found it difficult to abandon caste hierarchies entirely. At their insistence, walls were erected within churches, as well as cemeteries, to separate the casted from the 'impure'. These were not taken down until after the First World War.[40] Yet the French presence

---

39. 'Relevé', *MOEFI*, 1898; 'Relevé', *JOEFI*, 1928.
40. Saroja Sundararajan, *Glimpses of the History of Karaikkal*, Madras: Lalitha Publications, 1984, p.130; N. Gupta, 'Citizens of French India', p. 169; Miles, *Imperial Burdens*, p. 266; Francis Cyril Anthony (ed.), *Gazeteer of India: Union Territory of Pondicherry Vol I*, Pondicherry: Administration of the Union Territory of Pondicherry Press, 1982, p. 356.

offered other opportunites for social mobility to French India's *pariahs*. Among them were men and women who found opportunities to work for the French as domestic servants and who acquired a rudimentary knowledge of French in doing so.[41] The principle of equality in a French republican sense must surely have added to the appeal of renunciation for this group. It is likely too that it was *pariahs* with backgrounds in French domestic service who found their way to Indochina.

Renunciation in its most principled form, then, was a commitment to equality both with French colonisers and fellow Indians. Among renouncers overseas in Indochina, parity with French citizens was always the more pronounced of the two principles. Without denying these expatriate renouncers the conviction of their beliefs, there were pragmatic reasons for their emphasis on renunciation as citizenship. Many of the debates described in later chapters over their rights and privileges in Cochinchina turned on whether they could be considered French citizens. On occasion in the course of these debates renouncers maintained that they had rejected the notion of caste through their renunciation. 'No castes, only men. No *pariahs*, only equal citizens', was the cry of a 1907 pamphlet published by Saigon-based renouncers in support of Indian policemen whose contractual rights were under threat.[42] This was intended though, to demonstrate all the stronger the renouncers' commitment to French republican notions of equality and fraternity, rather than an indication of any associated anti-caste campaign in Indochina.

Renouncers' efforts to secure legal assimilation with the citizens of metropolitan France became a means of furthering opportunities for themselves within the French colonial system and came to precede the goal of fundamental social change within Indian society. Renunciation did not effectively lift the social stigma of untouchability for *pariahs* who chose to renounce. Proof of this is found in the establishment in Pondicherry in 1898 of the 'Progressive Society for Renounced Valangamougattars'. The *Réveil Social*, a renouncer-led society which similarly aimed to 'work for the welfare of the depressed classes', was established in 1907 (and exists to this day).[43] Further research into

---

41. Weber, *Pondichéry*, p. 39.
42. ANOM GGI 17248 Au sujet des agents de police indiens citoyens français de la ville de Saigon, 1910: Pamphlet entitled 'Ce qui se passe au Colonies, les Immortels principes! La question des Indiens Citoyens Français en Cochinchine' (and see Chapter Five).
43. Anthony, *Gazeteer*, pp. 356–357.

the working of these organisations might establish whether they received active support from renouncers from casted backgrounds. In Cochinchina, renouncers' pursuit of citizenship masked perceptions of caste distinction within the group for several decades. From what we know of renouncers' interactions with one another in the early decades of their presence in that colony, there is no firm evidence that they made sharp distinctions between themselves on the basis of caste. These distinctions resurfaced though, with the pressures imposed by the economic crisis of the late 1920s (see Chapter Seven).

Renunciation was understood by the people who undertook it as a declaration of equality. On paper though, it was expressed as their rejection of their indigenous civil practices in favour of the French Civil Code. Renouncers were generally more concerned, however, with clearly defining the rights they had gained, than with dwelling on the indigenous 'usages' they had renounced. Strictly speaking, renunciation should have meant giving up all practices relating to marriage, inheritance, and the structure of the family which did not conform to the French Civil Code, in exchange for French citizenship. The standard explanation for the modest number of (caste) Hindu renunciations is that Hindus considered it an affront to the caste system and its values.[44] Similarly, Muslim renunciations were very few because Muslims did not wish to forgo practices pertaining to marriage, inheritance, and paternity which they perceived to be decreed by Islam. Renouncing such practices would amount to a denial of their faith.[45]

For the majority of those who 'renounced', however, renunciation did little to change their marriage practices. Catholics continued legally to contract arranged and consanguine marriages, in particular a long-standing preferred alliance between maternal uncle and niece. These unions were quietly tolerated by the French authorities, assisted by special dispensations from the courts, despite being inadmissible under the French Civil Code (and despite the church's disapproval).[46]

French Indian Catholics eagerly renounced their personal status, but could quietly continue to marry as it suited them because of the ambi-

---

44. Annasse, *Les comptoirs français dans l'Inde*, p. 123.
45. Interview with J.B.P More, Paris, April 2004.
46. Weber, 'Accumulation et assimilation'; Annoussamy David, 'Le Mariage entre oncle et niece dans le sud de l'Inde', *Le Trait d'Union*, April 2002, p. 8.

guity surrounding their personal status. In 1881 when the renunciation decree was issued it was still not absolutely clear how an indigenous Christian's personal status was defined. In strictly legal terms, Hindu personal laws applied to them, yet through their conversion, and through moral pressures applied by the church, they were pressed to adopt 'usages' more closely aligned with the French Civil Code. One Saigon-based Catholic, pushing the notion of renunciation to its logical conclusion, wrote an absurdist text in 1890 begging authorities to have his renunciation rescinded and allow him to apply for naturalisation instead, on the basis that he had already given up his indigenous customs and usages in the act of converting to Christianity. He had, he claimed, reverted to his former personal status of 'paganism' through his renunciation.[47]

According to historian Jacques Weber, renunciation never became widespread in French India. He maintains that the movement 'had very little impact' and renunciations never became popular except among a 'small, marginalised minority'.[48] His assessment does not consider though the flow of Indians from the French possessions who started to leave to seek work in Indochina even as Laporte's renunciation movement was underway. The total number of migrants of Indian origin (which included not only renouncers, but also Indian French subjects and British Indians) never stood at more than 0.2% of Cochinchina's population at its peak in the 1920s. This amounted to approximately 8,000 migrants against a total population of nearly four million; the figure was lower in other parts of Indochina. Yet renunciation was far more popular among Indians away from home in Indochina than it was among those in Pondicherry. According to Weber, a mere 2% of Pondicherry's population had renounced by 1883.[49] The figure among Indians from the French possessions residing in Cochinchina in 1888 was 16%. By 1935 the percentage of Indians who originated from the French possessions and who held the status of renouncer in Cochinchina (79%) far surpassed the number who did not, the reverse of the situation in French India in the same period (see Table 1). Simply put, a lot of renouncers

---

47. T. P. Appavou, *Absurde renonciation des Indous chrétiens*, Saigon: Imprimerie Aug. Boch, 1890, p. 4.
48. Weber, 'Accumulation et assimilation', pp. 190, 209.
49. Ibid., p. 209.

Table 1: Population in Cochinchina of residents of Indian origin, 1888–1936

	Legal status		
Year	French citizens (renouncers)	French citizens (non-renouncers)	British subjects
1888	64*	342*	812
1921	700*	1,274#	4,000
1936	1,589	435	2,000

* Male voters. # In 1915.

Sources: As full figures on the Indian population according to legal status cannot be extracted from the colonial census, data here is drawn from a variety of sources. See VNA2 Goucoch IB.29/233 Élections coloniales, inscription des natifs de l'Inde sur les listes électorales 1887–1888; *Annuaire de la Cochinchine Française pour l'année 1888*, Saigon: Imprimerie Coloniale, 1888, p. 508; 'Le Cahier des vœux annamites. Naturalisation française', *Echo Annamite*, 1 December 1925; *Annuaire statistique de l'Indochine, Recueil des statistiques relatives aux années 1913–1922*, pp. 36–37; VNA1 L11: 'État numérique des Indiens sujets français non renonçants établis en Cochinchine, 1936'; *Annuaire statistique de l'Indochine*, Vol. 6, 1934–35–36, Hanoi: IDEO, 1937, p. 25; *Le Monde Colonial Illustré*, 164, Sept 1937.

found their way to Indochina. And as subsequent chapters reveal, their presence was more powerful than their numbers suggest.

MULTIPLE LINKS TO INDOCHINA

French reasons for endorsing renunciation were not completely transparent and Indian reasons for choosing to renounce were equally complex. Less opaque were the many forces which connected renunciation with the migration of Indians to Indochina. The reason for this pull towards Indochina lies partly in the kinds of people who chose to renounce. The first Indians from the French Establishments called to Saigon from the 1860s to work in the administration were the same kinds of people who went on to become the main supporters of the renunciation movement a decade later. Many were 'progressive' Catholics of the *Vellala* caste. Some were undoubtedly cohorts of Pounnoutamby Laporte, and Laporte's relatives and children were among those who fashioned careers for themselves in Indochina.[50] The debates over renouncers' electoral and civil rights in Cochinchina, described in Chapter Four, took place during the same period when supporters of Laporte and Chanemougan

---

50. Weber, *Pondichéry*, p. 253; Annasse, *Les comptoirs français dans l'Inde*, p. 41.

were pitted against one another in French India. Chanemougan's success in removing renouncers from 'European' electoral lists in French India in the 1880s, it has been claimed, even provided a direct motive for renouncers to seek refuge in Cochinchina.[51] No firm evidence proves that renouncers' intentionally removed themselves from Pondicherry to escape Chanemougan and his 'traditionalists'. Yet it remains that the height of the debate in Cochinchina over how renouncers' status was to be interpreted (early 1880s to 1907) coincides neatly with Chanemougan's extended term as Mayor of Pondicherry (1880–1908). Whether intentional or incidental, the positioning of Cochinchina's renouncers away from Chanemougan's adverse influence allowed them to more easily pursue their ambitions to become colonial citizens.

Colonial authorities in French India considered 'renunciation of personal status' to be of value in assuring the moral stature of Indians in the public service at a time when Cochinchina was coming to rely on Pondicherry and Karikal as sources of functionaries for its expanding administration. This raises the question of whether a legal instrument intended to stamp French values on Indian public servants (as flimsy an effort at social engineering as this may have been) was introduced with a view to its application beyond French India. The French wish for its Indian public servants to hold appropriate moral values cannot be explicitly linked to their hiring in French administrations in Indochina. Yet there are certainly powerful suggestions. Vennemani Cannoussamy, the Pondicherry magistrate whose promotion in 1879 first raised the question of moral guarantees, was transferred five years later to Cochinchina. There he became the first Indian Justice of the Peace in the colony, serving from 1884 at the tribunal in Mỹ Tho, and subsequently in Rạch Gí.[52]

Those who chose to renounce were primarily from the two extreme ends of the French Indian social scale. On the higher rungs of the status ladder were people of a small, Francophile, 'progressive' minority. At the bottom of the status ladder were *pariahs* deeply stigmatised by the rest of society. Although there was little in the way of French language education available to people native to French India, these two groups, despite

---

51. Marius, 'Les Pondichériens dans l'administration', p. 391.
52. NAIP DM 1883: MMC to GEFI, 12 May 1883; NAIP DM 1884: Decree of the President of the French Republic, 11 February 1884; *ACCH pour l'année 1887*, p. 208.

the social gap which separated them, were the most likely to receive it, and this education was a further factor tying them to Indochina.

French medium schools in the French Establishments were scarce because of French slowness to found them, but also because the majority of the Indian population saw little value in learning French. Those who managed to obtain an education in French were either among the Francophile elite, or conversely were *pariahs*. The former sought to enter the primary *Collège Calvé*, reserved for casted Indians and Muslims. Once it opened its doors to Indians in the latter half of the nineteenth century, they aimed to further their studies at Pondicherry's French *lycée*. Pariahs could enter a free school established by religious missions expressly to improve their lot; these provided French tuition even though they offered no more than a very basic primary education.[53] High caste individuals tended to stay longer in education, usually obtaining the *baccalauréat* and, if their families could afford it, going on to higher education either in Pondicherry or in France. In general, renouncers of low status origins continued to obtain little more than a primary school certificate at best. There were marked exceptions to this rule though. The lawyer Mathias Clairon was of humble status but he nonetheless managed to secure a higher education. He and other members of the Clairon family (several of whom held respectable positions in the professions and in business) were instrumental in the 1907 formation of the 'Réveil Social'.[54] It is no coincidence that the Clairon family progressed to Saigon, where opportunities to rise both economically and socially in spite of their origins were greater.

Regardless of the level of French education they obtained, opportunities for French-educated Indians were limited if they stayed at home. As the educationalist Valmaire observed in the 1920s, the small pool of Indians who had been educated in French was virtually obliged to leave India to find work:

> Those in our colony who really have need of French are but a small number. It is those who are preoccupied with local politics, those who seek places in the administration or who aim for certain liberal professions such as the bar,

---

53. M. Valmaire, *Rapport sur l'enseignement dans l'Inde Française du XVIIIe siècle à nos jours*, Pondicherry: Imprimerie moderne de Pondichéry, 1922. On caste segregation in Pondicherry schools, see Valmaire, *Rapport*, pp. 13, 27; Weber, *Pondichéry*, p. 302; NAIP DM 1908: petition 'Réveil Social' to MMC, 7 February 1908.

54. Antony, *Gazeteer*, p. 356.

teaching, etc., for which but a few places are available. The others, it must be admitted, have no use for French. There are nonetheless people who learn [French] but most of them do not remain in the Colony; neither industry, nor local commerce are sufficient to offer them prospects, so they emigrate to larger colonies and especially towards Indochina. It is this route which, in the last twenty-five to thirty years, nearly the entire *créole* element has taken and it is the route taken by more and more Indians who have through education become proficient in French.[55]

It was their French education, then, rather than their renunciation which initially made some Indians from the French Establishments employable in Indochina as France extended its influence there. This changed from the late 1880s, once renunciation became obligatory for Indians employed in the Cochinchinese administration who wished to continue to enjoy 'European' terms of service, with the paid leave, travel, and 'colonial' supplements which this included (see Chapter Four). Thereafter, renunciation had a value in Cochinchina which it did not have in India. Indian employees in the public service in Pondicherry or Karikal may have had a salary on par with their European counterparts, but they were not eligible for the array of extra benefits enjoyed by Europeans hired from overseas. The prospects, in Indochina, of so fully enjoying the benefits of French citizenship made employment there even more appealing. It was a factor binding together renunciation and migration to Indochina even more tightly.

One of the main obligations of French citizenship was the duty to fulfil military service.[56] In principle, renouncers too were obliged to serve in the French military. Until 1908, however, all French citizens in the French Establishments in India were exempt, including renouncers. The fact that they did not have to 'pay their debt' to France was one justification, prior to that date, for questioning the validity of their 'citizenship'. Yet after the policy changed, another difficulty remained. With the (Second) Treaty of Paris, signed in 1815, Britain forbade France from constructing military fortifications in French India and severely limited the troops it could retain on its soil in India.[57] From 1908 French authorities circumvented this restriction by recruiting men from French India who were eligible for military service to the nearest recruitment centre in the French overseas

---

55. Valmaire, *Rapport sur l'enseignement*, pp.17–18.
56. Michalon, 'Des Indes françaises', p. 39.
57. Annasse, *Les comptoirs français dans l'Inde*, pp. 107–108; Miles, *Imperial Burdens*, p. 5.

empire. This included renouncers as well as Indo-French and Europeans. The nearest recruitment centre was Saigon.⁵⁸

By the time renouncers began to be eligible for recruitment in the French army and called up to Indochina, many of the young French Indian recruits already lived there. Recruitment tables of all young men of Indian origin eligible for the draft in 1920 show that a single recruit out of a total of 62 men had been born in Pondicherry. Saigon was the birthplace of an astonishing 77 percent (48 recruits), with Haiphong in second place (five recruits). Other towns and cities named as the birthplaces of Indian recruits included Hanoi, Kratie (Cambodia), St. Denis (Réunion), Sénégal, Penang, Cape Town and Colombo. These figures included some Indo-French (based on their surnames, 37 recruits were renouncers, and fifteen were Indo-French), but the figure is still very high. The fact that by 1920 so many young male Indian French citizens were born in Indochina demonstrates again just how tightly renunciation was tied to migration.⁵⁹

Men native to French India, but who did not hold French citizenship, could voluntarily pursue careers in the military as auxiliaries (sepoys).⁶⁰ Few, however, remained auxiliaries for long. They were motivated to renounce their personal status by the considerably better pay, terms, and pensions which they stood to enjoy as French citizens. Those volunteers who did not renounce came to regret it, like the auxiliary Kichena who, having renounced his personal status 'a little late', wrote to Paris in 1931 to appeal for a raise in his meagre indigenous pension.⁶¹ One could be tempted to attribute these volunteers' renunciations solely to the pursuit of financial gain, but a glance at some of the surnames the new citizen-soldiers chose for themselves suggest that ideas of patriotic love for France, its republicanism, and its military genius cannot be entirely discounted in their motivations. Among soldiers who renounced in 1912 were those who chose surnames associating them with the statesmen of their time, including 'Freycinet' and 'Clemenceau'.⁶² In the

---

58. NAIP DM 1910: arrêtée interministerielle 19 April 1910.
59. NAIP C–372 État Civil Tableau de recensement des jeunes français, naturalisés et renonçants ayant atteint l'age de 20 ans révolus, Tableau de recensement des classes de 1887 à 1905.
60. Michalon, 'Des Indes françaises', p. 43.
61. NAIP DM 1931: S. Kichena, 'former voluntary soldier' to MMC, 11 February 1931.
62. 'Relevé', JOEFI, 1912.

1930s, the names of French Indian soldiers in Indochina read as a tribute to France's military strategists, its republic, and to glory in general. Applying for leave in September of 1930 were Messieurs 'Outtiriadassou Magnifique', 'Napoleon', 'Tricolore', 'Égalité', and 'Liberté'. So too could renouncers' surnames betray the force of the British presence across French India's porous boundaries. Both Aroquianadin Robaitche Claive and Andonissamy Robaitche Claive (presumably the 'Robert Clives' were brothers) were also among the applicants for leave in that year.[63]

Renunciation appealed to certain types of Indians in the French Establishments for reasons very closely intertwined with forces drawing them from French India to Indochina. The connections between renunciation and Indochina though did not end there. The decree on renunciation was also closely related to a similar decree issued in Cochinchina defining procedures for naturalisation in that colony.

INDIAN RENUNCIATION VS. *ANNAMITE* NATURALISATION

The introduction of naturalisation laws in France's new colonial possessions from the late nineteenth century may be understood as a signal from the recently established Third Republic of a renewed willingness to make the natives of its overseas possessions into Frenchmen. But the procedure for naturalisation, unlike renunciation, made citizenship a right which had 'to be earned individually' by those who could demonstrate their status as 'deserving French subjects'.[64] Decrees permitting naturalisation for the colonised peoples of France's 'new colonies', such as the regulation introduced for 'Annamites' in Cochinchina in 1881, effectively acted to severely reduce the number of people able to accede to the status of citizens. The Cochinchinese decree on *Annamite* naturalisation and the decree introduced in French India permitting renunciation of personal status together embody an important shift in French assimilationist thinking. So abrupt is this shift that the more restrictive Cochinchinese policy actually preceded – by a mere five months – the older more liberal policy.

From May 1881 people native to Cochinchina were given the right to apply for naturalisation. In their applications, they were obliged to demonstrate they had performed some service to France and had an

---

63. NAIP DM 1930: GGCCH to GEFI, 28 September 1930.
64. Conklin, *A Mission to Civilise*, pp. 104, 205.

attachment to French culture. The privilege was not readily granted. Indeed, the process became more difficult over time. By the 1910s Cochinchinese seeking French naturalisation were required to demonstrate guarantees of 'Frenchness' in their private life. Applications for naturalisation came to include questions as to whether the applicant wore western dress, ate rice or bread, and sat at a table with chairs.[65]

By contrast, Indians from the French Establishments were merely invited, if they so desired, to declare themselves 'renounced' of their personal laws and so become French citizens. They could choose to do so regardless of whether they had any knowledge of the French language. Even the suggestion of attachment to British rather than French imperial triumph, as the surname chosen by the brothers 'Robert Clive' implied, did not bar their renunciations from being legally recognised. Renunciation allowed people to freely and voluntarily submit to the French Civil Code, while naturalisation placed the colonial state as a gatekeeper, interceding to test the cultural and moral merit of candidates and pass judgement on their worthiness.

The modes through which two different groups of colonial subjects could obtain citizenship, depending on whether they were from an old colony or a new one, were vastly different. This difference was only heightened by the remarks of legal analysts at the time. They pointed out that the effects of renunciation as described in the French Indian law were a textual reproduction of the effects of naturalisation as described in the Cochinchinese law, a fact used later to support the idea that renunciation was equal to naturalisation in its legal effect.[66]

When the two forms of assimilation were brought together on Cochinchinese soil, they set in motion the troubles described in this book. Problems arose when people who were able to advance considerably their own position within an older French imperial project of assimilation came into a second French colony where local people were much more limited in their ability to pursue similar aspirations. The privileges enjoyed and

---

65. Hue-Tam Ho Tai, 'The Politics of Compromise: The Constitutionalist Party and the Electoral Reforms of 1922 in French Cochinchina', *Modern Asian Studies*, 18, 3, 1984, 371–391, p. 382. Naturalisation decrees for the Indochinese protectorates came later than in Cochinchina. The legal right to apply for French citizenship was introduced in Tonkin in 1887, while the naturalisation decree of 26 May 1913 later extended the right to all *indigènes* of Indochina, including the French subjects of Cochinchina and the *protégés* of Tonkin, Annam, Laos and Cambodia. See Girault, *Principes*, pp. 466–467.

66. Girault, *Principes*, p. 420; Clairon, *La renonciation*, p. 52.

obligations shouldered by Indian renouncers in Cochinchina by virtue of their legal status are described in the next section.

Legal rights of Indian French citizens in Cochinchina

Indians who had renounced their personal status were not firmly recognised in Cochinchina as full French citizens until the 1900s. Even after that date there were ongoing attempts on the part of the authorities in Cochinchina to undermine their status (see Chapter Four). In legal principle however, if not always in practice, renouncers were treated on an equal footing with other French citizens, in Cochinchina and throughout Indochina.[67]

There were many advantages to holding French citizenship in Cochinchina. These were advantages which outweighed for many their obligation to military duty. French citizens resident in Cochinchina could vote in local and council elections, and they were entitled to elect a Deputy to the French Parliament to represent their interests in the colony. These were electoral privileges which were extended to a very limited number of indigenous people in the colony. Where employed by the state, as many renouncers were, they were entitled to salaries at European levels, with paid passages for home leave, admission to European hospitals and other colonial 'supplements'. Like other French citizens, they were exempt from personal tax in Cochinchina and their children could benefit from the superior schooling reserved for French citizens.[68] Should renouncers end up in prison despite these advantages, they were entitled to the treatment reserved for those people classed as 'European'. For many 'European' detainees the most important aspect of this preferred treatment was the reprieve it gave them from the hard labour to which native Cochinchinese prisoners were subject.[69]

---

67. Evidence of renounced Indians being classed as French citizens in Tonkin and Cambodia, respectively, can be found in: VNA1 T.12 4919 Listes des patentes indigènes européens et asiatiques étrangers de la ville de Hanoi en 1932 et 1935; National Archives of Cambodia (hereafter NAC) 24842 Demande formulée par M. Pakiam tendant à obtenir sa nomination à un titre de Mandarin honoraire.
68. VNA2 Service Local personal files (*dossiers individuels*) of renounced Indians employed by the Cochinchinese administration; VNA2 GGI 42279 Charges fiscales des Indiens sujets français non-renonçants établis en Cochinchine 1915: GGI to MMC, 21 January 1915; VNA2 1A.6/244(6) Instruction Publiques…Demande de création d'une école indienne à Saigon présénté par Mme. Vve Pochont, 1907.
69. VNA2 1A.2/065(1) Prison Centrale…régime alimentaire des détenus indiens 1906.

Indians who held French citizenship had the right to travel freely and to reside in the Metropole. The most stark limitation on the full exercise of their citizenship was a regulation barring them from employment in the public service in metropolitan France.[70] Curiously, this restriction does not appear to have drawn sustained complaint from renouncers; their silence on the issue may reflect the concentration of their combative energies in Indochina and the sheer popularity of colonial postings there. There were other niggling bureaucratic prejudices to be faced in France though. A former employee of the Indochinese Civil Services, Mr. Samy, retired to the *rue de Rivoli* in Nice in the 1930s but occupied much of his time there appealing to the League of Human Rights to have his French pension paid in Nice rather than Saigon.[71]

Colonial societies of the late nineteenth and early twentieth centuries are noted above all for their racial divisions, yet people legally classified as 'French' or 'European' in French Indochina were much more heterogeneous.[72] Indians who had renounced (and who were later recognised as French citizens) were included in the legal category 'European and assimilated'. This category was 'a legal rather than an ethnic basis of distinction'. It included many people who were not European by birth or parentage, but nonetheless enjoyed the protection of European law.[73]

The economist Robequain claimed in the late 1930s that just under three quarters of Indochina's population classed as 'European and assimilated' were 'pure whites' (thus 30,000 out of the 42,000 people in Indochina who fell within the category 'European and assimilated'). He based this claim on census data from 1937, which for the first time gathered information on place of birth. Of those born in France, a large number were from peripheral areas of France, most notably Corsica. Also included within the category were migrants from other European countries, some naturalised as Frenchmen. Naturalised Indochinese were classed as 'European and assimilated'. So too were those *métis* who had obtained citizenship through their (French) father's recogni-

---

70. See Michalon, 'Des Indes françaises', p. 39.
71. Archive of the *Ligue des Droits de l'Homme*, Box 85 1938: M. Samy to Lt MMC, 28 March 1938.
72. Michael Vann makes this same point, although his treatment of 'Chetty' migrants is misleading. Michael Vann, 'The Good, the Bad and the Ugly: Variation and Difference in French Colonial Racism', in Sue Peabody and Tyler Stovall (eds), *The Color of Liberty: Histories of Race in France*, Durham: Duke University Press, 2003, 187–205.
73. Robequain, *Economic Development*, p. 22.

tion (*reconnaissance*) of paternity or, as later became possible, through naturalisation. The other significant group of 'Europeans' was the '*créole*' Frenchmen from the Mascarenes and the French Antilles. Some were pure-blooded Europeans but like the French Indian *créoles*, many were of mixed parentage. The 1937 census noted 2,000 persons born in French colonies other than French India. Robequain maintained that most of these came from Réunion and the Antilles (although he notes 'their numbers appear to have diminished since the beginning of the French occupation'). Census data for 1937 shows that approximately 1,000 persons classed as 'European and assimilated' were born in French India. Many French Indians by this time though were Indochina-born, and had been absorbed along with the *métis*, naturalised Vietnamese, Frenchmen of European origin, and others into the category of 'Europeans' born in French Indochina (a total of 15,000 people for all Indochina).[74]

Two other groups of Asians were classified with 'Europeans' in colonial Indochina. Japanese enjoyed the protection of European law by virtue of treaties guaranteeing 'equal treatment' (1858, 1907). 207 Japanese were counted in all of Indochina in the 1937 census.[75] Under a Cochinchinese decree of 1897, Filipinos (*tagals*) were also permitted to enjoy the rights of Europeans in that colony. Most were ex-soldiers who had fought alongside the French in the conquest of Cochinchina and subsequently settled. The number of *tagals* in Indochina was very modest. Their right to enjoy the protection of European law was repeatedly called into question, and contentions over *tagal* status fed into debates over renounced Indians' status in Cochinchina (see Chapter Five).[76]

---

74. Robequain, *Economic Development*, pp. 22–25. On Corsicans see also Brocheux, *The Mekong Delta*, p. 104, and Jean-Louis Pretini, 'Saigon-Cyrnos', in Philippe Franchini (ed.), *Saigon 1925–1945: De la 'Belle Colonie' à l'éclosion révolutionnaire ou la fin des dieux blancs*, Paris: Éditions autrement, 1992, 92–103, p. 101. Emmanuelle Saada (*Enfants de la colonie*) provides a detailed analysis of changes in regulations regarding citizenship pertaining to the *métis* of Indochina.

75. ANOM FM NF 164 Relations Extérieures Statut des Étrangers: Rapport du GGI sur le statut personnel des étrangers en Indochine 1908; Robequain, *Economic Development*, p. 23.

76. VNA2 Goucoch II.A45/271(2) Contrôle des asiatiques étrangers: Frères Amio 1915–1917; VNA2 GGI 20404 Extrait d'un arrêt de la cour de cassation condamnant le sieur Amio Martin sujet philippin à 50 F d'amende pour détention d'armes à feu sans permis 6 mai 1910; ANOM GGI 42315 Étrangers en Indochine, Décret du 30 juin 1929: Application du décret du 30 juin aux asiatiques non-énumérées à l'arrêté présidentielle du 30 août 1871; VNA2 CP 8768 (1) Séance 2-12-1872 Réclamation Sieur Rangassamy quant à l'impôt de capitation; VNA2 SL 2582 Liquidation de compte de prévoyance de M. Adicéam, comptable du 2e classe, 1888.

Indians migrants who did not hold French citizenship (Indians who were either French or British subjects) added further complexity to the question of who was legally 'European' in colonial Indochina. They too were considered to be assimilated with Europeans for certain provisions of the law, as I explain in the next section.

STATUS IN COCHINCHINA OF OTHER MIGRANTS OF INDIAN ORIGIN

Indians living in Cochinchina who were not French citizens fell into one of two categories. If they originated from the French Establishments in India but had chosen not to renounce their personal status, they were French subjects. This status was nevertheless distinct from that of French subjects native to Cochinchina. For example, until the close of the nineteenth century they carried over to Cochinchina the electoral rights they had been given in India, and voted for a time in elections in Cochinchina, until debates over the Indian vote put a stop to this (see Chapter Four). They were sometimes called 'non-renouncers' (*non-renonçants*). Migrants originating from parts of India under British rule were classified in Cochinchina with the Chinese, as 'Foreign Asians' (*asiatiques étrangers*).

For some purposes, however, neither French Indian nor British Indian subjects were legally 'Asian' in Cochinchina. The legal standing of Indians in Cochinchina was made more complex by the continued application of an 1871 presidential decree which determined that no one of Indian 'race' was classified as 'Asian' for legal purposes. The purpose of the decree was to define which 'racial' groups then present on Cochinchinese soil were subject to *Annamite* law and which to French law. All indigenous groups and 'races' of migrants considered to be present in Cochinchina prior to French rule were collectively considered to have become French *protégés* following the conquest, and were consequently subject to *Annamite* law. These included 'the Chinese, the Cambodians, the *Minh Hương*, the Siamese, the *Moïs*, the Cham and the "mixed bloods" (Malays from Châu Đốc)'.[77] 'All other individuals', the decree went on, 'regardless of the race they belong to, are subject

---

77. *Minh Hương* were the offspring of Chinese migrants and local Vietnamese women; *Moïs*, from 'savages' in Vietnamese, referred to the peoples of the Vietnamese Central Highlands.

to French law'.[78] Indian migrants fell into this latter category, although given the modest number of Indians in the colony at the time, they were probably placed there more by accident than design as they were not specifically named in the decree.

For Indians who had renounced their personal status, once they had secured recognition of their French citizenship, the 1871 decree came to hold little significance. But it continued to be important in determining the status in Cochinchina of both Indian French subjects and British Indians. Both groups remained 'legally assimilated' with Europeans, although changes in legislation altered this status over the years. One element which remained constant was the application of French commercial law to these categories of Indians. The ability to pursue debtors with the backing of the French legal system was particularly important to Indian moneylenders. Indian French subjects and British Indians were both assimilated with Europeans for the purposes of incarceration. Thus like Indian French citizens they were entitled if imprisoned to the relative comfort of quarters reserved for convicted Europeans and could forgo forced labour. The exercise of these privileges, however, depended upon whether the local authorities recognised them. Several cases document how Indian prisoners, particularly when they were incarcerated far from the urban centres, did not enjoy the 'European' treatment which was their legal right.[79]

In civil cases, Cochinchinese courts upheld the principle, dear both to French imperial law in India and to the British legal system in the subcontinent, that 'a Hindu or *Muhammaden* carries his personal law with him wherever he goes'.[80] This meant that Indian subjects (both British and French) were entitled to marry, legitimate their children, and

---

78. ANOM FM (B05) NF 164 Relations Extérieures: Statut des Étrangers. Rapport du GGI sur le statut personnel des étrangers en Indochine 1908.
79. See VNA2 IA.2/015(3) Affaire Chavanne – Leidou-Mogamadou 1874 Dossier Chavanne 1877; VNA2 IA.2/065(1) Prison Centrale … régime alimentaire des détenus indiens 1906; VNA2 GD 445 Peine administrative infligée par le Chef de la province de Cantho contre M. Yaccoumsah, indien sujet anglais, 1925; ANOM GGI 42329 Étrangers en Indochine. Dans quel établissement pénitencier les indiens sujet anglais doivent-ils purger leur peine 1930.
80. Quote from Legislative Council of Madras, quoted in John D. Kelly, 'Fear of Culture: British Regulation of Indian Marriage in Post-Indenture Fiji', *Ethnohistory*, 35, 4, 1989, 372–391, p. 374.

manage their estates and successions on Cochinchinese soil according to personal laws applicable to them as Muslims or Hindus in India.[81]

Indian French subjects were initially, like Europeans, exempt from the payment of personal tax. This right was soon withdrawn, and then reinstated in 1870 through the forceful petitioning of Rangassamy, a Saigon-based publican.[82] Their exemption from head tax was withdrawn a second time in 1915, due to wartime concerns that *Annamite* loyalty was being tested by 'the particularly privileged situation' from which 'non-renounced French subjects' benefited.[83]

The tax and immigration situation of British Indians, meanwhile, fell under rules pertaining to Foreign Asians. Unlike Indian French subjects, their obligation to pay personal tax was never in question. Their taxation, like their immigration, was regulated by the system of 'congregations' (French *congrégation*, *bang* in Vietnamese). These were migrant groups led by elected chiefs charged with guaranteeing the good conduct of their members. Congregations were originally organised under Nguyễn rule in the early nineteenth century to manage Chinese immigration, and were adapted in Cochinchina under French rule.[84] Formal congregations for British Indian migrants were introduced in Cochinchina in 1874. Indians were organised into congregations along religious lines, unlike their Chinese counterparts who were grouped by dialect.[85] Saigon and Cholon in the late nineteenth century supported between them at least two (Indian) Muslim and two Hindu congregations. Indians residing in the interior were made to join Chinese congregations if there were very few Indians in a given location. This arrangement was not always to their

---

81. See 'Pathmabivy versus Ka-Abdul Radjah 1902', in Pierre Dareste, G. Appert and Maxime Legendre, *Recueil de législation et jurisprudence coloniale*, Paris: A. Challamel, 1903 edition, pp. 32–34; 'Tran Thi Bu versus Aissouamalle and others', in Dareste et al., *Recueil* (1903), pp. 58–70.
82. VNA2 CP 8768(1) Séance 2–12–1872 Réclamation Sieur Rangassamy quant à l'impôt de capitation.
83. VNA2 GGI 42279 Charges fiscales des Indiens sujets français non-renonçants établis en Cochinchine 1915: Deliberations of Colonial Council, 11 November 1914.
84. John Clammer, 'French Studies on the Chinese in Indochina: A Bibliographical Survey', *Journal of South East Asian Studies*, 12, 1, 1981, 15–26, p. 21; Vimeux, *De l'immigration en Cochinchine et les taxes spéciales aux immigrants asiatiques*, Paris: Challamel Aîné, 1875, p. 18.
85. VNA2 SL 1825 Arrêté soumettant les Indiens et Malais non-sujets français au régime de la congrégation 1874.

liking.[86] Outside of Cochinchina, congregations were organised for a brief period in the 1910s in the French-controlled cities of Hanoi and Haiphong.[87] Otherwise, taxation and immigration matters for British Indians and Indian French subjects in the protectorates were the responsibility of their employers.[88]

A large proportion of Indian French subjects and of British Indians were Muslims. Most of them were from the Tamil region of South India, from the French town of Karikal and its surrounding villages, and from neighbouring Tanjore district in British India (in particular the towns of Koothanallur and Mayavaram). With the increased urbanisation of business centres in India, Madras gradually became an important base, too, for South Indian Muslim trade in Indochina.[89] In 1926 the colonial Security Service (*Service de la Sûreté*) counted approximately 1300 South Indian Muslims residing in Cochinchina, the majority living in Saigon and Cholon. Of that number only twelve were renouncers, showing the infrequency with which Muslims from the French territories in India chose to renounce their personal status.[90]

There were two broad social divisions within the overseas South Indian Muslim community. The largest group were 'Tamil Muslims' properly speaking. They claimed descent either from Arab Muslim traders and local Tamil women, or from local converts to Islam. They retained many Tamil cultural practices. *Marakkayar* (*Marécar* in French), *Lebbais*, and *Rawthers* were all Tamil Muslims and all were present in Cochinchina, although it remains unclear whether the latter two groups were branches of the larger *Marakkayar* group, or separate and

---

86. See VNA2 IA.12/164(1) Bạc Liêu: Demande présentée au nom des Indiens habitant Bạc Liêu à l'effet d'obtenir un chef de congrégation, 1897.
87. ANOM GGI 50951 Réclamation des Indiens de Hanoi et de Haiphong contre les procédés de service de l'immigration de Saigon 1916.
88. ANOM GGI 42303 Émigration en Indochine. Décret du 30 juin 1929. Réclamation du Consulat Général du Royaume-Uni relative à la procédure du remboursement des sommes consignés par quatre Hindous 1931; VNA1 RST 3711 Demande des certificats de départ à destination de leur pays d'origine formulée par des Indiens Asiatique étrangers résidents au Tonkin 1932; ANOM RST 02104 Expulsion des étrangers (indiens etc.) 1933.
89. Marcel Ner, *Les musulmans de l'Indochine française*, Hanoi: Bulletin de l'École Française d'Extrême-Orient, 1941, p. 52; Discussions with Mrs. M. Alam, Ho Chi Minh City January 1997; Interviews in Pondicherry with Raffiq Mohammed, August 2004, Tony Bui, October 2004, and G. M. Said family, November 2004.
90. ANOM GGI 65476 Service de sûreté, Rapports annuels: Service de sûreté, Rapport annuel (1926–1927) du commissariat spéciale de la port de Saigon-Cholon, pg. 349. And see Table 2 in Chapter Three.

hierarchised caste-like entities.⁹¹ A much smaller group of South Indian Muslims differed from the Tamil Muslims in claims of origin and purity. Some were of Turkish or Afghan descent (thus *Tulukars* and *Pattanis* respectively), and *Sayyids* claimed (Arab) descent from the Prophet. South Indian Muslims who were not ethnically Tamil had come to the Tamil country by way of northern India. Although these migrations had taken place several generations previously, they continued to keep Tamil culture at arms' length.⁹²

The largest group of Indians practising Hinduism in Cochinchina was the caste of Nattukottai Chettiars, from Chettinad in South India, known in Indochina as elsewhere in Southeast Asia for their banking activities.⁹³ Although the term 'Chetty' originated from the Nattukottai Chettiar presence in Cochinchina, it came in popular usage to mean anyone in Cochinchina from the Indian subcontinent.⁹⁴ In other contexts it could mean (often as a slur) any Indian moneylender, or any moneylender regardless of race. Thus a 'yellow Chetty' appeared in a cartoon in the Vietnamese newspaper *La Tribune Indigène* during the 1919 Chinese boycott.⁹⁵

As a suffix in South Indian usage, '-chetty' had a further meaning. It was added as a title to Tamil names to denote associations with finance or trade; there were some such 'chettys' by name in Cochinchina who were distinct from the specific caste of Nattukottai Chettiars.⁹⁶ They were among the small networks of other Tamil Hindus who operated

---

91. For these terms used as titles by expatriate Tamil merchants, see *Annuaire Générale de l'Indochine* (hereafter AGI) *1912*, p. 188. In French Indochina the term *Marikkayar* was used more often as a title than as a term to refer to Tamil Muslims as a group. The term 'Chulia', in common usage for Tamil Muslims in the Malay states, was unheard of in Indochina. See Nasution, *The Chulia in Penang*.

92. It is not always possible to reconcile the divergent claims about these groups made in the literature. The information here is based on Julien Vinson, 'Les musulmans du sud de l'Inde', *Revue du Monde Musulman*, 2, 1907, 199–204, p. 203; Delval, *Musulmans français*, pp. 135–136; J.B.P. More, 'The Marakkayar Muslims of Karikal, South India', *Journal of Islamic Studies*, 2, 1, 1991, 25–44.

93. See Michael Adas, *The Burma Delta: Economic Development and Social Change on an Asian Rice Frontier, 1812–1941*, Madison: University of Wisconsin Press, 1974; David West Rudner, *Caste and Capitalism in Colonial India, the Nattukottai Chettiars*, Berkeley: University of California Press, 1994; Rajaswary Ampalavanar Brown, *Capital and Entrepreneurship in Southeast Asia*, Houndmills, Basingstoke: Macmillan, 1994.

94. See for example Jean Marquet, *Les Cinq Fleurs, l'Indochine expliquée*, Hanoi: Directeur de l'instruction publique, 1928, p. 23.

95. *La Tribune Indigène*, 2 October 1919.

96. Anthony, *Gazeteer*, p. 360; Rudner, *Caste and Capitalism*, p. 423.

in small trades and enterprises in Cochinchina throughout the colonial period. They probably hailed from several castes which had begun to be upwardly mobile in India from the mid-nineteenth century.[97]

France's possessions outside of the Tamil country drew negligible numbers of people to Indochina. Key networks of Indian traders with interests in Indochina were the Bhoras, Parsis and Sindhi merchants; they came to be known collectively as 'Bombay' for the Indian port out of which they operated. Indochina's 'Bengalis' were similarly named for their place of embarkation; they were in actuality Pathans and Punjabi Sikhs who worked as night-watchmen, guards, and petty traders.[98]

Indians who did not hold French citizenship are not the main subjects of this study, but they feature in many of the incidents, events, and debates which form its substance. Their identities and lives as migrants in Indochina intersected with those of Indian French citizens in many ways. This is particularly true of those who were subjects of French India and to whom some of the same Indian legislation applied (particularly that concerning electoral rights). Even though it happened very rarely, British Indians too, did sometimes become French citizens. This was the case of the banker and landowner Ra. Soccalingam, born in Saigon to a British Indian. He applied for and was granted French naturalisation in 1906, and quickly became a vocal and influential supporter of the renouncer cause.[99]

Conclusion

The right of Indians from the French Establishments to 'renounce' their personal status issued both from a wider project of creating French citizens throughout the post-revolutionary French Empire, and from political and social conditions particular to the context of French India. The first Indians who asserted a right to renounce claimed to be seeking equality on two levels, both with their colonial masters and within Indian society. Later, renouncers laid more emphasis on the opportunities for social mobility which renunciation could offer them within the French

---

97. Based on Esquer, *Les castes*, and Thurston, *Castes and Tribes*. And see Chapter Three.
98. ANOM GGI 65476 Service de sûreté, Rapports annuels: Service de sûreté, Rapport annuel (1926–1927) du commissariat spéciale de la port de Saigon-Cholon, pg. 349. On 'Bengalis' in Southeast Asia see Metcalf, *Imperial Connections*, pp. 52, 128.
99. VNA2 IB.38/0711 Dossier relative aux demandes de naturalisation années 1902–1906. Soccalingam's brother applied shortly after him for French citizenship but was turned down.

colonial system. Historians of French India claim that renunciation was of little importance in French India itself. Yet Indian migrants to French Indochina were very keen to renounce. By the 1930s, the number of renouncers in Indochina was greater than the number of French Indians resident there who had not renounced. The renunciation movement got underway in Pondicherry, and French Indian renouncers were arriving in Cochinchina just as the indigenous people of Cochinchina were granted a legal means permitting them to seek French citizenship. The decree sanctioning Indians' right to renounce in French India and the regulation issued in Cochinchina were drafted using virtually the same wording. They made citizenship accessible through very different means. For the indigenous peoples of Cochinchina, French citizenship came only by the good graces of French authority. As later chapters show, it was only in Cochinchina that the question of whether Indian renouncers' status was equivalent to citizenship was fully resolved. Unlike the Cochinchinese, however, the Indian renouncers could gain equal status to French citizens through their own free choice.

This picture runs contrary to more generalised accounts of how France extended citizenship to the peoples of its overseas empire. Citizenships obtained in the old colonies do not fit the standard view that a firm hand directed assimilation policy from the Metropole down to the colony, or that citizenship was uniformly conferred in restrictive ways.[100] Instead, as Pondicherry's renouncers demonstrate, would-be-citizens intervened to a high degree in shaping the terms of their citizenship. The standard account, emphasising state authority and restriction, matches more closely how citizenship was obtained once processes of naturalisation were introduced in France's newly acquired nineteenth-century territories.

French Indians, many newly renounced or about to renounce, arrived in late-nineteenth-century Cochinchina just as a naturalisation decree was put in place there for the Cochinchinese. At the heart of the story of French Indians in Indochina is the sharp distinction between the rights of Indian renouncers, born out of an old colony context, and the rights of the Cochinchinese. The conflicts related in later chapters are a consequence, for the most part, of a situation where Indians could – with

---

100. Cf. Deming Lewis, 'One Hundred Million Frenchmen'; Aldrich, *Greater France*, p. 212.

ease – become Frenchmen in a colony other than their own, while very few Cochinchinese managed to obtain French citizenship.

While caught in conflicts over their legal status as French citizens in Cochinchina, renouncers participated at the same time in an overseas Indian, or more correctly Tamil, social and commercial world. The chapter which follows builds up a more detailed picture of how the broader community of Indian migrants were occupied in Cochinchina. From one perspective the renouncers, as French citizens, lived and worked apart from other Tamils, yet there are many ties too which connected them to a wider migrant community.

CHAPTER THREE

AT WORK IN INDOCHINA
INDIAN FRENCH CITIZENS AND TAMIL SPHERES OF ACTIVITY

Renouncers from French India were mainly employed in Indochina in areas which were closely connected to French colonial interests. Many of the kinds of posts they occupied, as legal clerks, tax collectors, lighthouse guards, or postmen, as policemen and soldiers, and even as accountants in the employ of private French companies, positioned them as an important intermediary group. Vietnamese commentators spilled more ink in protest at the economic domination and legal privilege of specific sectors of the Indian migrant community than they did at the Indians' role in carrying out the everyday tasks of French colonisation (see Chapter Six). It was nevertheless French Indians (alongside Indo-French and Antillean *créoles*, men from the Mascarenes and from Corsica) who enforced French domination in its quotidian forms over Indochina and its peoples.

Renouncers' employment was not confined to the sphere of French colonial interests. They were also involved, both directly and indirectly, in the numerous economic activities which characteristically occupied other Indian, or more precisely Tamil, residents of Indochina. Their French connections did not detract from their role as vital players in a world of Tamil migrants in Indochina, with Saigon at its hub. Indeed, French India's renouncers had a closer understanding of the French colonial system, and better French language skills, than most other overseas Tamils. They used this knowledge to the benefit of other Tamils and Tamil businesses in Cochinchina in a multitude of ways. When they ventured directly into entrepreneurial activities, they were almost always drawn into typically Tamil activities. The Chettiar bankers and South Indian Muslim merchants were among those South Asian migrants who operated long-distance business networks in Indochina. They have a reputation from studies elsewhere for being closed commercial networks whose success depended on the trust forged by strong bonds of religion or caste between men from a common locality. Yet in Cochinchina these commercial networks appear to have brought in outsiders to assist them, and their operations did not preclude the entry of other Tamils who did not fit these social profiles, including Indian French citizens, into the same occupational specialisations.

Social and political reform movements arose in South India in the 1920s and 1930s, built around ideas of a Tamil ethnic consciousness.[1] It is not a political Tamil community that is evoked here though, but a simpler bond of 'Tamilness' generated by everyday practice. It consisted of the many ways in which people with a common language and shared cultural references acted in conjunction with one another while resident overseas. Although a more self-conscious and politically charged sense of *Indian* identity began to emerge in Saigon from the 1920s, the direct influence of Tamil reform movements among the diaspora in Indochina is difficult to trace. It was the linguistic and cultural ties exercised through everyday interactions between Tamils which make it possible to identify a Tamil community in the longer term in colonial Saigon.

Unlike other parts of Southeast Asia in the same period, contract labourers were noticeably absent from Tamil migrant flows to Indochina. French Indochina fulfilled its growing demand for labour internally. It drew labourers from the overcrowded deltas and impoverished coastal areas of Annam and Tonkin to plantations and mines where they faced appalling conditions.[2] The class make-up of Indochina's Tamil community was shaped by these arrangements. Flows of South Indian migrants came to Indochina primarily to provide goods, services, and skills. They were people of bourgeois and petit-bourgeois backgrounds, who were sometimes joined by servants and employees from India. Although a segment of the French Indian renouncer community was of *pariah* origin, these individuals had already placed some distance between themselves and their marginalised backgrounds by virtue of the modest French education which was itself their ticket to Cochinchina.

---

1. On Tamil reform movements see Eugene F. Irschick, *Politics and Social Conflict in South India. The Non-Brahman Movement and Tamil Separatism, 1916–1929*, Berkeley: University of California Press, 1969; C.J. Baker and D. A. Washbrook, *South India: Political Institutions and Political Change, 1880–1940*, Meerut: Macmillan of India, 1975; Marguerite Ross Barnett, *The Politics of Cultural Nationalism in South India*, Princeton: Princeton University Press, 1976.
2. For a first-hand account see Tran Tu Binh, *The Red Earth: A Vietnamese Memoir of Life on a Colonial Rubber Plantation*, Athens, Ohio: Ohio Universiy Press, 1985.

The Plural society revisited

One of the most enduring models for explaining the dynamics of Southeast Asian urban colonial contexts is the notion of a 'plural society'. It was conceived by the British civil servant J.S. Furnivall, as a result of long experience in Burma and the comparative study of the Dutch East Indies. He proposed that order was maintained in the migration-dependent and racially diverse urban societies of colonised Southeast Asia by 'different sections of the community lining up side-by-side but separately' and a division of labour in the economic sphere along these lines.[3]

One criticism of Furnivall's conception is levelled at his characterisation of the main Asian migrant groups in colonial societies as broad undifferentiated categories. This analysis viewed from Indochina raises some problems. The term 'Indian' was used in everyday life by people across all sectors of Indochinese colonial society, including 'Indians' themselves, to refer to anyone originating from the Indian subcontinent. This did not necessarily indicate the person using the term was unaware of internal divisions within this broad category. The writings of both colonial authorities *in situ* and Vietnamese commentators indicate that both groups were able when the context required to distinguish between the legal and ethnic divisions within Indochina's broader category of Indians. Some recent scholars of Indian diasporas imply that the widespread use of the terms 'Indian' or 'Chinese' as broad referents for migrant communities simply led Furnivall to construct a model that was not sufficiently refined. They have sought to emphasise the internal divisions within larger Chinese or Indian groups and to insist upon the 'deeply segmented' nature of long-distance trading networks bounded by caste, ethnicity, religion, and localised place of origin.[4]

In Indochina, the term 'Indian' retained its usefulness even though the vast majority of Indians was ethnically Tamil. The strongest bond connecting Indochina's Indians to one another on a level higher than religious or caste bonds or (in the case of French citizens) shared legal status was their common Tamil linguistic and cultural ties. Within this

---

3. Furnivall, *Colonial Policy and Practice*, p. 304.
4. For Indian diasporas see the work of Markovits, *The Global World of Indian Merchants*; Rudner, *Caste and Capitalism*; Falzon, *Cosmopolitan Connections*. See also Claude Markovits, 'Indian Merchant Networks outside India in the Nineteenth and Twentieth Centuries: A Preliminary Survey,' *Modern Asian Studies*, 33, 4, 1999, 883–991, p. 902.

Tamil community, the Nattukottai Chettiar banking caste, and to a lesser extent the South Indian Muslim trading groups, built the strongest boundaries around themselves both in their social life and their business practices. Yet although these long-distance corporations in colonial Saigon clearly did have strong mechanisms of internal organisation, they were not nearly as tightly-knit as the literature on long-distance trade suggests, nor even as they made themselves out to be. Instead, there were multiple interactions between Chettiars, Indian Muslims, Indian French citizens, and other members of the wider community, both in the economic sphere and beyond.

A strict reading of a 'plural society' would have the different segments of colonial society centred completely on economic or working life, meeting only 'in the marketplace'.[5] This is yet another prescription confounded by many of Saigon's Tamil migrants. The number of male migrants outstripped the number of women who came to Indochina from India. Yet they did not always form the isolated adult male communities said to typify migrant social organisation in 'plural societies'. Indian French citizens often had wives and children from home join them in Indochina. They enjoyed very active Indochina-based family lives (described in the next section), while mixed unions between Tamil men and local women, most prevalent among South Indian Muslim merchants, led to the growth of an Indo-Vietnamese community (discussed in the last section of Chapter Six).

INTERMEDIARIES IN THE COLONIAL ADMINISTRATION

From the beginnings of the French conquest of Cochinchina, and throughout the period of French rule, the demand for French-speaking subordinate and middle-level functionaries in Cochinchina's colonial administration was met in part by Indians from the French *comptoirs* of Pondicherry and Karikal. They were also employed as functionaries elsewhere in Indochina, notably in the Governor General's administration in Hanoi, and in the French-controlled municipalities of Hanoi and Haiphong. Indochina's protectorates maintained much more modest French-run bureaucracies than did the colony of Cochinchina. Indian representation within protectorate bureaucracies was consequently more limited.

---

5. Furnivall, *Colonial Policy and Practice*, p. 304.

Many Indians working for the Cochinchinese administration were hired in posts normally reserved for Europeans, on European terms, and with European salaries (*à titre européen, à solde d'Europe*). This practice was in place from the mid-1860s, prior to the implementation of the renunciation law in India. While some Indians working in Indochina's administration were employed in relatively high positions, 'European status' did not denote necessarily a position of high standing. Many such posts were middle-ranking but required a mastery of French. By 1890, proof of renunciation had become a prerequisite for Indians to be hired to 'European' posts. While some Indians, usually those who were better-educated, were hired on 'European' terms, others took up subordinate positions which were classified as 'native'. Indians employed on 'native' terms were not obliged to renounce their personal status, but they had to content themselves with native salaries and conditions. This is not to say they did not renounce. Most did, in fact they appear to have done so without exception. The difficulties this created for colonial officials are discussed in Chapter Four. Thus although not all Indians employed in the Cochinchinese colonial administration were required to renounce their personal status, all Indians within the administration were renouncers, and held the status, once controversies over the issue were resolved, of French citizens.

Indian French citizens were not employed evenly across every sector of the Cochinchinese administration. Rather, there were clusters of Indian employment, in specific departments and in certain types of positions. While it is not stated explicitly in the colonial record, Indian civil servants and administrators were also placed in positions which suggest that deliberate decisions may have been made by colonial authorities to position men who were not 'completely' French as intermediaries in an attempt to diffuse tensions over French rule. Their positioning within the administration may also have reflected their reputation (which they shared with Corsicans) for lobbying to reserve administrative posts for their compatriots.[6]

'Writers' (in the proper sense, prior to the advent of the typewriter) were among the earliest Indian *fonctionnaires* to arrive in Cochinchina. Correspondence between the newly appointed Lieutenant General of Cochinchina, Admiral Ohier, and the Commissioner Governor

---

6. See Pretini, 'Saigon-Cyrnos', p. 101.

General of French India in May of 1868 reveals the French Governor to be engaged in 'recruiting the writers requested', 'young recruits from Pondicherry' who had signed engagements to work in Cochinchina and were due to sail for Saigon.[7] Interpreters of Tamil, like writers, were hired from the earliest days of French colonisation, suggesting the early presence of a critical mass of Tamil-speaking migrants in the new colony. Indians from the French possessions continued to fill clerical posts within many branches of the service right up until France's departure from Indochina.

French Indians helped to manage the colonial state's revenue flow in a number of ways. The Customs and Excise Service (*Douanes et Régies*) was staffed almost entirely by French Indians and French Indian *créoles*, under supervision which was largely Corsican.[8] All three *porteurs de contraintes* employed in Cochinchina's treasury in the 1880s were Indian French citizens.[9] Their role was to carry executive mandates to those who had not paid their taxes, pressing them to do so.[10] In the *Bureau de l'Enregistrement, des Domaines et du Timbre*, which managed the registration of property and collected stamp duty, Indians served as clerks, registrars, and bailiffs.[11]

Renouncers were particularly well represented in the colonial justice system. One of the highest ranking was the Pondicherry magistrate Vennemani Cannoussamy, whose case was associated with the establishment of renunciation in French India. He served as an appeal judge in Mỹ Tho from 1883.[12] The period between the two World Wars saw a general rise in the number of Indian French citizens in the justice service in Cochinchina, including several Indians who attained posts comparable to Cannoussamy's. By 1938, one third of the clerks of court (*commis-greffier* and *greffier-notaire*) in Saigon's Court of Appeal

---

7. ANOM GGI 10410 Personnel recruté aux Indes françaises 1868: GEFI to Lt-GGCCH, 6 May 1868 and 5 October 1868.
8. See for example *ACCH 1887*, pp. 122–127.
9. *ACCH 1884*, p. 176.
10. Leconte, Nadia, 'La migration des Pondichériens et des Karikalais en Indochine ou le combat des Indiens-renonçants en Cochinchine pour la reconnaissance de leur statut (1865–1954)', unpublished DEA thesis, Université de Haute-Bretagne, 2001, p. 95.
11. Respectively *commis*, *greffiers*, and *huissiers*. See for example the Tamil names listed under this heading in *AGI 1908*, Hanoi: IDEO, pp. 12–13.
12. See NAIP DM 1883: Minister of Navy and Colonies to GEFI, 12 May 1883, and *ACCH 1884*, p. 156.

and another third employed by the Saigon Tribunal were Indian French citizens. So too were three out of eleven judges (*juges suppléants*) within the Court of Appeal. In the provinces, nine out of thirteen provincial tribunals employed either Indian clerks of court or appeal judges.[13]

French Indians also served in the Cochinchinese administration as postmen and guardians of public services such as lighthouses and railways. These positions became typically 'Indian' jobs. The heading 'Indian postmen' was used in the colonial yearbook of 1938 to list the names (all Tamil) of the twelve men so employed.[14] Lighthouse guards too were primarily Indian. In 1897, nine out of a total of sixteen men assigned to Cochinchina's lighthouses had Tamil names.[15] Indians were also commonly employed as overseers during the construction of Indochina's railway networks, supervising local labourers. Typical of such employees was Gnanadicom Saverinaden, who oversaw the building of embankments at kilometres 142 to 200 on the main trans-Indochina line under construction in 1908.[16] Indians also staffed the railways and tramways as conductors and guards.[17]

Saigon's police force was made up in large part of Indian agents, as were Cochinchina's ranks of prison guards. In 1908, half the agents in the Saigon municipal police force were Indian. Virtually all of their colleagues, both their equals and their superiors, were Corsicans.[18] On the prison island of Poulo Condore in 1917, nine of the seventeen principal prisons guards (meaning non-native guards) were Indian. Here too, the men they worked alongside were mainly Corsican.[19] The guard killed during the serious rebellion on Poulo Condore the following year, and described in the press as French, bore a recognisable renouncer name, Simon-Jean.[20] Samy Beaumont and Saverinaden Dupas, both French Indian, were among four guards awarded medals of honour for good

---

13. *AGI 1938–1939*, pp. 62–67.
14. *AGI 1938–1939*, p. 858.
15. *AGI 1897*, p. 42.
16. *AGI 1908*, p. 65.
17. For example VNA2 Goucoch IB.29/233 Élections coloniales Inscription des natifs de l'Inde 1887: 'Ville de Saigon. 'Élections coloniales et Législatives Années 1887–1888'.
18. *AGI 1908*, pp. 336–337.
19. *AGI 1917*, p. 157.
20. 'Rébellion à Poulo-Condore: Un bagnard d'un coup de massette tua raide le gardien Simon-Jean', *La Tribune Indigène*, 25 March 1918. For an account of this rebellion see Zinoman, *The Colonial Bastille*, pp. 142–148.

conduct during the same uprising.[21] Once Indochina put in place an internal security service (*Service de la Sûreté*) in the 1920s, Indians were counted among its agents. The appointment of Evariste Marius as a Security inspector was announced in the pages of the *Indochine-Inde* in 1936. He was described as 'a child of the country (*un enfant du pays*) who is fluent in Vietnamese'.[22] At least one other Indian from the French Establishments worked for the Security Services.[23]

The types of posts taken up by renouncers in Cochinchina's administration reflected, doubtless quite logically, their levels of education. The better-educated were found in the higher- and middle-level posts, requiring professional or clerical skills and a mastery of French. Those in more subordinate posts (many – but not all – classed as 'native' posts) tended to be men with poorer qualifications and more rudimentary levels of French.

Renunciation was understood by Indians who renounced when the movement was at its height to signal a rejection of caste hierarchies. Despite this, organisation along the lines of caste continued to be evident in patterns of renouncer employment within the Cochinchinese administration. Throughout the French colonial occupation of Cochinchina, most renouncers in the higher- and middle-level administrative posts were of high-caste *Vellala* origin. They were joined by a small number of *Vannias*, another group who earned a reputation in Pondicherry in the late nineteenth century as a well-off, educated, and upwardly mobile group. *Naidoos*, another higher ranking caste, tended to favour careers in law and were predominate in the justice service.[24] The subordinate '*petit fonctionnaire*' posts requiring no more than a *brevet élémentaire* (for example lighthouse watchmen, postmen, prison guards) became the province of renouncers of low caste or *pariah* backgrounds. Renouncers in the ranks of the police appear to have been more mixed.[25]

Caste differences underlay Indian French citizens' patterns of employment even if caste in daily life appears to have genuinely been of little consequence to them until the Depression (see Chapter Six). By

---

21. 'Echos de la révolte de Poulo Condore', *La Tribune Indigène*, 6 June 1918.
22. 'Dans les polices', *Indochine-Inde*, 16 February 1936.
23. Interviews in Pondicherry with Dr. Claude Marius, September 2004, and Alfred Sinnas, October 2004.
24. Marius, 'Les Pondichériens dans l'administration', p. 393; Esquer, *Essai sur les castes*, p. 120.
25. Miles, *Imperial Burdens*, p. 266; Michalon, 'Des Indes françaises', p. 45.

contrast, official French communications about employees from French India show that French officials perceived differences between their renouncer employees to be distinctions purely of social class, opportunity, and education. This was very unlike the situation in the British Empire. British colonial officials both in India and beyond sought men of castes perceived to lend themselves to administrative work, or recruited men of recognised 'martial races' for the army.[26] French officials in Cochinchina appear to have neither possessed nor deployed a detailed knowledge of the caste differences which may have existed (or persisted) among renouncers or other Indians resident in the colony.[27]

Indian French citizens found work in Cochinchina in much the same way their metropolitan peers did. Some participated in the colonial examinations (*concours coloniaux*) and were contracted prior to arriving in Cochinchina. Others were hired locally, and sought positions in the administration through networks of friends and relatives already established in Cochinchina. The former route was relevant primarily to those applying for middle-level and higher-level positions requiring more advanced levels of French education. Official despatches between Pondicherry and colonial Indochina regularly included notices advising Indian functionaries that they had succeeded in their exams and been posted to Indochina.[28] Those hired through the *concours* were the most mobile, even though they tended to be re-assigned within Indochina. Members of renouncer families alive today speak of childhoods spent moving from Saigon, to Phnom Penh to Hanoi, or between towns in the Mekong Delta.[29]

Positions obtained through the *concours* were highly sought after. Those who succeeded could hope to enjoy the full advantages of European employment overseas. This comprised not only a European salary, but a 'colonial supplement' which doubled that salary. It also included paid passage to the colony for the employee and his immediate family and the

---

26. Metcalf, *Imperial Connections*, p. 17.
27. Based on the many personal files (*dossiers individuels*) of renouncers employed by the Cochinchinese administration (VNA2, series 'service locale') and by the Government of Indochina (archive of GGI in ANOM and VNA1).
28. NAIP *Dépêches Ministérielles* throughout the late nineteenth and early twentieth centuries.
29. Interviews in Pondicherry with Antoine Saint-Jacques, January 2002, Mrs. Amélie Marius Le Prince, November 2004, and Mrs. Lourdes Louis, November 2004.

right to a home leave (to India) of six months every three years.[30] These European-level benefits in a colonial context were advantages over and above what renouncers could hope to receive in Pondicherry.

Paid passage for wives and children was one employment benefit which had a significant impact on the lives of Indian French citizens in Indochina. The wives of Indian functionaries began to arrive in Cochinchina before metropolitan French women and children came to Indochina in any significant numbers. Anxieties that persisted at this time, among Indian Catholics as much as Hindus, over the risk of ritual pollution and the loss of caste in the act of travelling overseas (crossing the 'black water' or *kala pani*) are not evident here, even though some scholars have suggested that the risk of ritual pollution was sometimes transformed into a bar on travel for women.[31] Renouncers in the late nineteenth century were remarkably relaxed in their attitudes towards bringing their wives overseas. When Savere Conjondessamy's wife came to join him in Saigon in the 1870s, he expressed no concern that she should be travelling far from Pondicherry, only that she should be accompanied by people who could help her: 'Several families of Indian origin are due to come to Saigon on the ship which leaves Pondicherry next January and their assistance will be very helpful for my wife, who is unaccustomed to European habits.'[32]

The presence of a core of French Indian families in Cochinchina encouraged other Indian French citizens (in the administration and elsewhere) to bring their wives and families to join them, even if it meant paying the passage themselves. By the turn of the twentieth century many of the renouncers living in colonial Vietnam had been born there, of Indian parents.[33] While many men still returned to India to seek marriage partners, the pool of renouncer women residing in

---

30. Bertrand Camilli, *La représentation des indigènes en Indochine*, Toulouse: Imprimerie J. Fournier, 1914, p. 117.
31. On restrictions on the movements of Sindhi women see Markovits, *Global World*, pp. 266–267.
32. VNA2 SL 4269 Dossier Individuel de M. Conjondessamy, (Savere) Porteur de contraintes du trésor 1873–1882: Conjondessamy to Treasurer Paymaster (*Tresorier Payeur*), 14 December 1875; Also VNA2 SL 2110 Dossier Individuel de Apparayen, Pierre, sécretaire à la direction de 2ᵉ classe attachés au Haras du 21 nov 1871: Apparayen to Director of Interior, 9 March 1871.
33. See for example NAIP C–372 État Civil, Tableau de recensement des jeunes français, naturalisés et renonçants ayant atteint l'age de 20 ans révolus, Tableau de recensement des classes de 1887 à 1905.

Plate 2: An Indian functionary and his family, Hanoi, circa 1920. Courtesy of Maurice Sinnas, Pondicherry.

colonial Vietnam was large enough that marriages were arranged and took place in Indochina. Franco-Tamil newspapers published in Saigon in the 1920s and 1930s regularly carried notices of such unions.

Renouncers in the higher-ranking and middle-ranking administrative positions not only received the same benefits as their European peers but began to adopt for themselves the same trappings of a colonial lifestyle. Photographs from French Indian family albums, taken in colonial Indochina from the 1920s onwards, depict scenes of men in white linen suits and topees, children in sailor suits or white lace dresses, and infants held in the arms of Vietnamese nannies while other native domestic servants stand by. The subjects are frequently posed outside French-style colonial villas. Those in more subordinate positions, however, would have lived in the shop-front housing built in a style common to other colonial port cities of Southeast Asia. The only indication in these photographs that a French colonial lifestyle had not been unconditionally adopted was in the dress of women, who appear, with some exceptions, in saris.

While French Indian women were present in colonial Indochina, they very seldom worked in the public sphere. There is no evidence of Indian women employed in the administration in Cochinchina, but it was not entirely unheard of elsewhere. In Phnom Penh in the 1930s, Mme. Clairon (of the Pondicherry family who achieved success in Cochinchina despite caste barriers) was employed as a '*dame contractuelle*' in a clerical position. She was honoured in 1931 for her 'extraordinary zeal'.[34]

The growing presence of French Indian women and children in Saigon is reflected in the founding of several Franco-Tamil schools from the turn of the twentieth century. These schools were established in response to the desires of French Indian parents to have both a degree of Tamil-language schooling for their children and a segregated primary education for their daughters. The schools were run by women, either Indo-French or Indian French citizens. They were invariably widowed or had husbands who were unable to provide for them. While renouncers were capable of stridently and publicly embracing French values and could – at least as higher- and middle-ranking functionaries – adopt lifestyles which attempted to mirror those of their European colonial counterparts, these schools demonstrate that Tamil aspects of their lives remained important to them.[35]

If the apex of renouncer ambition was a secure job in the French administration which translated status as a French citizen into tangible benefits, this was only really fulfilled by the elite who succeeded in gaining the best contracts by winning the *concours*. The demand for jobs on local hire was just as fierce however. So intense was the flow of hopefuls from French India that from the 1890s through the 1900s Cochinchinese authorities became greatly concerned. The administration was obliged

---

34. NAC 32753 Gratification accordée à Mme. Clairon, dame contractuelle, en service au 4ième bureau pour zèle extraordinaire.
35. Interviews with Henri Isidore and family, Madras, October 2004; Ms. Lefort, Pondicherry, November 2004; Dr. Claude Marius, Pondicherry, November 2004. Documentation on Franco-Tamil schools in Saigon is found in VNA2 IA.6/244(6) Instruction Publiques… Demande de création d'une école indienne à Saigon présenté par Mme. Vve Pochont, 1907; VNA2 IA.6/244(4) Instruction Publique: Demande de Mlle. Isidore, Marie, d'ouvrir une école, 1900; VNA2 IA.7/234(4) Écoles privées…subvention accordée à Mlle. ISIDOU [sic], institutrice libre à Saigon 1904–1907; VNA2 IIA.8/111(19) Subventions accordées à Mlle. Marie ISIDORE pour le fonctionnement de son école privée sise rue Mac Mahon 1925–1926; VNA2 IIA.8/111(21) Subventions accordées à Mme. Simon-Jean (ex-veuve MANNAPIN) pour le fonctionnement de son école libre Franco-Indienne 1910–1932; VNA2 IIA.8/121(18) Demande de remboursement des frais de réparation locatives effectués à l'école Franco-Indienne par M. Benjamin Sinnassamy 1938–1939; 'Un grand philanthrope hindou: M. Xavier de Condappa', *Saigon-Dimanche*, 15 February 1931; 'Donnons un nom à nos écoles', *Saigon-Dimanche*, 8 January 1932.

to shoulder the cost of repatriating Indian French citizens who had come to Cochinchina and, unsuccessful in their pursuit of positions as functionaries, had succumbed to vagrancy.[36] In 1908 the Cochinchinese Governor Outrey asked his superior in Hanoi to advise the Governor for French India (as well as high officials in Réunion and Corsica) that 'there are no available jobs in the service in Cochinchina in the foreseeable future' and that those hopeful of employment in the public service were to be discouraged from coming.[37]

Another important avenue of employment for Indians from the French possessions was with French firms established in Cochinchina.[38] By the 1930s, Indians were employed as accountants and clerks in a wide variety of European firms and organisations, ranging from banks and oil companies to department stores and professional associations. Indians from the French Establishments were also employed in printing presses and later as newspaper staff with the growth of the press in Cochinchina (and see Chapter Seven).[39]

Indians working for private French firms were not exclusively Indian French citizens. One source has claimed that many such posts were filled by Hindus of the *Reddiar* caste who tended not to renounce, and who had earned a reputation in Pondicherry as 'good accountants'.[40] This niche of Indian employment appears to have been equally favoured by renouncers. Those with French citizenship who were unable to secure prized administrative posts settled for work with private French firms.[41] These jobs had fewer benefits but were nonetheless attractive in comparison to work in French India.

---

36. NAIP DM 1890: Sub Secretary of State for the Colonies to GEFI, 25 April 1890; *MOEFI 1882*, 25 July 1882, Extract of a letter to the Governor of French India from the French Consul at Singapore, 29 June 1882.
37. ANOM GGI 2276 Rapatriement des Indigents provenant de l'Inde, de la Réunion et de la Corse. 1908: Lt Gov CCH to GGI, 1 May 1908.
38. See employees listed for Charles Bonnet and Denis Frères in *Les adresses de l'annuaire de l'Indochine, édition du* 2ième *sem. 1913,* Hanoi: IDEO, 1913, p. 250–253.
39. For examples see VNA2 Goucoch IB29/233: 'Ville de Saigon. Élections coloniales et Législatives Années 1887–1888'; VNA2 GD 2997: 'Liste Nominative des Sociétaires de la Mutuelle Hindoue de Cochinchine', 1935.
40. Interview with Dr. Claude Marius, Pondicherry, October 2004. In an address to an audience of Indian French citizens in 1929 a speaker of metropolitan French origin referred to Indians from the French possessions more generally as trustworthy accountants. 'Un remarkable conference de M. Darles', *Saigon-Dimanche*, 1 September, 1929.
41. See VNA2 GD 2998 Mutuelle des Indo-Français Employés de Commerce et d'Industrie 1934: Procès-verbal de 22 Juillet 1934, Rapport Moral.

French India's renouncers were not present in large enough numbers in Indochina for local people to encounter them at every turn. Yet the niches of employment they occupied within the colonial administration in Cochinchina placed them at the interface of local engagement with French authority. The face of French authority for the indigenous residents of Cochinchina would not always have been that of a white metropolitan Frenchman, or even a Corsican, but that of a Tamil from Pondicherry or Karikal. In the services in which they were employed to undertake clerical duties or in offices where they were engaged with tax, customs, and registration procedures, Indians from the French Establishments were at the frontline of Vietnamese contact with French bureaucracy. Where they were charged with the delivery of mail or with the supervision of lighthouses, trains, or railway lines, they were visible to the Vietnamese as protectors of (French) public goods. In the colonial legal system, French law was filtered through not one but several Indian lenses. A Vietnamese brought before court by a Chettiar moneylender could find himself pleading his defence through a Tamil interpreter, in front of an Indian magistrate, and in the presence of Indian legal clerks and bailiffs.

Those most powerfully engaged in the business of colonial dominance were the Indians in the urban police forces, the penitentiary system, and the security services. In these positions they were both symbolically and effectively among those at the forefront of the surveillance and control of the local population. It would not have been unthinkable for a local Cochinchinese in trouble with the law to have been arrested by Indians, tried by Indians, and imprisoned under the watch of Indian guards. Even their food, as we shall see later, may have been supplied by an Indian contractor.

The French Indians' position as intermediaries enforcing colonial rule is equally evident in the role they played in the military in Indochina.

Career soldiers and military service

Military connections between the French Establishments in India and French Indochina go back to the earliest days of the French conquest of Cochinchina, when French troops stopped to draw supplies at the ports of Pondicherry and Karikal. Indians joined them aboard their ships, among them men who served as soldiers in the conquest of Cochinchina and the other Indochinese territories as these areas were brought under French 'protection'.

Some of these soldiers stayed on and settled. When Mougamadoucamy (or Mamoucani in the Vietnamese rendering of his name) wrote in barely literate French in 1902 to appeal to the colonial authorities for financial help, he described how, originally from Karikal, he had arrived in the colony in 1855 [sic], 'comme simpelle solda a la guer Saigon [sic]' ('as a simple soldier in the fight for Saigon'). He took up with a local woman who bore him ten children and he had been employed consecutively as a carter, a salesman, and a collector of market taxes, all jobs tied to Tamil networks in the Mekong Delta.[42]

Another class of Indians from the French possessions – those who could speak, read, and write in French – also came with the military in the days of the French conquest, and served as *magasiniers*, charged with managing the stores of the colonial troops. Men who served in such positions were often renouncers, or had children who renounced and followed careers in the Cochinchinese administration.[43]

Some Indians from the French possessions were posted to Cochinchina having entered the French military as career soldiers. Once they did so, they found it advantageous to renounce their personal status. Other Indians were called up once it became obligatory for French citizens in the colonies to fulfil military service. Because Britain had limited the number of troops France could keep in its Indian territories (through the 1815 Treaty of Paris), renouncers were called up from 1908 to the nearest recruitment station in the region, which happened to be in Saigon.[44] The colony appealed to many of these young men: it was a welcoming place where many already had family connections, and where decent employment could be found. Soldiers of French Indian origin preferred to be engaged in Indochina, or, if career soldiers, to serve out the end of their military service there in order to remain and seek civilian employment. Ministerial despatches held in the Pondicherry archive are riddled with requests from Indian soldiers asking to be allowed to serve in Indochina, and preferably Saigon. Senior military officials were not always happy with this arrangement, but such requests were rarely refused.[45] As one

---

42. VNA2 IA.12/149(11) Tân An demand de dégrèvement d'impôt demandé par le sieur Mamoucani (Indien) 1902.
43. Marius, 'Les Pondichériens', p. 392.
44. Clairon, *La renonciation*, p. 100.
45. See NAIP DM 1926: Minister of Defence to Commander of the Indian Sepoy Corps, 7 May 1926, and numerous requests of this nature from the 1910s through the 1930s.

soldier, Christophe, put it in his request, he hoped in Saigon to 'find a job more easily than in Pondicherry'. The free passage the army provided was clearly an added benefit.[46]

The Eleventh Colonial Infantry Regiment (*régiment d'infanterie coloniale* or R.I.C.), with its barracks adjacent to the Botanical Gardens in central Saigon, was so popular with French Indian soldiers that the Franco-Tamil newspaper *Saigon-Dimanche* ran a column in the early 1930s entitled 'Gossip from the 11th R.I.C.'[47] The presence of young French Indian soldiers in the heart of the city added both to the growth of the community of renouncer families in Saigon and the development of a Tamil community in the city. At higher levels of service recruits could seek permission to marry. Some were entitled to free passage for their wives and families to join them in the colony, while others found partners with ease within the local pool of eligible French Indian young women. A restriction on marriage for soldiers in the lower orders of the service was also a spur to less formalised unions with local women.[48]

A SUPPRESSED PROFESSIONAL CLASS

Although some Indians held positions of high standing within the administration, two groups with professional training were unable to further their careers in Cochinchina. The qualifications of those with legal or medical training obtained in the French Establishments were not fully recognised in Indochina.[49] The reasons for these restrictions are not completely clear. They appear to lie more in a concern that French Indian qualifications were lower than metropolitan standards than in any official desire to protect the interests of the modest cadre of professionally trained indigenous Indochinese.

Indians trained in the French Establishments could take up positions as legal clerks and even magistrates within the Cochinchinese administration. Any Indian who wanted to open a private legal practice, however, had to have been trained in France. Many settled for working as legal

---

46. NAIP DM 1913: MMC to GEFI, 8 March 1913.
47. See NAIP DM 1910: Correspondence 19 April 1910; 'Cancans du 11ième R.I.C.', *Saigon-Dimanche*, 7 June 1931.
48. NAIP DM 1910: Re Filatriau (A.F.), 1 May 1911 (The soldier in question was a *créole*, but marriage regulations applied equally to all recruits); 'Un crime à Saigon. Le soldat Francisque tombe sous les coups d'une vengeance', *Réveil Saigonnais*, 6 February 1923.
49. ANOM GGI 2786 Les médecins de l'école de Pondichéry ne peuvent exercer la médecine en Indochine (requête Mariadassou) 1907.

Plate 3: Indian magistrate and his wife in Cochinchina, 1925. Courtesy of National Archives of Cambodia.

clerks in private French practices, where some specialised in serving an Indian clientele. Louis Sinnaya, employed by the lawyer Thiollier in the 1900s, received 'twenty percent on Indian affairs' as a supplement to his monthly salary.[50] The bulk of this work is likely to have been in Chettiar foreclosure cases. Joseph Xavier, the one Pondicherry lawyer who is known to have run a private practice in Saigon (in the 1920s), had obtained his degree in France.[51]

Likewise, the qualification obtained by graduates of the Pondicherry Medical School (*officier de santé*) did not permit them to practise civil medicine in Indochina. One renouncer, Paramanada Mariadassou, pressed the authorities in the 1900s to allow him to practice in Cochinchina, but had to settle for a post with the medical army corps.

---

50. VNA2 GD 2997 Mutuelle Hindoue 1935: 'Liste Nominative des Sociétaires de la Mutuelle Hindoue de Cochinchine', 1935; VNA2 SL4585 Réhabilitation formulée par M. Sinnaya (Louis) demeurant à Saigon 1902.
51. Interview in Pondicherry with Ms. Anna Xavier, November 2004.

He served in Saigon and subsequently in Poulo Condore.⁵² The *créole* Édouard Marquis, who later became a journalist, was similarly qualified. In 1918, a decade after Mariadassou, Marquis too was employed as a medic (*agent sanitaire*) in Poulo Condore.⁵³ Only one Indian doctor is known to have worked in civil medicine in Indochina. Dr. Tirouvanziam was able to do so because he had trained in Montpellier. He practised in Saigon and Phnom Penh in the late 1920s and 1930s.⁵⁴

Indian lawyers and doctors who were unable to exercise the professions in which they were trained were often successful in Cochinchina in other fields. Several such men reinvented themselves as entrepreneurs and journalists, and as community leaders taking active roles in French Indian mutual societies and within renouncer politics in Cochinchina. The legal clerk-turned-entrepreneur and publisher Louis Sinnaya was an example of such a figure at the turn of the twentieth century. Doctor-turned-businessman Samy Appassamy and lawyer-turned-landowner Xavier de Condappa both epitomised this trend between the wars. Although the doctor-turned-journalist Édouard Marquis was a *créole* and not a renouncer, he may be included among this group for his close commitment to renouncer causes.

'Indian shops' and related niches of Muslim enterprise

From an early date, 'Indian shops' were ubiquitous in the large urban centres of Saigon and Cholon. They were also spread through the smaller towns of the Cochinchinese interior, and in towns and cities elsewhere in Indochina. Imported cloth was the mainstay of these shops, which also stocked garments, as well as fancy and general goods.⁵⁵

The great majority of 'Indian shops' were run by Muslims from the Tamil region of South India. The total number of South Indian Muslims residing in the colony was just over one thousand in 1926, most of them coming expressly to engage in trade. The value of this trade is

---

52. ANOM GGI 2786 Les médecins de l'école de Pondichéry ne peuvent exercer la médecine en Indochine (Requête Mariadassou); VNA2 SL533 Dossier Individuel de Paramanada Mariadassou.
53. ANOM GGI 33987 M. Marquis (Édouard) engagé comme Agent sanitaire contractuel à Saigon-Cholon.
54. Interview with Mrs. Lourdes Louis, Pondicherry, November 2004.
55. VNA2 Goucoch IA.7/175 (9): Musée Commerciale: Marchandises Étrangères 1886.

Plate 4: Tamil Muslim merchants in Cochinchina. Postcard, Éditions Melle Cauvin, circa 1900.

uncertain, although it covered extensive areas of Cochinchina. The Cochinchinese trade supported the growing urban centres of Saigon and Cholon, as well as Gia Định, Saigon's north-western extension. South Indian Muslim trade also flourished in the rice-growing regions and their transport hubs in the Mekong Delta and in centres of rubber production, reflecting their role in bringing supplies to the expanding agricultural frontier and developing industrial areas.[56] These patterns can be seen in the distribution of the South Asian Muslim population in Cochinchina in 1926 (see the table below).[57] Although Châu Đốc was, and remains, the centre of Cham Islam in the south of Vietnam, South Indian Muslim trade there was surprisingly limited.[58] The second larg-

---

56. And see C.J. Baker, 'Economic Reorganization and the Slump in South and Southeast Asia', *Comparative Studies in Society and History*, 23, 3, 1981, 325–349.

57. Mekong Delta towns connected to commercial rice production include Mỹ Tho, Trà Vinh, Cần Thơ, Sa Đéc, and Rạch Giá. Thủ Dầu Một, north of Saigon, was a seat of rubber production.

58. Intermarriage between South Indian Muslim men and Cham women was less prevalent than one might imagine, probably, as Ner notes, because of Cham resistance to such unions, even with outsiders who shared their faith. See Ner, *Musulmans de l'Indochine*, p. 163.

Table 2: Population and distribution of South Indian Muslims in Cochinchina, 1926

City/province	British subjects	French subjects	French citizens ('renouncers')	Total
Saigon	370	123	7	500
Cholon	175	31	4	210
Tây Ninh	15	0	0	15
Bà Rịa	7	3	0	10
Tân An	13	2	0	15
Gia Định	45	15	0	60
Lái Thiêu	20	5	0	25
Thủ Dầu Một	30	20	0	50
Biên Hòa	5	10	0	15
Mỹ Tho	50	20	0	70
Bến Tre	12	8	0	20
Trà Vinh	50	10	0	60
Cai Lậy	5	0	0	5
Vĩnh Long	20	5	0	25
Cần Thơ	40	10	0	50
Sóc Trăng	10	10	0	20
Bạc Liêu	20	5	0	25
Sa Đéc	30	0	0	30
Long Xuyên	13	2	0	15
Rạch Giá	30	10	0	40
Châu Đốc	3	6	1	10
TOTAL	963	295	12	1,270

Source: ANOM GGI 65476 Service de Sûreté, Rapport Annuel (1926–1927) du Commissariat spécial du port de Saigon-Cholon.

est centre in Indochina for South Indian Muslim trade was Hanoi. In the 1920s, 280 South Indian Muslim men resided there.[59]

South Indian Muslim merchants came from both British and French parts of India, but British Muslims by the 1920s far outnumbered their French peers. British Indians were considered in Indian circles to be the more successful businessmen and were generally better-off. The

---

59. ANOM GGI 65476 Service de sûreté, Rapports annuels: Service de la Sûreté, Rapport Annuel de Commissariat spécial pour la port de Saigon-Cholon (1927–1928): Action Indienne.

Koothanallur firm of J.M.M. Ishmael Brothers, the most prosperous Indian Muslim enterprise in colonial Saigon, proved this rule. Providing the exception was the powerful Pondicherry firm of G.M. Said which held fast as the largest Indian Muslim firm in Hanoi, with interests across Tonkin. These larger firms generated employment for lower classes of overseas Tamils as their shopkeepers, cashiers, and servants.[60]

Many of these employees were South Indian Muslims from the French possessions.[61] They were valued for their French language skills and their knowledge of the French commercial bureaucracy by employers more familiar with such matters within the British Empire.[62] Although South Indian Muslims seldom filled administrative posts in Indochina (connected to the fact that few renounced), there were exceptions. Mouhamed Haniff was a close relative of the G.M. Said trading family who was employed within the Indochinese administration from the 1900s. By the 1920s he held a top clerical position at the central tax office in Hanoi (*Bureau de l'Enregistrement, des Domaines et du Timbre*). He would have been required to renounce his indigenous personal status to hold this post.[63]

Cloth was the principal trade of Saigon's 'Muslim brotherhood' (as a French Security report of 1928 called it), but it was invested in other commercial activities besides.[64] South Indian Muslims dealt in the import of diamonds, but while this was surely a financially lucrative trade, there is little in the historical record to enlighten us further.[65] We know more about Muslim-run financial services. By 1910, South Indian moneychangers were installed the length of Catinat Street, Saigon's main thoroughfare, with networks of smaller-scale agents working for larger ones. In addition, Muslim trading networks offered remittance services and were involved in money-lending. The latter was mainly in the form of purchases advanced on credit; this was likely due to the

---

60. ANOM RST 02104 Expulsion des étrangers (Indiens etc) 1938.
61. VNA2 GD 2995 Plainte au sujet de l'administration de la mosquée musulmane rue Amiral Dupré, 1933: 'Août 1933: Note sur l'Affaire de la mosquée de Saigon.'
62. Interviews in Karikal with Hajee Abdoul Hameed Maricar, Regional Kazi, September 2004; S.M. Basheer Marécar, Deputy Regional Kazi, September 2004.
63. *AGI 1926*, p. 37; Interview with Said family, Pondicherry, November 2004.
64. ANOM GGI 65476 Service de sûreté, Rapports annuels: Service de la Sûreté, Rapport Annuel de Commissariat spécial pour le port de Saigon-Cholon (1927–1928): Action Indienne.
65. 'Hột Xoàn!' [Diamonds !], *Saigon-Dimanche*, 28 August 1927.

illegality in Islamic law of lending or borrowing with interest (*riba*). Bankruptcy notices provide clear evidence of this practice, as does a 1910 advertisement for French cigarettes depicting a Tamil shopkeeper and his Vietnamese customer. As I mention later, Tamil Muslims based in Cochinchina's interior also acted on occasion as informal agents for Chettiar lenders.[66]

Tamils who were modest entrepreneurs or petty traders were usually connected to or sustained by the larger Muslim businesses. Tamil tailors were regularly listed in the colonial yearbook from the 1890s, their shops in Saigon routinely located in streets adjacent to areas where the cloth merchants conducted their trade.[67] Tamils who plied Cochinchina's waterways carrying cloth and general goods into the more remote areas of the interior relied on South Indian Muslim trading houses for their stock. Itinerant Cham traders were operating along the same lines right up until the mid 1970s, carrying the cloth of South Indian traders into the Central Highlands to sell.[68]

Certain streets of Saigon were, from an early date, clearly zoned as areas of South Indian Muslim enterprise. Tamil businesses were already concentrated on the *rue Vannier* near to the Saigon River in the 1880s. By 1908, nearly two thirds of the premises on Vannier Street were occupied by Tamil cloth merchants, moneychangers, or 'retail vendors' (*marchands au détail*). Viénot Street, facing the *Halles Centrales* or Central Market, became another important location for Tamil trade. Throughout the colonial period, Indian money changers continued to occupy the same single block of Catinat Street.[69]

Muslims dominated these trading networks, but this did not preclude the involvement of other Tamils in the same types of business. The majority of cloth traders and moneychangers were South Indian

---

66. Sources on Muslim financial services include: *Les adresses 1913*, pp. 278–279; ANOM GGI 65475 Service de la Sûreté Cochinchine Rapport Annuel 1924–26: rapport annuel 1er juillet 1926 à 1er juillet 1927, Les Indiens; 'Avis', *Réveil Saigonnais*, 3 May 1924; 'Avis', *Réveil Saigonnais*, 14 May 1924; *LTTV*, 12 March 1914; Interview with R.M. Krishnanchettiar, Tiruchchirapalli, September 2004. *Riba* and other rules pertaining to *Dar al Harb* (the community of the faithful overseas, literally the 'land of war') were contentious topics among Cochinchina's expatriate Muslim community in the late 1920s and 1930s. See VNA2 GD 2995 Plainte au sujet de l'administration de la mosquée musulmane rue Amiral Dupré, 1933: 'Notice sur le sieur Mouhammed Aboubakare'.
67. *Les adresses 1913*, p. 270.
68. Discussion with Hajjah Basiroh bin Haji Aly, Ho Chi Minh City, May 1997.
69. *ACCH 1887*, p. 106; *AGI 1908*, pp. 410–411.

Plate 5: Map of central Saigon, 1928. Guides Madrolle, 1928.

Muslims but they did not all fit this profile. In 1887, the Hindu (or possibly Christian) 'retail merchant' Kichenassamy occupied premises on Vannier Street alongside eleven South Indian Muslim competitors. In 1889 Annasinnapoullé and Leupragalannaiker, most probably Hindus, ran their Catinat-based money-changing shops next to their Muslim compatriots and competitors. Kayappa Adicéam, whose surname suggests he was from a renouncer family, was a cloth merchant on Saigon's Vannier Street in the 1900s. His shop was situated alongside those of his Muslim compatriots.[70]

Nattukottai Chettiars and other Tamil bankers

Tamil moneylenders played an important role in financing rice production in the Mekong Delta and in extending both credit and savings ser-

---

70. *ACCH 1887*, p. 106; *ACCH 1889*, p. 68; *AGI 1908*, p. 390.

vices to merchants and functionaries in Cochinchina. The best-known of these bankers were members of the Nattukottai Chettiar banking caste, who began to arrive in Cochinchina in the 1870s. By 1930, 110 Chettiar banks were registered in Cochinchina. This number dropped following the economic crisis of the 1930s, but by 1937 there remained fifty-five banks, with a total of 170 Chettiars resident in the colony, including bank owners, agents, and employees.[71]

The Nattukottai Chettiars' main sources of income in Cochinchina were from money-lending and rental properties. Barring the losses they suffered during the economic crisis from 1929, they did very well out of their enterprises in Cochinchina. The total Chettiar credit amounted to fifty million piastres before the economic crisis, and had reduced by 1937 to twenty million piastres. Chettiars held a third of the total rice credit in Cochinchina in 1937.[72]

The Nattukottai Chettiars gained a reputation as usurers in Indochina because of the high interest rates they charged, and their presence spurred debate across the early decades of the twentieth century.[73] Many clients nevertheless valued Chettiar services, which enabled them to borrow on low security.[74] Chettiar bankers were frequently accused of further impoverishing poor farmers, even though patterns of lending appear to have been more complex. The larger landowners of the Mekong Delta were the Chettiars' biggest clients; the substantial sums they borrowed were often on-lent to their tenant farmers.[75] Indigenous public servants and

---

71. *ACCH 1877*, p. 134; VNA2 GD 2992 Situation et rôle des chettys en Indochine, 1937: Report of Police service, Second Section, 30 August 1937.

72. This amounted to over six million piastres of a total of nearly twenty million piastres. VNA2 GD 2992 Situation et rôle des chettys en Indochine, 1937: Report GGCCH to GGI, 9 December 1937; see also ANOM GGI 65475 Service de la Sûreté Cochinchine Rapport Annuel 1924–26: rapport annuel 1er juillet 1926 à 1er juillet 1927, Les Indiens.

73. See VNA2 IB.24/147(3) Conseil Colonial: Cahiers des colons de l'Inde Française 1907: *Ligue Française pour la Défense des Droits de l'Homme et du Citoyen* to Canavaggio, VP of Colonial Council, 30 July 1907; E. Mathieu, *Les Prêts Usuaires et le Crédit Agricole en Cochinchine*, Paris: Recueil Sirey, 1912; Ch. Leonardi, 'L'Usure en Cochinchine', *Extrême-Asie*, May 1926, 226–231; Ernest Outrey, 'L'Intérêt bien compris de la Cochinchine doit nous engager à aider les banquiers indiens installés dans cette Colonie à reprendre leurs affaires de crédit', *Midi Colonial*, 19 December 1935.

74. VNA2 GD 2992 Situation et rôle des chettys en Indochine, 1937: Report GCCH to GGI, 9 December 1937; Interview with R.M. Krishnanchettiar, Tiruchchirapalli, September 2004.

75. See Mathieu, *Les Prêts Usuaires*, p. 90; Phan Trung Nghĩa, *Công tử Bạc Liêu Sự thật và giai thoại* [*Bạc Liêu Playboy, Truth and Myth*], Ho Chi Minh City: Youth Publishing House, 2006, p. 27.

Plate 6: 'Chetty types', Saigon. Postcard, Mottet et Cie, circa 1910.

other colonial *petits fonctionnaires* also frequented the Chettiar bankers. Their modest salaries forced them to rely on the Chettiars to 'make ends meet'; many also entrusted their meagre savings to the banking caste.[76]

Posted overseas for three-year stints, Chettiar men lived and worked in the same sparse, communal quarters. Despite the fortunes they amassed in Cochinchina, they adopted an outwardly modest appearance. In conspicuous contrast to the European dress worn by Indian French citizens employed in the colonial administration, Chettiars wore simple long loincloths (*vershti*), shaved their heads, and smeared their foreheads, bare chests and arms with temple ash.[77] They made little concession to 'modern' European trends in dress until the late 1920s.

Ohier Street in Saigon was the headquarters of the Nattukottai Chettiars in Cochinchina. A temple at one end of the street was dedicated to Sri Thenday Yuttapani (the god Murugan). Constructed in 1881, it was

---

76. Quote from 'La Situation des Fonctionnaires et Employés Indigènes', *Echo Annamite*, 17 January 1920; VNA2 GD 2992 Situation et rôle des chettys en Indochine, 1937: Report GGCCH to GGI, 9 December 1937.

77. S. Muthiah, Meenakshi Meyappan, and Visalakshi Ramaswamy, *The Chettiar Heritage*, Chennai: Madras Editorial Services, 2002, p. 268.

both a centre of spiritual life and an integral part of banking operations. Banking establishments with barred windows (*kitangis*) served both as home and bank for the Chettiar agents. A temple choultry (*chattiram*) provided a resting place for visiting members of the banking caste, and a building housing the Indochinese Association of Nattukottai Chettiar was added in the 1930s.[78]

Aside from the Nattukottai Chettiars, there were other Tamils who operated as bankers in Cochinchina but were not part of the Chettiar caste or corporation. The banker Ra. Soccalingam is an interesting case. He was a naturalised French citizen (rather than a renouncer). He may have had Chettiar origins (most likely a Vietnamese mother and an Chettiar father) but he associated more closely with the Indian French citizens and appears to have worked independently of Chettiar banking circles. Nor was he alone as a banker operating outside of the Chettiar corporation. There were at least three others, the Cholon-based bankers Paquéry, Nadessapillai and Virapillai. Paquéry appears elsewhere as a surname adopted by renouncers; the other two were probably caste Hindus who had not renounced.[79]

The Franco-Tamil newspaper *Saigon-Dimanche* stated explicitly that during the 1920s ('in the times of prosperity'), 'there were in Saigon twelve moneylenders, French subjects [sic], who should not be confused with the Chetties'. Another source, the Chettiar banking enquiry conducted in Cochinchina in 1937, listed André Rocke, an Indian French citizen employed in the local press, and Appapoulé, a landowner well-known in French Indian circles, among '*Chettys* who appear to specialise in loans to functionaries'. One of the first Indian bankers to declare bankruptcy when the world economic crisis hit Cochinchina in the late 1920s was a French subject, Candassamy. As one of Saigon's Tamil bankers with whom many functionaries deposited their savings, his bankruptcy caused alarm among his clientele. His operation's col-

---

78. Ohier Street is now named Tôn Thất Thiệp. The sign of the Association Indochinoise des Nattukottai Chettiars was visible until 2005 when the façade was taken down. The temple choultry, still standing, now houses two up-market restaurants and an ice-cream parlour (2015). VNA2 CP 8372 Arrêté du Gouvernement concédant un immeuble domaniale… aux Indiens sectateurs de Brahme pour y construire un temple 1881; Interview with R.M. Krishnanchettiar, Tiruchchirapalli, September 2004; Muthiah et al., *Chettiar Heritage*, p. 63.
79. VNA2 IB.38/0711 Dossier relative aux demandes de naturalisation années 1902–1906; 'Banquet donné par M. Ra. Soccalingam en l'honneur de M. François Deloncle', *Réveil Saigonnais*, 16 April 1910; AGI 1912, p. 182.

lapse heightened emotions to such an extent that he was pursued by a distraught client (a Karikalais, as it happened) armed with a knife.[80]

Anthropologist David Rudner has argued that the strong caste and clan organisation of Nattukottai Chettiars was the key to their ability to organise their banking business over long distances.[81] While this might hold for the internal workings of the complex Chettiar financial network, there was a myriad of everyday forms of Chetty reliance on other non-Chettiar Tamils in Cochinchina. The peculiarities of Chettiar legal status in Cochinchina (as 'Foreign Asians' who were not legally 'Asian' in commercial courts) meant that the presence of francophone Tamils at sites of French authority was particularly useful to them. Chettiars did not always speak Vietnamese or French, due to the short stays many of them undertook in Cochinchina. They relied when they made use of French courts on Tamil interpreters provided to the courtroom by the colonial government. Even though proceedings were conducted in French, Chettiars often shared a mother tongue with many of those present in the courtroom, including the legal clerks, bailiffs, process servers, and possibly also the lawyers and the judges. In the 1930s, the Pondicherry lawyer Joseph Xavier was regularly employed by theIndochinese Association of Nattukottai Chettiars. As the French security bureau carefully noted, he came daily at six o'clock in the evening to the Saigon office of the association. He advised the Chettiar bankers on legal matters and was charged with translating for the president of the association whenever necessary.[82] A second lawyer working to defend the Nattukottai Chettiar position at the time of the economic crisis was of metropolitan origin, but he was assisted by a renouncer, Mr. Mouttayah, who was also trained in law. The daughter of one Chettiar who worked in Saigon described Mouttayah as

---

80. 'La Crise et les prêteurs d'argent', *Saigon-Dimanche*, 18 December 1932; VNA2 GD 2992 Situation et rôle des chettys en Indochine, 1937: Report GGCCH to GGI, 9 December 1937.
81. David Rudner, 'Banker's Trust and the Culture of Banking among the Nattukottai Chettiars of Colonial South India', *Modern Asian Studies,* 23, 3, 1989, 417–458.
82. VNA2 GD 2994 Demande de capacité juridique presenter par l'Association Indochinois de Nattukottai Chettiars 1940: Note from Special Commissioner for Saigon-Cholon ports to Chief of Security, 11 October 1930. According to his daughter he also advised the Ishmael brothers during the Great Depression. Interview with Anna Xavier, Pondicherry, November 2004.

'a Pondicherry lawyer' and friend of her father's who negotiated on behalf of Saigon Chettiars.[83]

In addition to their reliance on Tamils from French India employed in the French Justice Service and in the legal profession, Chettiars had commercial connections with South Indian Muslim traders established in the provinces of Cochinchina. In at least one case, Tamil Muslims acted, albeit informally, as agents to Chettiar bankers. In 1906 two Chettiar bankers, both holding trading licences in Sóc Trăng, were accused of extending their operations to Bạc Liêu without paying the necessary licensing fee (*patente*) in that province. A closer investigation of their activities found that they stayed during their regular journeys to Bạc Liêu with South Indian Muslim cloth merchants. One of the bankers, Sivaramanechetty, had another Muslim, Mougamadoumadarsah, working as an agent for him in Bạc Liêu: 'Through this agent he is alerted, by post or by telegraph, of new requests for loans which he processes on his next visit.'[84]

These cases show Chettiar bankers to have been less self-reliant than some scholars suppose. Yet the Chettiars relied not only on other non-Chettiar Tamils in Cochinchina in various ways. The preponderance of Chettiars and their business interests on Ohier Street in Saigon encouraged the presence of other Tamils as tenants and entrepreneurs. A street directory of 1913 reveals that Tamils occupied virtually every address on Ohier Street in that year. Besides numbers 21 to 31, which were listed as 'Chetty houses', eight Indian policemen lived there, all with surnames typical of renouncers. So too did the dry goods merchant (*épicier*) Mouttou. Three Tamil jewellers (Souppayapatter, Kamatchy, and Aroquiassamy) also occupied premises in the street in the same year. The shop of a fourth jeweller, Lazare Adécalamadin, was located in an adjacent alley. A petrol station belonging to the wealthy renouncer businessman Samy Appassamy was positioned at the top of the street at Number One. He lived at Number Three and the mutual association *Mutuelle de Karikal* was located a few doors down.[85]

---

83. 'Hindoue Tamoule Djana Sangam', *Indochine-Inde*, 8 March 1936; Discussion with Mrs. Meenakshi Meyappan, Karaikkudi, September 2004.
84. VNA2 IA.12/162(5) Bạc Liêu, Deux Chettys patentés à Bạc Liêu, 1906: *Contributions directes* to Lt GCCH, 30 October 1906.
85. *Les adresses* 1913, p. 286.

Livestock, transport, and milk

The earliest reference in French sources to any overseas Indian presence in Cochinchina comes from the Cochinchina Yearbook (*Annuaire de la Cochinchine*) of 1865. It reads as follows:

> The 200 Indians whom we possess [*que nous possédons*] have managed to make themselves useful, and it is desirable that their numbers increase. Thanks to them the care of livestock is seen to, numerous carts [*chariots*] circulate, and some carriages for hire [*voitures de louage*].[86]

The little that is known about this group of migrants is enough to maintain that they probably arrived initially from Pondicherry and Karikal, coming with the French military during its conquest of Cochinchina, on ships taking supplies at Pondicherry before proceeding to Cochinchina.

In late nineteenth-century Cochinchina Tamils operated bullock carts (*chariots*) for the transport of goods, coaches (*voitures*) for the transport of people and mail over longer distances between towns and cities, and small horse- or pony-drawn carriages for short journeys within urban areas. The latter vehicles came to be called *malabars* because of the widespread but erroneous use in late nineteenth-century Cochinchina of the term 'Malabar' for the Tamils who originally drove them. In the 1870s the French traveller Morice was pursued through Saigon's central market by 'black *Hindus* from Malabar [sic]' who cried 'Carriage, captain, carriage!'. By 1907, when the Englishwoman Gabrielle Vassal travelled through Saigon, the 'queer little vehicles' were being driven by 'native [Vietnamese] sais'.[87]

In the latter half of the nineteenth century, Tamils filled service contracts in Cochinchina to supply bullock carts and drivers to government, and to run long-distance coach services. Beyond the turn of the twentieth century, though, there is little trace of these Tamil-run means of transport. It is likely that, like the Malabar carriages, these services gradually moved out of Tamil hands; technological changes and improvements in transport links also made these types of service less crucial. At least three expatriate Indians were 'proprietors of transport autos' in 1936, but there is no discernible link between the Indians running automated

---

86. *ACCH pour l'année 1865*, p. 68.
87. Dr. A. Morice, *People and Wildlife in and around Saigon, 1872–1873*, Bangkok: White Lotus, 1997 [1875], pp. 6, 8; Gabrielle M. Vassal, *Three Years in Vietnam (1907–1910)*, Bangkok: White Lotus, 1999 [1910], p. 19.

Plate 7: Tamil carters, Cochinchina. Postcard, Mottet et Cie, circa 1900.

cars and the Tamils of the previous century driving horse carriages and bullock carts.[88]

From the beginning of the French colonial presence in Cochinchina, a demand for milk and dairy products created by the European presence was filled by Tamils who tended cattle and sold milk door-to-door. In

---

88. Numerous files in Ho Chi Minh City's National Archive Number Two address Tamil transport services: See VNA2 CP 7979 Cahier des charges pour la fourniture des voitures à boeufs à la journée [1869]; VNA2 CP 8042 Constructions navales: marché pour l'entreprise générale des charrois et transports...soumission de POUNOUSSAMY...15 May et 12 juin 1869; VNA2 CP 8005 Pont et Chausée, marché de gré à gré avec l'entrepreneur NAGALINGAPOULLÉE pour l'achèvement des remblais du Blvd Bonnard. 15 avril 1874; VNA2 IA 20/186 (10) Voitures publics Saigon – Thủ Dầu Một – Resiliation du marché Mou-Moussat. 1885–1891; VNA2 IA.20/224(4) Voitures Publics Biên Hoà – Bà Rịa. Service journalier de voitures publics (correspondence – colis postaux – voyageurs). Marché de gré à gré. (adjudication: un indien) 1898–1899; VNA2 IA.20/244(3) Voitures Publics Saigon – Tây Ninh, Saigon – Trang Bang. Service correspondance et voyageurs. Marché de gré à gré avec M. Fabule et sieur Pajaniappatevane en vue d'assurer le même service. 1890–1897; VNA2 IA20 244 (8) Voitures Publics Biên Hoà – Long Thanh. Marché de gré à gré...Actes de substitution au nom de Sepakyry Mahamed entrepreneur 1900–1906; VNA2 IA.20/252 Voitures Publics Service de voitures publics pour le transport des voyageurs et de la poste entre Saigon – Tây Ninh, Saigon – Biên Hoà– marché de gré à gré avec M. Trigaut, concurrence avec M. Pajaniatevane (Saigon –Tây Ninh et vice-versa), 1898–1899. On Indians running automated transport services in the late 1930s, see VNA1 L1 1. Non-reconnaisance du droit de l'eligibilité des indiens sujets français aux chambres de commerce, 1938. 'État numérique des Indiens sujets français non-renonçants établis en Cochinchine, 1936'.

1884, when a list of 'merchants of milk' (*marchands de lait*) began to be included in the commercial section of the colonial yearbook, it consisted of no less than twenty-six Tamil names in Saigon, and seven in Cholon. The great majority, like those Tamils using livestock for transport, were probably caste Hindus, although one or two Muslims also supplied milk in Saigon and Phnom Penh in the 1880s.[89]

Tamils supplied milk door-to-door, but also filled contracts to supply fresh milk, mainly to government hospitals. They continued to produce and sell milk in Cochinchina throughout the French colonial period. A woman from a French Indian family who grew up in Saigon and Phnom Penh just prior to the Second World War could remember Tamils bringing milk to her family home in both places.[90] Yet from the 1930s, most Tamil milkmen 'could barely make ends meet'.[91] From the early twentieth century they lost much of their metropolitan clientele to European competition and a preference for hygienic packaging and pasteurisation. A 1905 report on milk in Indochina stated that fresh milk was produced mainly for military hospitals by 'Indians and Annamites' who kept herds of cows. It noted that fresh milk was not part of the indigenous diet. By contrast, 'Condensed milk, sweetened or plain, sold in small tins, and fresh pasteurised milk displayed in shops in tins and bottles are more widely consumed, due to their modest price and their easier conservation.'[92] Not long afterwards, the scores of Tamil milkmen listed in the commercial pages of the colonial yearbook disappeared, replaced by a single name: 'Nestlé and Anglo-Swiss Condensed Milk Co., 19 Mac Mahon Street.'[93] Around the same time, some French milk companies were employing aggressive advertising in attempts to wrest those Vietnamese who had developed a taste for dairy products from the grip of the Tamil milk merchants (see Plate 8 and also Chapter Six).

Identifying the social origins of these men of livestock, transport, and milk is partly guesswork. Some Muslims were involved, but most were Hindus. They were possibly from three South Indian castes which in the late nineteenth century, in Pondicherry as well as the surrounding

---

89. *ACCH 1884*, pp. 386, 392; 'Relevée des actes de renonciation', *JOEFI 1898*, p. 400.
90. Interview with Mrs. Julienne Paul Ambroise, Pondicherry, October 2004.
91. 'Taper sur les pauvres hindous est si facile!', *Saigon-Dimanche*, 6 December 1931.
92. VNA1 L.413423 Renseignements sur l'importation et la production du lait en Indochine, 1902–1906.
93. *Les adresses* 1913, p. 261.

Plate 8: Tamil milkman admonished by a Vietnamese servant. Advertisement for 'La petite fermière' milk, LTTV 26 February 1914. Courtesy General Sciences Library, Ho Chi Minh City.

British areas of the Tamil country, were noted for their enterprise and drive for upward mobility. These castes included *Yadavals* (specialising in the period in raising cows and milk production), *Pattanavans* (originally fishermen but branching out into other enterprises), and *Pallis* or *Vannias* (variously merchants, bullock and pony cart drivers, and oil pressers).[94]

Carters and drivers of carriages had connections to Tamils who raised cows and produced milk. They were probably also associated with Tamil oil pressers, who used cattle-driven presses, and are described in a later section of this chapter. These various occupations were linked to the contracts held by Hindu businessmen in the late nineteenth century to furnish supplies and labour to the colonial administration. Many of these connections come together in the career of the entrepreneur Pajaniappatevane. When he brought a complaint in 1899 against the

---

94. Esquer, *Les castes*, pp. 105, 115, 120, 127; Thurston, *Castes and Tribes*, pp. 14, 17, 179.

local authorities for non-payment of his transport contract, he was described as both 'a merchant of milk, residing in Saigon' and as 'a former contractor of a public transport service, between Saigon and Tây Ninh'.[95]

The decline of Tamil livestock-related services led to the disappearance of Indian carters and carriage drivers. Although Tamil milkmen continued to operate in Cochinchina throughout the colonial period, they were an increasingly impoverished class of migrants whose trade was no longer lucrative. However, some men of livestock, transport, and milk who contracted to the government met with considerable financial success. Their names, as well as those of their descendants, appear again between the wars associated with property dealing, as described later in this chapter. The name of Pajaniappatevane is among them.

Tax farms and government tenders

Revenue farms or tax farms were arrangements whereby private bidders won the right to collect taxes from the public for specific services in return for a lump sum payment from government. They were prevalent elsewhere in Southeast Asia in the late nineteenth century, where they have been described as transitional institutions which 'sowed the seeds of their own dissolution' by helping to finance modern state-run bureaucracies.[96] In Cochinchina, however, many types of revenue farm persisted well into the twentieth century. Tax farms for markets, ferries, and moorings in the colony were managed by Tamils from the 1870s right up until the end of colonial rule. Tamils were also involved in a number of different types of government supply contract, among them contracts involving milk and livestock. Unlike the tax farms, the Tamil role as purveyors to the colonial government was short-lived.

The first Tamils known to be involved in market tax farms in Cochinchina were Souprayapoullé (presumably a Hindu) and a Catholic renouncer, Samy Appassamy. Souprayapoullé was listed in the Colonial Yearbook for 1876 as a '[tax] farmer of the central market'.[97] Samy Appassamy became involved in the tax farming of Cholon markets in the late 1880s or 1890s; a

---

95. VNA2 SL 3940 Transaction dans l'affaire PAJANIAPPATEVANE, adjudicatiare du service des voitures publiques entre Saigon et Tây Ninh, contre l'administration pour paiement de diverses sommes 1898–1899.
96. John Butcher and Howard Dick, (eds), *The Rise and Fall of Revenue Farming*, Houndsmills, Basingstoke: Macmillan, 1993, p. 3.
97. *ACCH 1876*, p. 137.

Franco-Tamil newspaper claimed he developed the Cholon revenue farms when they 'did not exist at the time'.[98]

Tamils were especially active in the management of market taxes in the Mekong Delta. They went on to carve out similar niches tendering charges for ferry services, for mooring, and for loading along quays. These areas of revenue farming, while they remained securely Tamil, quickly became distinctly Muslim niches of operation. There were good reasons for this. All these types of tax farm were well suited to the merchants, whose shops were located in market towns throughout the Mekong Delta, and who had good access to the waterways criss-crossing the Delta. From the late nineteenth century it was South Indian Muslims who routinely won bids to farm taxes in Mekong Delta towns and districts.[99] Other areas of revenue farming in which Tamils (but not always Muslims) occasionally became involved were tax farms on slaughterhouses, and taxes on rubbish collection in towns and cities.[100]

Tamils also filled contracts for various supplies and services to government. The networks of Tamils associated with livestock raising were associated with many of these contracts, some of which were dependent upon access to livestock. Tamil contractors provided transport and labour for early French urban construction projects and for the development of public transport links in colonial Cochinchina. Contracts such as the one Tirouvingadame signed in 1869 to furnish bullock carts to the Civil Works department are testimony to the Tamils' role in constructing Saigon as a colonial city.[101] Other Tamil contractors helped to develop communications links with the interior. Livestock-related contracts extended to the provision of animal feed and milk, and Tamils serviced a variety of other contracts, including supplying wood for heating to local administrations, and food to prisoners and college students.[102]

---

98. 'Depart de M Samy Appassamy', *Saigon-Dimanche*, 13–16 July 1933.

99. See *AGI 1908*, pp. 342–345.

100. VNA2 IA.9/243(9) Trésor – Demande de main-levée d'opposition sur les mandates des paiements de patents de M. Madjagabalanchetty, fermier des abattoirs de Saigon, fournisseur de bois de chauffage du Service Locale et fermier des marchés de Dakao et de Nam Chon, 1895; VNA2 GD 2995 Plainte au sujet de l'administration de la mosquée musulmane rue Amiral Dupré, 1933: 'Notice sur le sieur Mouhammed Aboubakare'.

101. VNA2 CP7979 Cahier des charges pour la fourniture des voitures à boeufs à la journée [1869].

102. See references in footnote 88, as well as: VNA2 CP 8111 Marché de gré à gré avec le sieur NARAYANIN pour la fourniture du paddy nécessaire à la nourriture des bœufs... 7 décembre, 1878; VNA2 CP 8143 Hôpitaux: Cahier des charges pour la fourniture du lait

Prior to the introduction of electricity in the two cities, two renouncers played important roles providing lighting to Saigon and Cholon. In the 1900s, Samy Appassamy was contracted to provide petrol lighting to public buildings in both cities. Xavier de Condappa, presumably taking over from Samy, took charge of petrol lighting for the city of Saigon from 1908 to 1911. Both men had professional training, the first medical and the second legal; both had been previously employed in the administration, Samy as a health officer (*officier de la santé*) in the 1880s, and de Condappa as a legal clerk around the turn of the twentieth century.[103] They are typical of French Indians who could not use their professional training to its fullest extent in Cochinchina, and instead pursued other interests.

Tamils continued to maintain control of certain types of market tax farming throughout the period of French colonial rule, but not without the threat of competition from the Chinese, who were even more heavily involved in revenue farming. Writing in 1939, the economist Robequain made mention of the Chinese collecting taxes in the markets and feeding prisoners (roles he described as 'too distasteful for Europeans').[104] Technological change no doubt played a role in the decline of some types of government service contracts. Livestock-related transport contracts fell off with the introduction of motorised transportation, and contracts for gas lighting declined as electricity came to light city streets. Diminishing Tamil involvement in official supply contracts after the 1900s, however, can also be attributed to Chinese competition. Many tenders from the late nineteenth century show Chinese entrepreneurs bidding against Tamil hopefuls. Yet there are also examples of Chinese and Tamils submitting joint bids for contracts. The 'plural society' in which different groups acted only in their ethnic or proto-national interest is a model which clearly cannot capture these more complex interactions on the ground.

---

pendant l'année 1880; VNA2 IA.9/243(9); VNA2 IA.9/292(12) Marchés et adjudications –Fournitures des ratios de mires nécessaires à la nourriture des élèves du Collège de Mỹ Tho. Marché Oussanessaheb, 1905; VNA2 GD 2995 Plainte au sujet de l'administration de la mosquée musulmane rue Amiral Dupré, 1933: 'Notice sur le sieur Mouhammed Aboubakare'.

103. 'Depart de M Samy Appassamy', *Saigon-Dimanche*, 13–16 July 1933; VNA2 IA.9/292(6) Marchés adjudications – Éclairage au pétrole des batiments du service locale: marché Samy Appassainy [sic] (cahier des charges), 1905–1907; 'Un grand philanthrope hindou: M. Xavier de Condappa', *Saigon-Dimanche*, 15 February 1931.

104. Robequain, *Economic Development*, p. 38.

Urban and rural land investments

The Chinese were the largest foreign landowners in colonial Cochinchina by a long measure, but Indians came a respectable second. Figures for foreign land ownership in Cochinchina from 1921 (thus at the beginning of the building boom in Saigon and Cholon) showed that the Chinese held some twenty million piastres worth of land, against 1.7 million held by the much smaller Indian population. The larger-than-proportional Indian share of the market was mainly in urban land.[105]

The Nattukottai Chettiars comprised the biggest group of Indian landowners in the colony. The value of all Chettiar-held property prior to the economic crisis of 1929–1930 was 2,045,000 piastres (at 1937 values).[106] The Chettiars actively invested in urban properties right from their arrival in the colony in the 1870s; they were generally averse to owning and managing rural land.[107] In the late 1920s, individual Chettiars' annual incomes from property averaged from 60,000 to 100,000 piastres. They received further rental income from properties belonging to the temple fund, in collective Chettiar possession; this amounted to a sum of 3,000 piastres monthly.[108] At the onset of the Depression Nattukottai Chettiars acquired vast tracts of agricultural land through debt foreclosure. By 1937 they owned 30,000 hectares of land, worth 3,300,000 piastres. Seventy-three percent of the area they possessed was in the fertile Transbassac rice tracts.[109]

The single most wealthy Indian landowner between the wars was not a Chettiar, however, but a South Indian Muslim merchant. Saigon-based J.M.M. Ishmael, in partnership with his brothers Mohamed Abdoullah and (somewhat later) Abdul Aziz, acquired property in the interwar years consisting of blocks of shop houses, commercial properties, and empty lots on ten different streets in central Saigon. Their holdings were valued in 1933 at 891,000 piastres with an annual income of 111,328

---

105. ANOM GGI 60909 Renseignements fournis au Département au sujet propriété foncière: droit des étrangers 1921.
106. VNA2 GD 2992 Situation et rôle des chettys en Indochine, 1937: *Directeur des Services des prêts fonciers à longue terme* to Director Finance Indochina, 29 September 1937.
107. Interview with A.M.A. Meyapachettiar, Karaikkudi, September 2004; See also VNA2 GD 2992 Situation et rôle des chettys en Indochine, 1937: lists of 'properties held by *Chettys*'.
108. ANOM GGI 65475 Service de la Sûreté Cochinchine Rapport Annuel 1924–26: Rapport Annuel 1924–25, and rapport annuel 1er juillet 1926 à 1er juillet 1927, Les Indiens.
109. VNA2 GD 2992 Situation et rôle des chettys en Indochine, 1937: *Directeur des Services des prêts fonciers à longue terme* to Director Finance Indochina, 29 September 1937.

piastres.[110] A descendant has claimed that at its height the family's property empire was second only to that of the Chinese Hui Bon Hoa, the largest landowner in Saigon.[111] This view went unchallenged in my interviews with older Tamils in Pondicherry, who continue to remember the Ishmael brothers as legendary figures with legendary fortunes.[112] Although other South Indian Muslim merchants also acquired properties between the wars, their holdings and incomes were somewhat more modest than those of the Ishmael brothers.[113]

Chettiar and Muslim landholdings were impressive, but a few Indian French citizens could also hold their own in this field. Some were men who arrived in Cochinchina in the late nineteenth century and benefited (probably much like the Chettiars) from buying urban land before Saigon and Cholon's colonial development got underway in earnest. Men employed in the administration in the Offices of Public Works or Land Registration may have acted on information obtained in their places of work to make wise and timely purchases. One Indian French citizen who acquired significant land holdings was Rattinam Sinnas. He arrived in Saigon in 1889 and was employed shortly thereafter by the Office of Public Works. According to his grandchildren and great-grandchildren, all raised in Saigon or Hanoi, he purchased land cheaply in the area which then became developed as the Central Market. Rattinam's son Evariste constructed shop houses on this land in the 1920s, where a 'Sinnas alley' (*ruelle Sinnas*), the family maintains, gave access to housing.[114] Evariste Sinnas' entry into the world of business is yet another example of how certain ambitious renouncers shunned secure employment in the colonial administration. As a young recruit posted in 1927 to the forestry service in Kampung Thom (Cambodia), he resigned just days after beginning work in the remote village. He declared upon quitting that he was 'sufficiently

---

110. VNA2 GD 2995 Plainte au sujet de l'administration de la mosquée musulmane rue Amiral Dupré, 1933: 'Notice sur les sieurs J.M. Mohamed Ishmael et J.M. Mohamed Abdoullah.'
111. Interview with Mrs. Mumtaz Alam, Saigon, January 1997.
112. Interviews in Pondicherry with Mr. Abdoul-Gaffour, January 2002 and September 2004, and members of the Said family, November 2004.
113. See ANOM GGI 65476 Service de sûreté, Rapports annuels: Service de la Sûreté, Rapport Annuel de Commissariat spécial pour la port de Saigon-Cholon (1927–1928): Action Indienne.
114. Interviews in Pondicherry with Alfred Sinnas and Maurice Sinnas, October 2004.

wealthy to have no need to bow down before the drudgery of making [his] living as a functionary'.[115]

The entrepreneur Xavier de Condappa was another French citizen of Indian origin who acquired considerable land holdings in Cholon either during or shortly after the First World War. A Sinnas descendant recounted:

> In Cholon it was de Condappa...If his name was on the map, it was because he had even more shop houses [*compartiments*] than my grandfather. There was a boulevard Xavier de Condappa in Cholon...[116]

I have been unable to verify the claim that one of Cholon's boulevards once carried the name of an Indian French citizen, but it is not entirely unlikely. An article in the Franco-Tamil *Saigon-Dimanche* outlining de Condappa's achievements stated that in 1928 he had donated large tracts of land in Cholon to the municipality to develop a market and widen roads.[117] It is possible that one of these avenues was then given his name.

The contractor Samy Appassamy also saw his fortunes take off during the building boom of the 1920s; he is said to have entered into construction at a time when Saigon 'was growing like a mushroom'.[118] Yet another big landowner in the late 1920s was Savéricom Prouchandy. His holdings included shop houses and vacant lots in both Saigon and Cap-St-Jacques (Vũng Tàu). Léon Prouchandy, Savéricom's nephew, himself became a property owner and entrepreneur of some note.[119]

Some caste Hindus involved in the livestock networks also amassed significant land holdings in Cochinchina. In 1881 the entrepreneur Nagalingapoullé owned a large lot bordering the Murugan temple on Ohier Street.[120] By the late 1920s, the milk merchant Pajaniappathévar had a monthly rental income of 6,000 piastres, large enough to warrant mention in the Security Bureau's annual report. In the same year the Security Bureau noted the rental income of Kathéappathévar as 2,500 piastres monthly; by the 1930s he was a well-known personality in Saigon's Tamil expatriate circle, lauded in the Franco-Tamil newspaper

---

115. NAC 13468 Dossier Personnel Evariste Louis Sinnas, agent journalier 1921–1927.
116. Interview with Alfred Sinnas, Pondicherry, October 2004.
117. 'Un grand philanthrope hindou: M. Xavier de Condappa', *Saigon-Dimanche*, 15 February 1931.
118. 'Depart de M Samy Appassamy', *Saigon-Dimanche*, 13–16 July 1933.
119. Interview with a descendant, Paris, April 2004.
120. VNA2 CP 8372 Arrêté du Gouvernement concédant un immeuble domaniale...aux Indiens sectateurs de Brahme pour y construire un temple 1881.

Indochine-Inde for his philanthropy and his 'exquisite urbanity, cordiality and amiability'.[121] Appapoulé emerges from a listing of Indian moneylenders (not all of them Nattukottai Chettiars) in the 1937 Chettiar banking enquiry as a man who had acquired massive tracts of land in Gia Định and Gò Vấp provinces following the economic crisis, apparently through mortgages he extended directly. In this same document Nadimouttouppoullé and Varadappoulé are listed as co-owners of a tract of land that had been 'bequeathed [to them] by Pajaniappathévar in his will of 4 November, 1922', a fact which connects them to the former milk merchant and the Hindu livestock networks.[122]

Aside from urban properties, some Indians secured concessions of rural land. Such concessions were reserved for French citizens, indicating that the landowners in question were largely renouncers.[123] According to notary records, Indians Andoninadin Guanadicom (Bạc Liêu, Bà Rịa), P. I. Tetta (Bà Rịa), and Marie-Joseph Ponnou (Châu Đốc and Long Xuyên) all held concessions in Cochinchina in the 1900s.[124] Mr. Mouttou was known in the 1930s as 'a well-known colonist (*colon*) from Mỹ Tho', where he kept paddy fields and coconut groves. At least one South Indian Muslim, one of the few of his faith who renounced, was a 'colonist and entrepreneur', in Châu Đốc in 1926.[125]

One Tamil bid for a land concession is particularly interesting for what it reveals of the interdependence of overseas Tamils both within Cochinchina and beyond its borders into the French protectorate of Cambodia. Henri Djeganadin Saint-Jacques was a French citizen, a legal clerk and Justice of the Peace in Saigon when he applied in 1926 for a land concession in Soai Rieng on the Cambodian–Cochinchinese border. Obliged to demonstrate his financial resources as part of his application, the deeds he enclosed indicated he held deposits with two Tamil bankers

---

121. ANOM GGI 65476 Service de sûreté, Rapports annuels: Service de la Sûreté, Rapport Annuel de Commissariat spécial pour la port de Saigon-Cholon (1927–1928): Action Indienne; 'Le départ de M. Katthéappathévar', *Indochine-Inde*, 2 and 9 May 1937.
122. VNA2 GD 2992 Situation et rôle des chettys en Indochine, 1937: 'Province de Gia Dinh, Liste des biens immeubles des chettys'.
123. Ngô Vĩnh Long, *Before the Revolution*, pp. 11–14.
124. Centre d'accueil et de recherche des Archives nationales (CARAN) SOM NOT Indochine SOM/02.
125. 'Le retour de M. Mouttou', *Saigon-Dimanche*, 27 April 1930; ANOM GGI 65475 Service de la Sûreté Cochinchine Rapport Annuel 1924–26: rapport annuel 1er juillet 1926 à 1er juillet 1927, Les Indiens.

(Si-Mou-Ta-Candassamy and Sa-Covindassamy) as well as an account with the Bank of Indochina. Further interconnections between different Tamil migrants are revealed in Saint-Jacques' appointment of a Mr. Mougamadou (no doubt a Tamil Muslim trader in the local area) as his representative in Soai Rieng while his application was being processed.[126]

The Chettiars were criticised the most loudly for taking money out of Cochinchina to invest in India, but all groups of Tamil migrants did so, on scales both large and small. Although they are difficult to quantify, many land investments in India were financed by gains from Cochinchina. The renouncer Xavier de Condappa began to acquire and develop agricultural land in Tavalacoupam (Pondicherry district) in the 1900s, around the same time he was investing in urban land in Cholon. He also bought urban property in Pondicherry.[127] The J.M.M. Ishmael brothers, too, made significant land investments in India.[128] Similarly, Savéricom Prouchandy purchased at auction between the wars one of the grandest houses in Pondicherry, the Villa Aroumé.[129] Other descendants of Indochina-based Tamils routinely told me that family properties in Pondicherry were purchased by their forebears with capital brought back from Indochina.

Purveyors to Saigon's expatriates

In the late nineteenth and early twentieth centuries a preponderance of bars, public houses, cafés, and small drinks shops (*débit de boissons, cabarets, cafés,* and *buvettes*) in Saigon were run by Tamils. Some of these enterprises appear to have been based on European models; their owners, like the vendors of milk, capitalised on demands created by the French presence, and the presence of French tastes.

At least three French citizens of Indian origin ran establishments in Saigon serving drink to French clients in the late 1800s. Rangassamy-

---

126. NAC 4331 Demande de Concession 800Ha formulée par M. Saint-Jacques. 1926–1928: 'Traduction de l'obligation souscrite au recto en caractères tamouls par le sieur Si-Mou-Ta-Candassamy, banquier indien, demeurant à Saigon, rue Ohier, No.20, au profit de M. D. Saint-Jacques.' And in the same file, 'Traduction de l'obligation souscrite à la page précédante…en caractères tamouls par le sieur Sa Covindassamy, banquier indien, demeurant à Saigon, rue Ohier, No. 9, au profit de M. D. Saint-Jacques', and Saint-Jacques to French resident, Soai Rieng, 31 July 1926.

127. 'Un grand philanthrope hindou: M. Xavier de Condappa', *Saigon-Dimanche*, 15 Febuary 1931; Discussion with Raj de Condappa, Pondicherry, September 2004.

128. VNA2 GD 2995 Plainte au sujet de l'administration de la mosquée musulmane rue Amiral Dupré, 1933: 'Notice sur les sieurs J.M. Mohamed Ismael et J.M. Mohamed Abdoullah.'

129. Interview with a descendant, Paris, April 2004.

Naiker (known as Casimir upon his renunciation) served a French clientele at his bar on Catinat Street from the late 1860s.[130] Ayassamy Beaumont, proprietor of the *Café des Messageries Maritimes* in 1880s Saigon, was also a French citizen.[131] The Portuguese (or Macanese) wife of entrepreneur Darmanaden Prouchandy owned a drinks shop in the 1890s; a few years later the couple deepened their investment in the potential market for European drink by founding a plant to produce carbonated drinks and lemonade. Robequain noted that both products, along with ice cream and beer, 'were created in the first place for a European clientele'.[132] French authorities initially observed of the Prouchandys' operation that: '[it] appears to prosper and has made [them] relatively well off'. Yet Darmanaden's 1902 request to the Governor General of Indochina to prohibit the import of 'lemonades' fell on deaf ears, suggesting that his enterprise, like that of the Tamil milkmen, succumbed to European competition.[133]

During the same period, other Tamil-run drinks shops and various small-scale services were located in areas of Saigon where Tamils lived and worked. In 1889 Samdapoullé ran a shop serving drinks (*buvette*) in Batavia Street; it probably catered to the Tamil milk merchants with whom the street was then associated. The yearbook of 1891 noted another Tamil drinks stall, that of a Mme. Coupamalle, on the same street. In the same period Zeinabou and Sandjivinadivi-Ajaguianadin ran *buvettes* in Adran and Ohier Streets respectively. Properties in both streets were by then primarily Chettiar-owned, while most residents were ethnic Tamils with varied social profiles. Thus when Mouttou set up shop on Ohier Street to sell spices in 1912, he centred his business in the midst of his best customers.[134]

---

130. VNA2 CP 8768 (1) Séance 2–12–1872 Réclamation Sieur Rangassamy quant à l'impôt de capitation: Rangassamy to Governor CCH, 23 September 1872.

131. *ACCH 1889*, p. 488.

132. Robequain, *Economic Development*, p. 279.

133. On the Prouchandys' enterprises see ANOM GGI 8644 Demande formulée par Mme. Veuve [sic] Prouchandy tendant à obtenir l'interdiction de l'importation des limonades gazeuses originaires de Singapore 1902; VNA2 SL 4577 Demande de réhabilitation formulée par M. Prouchandy (Darmanaden), demeurant à Saigon 1905; VNA2 Goucoch 1A6/015 Deputy Outrey to GCCH, 14 February 1916. I am grateful to Christina Firpo for drawing my attention to the latter document.

134. *ACCH 1889*, p. 402; *AGI 1891*, p. 412; *AGI 1912*, p. 398.

Plate 9: Tamil sesame press, Cochinchina. Postcard, Nadal, circa 1930.

For other Tamil businesses, we can only speculate who their customers were. It is difficult now to know to whom Ayassamy, of the 'Ayassamy Patisserie' on Chaigneau Street circa 1908, or Annamalechetty, 'fixed-post merchant of sweets' in 1912, served their confections.[135]

Between the wars, there was a rise in the number of small-scale Tamil businesses in Saigon catering more obviously and more directly to a Tamil clientele. The decline of Tamils providing 'French' services and the increase in services directed at Tamils could be explained by competition which pushed Tamils out of niches which they had earlier filled in the absence both of small-scale European entrepreneurs in Cochinchina, and of organised channels of import. It was also, no doubt, due to the growth in the Tamil and the wider Indian population in Saigon, which made it worthwhile to cater to an Indian clientele.

In the 1920s and 1930s, Saigon-based businesses catering to Tamil expatriates included importers of Indian spices and providers of specially prepared Tamil foodstuffs. Nadarassin, on the *rue d'Espagne*, was one dry goods merchant (*épicier*) whose products were sought after by Tamil expatriates in this period. Tamils located in the outskirts of Saigon pressed sesame oil and prepared rice and tamarind by Tamil methods to supply the Indian expatriate community. These services were certainly

---

135. *AGI 1908*, p. 470; *AGI 1912*, p. 398.

in place by the 1930s, but likely began earlier. Postcards from about the 1910s show bullock-driven Tamil oil presses in Cochinchina. One Pondicherry woman who grew up in Saigon in the 1930s can recall how her family continued, after a move to Phnom Penh in the early 1940s, to have all three products sent by bus to Cambodia, until wartime conditions made it no longer possible.[136]

Between the World Wars, as in the previous decades, many small Tamil enterprises were located in streets occupied by Tamils in Saigon. Although in the 1880s it was lined with Tamil milkmen, by the First World War Lagrandière Street had come to be the preferred place of residence of many Indians employed in the administration. The street increasingly attracted importers of Tamil foodstuffs and restaurants serving Indian food. In the early 1930s the dry goods merchant *Au Comptoir Hindou* was a fixture on Lagrandière Street. It enticed customers in its advertising with 'Garouda curry powders' and arrack ('as good as Gin, Cognac and other spirits. Ask for it at the *Comptoir Hindou*... sole agent in Indochina').[137]

THE STEAMBOAT VENTURES OF DARMANADEN PROUCHANDY

Indian French citizens who eschewed the secure life of a functionary in Indochina and struck out instead in private business tended to gravitate towards characteristically Tamil enterprises. One notable exception to this rule was the renouncer Darmanaden (Pierre) Prouchandy, who attempted to establish a steamboat service on the Mekong Delta waterways in the 1890s. His story reads as a cautionary tale of the difficulties faced when a 'so-called' Frenchman tried to compete directly with French interests. Prouchandy aimed to do business just like his metropolitan compatriots, by pursuing state subsidies which he felt he deserved as much as they did. The cool reception he faced goes some way to explaining why most renouncers resident in Cochinchina may have felt they had more to be gained by entering into commerce alongside their Tamil peers.[138]

---

136. Interview with Mrs. Amélie Marius Le Prince, Pondicherry, November 2004; see also VNA1 Goucoch III59/N44(11) Authorisation d'éxportation de Pondichéry d'un produit alimentaire dénommé 'mantèque' solicitée par l'épicier Nadarassin 1939.
137. *Saigon-Dimanche*, 9 October 1932; *Saigon-Dimanche*, 12 March 1933.
138. For an analysis of Prouchandy's story within the wider context of South Indian-owned steam navigation lines, see J.B.P. More, *Indian Steamship Ventures, 1836–1910: Darmanathan Prouchandy of Pondicherry, First Steam Navigator from South India, 1891–1900*, Pondicherry: Leon Prouchandy Memorial Sangam, 2013.

Darmanaden Prouchandy arrived in Saigon from Pondicherry in 1870.[139] Like several of his Tamil compatriots, he was involved in supply contracts in the 1870s and 1880s. He filled orders for milk and other diverse items (including matches, corks, mosquito nets, and soap) to military hospitals in Baria and Saigon.[140] His entry into the business of transport began around the same time that he established with his wife the enterprises described in the previous section.

Prouchandy owned two steamboats. The 'Prouchandy' was registered in Phnom Penh from at least 1892. The 'Alexandre' ran a passenger service through the 1890s from Phnom Penh to Hà Tiên via Châu Đốc and was also contracted to carry the post.[141]

Prouchandy persisted in requesting government subsidies to run his service over this period, while complaining that the *Compagnie des Messageries Fluviales* was being unfairly favoured in receiving such subsidies. Some of the evidence supports Prouchandy's case. When he established his service in October 1891, local administrators agreed to provide him with a subsidy to serve the route Hà Tiên–Châu Đốc. By March of the following year, however, the *Messageries Fluviales* had proposed to establish a competing service between the same two ports. The company insisted upon, and obtained, a higher subsidy than that which Prouchandy had applied for but had yet to receive. Prouchandy also repeatedly failed in his attempts to wrest control of another government subsidised route, the Saigon–Bangkok line, from the *Messageries Fluviales*. He was granted short-term aid (*secours*) a few times to run the 'Alexandre', but on each occasion this was accompanied by a nervous statement on the part of colonial authorities that the *secours* should not be considered a subsidy (*subvention*) for fear that it might constitute a breach of the government's contract with the *Messageries Fluviales*.[142]

---

139. VNA2 SL 4577 Demande de réhabilitation formulée par M. Prouchandy (Darmanaden) demeurant à Saigon 1905.

140. VNA2 CP 8133 Cahier des charges relatifs à la fourniture des matériels et matières grasses … soumission Darmanaden 1879; VNA2 CP 8143 Hopitaux, Cahier des charges pour la fourniture du lait pendant l'année 1880.

141. VNA2 I.A/5/124(4) Transports Fluviaux, dossier Darmanaden (1898); VNA2 IA.5/124(7) Subvention Prouchandy 1893: Administrator Châu Đốc to General Secretary Colonial Council, 2 December 1891.

142. VNA2 IA.5/124(7) Subvention Prouchandy 1893: Messageries Fluviales to Colonial Council, 2 March 1892; VNA2 IA.5/124(8) Prouchandy service de chaloupes entre Hà Tiên et Bangkok, 1893–1894; VNA2 IA.5/124 Navigation … Demande de subvention pre-

The other side of the story emerges in officials' highly critical assessments of the steamboat 'Alexandre'. They claimed Prouchandy's inability to compete with the *Messageries Fluviales* was due not to favouritism but to the poor quality of service he provided. In 1894 the Administrator of Hà Tiên, in supporting the rejection of yet another request from Prouchandy, deplored the condition of the 'Alexandre': 'If Mr. Prouchandy, for want of a subsidy, ceases to run his boat from Châu Đốc to Hà Tiên and vice versa, the *arrondissement* of Hà Tiên will not only not suffer, but will even rejoice.' A safety check on the 'Alexandre' in the same year concluded that 'the speed reached was barely superior to that of the current'. A navigation permit was nonetheless granted on the grounds that the feeble power of the craft did not actually constitute a danger. Reports from Hà Tiên under a new administrator in 1898 continued to describe the 'Alexandre' as 'old, infected and completely inadequate in comfort or speed'.[143]

The abrasive nature of Prouchandy's relationship with the colonial authorities implies that they considered him out of place in this 'European' role and that he was all too aware of this judgement made against him. In response to a complaint in 1893 from the postal master in Phnom Penh, that Prouchandy's boat had failed to take the post on board before its departure, Prouchandy retorted, 'Why does [the Phnom Penh post master] think he is addressing an inferior?'[144] In 1894 the Administrator at Hà Tiên proposed that Prouchandy's rightful competitors were Chinese and Vietnamese boat owners rather than the French-run services. In this letter the administrator made mention of several Chinese vessels and one run by an '*Annamite* from Cholon' who also plied the route between Châu Đốc and Hà Tiên, and 'never asked for subsidies'.[145]

The remarks of Kieffer, a planter from Kampot and would-be passenger of the 'Alexandre' spell out most clearly the uncomfortable relation-

---

sentée par M. Prouchandy pour un service de chaloupe... 1893–1898; VNA2 IA.4/207(30) Navigation: Un secours de $200 accordé au Sieur Prouchandy 1893.

143. VNA2 IA.5/124(6) Demande d'indemnité formulée par le Sr. Prouchandy (1894): Administrator Hà Tiên to GGCCH, 17 December 1894, and in the same file, 'Procès-verbal d'essai de la chaloupe à vapeur 'Prouchandy' appartenant au Sieur Prouchandy demeurant à Cholon, 12 décembre, 1894'; VNA2 IA.5/124(4) Transports Fluviaux, dossier Darmanaden (1898): Administrator Hà Tiên to GGCCH, 1 September 1898.

144. VNA2 IA.5/124(5) Demande d'une prime d'encouragement – Prouchandy 1893.

145. VNA2 IA.5/124(6) Demande d'indemnité formulée par le Sr. Prouchandy (1894).

ship between Prouchandy and his European clientele. In January 1895, Prouchandy refused to make his craft wait in dock at Hà Tiên while Kieffer's baggage and servants were unloaded from an incoming boat from Kampot. Kieffer wrote to complain:

> I find that this race [*race*] who appears to be very concerned by the defective service it offers, could be more amenable in order to attract the good will of the administration and the business of the *colons*... [it needs to be able] to do sufficiently good business [in order to] pass up the subsidies that it does not cease to request, although it does not merit them. In addition, I have heard the *Malabar* patron employ vulgar expressions when speaking of senior French *serviteurs*, no doubt because he thinks he has the right to call himself French, which, unfortunately, is the case.[146]

Kieffer may have been jealous of, as well as hostile to Prouchandy's citizenship. His own application for French naturalisation – he was from Luxembourg – had been turned down two years previously, and resulted in him being denied a land concession in Kampot. He had also been previously employed with the *Messagerie Fluviales*.[147]

The captain of the 'Alexandre' refuted Kieffer's view, by maintaining that the boat had already gone nearly a kilometre when it was signalled by Kieffer on the jetty demanding it return to fetch him. 'Given the great distance and out of fear of missing the tide M. Dairy [Dairy Prouchandy, a relative employed by Darmanaden] informed me it was impossible to return, given that Mr. Kieffer was not even ready to depart.'[148]

Prouchandy's venture into river transportation was resisted by both the Frenchmen he was aiming to compete with and those to whom he was attempting to cater. While his efforts to appeal to French tastes in the urban setting of Saigon met with somewhat greater success, his steamboat ventures fell victim to a particularly incestuous form of French competition which saw metropolitan private businesses 'competing' by capturing state subsidies.

Conclusion

The main Tamil migrant groups to Cochinchina were Indian French citizens employed in the colonial administration, South Indian Muslims

---

146. VNA2 I.A/5/124(2) Affaire Prouchandy 1896: Kieffer, planton in Kampot, to Administrator of Indigenous Affairs, Châu Đốc, 10 January 1896.
147. VNA2 IIB.38/078 Dossier relatif à la naturalisation années 1885–1894.
148. VNA2 I.A/5/124(2) Affaire Prouchandy 1896: Commandant 'Alexandre' to Administrator Châu Đốc, 17 January 1896.

in textile and other trades, Nattukottai Chettiars in banking, and certain other Hindus in livestock rearing, transport, and the provision of milk. Despite these 'occupational specialisations', there was scope for Tamils to enter into fields that were apparently the preserve of other compatriots. Most notably, some ambitious renouncers eschewed their accepted employment as colonial functionaries and undertook business ventures. When they did so these ventures were almost always – Prouchandy's is the exception – characteristically Tamil.

There were also many everyday ties between Indian French citizens and the wider overseas Tamil population. Even when they were not directly engaged in 'Tamil' commerce, renouncers were involved in various ways in Tamil commercial networks. Renouncer functionaries assisted other Tamils in negotiating their way through the French colonial bureaucracy. They facilitated the conduct of Tamil business in Cochinchina because of their positioning in key areas of the administration (immigration, customs and excise, public works, the legal system). They shared a language and cultural references with the Indian entrepreneurs, and at the same time understood the workings of the French system. Their presence within the administration was therefore important to other Tamils who operated at a greater distance from French power. But this assistance was reciprocated too, as renouncers are also known to have sought the assistance of other Tamils to further their own business interests. This sense of a Tamil community also developed with the decline of Tamil-run services aiming to cater to European tastes and the growth of services catering specifically to the tastes and preferences of a growing Tamil population.

If we focus on the more tightly organised Tamil migrants groups, the Chettiars and the Muslim merchants, it appears to be legitimate to speak of migrant groups as part of a 'plural society' with closely-guarded internal economic interests. Yet this model collapses when subjected to closer scrutiny. Tamil migrants existed as a coherent group in colonial Cochinchina by regularly crossing the boundaries between one supposedly 'highly stratified' migrant group and another. They were unified not by tightly guarded economic interests, but through shared cultural and linguistic ties in the many small but significant ways outlined in this chapter.

Renouncers were very much part of this Tamil world. And yet, in the bureaucratic, policing, and security positions in which they were employed by the French state, they very visibly represented the face of French power and authority. Moreover, in debates over renouncers' political and civil rights in Cochinchina they made very self-conscious claims to their French-ness (Chapters Four and Five). These two hats they wore, and the complex network of ties between different Tamil migrants, are one reason why Indian migrant identities in Indochina have been so difficult to unpick. Renouncers' ability to be mistaken for other Indian migrants, and their own ambiguous existence as both French and Tamil, became important in themselves in Vietnamese reactions to the presence of Indian French citizens (Chapter Six), in renouncers' efforts to raise their public profile in Cochinchina in the interwar years (Chapter Seven), and in their attempts to negotiate the complex web of loyalties produced in Indochina from the Second World War through to Vietnam's independence (Chapter Eight).

CHAPTER FOUR

THE INDIAN VOTE IN COCHINCHINA

French attitudes towards native political franchise in the 'old colonies' and in the territories France later claimed from the mid-nineteenth century were vastly different. So much so that, as one observer remarked in the 1930s, the development of colonial representation '[did] little to increase the French reputation for logic and order'.[1] When Indians moved from the French Establishments to Cochinchina they tested French logic and order by highlighting the marked imbalance between the electoral privileges of the Indians and the poor political representation of peoples native to Cochinchina. French Indians resident in Cochinchina played no small part not only in highlighting but in heightening this imbalance. They ardently defended the idea that they should continue to enjoy in Cochinchina the same political rights they had been granted at home in French India. Even as French India was embroiled in arguments over the structure of its electoral colleges, Indians based in Saigon became engaged in debates about their electoral status in Cochinchina. In the last two decades of the nineteenth century Cochinchina became a ground for testing whether the voting rights of Indians from the French Establishments, be they renouncers or non-renouncers, were transferable to other parts of the empire.

The political rights of Indians residing in Cochinchina were eventually secured for those who had obtained French citizenship through their acts of 'renunciation', although Indians who had not renounced were denied the right to vote in Cochinchina. Yet the resolution of the question of Indian voting rights in Cochinchina did not make the Indian vote in Cochinchina any less problematic. The form of Cochinchina's political institutions, the aspirations of its French politicians, and the

---

1. Rudolph A. Winnacker, 'Elections in Algeria and the French Colonies Under the Third Republic', *American Political Science Review*, 32, 1938, 261–277, p. 262.

desire of Indian French citizens to find people in power who could intervene on their behalf, all conspired to create in the colony a special form of electoral patronage.

NATIVE SUFFRAGE IN THE 'OLD COLONIES' AND THE 'NEW'

The political representation granted to natives of France's 'old colonies' was serially rescinded and reinstated throughout the nineteenth century; yet a measure of the greater generosity with which political assimilation was first granted in the heightened and heated contexts of the French revolution and the abolition of slavery was retained in these older tracts of the French Empire. This stands out in marked contrast to the far less generous political rights granted to the indigenous people of colonial possessions acquired in the second wave of French acquisitions from the mid-nineteenth century. While Algeria is in some ways a transitional case (see Chapter Two), in Cochinchina a 'clean slate' allowed for less liberal arrangements to be inscribed upon it.[2]

Indians from the French Establishments were granted the right to elect a Deputy to represent their interests in the French parliament for a brief period from 1848. Inhabitants of the French Establishments merely had to prove that they had been resident in the French territories for at least five years in order to be able to vote. Parliamentary representation was rescinded in French India in 1852, as it was in the other French colonies. In 1871, with the downfall of Napoleon III and the declaration of the Third Republic, it was again reinstated. A year later, in 1872, local councils were established in each of the French Establishments in India; both Indian and European men were entitled to participate in the election of councillors.[3]

In post-revolutionary France, electoral franchise and civil equality went hand-in-hand as the two inseparable rights of the citizen. Contrary to this metropolitan conception of citizenship, the right of French Indians to political representation did not flow from their French citizenship. It was, rather, the other way round: the colonial state offered electoral rights as a means of moving its colonised people in India more

---

2. Winnacker, 'Elections in Algeria', p. 263.
3. Lewis, 'One Hundred Million Frenchmen', pp. 134–135; Clairon, *La renonciation*, p. 79; H. Ternisien, 'La Question Électoral en Cochinchine', Supplement of *Journal d'Outre Mer*, 21 February 1888; Weber, *Pondichéry*, pp. 218–221.

gradually towards legal equality with citizens in the Metropole. People indigenous to French India, as I have emphasised in Chapter Two, exercised their political rights *independently* of their civil rights; in their own colony they were allowed to enjoy the political rights belonging to French citizens while retaining their indigenous personal status.[4] Even once advocates of renunciation pushed the citizenship debate forward by voluntarily renouncing their personal status, those Indians who had not renounced continued to retain their electoral rights in French India.

Electoral rights for the peoples of Cochinchina were far more restricted. Cochinchina was granted its own representative in the French National Assembly from July 1881, but the right to vote for the Deputy was limited to those who counted as French citizens.[5] Unlike their Indian counterparts in the French Establishments, the indigenous people of Cochinchina had no access to political representation in the Metropole unless they were among the select few who were given French citizenship through naturalisation.

The Vietnamese college of electors for colonial council elections comprised a small group of men handpicked by collaborating local elites. While the municipal council elections for both Saigon and Cholon were open from 1881 to 'universal' indigenous suffrage, in practice this meant that a tiny native electorate participated in selecting only a small number of native councillors. Their power was negligible at best and they were overshadowed by a much larger majority of (French-elected) French councillors.[6] Reforms introduced in 1922 were intended to correct this situation, but had little impact.[7] The first colonised people to argue for the right to political representation in Cochinchina, however, did so well before the 1920s, and were not Vietnamese, Cham, or Khmer, but Indian migrants from the French possessions in India.

Although the political rights of the peoples of French India were more generous than those of their counterparts in Cochinchina, elections in the French Establishments did not stand up to any real test of democ-

---

4. See Girault, *Principes*, p. 566.
5. A. Bouinais and A. Paulus, *L'Indo-Chine Française contemporaine*, Paris: Challamel Aîné, 1885, p. 88.
6. Camilli, *La représentation*, pp. 89–92.
7. See Tai, 'The Politics of Compromise', and R. B. Smith, 'Bui Quang Chieu and the Constitutionalist Party in French Cochinchina, 1917–1930', *Modern Asian Studies*, 3, 1969, 131–150, p. 137.

racy. With the reintroduction of political franchise for French Indians in 1871, two electoral lists were established. One was for Europeans and the other for natives; the European list carried the same weight as the native list despite the obvious difference in size of the two populations. The system of lists was introduced, as one commentator expressed frankly, 'to avoid as much as possible the danger of *hindou* domination'.[8]

Once renunciation was formally recognised a decade later, French India's system of electoral lists underwent almost constant revision. For a brief period renouncers were allowed to vote on the 'European' list. 'Political considerations', however, 'quickly led to reform', and for four years (1881–1884) renouncers and non-renouncers shared the same electoral list. In 1884, the electorate was separated into three lists, one for Europeans, one for renouncers, and one for non-renouncers. To complicate matters, this change affected only local council elections, and neither this nor the previous decree had any retroactive effect, 'leaving on the European list Indian renouncers who had already been registered there'. In 1899, French India reverted to two electoral lists for local councils, one for Europeans and one for non-Europeans. Renouncers were permitted to register on the European list only if they could demonstrate that they had renounced at least fifteen years earlier, that they were proficient in French, and that they held either a French diploma, an administrative or judiciary function, an elected position, or a French honour. All of these changes were led by the obliquely-termed 'political considerations' mentioned above. These consisted of on-going attempts by both the 'Indian' and 'French' parties in Pondicherry to shift the weight of the electoral colleges in their favour in order to gain influence through the ballot box.[9]

The changes brought in 1899 were intended to put paid to accusations that the renouncers' list was being used to form coalitions to swing the vote, and that renunciation was being appropriated for 'purely electoral considerations'.[10] Proof that the reforms of 1899 did not manage to achieve this fills many boxes in the colonial archives in Pondicherry, in

---

8. Clairon, 'La Renonciation', p. 79.
9. Girault, *Principes*, p. 568 (all direct quotes); Clairon, 'La Renonciation', p. 81, 96; ANOM GGI 50927 Situation des Indiens en Cochinchine au point de vue électorale 1900–1901; Weber, *Pondichéry*, p. 241.
10. Clairon, 'La renonciation', p. 89.

the form of court cases brought by Europeans, *créoles*, and Indians alike, contesting the results of colonial elections well beyond this date.[11]

Early licence at the Cochinchinese ballot box

Indians from the French Establishments enjoyed full and unhindered participation in the political life of Cochinchina when the colony was first established. They were registered on electoral rolls from the moment municipal councils were formed in Cholon and Saigon in the 1870s. A Mr. Douressamy-Naiker even served for six years as a municipal councillor for Saigon in the late 1870s and early 1880s. Moreover, Indians living in Cochinchina, unlike in French India, were included without exception in the same electoral colleges as European voters.[12]

Indians from the French Establishments were similarly permitted, when parliamentary representation was first introduced to Cochinchina, to participate in elections to choose a Deputy for the colony. Nor was their participation a fact quietly hidden from view. Indeed, a petition drafted in the wake of the introduction of parliamentary representation, which pressed the Senators and Deputies of France to approve a Cochinchinese Deputy, was signed by 154 'inhabitants of Cochinchina', thirty of whom were Indians.[13]

Further evidence of the active participation of Indian voters in early Cochinchinese colonial politics is seen in the championing of Indian causes by the colony's first Deputy, Marie Jules Blancsubé. Blancsubé, a *métropolitain* from the high Alps, began his Cochinchinese career as a lawyer in Saigon. He was Saigon's Mayor from 1879 to 1881, prior to his entry into legislative politics. Serving as Deputy from 1881 until his death in March of 1888, he was the first in a line of Deputies who used the Indian vote in Cochinchina to their advantage. Blancsubé's time in local politics served as his training ground; as Mayor he was already noted for his support of Indian causes. In Brébion's biography of Indochinese personalities, Blancsubé is portrayed as, 'very popular amongst the nu-

---

11. See, for example, NAIP DM 1928.
12. On Indian participation see ANOM FM Indo af carton 53 Droits électoraux des Indiens établis en Cochinchine: Laurans to Senator for French India, 15 March 1888; Ternisien, 'La Question Électorale en Cochinchine', Supplement of *Journal d'Outre Mer*, 21 February 1888. On the establishment of electoral colleges in Cochinchina: Tai, 'The Politics of Compromise', p. 377; Camilli, *La représentation*, pp. 90–92.
13. ANOM FM Indo af carton 52 Élections: 'Pétition addressée à Messieurs les Sénateurs et à Messieurs les Députés de France par les signataires' [n.d.].

merous *Malabar* cloth merchants of Saigon'. This points to the diverse Indian electorate he patronised, which would have included merchants who for the most part would choose to remain French subjects, as well as French Indians employed in the administration. The latter had renounced or were poised to make a decision whether to renounce in this period. Because Blancsubé:

> always upheld [French Indian interests] in the municipal councils and in front of tribunals ... his name became for the natives of India a superlative for comparison. Thus, to a client who cast in doubt the quality of their merchandise on display [the Indian merchants] would say with conviction: 'This first quality, better even, same thing Blancsubé!' [*Cela première qualité, plus meilleur, même chose Blancsubé!*][14]

Osborne describes Blancsubé as 'the French spokesman in the Colonial Council of Cochinchina for the Indians resident in that colony'.[15] He enjoyed nearly three terms as Deputy, tapping into the strength of this small but powerful group of voters, before the legitimacy of Indian participation in Cochinchinese elections was questioned.

THE INDIAN VOTE CONTESTED

In 1887, the Director of the Interior for Cochinchina, Noel Pardon, noted that Saigon's Mayor had newly registered 345 Indians resident in the city alongside Europeans in his annual exercise to draw up lists for colonial and legislative elections. Alarmed at the sudden increase in the size of the 'French' electorate, Pardon penned a series of complaints questioning the Mayor's action. Asking that 'Indians who could not prove their French citizenship' be struck from the electoral rolls in Cochinchina, he set in motion a protracted debate over which Indians from the French Establishments, if any, were true 'citizens' and whether they could exercise their voting rights in Cochinchina.[16] The arguments he raised illustrate several of the problems faced by French colonial authorities pressed to respect regulations prevailing in other parts of France's colonial empire.

---

14. Antoine Brébion, *Dictionnaire de Bio-Biographie Générale de l'Indochine Française*, Paris: Société d'Éditions Géographiques Maritimes et Coloniales, 1935, p. 33.
15. Milton E. Osborne, *The French Presence in Cochinchina and Cambodia*, Bangkok: White Lotus Press, 1997 [1969], p. 191.
16. VNA2 Goucoch IB.29/233 Élections coloniales Inscription des natifs de l'Inde 1887: Director of Interior to Municipal Commission of Saigon, 31 January 1887, and in the same file, 'Mémoire à l'appui', signed Government Advocate, 2 May 1887.

Pardon's main argument was that renunciation did not confer citizenship and as a consequence was not transferable to another colony. Using the wording of the decree on renunciation to make his case, he pointed out that renouncers acquired, 'the civil and political rights applicable to the French *in the colony of French India*' [my emphasis].[17] Similarly, Pardon argued, the political rights given to non-renouncers in Pondicherry or Karikal could not be exercised outside of French India.[18]

A further objection Pardon put forward, which would be raised again by other Cochinchinese officials trying to grapple with Indian voting rights, was the question of establishing equivalence between the French Establishments, with their complicated and ever-changing system of electoral colleges, and the electoral structure in Cochinchina. At the time of Pardon's writing, three electoral lists were in place in French India (one 'European', one renouncer, and one non-renouncer). In Cochinchina, for lack of any alternative, Indians simply voted with Europeans (and any naturalised Frenchmen) for both colonial and parliamentary elections. If Indians were to remain on European electoral lists in Cochinchina, Pardon worried, 'their electoral condition in Cochinchina would be infinitely superior to their condition in India.'[19]

Pardon backed his arguments with the claim that the exercise of Indian electoral rights in Cochinchina risked offending the native Vietnamese, 'who for their part are in their own country, who pay taxes, who furnish the coffers of the local budget of the colony and who give generously when it is necessary of their blood for the defence of the greater interests of France in Indochina'.[20] Pardon was astute, and forward-thinking, in recognising that Indian electoral privilege would store up political resentment in Vietnamese quarters. Yet the obvious parallel implication, that the privileges of Cochinchina's European masters might be an even greater affront to the largely disenfranchised peoples of Cochinchina, was lost on Pardon, as it was on those who would later make arguments similar to his.

---

17. *Annuaire des Établissements français dans l'Inde pour l'année 1881*, pp. 472–473.
18. VNA2 SL 120 Reinscription des Indiens sur les listes électorales, 1887–1888: 'Conclusions', signed Director of the Interior, 15 February 1887.
19. VNA2 Goucoch IB.29/233 Élections coloniales Inscription des natifs de l'Inde 1887: Director of the Interior to President and councillors of the Civil Chamber of the Court of Appeal, 9 July 1887.
20. Ibid.: 'Mémoire à l'appui', signed by public prosecuter 2 May 1887.

As Director of the Interior Noel Pardon made multiple pleas to strike Indians from Cochinchina's electoral registers. He appealed to the Municipal Commission (February 1887), to Saigon's Justice of the Peace (March 1887), and finally to the Supreme Court in Paris (July 1887). The Municipal Commission maintained that both renounced and non-renounced Indians had been granted the same political rights as French citizens, and therefore should retain the vote and remain on European electoral lists in Cochinchina. The Justice of the Peace rejected Pardon's claim in the same terms. With this latter judgement though came the first indication of Indian involvement in the debate. The Justice of the Peace delayed his decision on Pardon's appeal, because, as he stated: 'Mr. Laurans, defence lawyer, has just informed me that he was charged by the natives of India to defend their cause before my tribunal.'[21]

By the time that he approached the Supreme Court, Pardon had begun to concede that Indians who had renounced might remain on electoral lists. He continued, however, to oppose the participation of the larger group of non-renouncers in Cochinchina's electoral processes. Disturbed perhaps by the Indians' own legal challenge, Pardon now emphasised the threat that Indian suffrage posed to European power in Cochinchina. The presence of non-renouncers on electoral lists alongside Europeans risked tipping the balance out of European favour:

> The non-renounced Indians...registered on the same electoral lists as the Europeans, enjoy identical rights [to Europeans] for the election of the colonial and Municipal councillors ... thanks to their continually increasing numbers and to the restrained number of the rest of the electoral body in Cochinchina, they could soon come to impose [their own people as elected representatives] on French electors from Europe and on an indigenous *Annamite* population.[22]

In numerical terms, Pardon was not wrong to anticipate that electors from French India could come to dominate the European vote. Figures for the Deputy election of 1888 (drawn from the lists which initially alarmed Pardon) show that the total number of French citizens (including naturalised citizens) in the colony came to 1,752. French Indians

---

21. VNA2 SL 120 Reinscription des Indiens sur les listes électorales, 1887–1888: 'Conclusions', signed Director of the Interior, 15 February 1887, and in the same file, Justice of the Peace Saigon to Director of the Interior CCH, 23 February 1887.
22. VNA2 Goucoch IB.29/233 Élections coloniales Inscription des natifs de l'Inde 1887: Director of the Interior to President and councillors of the Civil Chamber of the Court of Appeal, 9 July 1887.

registered on the electoral rolls included 64 renouncers and 342 who had not renounced.[23] Although the number of renouncers and non-renouncers, taken together, still fell short of a quarter of the electorate, this was pushed higher by the numbers of Europeans who could be expected to be away on leave at any given time.[24] Moreover, the number of Indians from the French Establishments present in Cochinchina was expected to increase, and was indeed, from some French colonial quarters, actively encouraged to do so.[25]

Pardon was concerned that Indian voters could come to outnumber the European electorate, but he also doubted that the Cochinchinese authorities were absolutely sure of the status of those Indians already registered on their electoral rolls. This was despite immigration controls which directed all British Indian residents to be registered in congregations, and Indians originating from the French possessions to be subject to formal registration.[26] To clarify the situation, the Governor of French India was asked to examine the electoral status of the 345 Indian voters against whom Pardon had initially objected. The Governor replied that twenty of the individuals in question were registered to vote on the European list in French India, twelve were registered on the renouncers' list, and another twelve on the list of non-renouncers. A full 118 persons, however, were 'unknown' in French India, and of the remaining 103 the Governor conceded he had 'insufficient information'.[27]

With his appeal to Paris Pardon succeeded in barring non-renouncers from voting in Cochinchina. The Supreme Court ruled: 'Non-renounced Indians do not, contrary to the opinion put forward up until this date, have the right to exercise outside of the French Establishments in India,

---

23. VNA2 SL 120 Reinscription des Indiens sur les listes électorales, 1887–1888: Secretariat, City of Saigon to Head of Electoral Commission Torcapel, [n.d.].
24. VNA2 Goucoch IB.29/233 Élections coloniales Inscription des natifs de l'Inde 1887: 'Mémoire a l'appui', 2 May 1887.
25. Ternisien, 'La Question Électorale en Cochinchine, *Journal d'Outre Mer,* 21 February 1888.
26. VNA2 SL 1825 Arrêté soumettant les Indiens et Malais non-sujets français au régime de la congrégation, 1874; ANOM Fonds de la mairie de Saigon 127 MIOM1 Registre destiné à l'inscription des asiatiques qui ont justifié de leur qualité de français 1880–1948.
27. VNA2 Goucoch IB.29/233 Élections coloniales Inscription des natifs de l'Inde 1887: Director of the Interior to President and councillors of the Civil Chamber of the Court of Appeal, 9 July 1887.

the electoral rights which the legislation has permitted them to enjoy within their own country.'[28]

This might have resolved the issue, with renouncers retaining their right to vote in Cochinchina and non-renouncers relinquishing theirs. However, the Governor General of Indochina, Ernest Constans (placed provisionally in the newly-established post), interpreted the Supreme Court's decision in a much broader sense than it had been intended. He issued the following order:

> According to the terms of the order of the Supreme Court of Appeal, non-renounced Indians are not electors. The order also states implicitly that the same applies to renouncers. Ensure actions are taken to strike one and the other from the electoral lists.[29]

It is difficult to justify Constans' action other than to say that his term of office was short and troubled. He resigned after six months and, according to the biographer Brébion, was violently criticised by his successor.[30] With no previous experience of either Cochinchina or French India, he might not have been expected to appreciate fully the complexities of the case. The man most likely to have challenged Constans' order and ensured a more accurate interpretation of the Supreme Court ruling, however, was lawyer and Deputy Blancsubé. He died in the very week in which Constans' order was issued. Two months' later, in May 1888, an election was called for a new Deputy to replace him.[31] It was Indians themselves at this point, or more precisely renouncers, who began to play a prominent role in defending their own case.

THE 1888 DEPUTY ELECTIONS

The feebleness of Indochina's first Governor General in the area of legal interpretation was matched only by the impetuousness of Saigon's Mayor, Carabelli. By the time Constans' order to strike all Indian voters off the electoral rolls was received in Saigon, it was mid-March, and two short months away from the election. Mayor Carabelli hesitated at first to comply. Despite the pressing deadline, he objected, the Indians' reinstatement had to follow regulations and legal procedure and would take

---

28. VNA2 Goucoch IB.29/233 Élections coloniales Inscription des natifs de l'Inde 1887: Supreme Court of Appeal Decision [*arrêté*], 3 January 1888.
29. Ibid.: Telegram GGI to Lt GCCH, 3 March 1888.
30. Brébion, *Dictionnaire*, p. 93.
31. Ibid., p. 404.

time. He also declared he needed time to decide whether he was even going to follow the order: 'Your order, Mr. Lieutenant Governor, has perplexed me; I need to think seriously, and at length. I must act with the greatest patience… and I will give you my decision in due course.' Yet the very next day, he penned a second letter which stated he would go ahead and strike all Indians off the list. He made no mention of legal barriers, and expressed no further hesitation.[32]

A group of Indians resident in Cochinchina hired the lawyer Laurans in March of 1888 to fight Mayor Carabelli's decision.[33] The day after Carabelli acted to remove all Indians from Cochinchina's electoral lists, Laurans wrote to Jacques Hébrard, Senator for French India, seeking support. Laurans asked the Senator to 'repair the injustice' done to the renouncers, who Laurans insisted should be treated as full French citizens. Some days later, fifty-two 'citizens of the French Establishments in India' petitioned Hébrard. They appealed to the Senator's 'high influence', and asked him, no doubt with a view to shaming Carabelli, to 'indicate to the Chamber and the country how the local authorities in Cochinchina understand respect for the law and universal suffrage'.[34]

The next ruling on Indian voting rights in Cochinchina was issued in Paris but did not reach the colony until 10 May 1888, three days short of the planned election. This order suddenly reversed again the most recent instruction. All Indians resident in Cochinchina who originated from the French possessions, renouncers and non-renouncers alike, were to be re-registered on electoral lists and given the chance to vote. Striking the Indians from Cochinchina's electoral rolls, the newest order stated, had been 'irregular'.[35] The lawyer Laurans lost no time in taking his share of credit for the outcome. In a notice addressed to 'Indian voters' which appeared a day later in the *Courrier de Saigon*, Laurans maintained that it was 'on the request of Hébrard, Senator for French India' that Indians had been put back on the electoral lists in Cochinchina. 'Therefore', he

---

32. VNA2 Goucoch IB.29/233 Élections coloniales Inscription des natifs de l'Inde 1887: Mayor Saigon to Lt Governor Cochinchina, 13 March 1888, and in the same file, Mayor Saigon to Lt GCCH, 14 March 1888.
33. This may well have been the same group who had hired Laurans a year earlier, although it is not made clear.
34. ANOM FM Indo af carton 53 Droits électoraux des Indiens établis en Cochinchine: Laurans to Senator for French India Hébrard, 15 March 1888, and in the same file, French citizens of India to Senator Hébrard, 24 March 1888.
35. ANOM GGI 9230 Élections legislatives, 1888–1893: Report GCCH to GGI, 18 May 1888.

continued, 'it is thanks to our joint efforts that you are able to exercise your political rights.'[36]

Renouncers' insistence that they should be recognised as French citizens provided some justification for the decision to allow them to exercise their electoral rights in Cochinchina. The basis upon which the court in Paris chose to uphold non-renouncers' electoral rights is less clear, but may have been grounded in the type of argument presented by Henry Ternisien, another Saigon-based lawyer. He had penned a defence of Indians' voting rights more generally, and non-renouncer rights specifically, in an open letter to the Secretary of State some months' earlier. Any question of retracting Indian voting rights in Cochinchina, in his view, was 'regrettable': 'It affects *Frenchmen* who have contributed to the [Cochinchinese] economy with intelligence, industry, and capital, by taking away the rights we have given them in their country of origin.' Ternisien's interpretation of what constituted French citizenship was the most liberal of any in the extended debate. He maintained that in 1819 when Indians had first been granted the right to be judged by their own personal laws, this had amounted to 'status naturalisation'. That is, the Indians had acquired French citizenship even while retaining their personal laws. Ternisien insisted these rights had never been clearly rescinded in law: 'The *Indous* have remained in 1888 what they were in 1819; that is, citizens able to exercise their civic rights, in India as much as in Cochinchina.'[37]

Whether it was Ternisien's letter or another intervention that prompted the court once again to include non-renouncers on electoral lists we do not know. The consequences of the court order to restore French Indians to Cochinchina's electoral lists, however, are much clearer. As a result, the 1888 Deputy election was fought over the single issue of whether migrants from the French Establishments in India could vote in Cochinchina.

The three candidates for the 1888 Deputy elections in Cochinchina were all compromised in some way in their bid for Cochinchina's seat in the National Assembly, but none more so than Saigon's Mayor Carabelli. Carabelli, of Corsican origin, had arrived in Cochinchina as a defence lawyer in 1881 and served as a municipal counsellor in Saigon until he

---

36. Laurans, 'Aux Électeurs Indiens: renonçants et non-renonçants', *Courrier de Saigon*, 11 May 1888.
37. H. Ternisien, 'La Question Électoral en Cochinchine', Supplement of *Journal d'Outre Mer*, 21 February 1888.

was elected Mayor in 1884. He retained the office of Mayor until 1890. This despite, as Brébion notes, his 'notorious incompetence and lack of comportment which made him the subject of scorn'.[38]

It is not clear whether an election had yet been called formally, nor whether Carabelli had already decided to run for the position of Deputy when he was ordered in March 1888 to strike Indian voters from the electoral lists. Blancsubé had died on 11 March, only two days before Carabelli wrote to the Lieutenant Governor expressing his initial hesitation. Nor is it clear whether Carabelli had weighed up his own prospects as a candidate when he decided to exclude the Indians from voting. It was Carabelli who had signed the letters Indian voters received in March informing them that they had been struck once again from the electoral rolls. This can have done nothing to improve his chances with these voters when they were placed back on the electoral lists in early May.[39]

Carabelli resisted the order to re-register Indians on the electoral lists in mid-May, claiming it was illegal: 'The law is categorical on this subject.' His reaction, which could be read as self-serving in his position as an electoral candidate, amounted to an act of insubordination in his role as Mayor. Three days away from the opening of the polls, Carabelli was still refusing to register the Indian voters, and the Governor General threatened to remove him from his post if he persisted in disobeying orders. The same day, the Lieutenant Governor of Cochinchina gave the Mayor a deadline of ten o'clock that morning to put the Indians back on the electoral lists: 'Do not see this as a threat, time is pressing.' The Mayor finally gave in, albeit insisting there was 'no bias' on his part, and that he would hold the Governor responsible for an act he considered to be 'illegal'.[40] The characteristic traits which emerged in Carabelli in his handling of the electoral lists – a resistance to the authority of his superiors and an erratic, about-face style of decision making – were to stay with him throughout the electoral campaign.

The two other candidates for Cochinchinese Deputy, lawyers Ternisien and Laurans, had both publicly defended the rights of Indians to vote in

---

38. Brébion, *Dictionnaire*, p. 61.
39. VNA2 Goucoch IB.29/233 Élections coloniales Inscription des natifs de l'Inde 1887: Mayor Saigon to Agnissamy de la Perle, Gerard, and Blanpain, 20 March 1888.
40. Ibid.: Mayor Saigon to Lieutenant Governor Cochinchina, 9 May 1888, and in the same file, GGI to Lt GCCH, 10 May 1888, Lt GCCH to Mayor Saigon, 10 May 1888, and Mayor Saigon to Lt. GCCH, 10 May 1888.

Cochinchina before declaring their candidacies. Henry Ternisien was a *créole from the* West Indies, although whether he was of 'pure' European or of mixed origins is unclear. He had served as a magistrate in Cochinchina, making a previous unsuccessful bid for the post of Deputy in 1885 (losing to Blancsubé, an 'avowed adversary'). He was among the colons and merchants who made up Norodom's 'cosmopolitan court' in the early 1880s, a group which had been held responsible for the revolt which followed the Cambodian king's forced signing of the treaty of June 1884 ceding key powers from the Cambodian throne to France. With the backing of the Cambodian monarch, Ternisien had become involved in the construction of the railway in Cambodia and obtained a vital mining concession as part of the deal.[41]

Little is known about Laurans other than that he practised law in Cochinchina. We do not know precisely when he declared his candidacy, save that it had been made public by the time he published his notice congratulating himself. From that notice it was already evident that there was little subtlety about him. 'In casting all your votes for me', he stated baldly, 'you will show just how grateful you are. To Sunday then! And no abstentions!'[42] In a campaign poster directed at Indian voters he again insisted on their gratitude, asking them to thank him for his legal assistance by casting their votes in his favour.[43]

Laurans focused his energies on attacking Ternisien, having decided perhaps that Carabelli was already too discredited to be a real contender. If Laurans was crude in his assumption that Indian voters were completely venal, he was just as capable of changing course. It is difficult to explain why he did so, but this is precisely what he did. Part way through the campaign he suddenly abandoned his efforts to court the Indian vote. He began to attack Ternisien as a 'stooge' (*féal*) of the Indians, adding insinuations of Ternisien's 'suspect' past in Cambodia and his 'traffic with Norodom'.[44] There is no record of what prompted this abrupt change of tactic, but the transformation was indeed complete. Styling himself now as the protector of 'French dominance', he warned voters:

---

41. Brébion, *Dictionnaire*, pp. 403–404; Osborne, *French Presence*, pp. 175–205, 218; 'Le Passé de Ternisien: Extraits du *Saigonnais* du 30 avril 1888', *Courrier de Saigon*, 11 May 1888.
42. Laurans, 'Aux Électeurs Indiens: renonçants en non-renonçants', *Courrier de Saigon*, 11 May 1888.
43. ANOM FM Indo af carton 53 Droits électoraux des Indiens établis en Cochinchine: Campaign poster 'Citoyens', signed 'Laurans'.
44. Ibid.: Campaign poster 'Citoyens … le candidat de l'idée française', signed 'Laurans'.

> If you want to see the Indian element invading the Colony; if you want to see cargoes of Indians arriving here with the aim of voting, of occupying positions that the French could fill, then vote for Mr. Ternisien.[45]

This sudden change of strategy did nothing to help Laurans' bid for a seat in Parliament. He was eliminated in the first round of voting.

Carabelli, for his part, made full use of Ternisien's Cambodian past to discredit his candidacy. He claimed Ternisien had supported the re-registration of Indians on the electoral rolls only in an opportunistic attempt to re-establish himself after his 'anti-patriotic' acts in Cambodia. One election poster accused Ternisien of hoping 'to turn [the Indian votes] to his profit on election day and to use them to counterbalance the European and *créole* votes which he has definitely lost'.[46] Another poster described Ternisien as a 'poor citizen' and a 'candidate for the *Malabars*'.[47] Yet another depicted Ternisien as instrumental, 'because of his repeated claims', in 'the re-inscription on Cochinchinese electoral lists of 420 Indians who had been struck off'. This poster openly proclaimed the election was to be fought along racial lines:

> Those who still have their doubts should now open their eyes. Mr. Ternisien wants to establish his political influence in the colony by supporting the Indians. He is putting forward the question of colour and of race. Electors now find themselves in the presence of two candidates: Mr. Ternisien, representative of the black element, and Mr. Carabelli, [representative of] the opinion and the policies of the white. Under these conditions…European and *créole* electors…[must] join forces in an act of preservation and defence. Let Mr. Ternisien stay then, as he wishes, the candidate for the blacks (*noirs*) of India; Mr. Carabelli carries with confidence the flag of the whites. Let us rally behind him and with him and fight the good fight.[48]

The complexity of colonial society is encapsulated in the Carabelli camp's attempt to exploit *créole* anxieties over their ambiguous identities by pressing them to side with the 'whites'. Given Ternisien's Caribbean origins, this tactic may be understood as a questioning of these origins, and a further attempt to 'blacken' his campaign.

---

45. Ibid.: Campaign poster 'Citoyens, Deux politiques …', signed 'Laurans'.
46. Ibid.: Campaign poster 'Citoyens', signed 'R. Carabelli'.
47. VNA2 Goucoch IB.29/233 Élections coloniales Inscription des natifs de l'Inde 1887: Campaign poster 'Aux Électeurs !', signed 'R. Carabelli'.
48. ANOM FM Indo af carton 53 Droits électoraux des Indiens établis en Cochinchine: Campaign poster 'Aux Électeurs de Cochinchine', signed 'Un Groupe d'Électeurs'.

Ternisien's defence of Indian voting rights is amply documented in his correspondence with colonial authorities leading up to and during the election. His support for the Indian cause is not as prominent in his public election campaign, however, as it is in his rivals' attacks against him. Ternisien referred only subtly to Laurans' participation in securing the Indian vote, and went on to attribute baser aims to his rivals, claiming that both Laurans and Carabelli had been 'taxed by the drop in rents' and would, if elected, use municipal funds to build strategically placed boulevards to raise the value of the properties they owned.[49]

It was the Indian electorate, rather than Ternisien himself, who used public notices to attack his rival Carabelli. A poster signed 'A group of Indian voters' accused Carabelli of hypocrisy, maintaining that only a few months previously he had 'demonstrated no repugnance' for them. The poster claimed he had defended their rights to a colonial pension in a speech to the Colonial Council in 1885, and had even communicated with Pounnoutamby Laporte (the 'father' of the renunciation movement in Pondicherry) to assure him that Saigon's Mayor 'paid particular attention to the Indian cause'. Yet now, 'it is this same man, who has the sad courage to repudiate us', and who 'dares to call himself a Republican… 'Pouah!!!' The message ended with a reference to Ternisien: 'For our part… We invite all voters to rally around a candidate who does not seek to satisfy his own appetites with the trust we place in him.'[50]

After Mayor Carabelli had reluctantly agreed on 10 May to restore Indians to the electoral lists, their names were hastily added to the roll. This enabled them to vote in the first round of Deputy elections held three days later. Carabelli won the greatest number of votes but did not secure a majority; consequently, the election went to a second round. A report on the first round of voting noted that some Tamil names were so disfigured on the electoral rolls (because of their 'length and spelling'), that it was impossible to tally them with names on the electoral cards of the voters. Ternisien registered a complaint and requested that the lists be corrected prior to the second round, due to be held on 27 May.[51]

---

49. ANOM FM Indo af carton 53: Campaign poster signed Ternisien.
50. Ibid.: Campaign poster 'Aux Électeurs de Cochinchine'. The affair of colonial pensions (*compte de prévoyance*) is taken up in the next chapter.
51. VNA2 SL 120 Reinscription des Indiens sur les listes électorales, 1887–1888: Draft report Electoral commission to Governor General, 4 June 1888.

AUX ELECTEURS

DE COCHINCHINE

Nous avons lu hier, sur les murs de Saigon, des affiches signées : *Un Groupe d'Electeurs,* dans lesquelles on reproche à M. Ternisien de « fonder son influence politique dans la Colonie « en s'appuyant sur les Indiens. »

Nous n'entreprendrons pas de défendre ici le candidat ainsi calomnié. Il sait se défendre mieux que nous ne saurions le faire. Il n'est pas, heureusement, de ceux qui ont horreur de la discussion publique. Tous ceux que l'amour de la vérité ou que le parti-pris n'aveugle pas, le savent. Passons.

Nous rechercherons seulement si le groupe d'électeurs qui patronne si chaudement la candidature de M. Carabelli peut décemment se réclamer des principes républicains, alors que ses tendances qui consistent à établir une distinction entre des Français soumis aux mêmes lois (distinction basée sur la couleur de l'épiderme) sont comme un outrage aux principes mêmes qu'il invoque.

Il suffira du plus vulgaire bon sens pour faire justice de la *manœuvre d'un Groupe* dont le candidat n'a éprouvé aucune répugnance, il y a quelques mois à peine, à aller quêter de porte en porte les suffrages de ce qu'on appelle aujourd'hui dédaigneusement les noirs de l'Inde.

Qui donc ne se rappelle le discours prononcé par M. Carabelli en 1885, au sein du Conseil colonial, pour revendiquer le droit des Indiens au compte de prévoyance que le Gouvernement leur conteste encore aujourd'hui.

A-t-il donc oublié, depuis cette époque, ce qu'il écrivait à M. La Porte, avocat à Poudichéry et chef du parti libéral de l'Inde française:

« J'ai, disait-il, puisé plus particulièrement ma force parmi les Indiens. » (lettre du 31 janvier 1885).

Et c'est ce même homme qui a, aujourd'hui, le triste courage de les répudier. Pouah !!!

Ces Noirs de l'Inde, M. Carabelli n'en a que faire en ce moment !!!

M. Carabelli ou son groupe (ce qui est tout comme) cherche à établir une caste dans la grande famille française, et il ose se dire républicain. Pouah !!!

Quant à nous qui ne voulons qu'un drapeau, le drapeau de la France républicaine, abritant tous ses Enfants, sans distinction aucune, nous invitons tous les Electeurs à se grouper autour d'un candidat, quel qu'il soit, qui a le respect de la parole donnée, qui ne trahira pas les intérêts de la Colonie, qui ne trouvera pas, dans la confiance que nous placerons en lui, le moyen de satisfaire ses appétits.

AUX URNES!

Pas d'abstentions!

Vive la République!

Vive la Cochinchine!

Un groupe d'Electeurs Indiens.

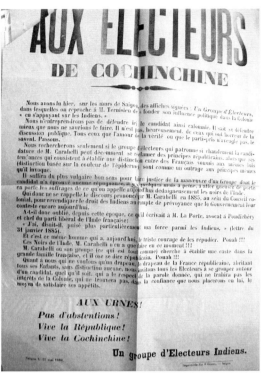

Plate 10: Public bill printed in Saigon by 'a group of Indian voters'. Courtesy French National Overseas Archive (ANOM).

RÉPUBLIQUE FRANÇAISE

LIBERTÉ — ÉGALITÉ — FRATERNITÉ

COCHINCHINE FRANÇAISE

ÉLECTIONS LÉGISLATIVES DU 13 MAI 1888.

SECTION de Saigon-Ville

CARTE D'ÉLECTEUR

Durée du scrutin : de 8 heures du matin à 6 heures du soir.

NUMÉRO D'INSCRIPTION d'après la liste.	NOM ET PRÉNOMS.	DOMICILE.
1896	Virassamipoullé	Saigon

NB. Les Électeurs sont invités à se munir de leur carte et à la conserver pour le cas où il serait nécessaire de procéder à un nouveau tour de scrutin.

LIEUX DE RÉUNION :

Section de Saigon-ville : *Hôtel de ville de Saigon, rue Catinat.*

Section de Cholon-ville et inspection : *Mairie de Cholon.*

Autres sections : *cap Saint-Jacques, Poulo-Condore, Bureaux des Inspections.*

Saigon, le 1er mai 1888.

Le Maire empêché

Plate 11: Voting card of an Indian, Virassamipoullé, Cochinchina legislative election 1888. Courtesy French National Overseas Archive (ANOM).

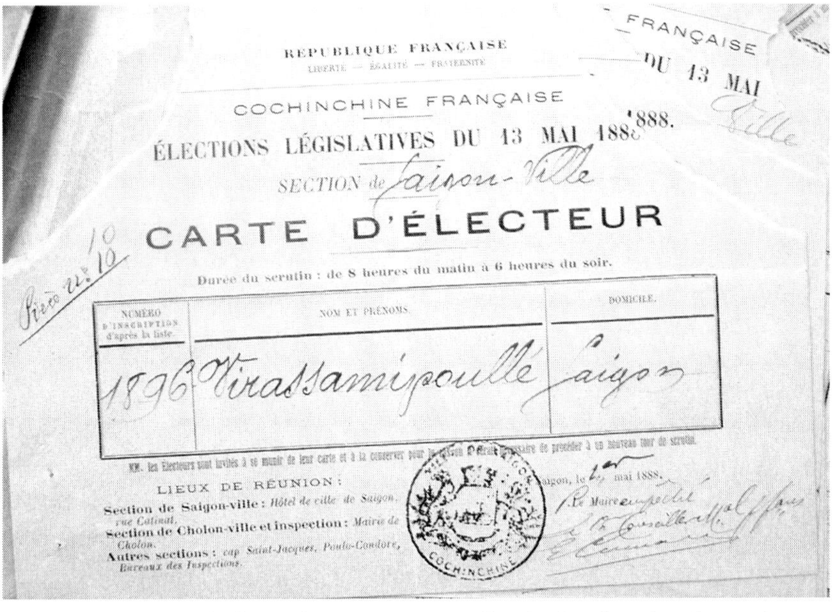

The first electoral round took place with relative calm, the candidates' personal attacks on one another notwithstanding. The second round, however, was more dramatic. On the morning of the election Carabelli summoned Saigon's Police Commissioner to the Municipality, and ordered him to take personal charge of the police officers stationed there. The reason for the summons was that Carabelli had once again abruptly changed his mind:

> I have decided not to allow the Indians to vote. I have already informed the Governor General. It is possible that some agitated or poorly advised spirits may put up resistance. You will undertake the means to prevent them once they appear, and you must take care not to permit any gathering of Indians or of Europeans in front of the Municipality. All your European agents must be put into service and at your disposal. You must arrest any Indians who are too recalcitrant and conduct them to the nearest post. Towards the Europeans, behave properly but be firm. You must remain constantly at my disposal in the polling room ... I will give you further orders as circumstances warrant.[52]

When the District Commissioner on morning duty arrived at the polling station in City Hall, he found that Carabelli had ousted the committee set up to guard the ballot box, and had put himself in charge. As the polls opened, two Frenchmen (they appear to have been of metropolitan origin) questioned the legality of an armed police presence at the polling station, and expressed their outrage at Carabelli's flouting of the law. Despite their complaints, the policemen stayed on. Others present in the room included Ternisien, as well as:

> about two hundred other people, among whom were many *Malabars* who protested energetically against the makeup of the polling office and mostly against the presence of Mr. Carabelli. He had just torn up the voting ballot of Mr. Pharod-Nemour, an Indian registered on the supplementary list of Indians as number 1474.[53]

According to the same account, when asked why he had ousted the committee, Carabelli simply replied, 'I had second thoughts.' This caused those present to erupt with cries of 'Take him away, we will not vote!' The room was cleared by the police and voters were then asked to enter two at a time to cast their ballots. Five Indians who presented themselves to vote, Arrokiassamy, Leroy, Mikel, Filon, and Samy

---

52. VNA2 Goucoch IB.29/233 Élections coloniales Inscription des natifs de l'Inde 1887: Mayor Saigon to Central Police Commisioner, 27 May 1888.

53. Ibid.: Police Commissioner 1st District to Central Police Commissioner, 28 May 1888.

Gnanapoullé, were reportedly refused; Carabelli told them that they 'did not have the right'. These men left and, according to the District Commissioner, 'went to find Mr. Ternisien', who 'objected against such a measure and advised them as well as other Indians out in the street to follow him to the Lieutenant Governor to claim their rights'. Ternisien 'then mounted into the Tilbury of Mr. Faciolle; others took *Malabar* carriages and still others followed on foot'.[54]

The Lieutenant Governor gave the Indians permission to vote in Gia Định, north-west of Saigon, 'to avoid disorder in the centre of the city'. Returning to the municipality, 'Mr. Ternisien hired nearly all of the carriages called "Malabars"'. He invited everyone to get into the vehicles, which he paid for, to take them to vote in Gia Định.' One Indian shouted from his carriage as they departed, 'Everyone who voted for Carabelli is a coward!' A Mr. Perrin, leaving the polling station at the time, yelled in return, 'I am no more of a coward than you! Have you paid your debt to the country? [a reference to the Indians' exemption at the time from military duty] … No? Well then… what do you have to say?' Another District Commissioner witnessed the Indian voters returning from Gia Định, and described the lively procession of '*Malabars*' in '*Malabar* coaches': 'All evening numerous carriages full of Indians passed in front of the Municipality and these people… did not waste the opportunity to show their satisfaction and defiance to the polling office with shouts and cries.'[55]

Ternisien emerged the victor in the 1888 election, defeating Carabelli in the second round of voting by 664 votes to 488. Yet he never assumed the position of Deputy. The Chamber of Deputies annulled the 1888 Deputy election in November of the same year, on the grounds that the participation of non-renouncers had been illegal.[56] No subsequent election in Cochinchina was run quite so blatantly on the singular issue of the Indian vote. It was to be another ten years, however, before the ques-

---

54. Ibid.: Police Commissioner 1st District to Central Police Commissioner, 28 May 1888.
55. Ibid.: Administrator Marquis to Director of Local Services, 4 June 1888. Also in the same file, Police Commissioner District Two to Central Police Commissioner, 28 May 1888.
56. The breakdown of Indian votes in the second round of the 1888 Deputy election was as follows: 244 Indians cast a vote in Gia Định, where 258 votes were cast in total; Ternisien secured 250 of these votes. No Indian votes were registered in Saigon or Cholon. In the other towns of Cochinchina, a total of 18 Indian ballots were cast. See VNA2 Goucoch IB.29/233 Élections coloniales Inscription des natifs de l'Inde 1887: Administrator Marquis to Director of Local Services, 4 June 1888. Also Brébion, *Dictionnaire*, p. 404.

tion of Indians' eligibility to vote in Cochinchina was finally resolved in the courts.

A CONTINUING STRUGGLE FOR ELECTORAL RIGHTS: 1889–1899

A decision of the Saigon Justice of the Peace, on 27 February 1889, removed both renouncers and non-renouncers once again from Cochinchina's electoral lists. Two groups of French Indians appealed to the Supreme Court in Paris against this decision. One appeal was brought by the renouncer Adicéam and a group of eight other Indian renouncers. A non-renouncer, Cadarsah, led the second appeal, representing thirty-eight other non-renounced Indians.[57]

Cadarsah's plea on behalf of the non-renouncers was rejected. The court maintained that this group's electoral franchise in French India was a 'concession of a specific and localised right'. It did not extend to them the right to vote in another colonial territory or in the Metropole.[58] This remained the final word on non-renouncers' right to exercise their electoral rights outside of French India.

Adicéam, who had led the renouncers' 1889 appeal, had already demonstrated he was well-attuned to colonial law and able to present its contradictions to his colonisers. Shrewdly, he had submitted an application for naturalisation in Cochinchina during the 1888 Deputy Election. Cochinchinese authorities had rejected this application on the basis that his renunciation 'already gave him the rights he solicited', thus inadvertently admitting that his renunciation was equal to French citizenship.[59] The Supreme Court upheld the renouncers' 1889 appeal for the right to vote in Cochinchina. In doing so, it endorsed the point Adicéam had made in his request for naturalisation. The court ruling made a direct connection between the effects of renunciation on natives of French India and the effects of naturalisation on the peoples of Cochinchina:

> The Indian after his renunciation, like the *Annamite* after his naturalisation, is subject to the civil status and the political laws of the French. [He is] no longer merely a French *subject* protected by treaties or local decrees, but a

---

57. VNA2 Goucoch IB.29/233 Élections coloniales Inscription des natifs de l'Inde 1887: Supreme Court of Appeal ruling, 29 July 1889.
58. Ibid.; also Girault, *Principes*, p. 566.
59. Clairon, *La renonciation*, p. 53.

French citizen who has the right to claim his place on the electoral list in all the territories of France.[60]

This ruling recognised French India's renouncers as French citizens, with the right to vote as French citizens in Cochinchina. Renouncers voted on par with other French citizens in Cochinchina for a decade following this decision. It was not to be the last word, however, on the subject of Indian voting rights.

When electoral colleges in French India were reorganised in 1899, and renouncers there placed back among the 'native' voters for local council elections, the Indian vote in Cochinchina was called into question once again. Indochina's Governor General Doumer complained to the Minister of Colonies that renouncers in their country of origin were now 'on the same footing as the non-renouncers' for local council elections, whereas in Cochinchina they continued to be included on a single electoral list alongside 'Europeans, descendants of Europeans and naturalised *Annamites* and Chinese'. He reasoned that the renouncers' situation should not 'be more favourable outside of their own country'. And his conclusion? They should quite simply be barred from voting in local council elections in Cochinchina.[61]

The Minister of Colonies placed the decision in the hands of the Supreme Court, while Doumer instructed the Lieutenant Governor of Cochinchina, Édouard Picanon, to bar renouncers from participating in local elections. These instructions met with resistance when they were passed down by Picanon to Saigon's new Mayor, Paul Blanchy. He refused to comply, insisting that renouncers' French citizenship had already been legally recognised. Blanchy argued that Picanon was exceeding Hanoi's orders and attempting to eliminate Indians entirely from political life in Cochinchina. Picanon meanwhile continued to issue orders stating that all French Indians were to be barred from both local and legislative elections in the colony.[62]

---

60. VNA2 Goucoch IB.29/233 Élections coloniales Inscription des natifs de l'Inde 1887: Supreme Court of Appeal ruling 29 July 1889.
61. ANOM GGI 50927 Situation des Indiens en Cochinchine au point de vue électorale 1900–1901: GGI to MMC, 12 April 1900, and GGI to Lt GCCH 23 September 1900. Also Girault, *Principes*, p. 568; Clairon, 'La Renonciation', p. 96.
62. ANOM GGI 50927 Situation des Indiens en Cochinchine au point de vue électorale 1900–1901: MMC to GGI, 12 July 1900. And in the same file, GGI to Lt GCCH 23 September 1900; Saigon Mayor Blanchy to Lt GCCH Picanon 11 January 1901; Order of Lt GCCH 1 February, 1901.

This final struggle over Indian voting rights in Cochinchina revealed the battle to be one between the rule of law in France, and the ability of French officials in Cochinchina to decide for themselves what was best for the colony. Throughout the course of the debate, Indian petitioners strategically directed their case to their elected representatives in French India and Cochinchina, parties whom they felt would uphold their legal claims. In the hands of these elected representatives, and subsequently in the hands of the Supreme Court, it was the rule of law which carried the argument. A Supreme Court decision, of 13 May 1901, ruled that the restrictions imposed by the system of electoral lists in French India applied only to that colony. 'Elsewhere in French territory', as described by the French Indian lawyer Clairon, 'and notably in Cochinchina, the Indian who has renounced his personal status has the right to be registered on the electoral lists as a French citizen.'[63] The right of Indian renouncers to participate in Cochinchinese elections was now firmly established in law. Indian participation in Cochinchinese politics now rapidly revealed itself, however, to be a rich source for electoral manipulation.

The 'legend' of Indian voters

Through to the Second World War, the Indian French citizens of Cochinchina gained a reputation as a sector of the electorate willing to vote *en bloc* for the candidate who presented them with the most attractive favours. In her 1937 book *French Indo-China*, the British journalist Virginia Thompson claimed that Indian French citizens formed, 'a large slice of an exceptionally venal electorate'. She even charged that, 'while some of them are Catholic', the 'Muslims and Hindus' who formed the majority pretended, 'through a remarkable industry in counterfeit papers ... to be French citizens', and thereby to influence the elections.[64] The 'legend' of Indian voters, as it became known, included talk of boatloads of Indians being sent out from Pondicherry to Cochinchina expressly for the purpose of voting. French politicians' established practice of 'importing natives from French India' was one of the main characteristics of Cochinchinese elections according to American commentator Winnacker in his 1938 analysis of elections in the French

---

63. Clairon, *La renonciation*, p. 103; See also Girault, *Principes*, p. 420.
64. Virginia Thompson, *French Indo-China*, London: George Allen and Unwin, 1937, p. 172.

Empire.⁶⁵ The practice is mentioned in more recent histories too. Historian Hue-Tam Ho Tai has commented, in reference to the 1919 Deputy elections, that 'as usual, some French electors imported boatloads of Indians with French citizenship from the French Territories of Pondicherry and Chandernagore to make absolutely sure that their man would win.'⁶⁶ Hard evidence to support rumours and suggestions of either 'counterfeit' renunciations or the purposeful 'import' of Indian voters to participate in Cochinchinese elections is difficult to come by. It is nevertheless undeniable that Indian French citizens, when they acted together, became a political force which had the power to determine the outcome of a given election.

Part of the strength of Indian voters lay in the sheer force of their numbers. These numbers were albeit modest, but became meaningful when compared to the population of naturalised French and French of metropolitan origin in the colony. Indian French citizens registered on Cochinchina's electoral rolls always managed to make up a sufficient proportion of the electorate to influence the outcome of an election. In 1922 there were approximately 2,000 (male) French citizens eligible to vote. Of these, 700 were Indian renouncers, and a mere 350 were naturalised Vietnamese or Chinese. The remaining 1,000 Frenchmen, from the Metropole and other colonies, could not be relied on to be present in the country on a given polling day.⁶⁷ In this situation it is easy to see how a candidate could find renouncers to be powerful political supporters, should he manage to capture their loyalty as a group. The yawning gap between the power of Indian French citizens as voters in Cochinchina, and the almost non-existent political participation of Vietnamese in the affairs of their own country is a story in itself, which I take up in Chapter Six.

A further reason why the Indian electorate in Cochinchina became an appealing *coterie* for some politicians was because it provided a foil for exploiting weaknesses intrinsic to Cochinchina's political institutions. Cochinchina's politicians could publicly claim to support the principles of justice and equality dear to the Metropole, and equally dear to so many renouncers, while cynically building a compliant base of voters. Politicians' use of Indian voters to exploit weaknesses in

---

65. Winnacker, 'Elections in Algeria', p. 277.
66. Tai, 'The Politics of Compromise', pp. 387–388.
67. 'La Question Indienne', *La Tribune Indigène*, 30 December, 1922.

the system is illustrated in the harsh criticism Governor General Paul Doumer reserved for Cochinchina's Colonial Council. His critique casts in a different light his eagerness, seen in the previous section, to bar Indian renouncers from voting for the Colonial Council and other local assemblies following changes to the electoral lists in French India in 1899. Doumer claimed in the same period that of 2,000 French citizens in the colony, 1,500 lived off a budget produced from taxes raised within the colony. As one of the main functions of the Colonial Council was to vote on how the budget was to be spent, 'a majority of agents whose salaries were paid out of the budget decided on the expenditures to be made and decided on the level of taxes to exact'. Without entering too deeply as yet into the lack of Vietnamese political representation, it is worth adding the succinct comments of de Lanessan, another former Governor General, whose analysis was similar to Doumer's:

> As it is currently made up, the Colonial Council represents not the taxpayers [who contribute to the budget] but just about exclusively the functionaries, entrepreneurs and merchants who consume the budget ... thus we can define [the Colonial Council as] ... an elected assembly which pays its electors with the money of those who cannot elect it.[68]

Saigon's Mayor Paul Blanchy may have appeared as a righteous defender of equality when he resisted Doumer's 1899 order. Yet in Doumer's opinion, Blanchy was using the Indian electorate to milk this system and held most of the electorate of Cochinchina in the palm of his hand. Blanchy was head of the Colonial Council in the 1890s; Doumer claimed he had expressly given subordinate posts in the administration and the municipal police force to 'three hundred French negroes (*nègres*)' with the purpose of making of these 'blacks (*noirs*)', a 'docile herd', which he 'led to the ballot-box'.[69]

Doumer's overtly racial references to the 'blacks' of India delineate the limits of his regard for republican principles of equality. They also suggest that the racial prejudices of some Cochinchinese politicians were strong enough for them to forego the rich political gains to be made by courting the Indian vote. Doumer's analysis of the malleability of Cochinchina's political institutions remains, however, a legitimate call to be cautious of those colonial politicians who stridently supported

---

68. Camilli, *La représentation*, p.115, p. 118 (quoting both men).
69. Ibid., p.116.

Indian French citizens in Cochinchina. They can be read as enlightened men of moral integrity, but they can also be seen as great manipulators.

Devoted deputies

If the members of the Colonial Council secured their seats by keeping functionaries well-paid and in work, then the Deputy in the French parliament, in Paul Doumer's analysis, acted as an 'accomplice', drawing his power, too, from advocating in Paris for the rights and needs of those living off of the colony's budget. Two men who represented Cochinchina in the Chamber in Deputies in the twentieth century, François Deloncle (1902–1910), and Ernest Outrey (1914–1936), were particularly noted for their support of Indian causes.

François Deloncle was a diplomat by profession. Sent to India by Jules Ferry in the early 1880s to study the political situation under British domination, he returned convinced of the need to expand and reinforce French colonial and commercial interests. He saw this as a means to counter British imperialism, by opposing the brutality of British rule with the 'democratic ideal' of a civilising respect for men and culture which he felt had been achieved in Pondicherry. He continued to express his support for colonial expansion as a prominent member of the *Groupe colonial* in the French Chamber of Deputies and he was allied with the moderate left *Gauche démocratique* throughout his political career. A scholar who has studied his reports from India has labelled him, 'an ambitious political opportunist', calling his notion of diffusing democracy, 'an ideal too pretty not to be suspect'.[70] Nonetheless, his terms as Deputy for Cochinchina show he supported Indian renouncers in their efforts to press the administration for contractual terms which reflected their status as citizens (see the chapter which follows).

Deloncle was strongly supported by renouncers, as revealed in the description in the Franco-Tamil newspaper *Réveil Saigonnais* of a banquet held by the banker Ra. Soccalingam in Deloncle's honour in 1910. The banquet took place prior to an upcoming election (which

---

70. Pierre Michel, 'Les Mystifications Épistolaire d'Octave Mirabeau', University of Angers, 1990, 1–6, pp. 3–4. at http://mirbeau.asso.fr/darticlesfrancais/PM-Les%20mystifications%20epist.pdf. On Deloncle see also C.M. Andrew and A.S. Kanya-Forstner, 'The *Groupe Colonial* in the French Chamber of Deputies, 1892–1932', *The Historical Journal*, 14, 4, 1974, 837–866, p. 859; C.M. Andrew and A.S. Kanya-Forstner, 'The French "Colonial Party": its Composition, Aims and Influence, 1885–1914', *The Historical Journal*, 14, 1, 1971, 99–128, p. 110.

Deloncle lost in spite of renouncer backing). At the banquet, attended by 'so many Frenchmen of India that it is impossible to name them all here', Ra. Soccalingam spoke of 'all the good deeds that the Deputy of Cochinchina has bestowed with such generosity on the Frenchmen of India', after which he 'raised his glass to the successful candidature of Mr. Deloncle'. For his part, Deloncle, broaching the question of the upcoming election, expressed his 'unerring devotion' to the cause of the French of India and insisted:

> I have not failed to take the opportunity on any occasion to protest against the numerous injustices of which you have been victim and to defend your rights against your enemies...even before I held the legislative mandate in Cochinchina.

'This is true', paused the author of the piece to comment, '...and we can be assured that no [Indian] voter can forget this in front of the ballot box any more than he can forget that [Deloncle's] competitor, Mr. Pâris, has done nothing.' In concluding his speech Deloncle declared:

> ...that he had the firm assurance that the Frenchmen of India would always be loyal to the superior principles of French democracy, this regime of equality which destroys prejudice, turns over the barriers and which Mr. Laporte has spread through the population in India... A Thunderous applause and cries of 'Long Live Deloncle! Long Live Cochinchina!' saluted the speech of this brilliant orator.[71]

The period in which Deloncle held the position of Deputy for Cochinchina coincided with a time when the debates over renouncers' legal status in the colony were most heated. However, it was the 'perennial Deputy' Ernest Outrey, who was the more avid supporter of Indian causes in Cochinchina, and whose support was even more explicitly connected, until the late 1920s at least, with his success at the ballot box.[72]

The entire career of Ernest Outrey was spent in the service of the French in Indochina. Entering the Cochinchinese administration in 1884, he worked for a brief spell in the cabinet of Governor General Étienne Richaud in Hanoi, and subsequently in the Cochinchinese administration under Henri Danel. His experience in provinces throughout Indochina was broad-reaching. He was administrator of

---

71. All references to this banquet are from Rose Quaintenne, 'Banquet donné par M. Ra. Soccalingam en l'honneur de M. François Deloncle', *Réveil Saigonnais*, 16 April 1910.
72. Quote from Thompson, *French Indo-China*, p. 311.

the Cochinchinese provincial town of Thủ Dầu Một in the 1890s, he established the province of Djiring in Annam, and was charged by Paul Doumer with founding the seaside town of Cap-St-Jacques (Vũng Tàu), all before the turn of the twentieth century. Prior to being elected Deputy in 1914 he had served briefly as Lieutenant Governor of Cochinchina (1908–1909), as interim French resident of Laos (1910–1911), and as Resident Superior of Cambodia (1911–1914). He was allied with political parties of the republican left (*Gauche radicale, Gauche républicaine démocratique*) during his five terms as Deputy for Cochinchina (1914 to 1936).[73]

Outrey's efforts to draw attention to Indian causes pepper French colonial archives from Aix to Pondicherry, and beyond to Saigon, Phnom Penh, and Hanoi. He has been noted for his lack of support for Vietnamese claims to equality or autonomy; historian Hue-Tam Ho Tai refers to him as, 'a vociferous champion of *colon* supremacy'.[74] He was already defending the causes of Indians domiciled in Cochinchina and Cambodia though for some time before he became Deputy. His interventions on behalf of groups of Indian employees of Cochinchina's colonial administration are the substance of the chapter which follows. Outrey was equally prone to writing references to promote the prospects in Indochina of individual Indians. In 1912, he backed the request of Mr. Alosius Conjondessamy for a position as an immigration agent in Phnom Penh. Mouttou, a renouncer and colonist long established in Mỹ Tho, specifically thanked his 'friend Ernest Outrey', when he accepted his Legion of Honour in 1931, for the Deputy's efforts in obtaining the distinction for him. And it was Outrey's recommendation, in 1934, which finally persuaded King Monivong to bestow the title of Honorary Mandarin on a Phnom Penh businessman of Pondicherry origin.[75]

These efforts to garner Indian support paid off, if that is what they were intended to do. Starting from the 1910s, until the effects of the Depression began to make themselves felt in Saigon, the Indian French citizens of Cochinchina rallied faithfully around their loyal Deputy, with few excep-

---

73. Brébion, *Dictionnaire*, p. 288.
74. Quote from Tai, 'The Politics of Compromise', p. 387.
75. NAC 34611 Demande de M. Alosius Conjondessamy, postulant pour le poste d'identificateur à l'immigration, 1912–1913; 'Colonie hindoue fête la Légion d'honneur de M. Mouttou', *Saigon-Dimanche*, 10 May 1931; NAC 24842 Demande formulée par M. Pakiam tendant à obtenir sa nomination à un titre de Mandarin Honoraire.

tions. He in turn was willing, at least immediately prior to elections, to defend their rights as French citizens. Around the time of legislative elections in the 1920s, the Franco-Tamil press was punctuated with references to rallies held in Outrey's honour. It also gloried in publishing denunciations of other electoral candidates from whose mouths racial slurs against the Indian population had emerged, or whose losses had been blamed on the pernicious effect of the 'Indian vote'. As one renouncer put it in later, more cynical times, 'After each election, it is customary, indispensable even, that the defeated candidate and his partisans console themselves with the thought, "It is the fault of the dirty *Malabars*".'[76]

Renouncer devotion to their Deputy was much evident in a meeting in November of 1919 of the *Union Amicale Indo-française* ('Indo-French Friendship Society'). Deputy Outrey was invited by the society to speak just prior to the legislative election in which he ran for a second term. At the event the society's president profusely thanked the Deputy for a recent parliamentary intervention in the Indians' favour. He spoke of the 'esteem mixed with respect and devotion' that 'all those originating from India, without distinction, hold for Mr. Ernest Outrey'. With the Deputy election upcoming, the first following peace in Europe, the president made specific reference too, to Outrey's assistance to Indian servicemen who had been stationed in France during the war, both those resident in Indochina and those in French India. The audience of Indian French citizens then listened to Outrey present his electoral mandate. Certain amendments were requested on behalf of the 'French of India' before the meeting closed with cries of 'Long Live France! Long Live Indochina! Long Live India! Long Live Outrey!'[77]

Outrey secured a third term in the April election of 1924. This victory was preceded by his interventions drawing attention to the working conditions of French Indian lighthouse guards in Cochinchina (beginning in early 1923), postmen (from February 1924), soldiers (from March), and interpreters (also from March).[78] The Franco-Tamil *Réveil*

---

76. 'M. Outrey, les Français de l'Inde ne mérite pas l'affront que vous leurs faites!', *Saigon-Dimanche*, 21 April 1932.
77. All references to this meeting from 'Union Amicale Indo-française', *Réveil Saigonnais*, 28 November 1919.
78. 'Les guardians de phare indiens', *Réveil Saigonnais*, 3 February 1923; 'Les guardians de phare', *Réveil Saigonnais*, 15 March 1924; 'Une injustice à réparer', *Réveil Saigonnais*, 25 February 1924; 'Une intervention de M. Outrey', *Réveil Saigonnais*, 20 March 1924; 'Les interventions de M. Outrey', *Réveil Saigonnais*, 5 May 1924.

Saigonais criticized colonial councillor Paul Monin, Outrey's rival, for voting to bar entry to any Indian who arrived in Cochinchina without employment. Monin's sole intention, the paper charged, was to reduce the Indian majority whose votes he could not hope to win from Outrey. Meanwhile, the candidate Augustin Séraphim Foray, who as former Mayor of Saigon had proposed the above vote in the colonial council, had lost any Indian support that might have remained to him. He had done so by letting slip in public that he had resigned from his post as Mayor because he had been 'a victim of the *nègres*', a crude reference to the Indian voters. Foray then claimed that the new Mayor, an avid supporter of Outrey, had granted several posts within the administration to Indians just days before the election.[79]

Outrey managed to secure one more term in the legislative election of 1928. Following the pattern of both local and legislative elections in Cochinchina through the 1920s, the defeat of Outrey's opponent, Raymond Rouelle, was attributed by his supporters to the 'Indian bloc'. This was despite Rouelle's victory in Saigon's Mayoral election of 1925, in which there were suggestions that he himself had bought the collective support of Indian voters with 'rum' and 'piastres'.[80]

Disillusion

The Rouelle camp tried to dismiss Outrey's renewed electoral success in 1928 as just another win for the Indian vote. Yet Outrey's star was beginning to fade in the eyes of the Indian French citizens themselves, and he could no longer rely on their unequivocal support. Although measured in its criticism, the *Réveil Saigonnais* strayed from its usual effort to rally support behind the chosen 'candidate of the Indians'. It now admitted that renouncers had been divided in their choice. The *Saigon-Dimanche*, a recently-launched second Franco-Tamil newspaper, expressed more vigorous opposition to Outrey, and threw its support behind Outrey's

---

79. Édouard Marquis, 'La manoeuvre de Paul Monin pour se débarrasser des électeurs de l'Inde', *Réveil Saigonnais,* 1 May 1924; Édouard Marquis, 'Le Citoyen Foray se dit victime des nègres et leur manifeste publiquement son dédain', *Réveil Saigonnais,* 30 April 1924; Édouard Marquis, 'Victime des nègres', *Réveil Saigonnais,* 8 May 1924; 'Français de l'Inde', *Réveil Saigonnais,* 6 May 1924.

80. Le Réveil, 'Politique de Concorde: en tout; la Juste mesure', *Réveil Saigonnais,* 4 May 1928; 'La Politique', *Réveil Saigonnais,* 12 May 1925; 'Les Français originaires de l'Inde, fidèles à la parole donnée, voteront en bloc pour les huits membres de la liste Rouelle', *Réveil Saigonnais,* 9 May 1925.

rival Henri Goudron. This paper too, though, indicated that renouncer support for Goudron was not unanimous.[81]

In spite of the venom which she otherwise reserved for the Indian community resident in Cochinchina and their role in electoral politics, the journalist Virginia Thompson only partially credits the Indian vote as the source of Deputy Outrey's long stay in power. Henri de Lachevrotière's backing was also significant. Perhaps Saigon's most active press baron in the 1920s and 1930s, de Lachevrotière used his position to gain political leverage at a time when newspapers began to play an important role in urban political life. Through his newspapers *La Dépêche* and *L'Impartiale*, he helped Outrey to secure re-election three times between 1919 and 1928. De Lachevrotière was himself no stranger to local politics and the uses of the Indian vote. As a candidate for the colonial council elections in 1926, his electoral list was elected in its entirety in the first round, in the wake of his firm opposition to then Mayor Foray's proposal to control Indian immigration, and amidst accusations from his opponents of Indian vote buying. 'Through years of journalism', wrote Thompson, 'he has built up a highly personal clientele, mainly among the *Hindu* electorate, through whom he can support candidates of his own choice.'[82]

Although Outrey managed to secure a final term in the 1932 Deputy election, the period from 1928 through the 1930s marked a cooling-off period in his relationship with the Indian renouncers. There is little indication of the views of those renouncers who continued to back him, although we know that some did so. They included the *colon* Mouttou, whose Legion of Honour had been gained with Outrey's assistance.[83] Those who finally turned against their long-standing Deputy, however, appear to have been disillusioned by his business dealings with de Lachevrotière. Outrey and de Lachevrotière's relationship ended on a sour note when de Lachevrotière took over the Deputy's shares in the *Dépêche*, all the while accusing 'the ingrate Outrey' of trying to 'oust

---

81. Le Réveil, 'Politique de Concorde…', *Réveil Saigonnais*, 4 May 1928; 'L'homme d'aujourd'hui: M. Henri Gourdron prend l'avance car son programme est clair et complet', *Saigon-Dimanche*, 12 April 1928; 'Nous voterons pour Goudron', *Saigon-Dimanche*, 12 April 1928; 'Les Français de l'Inde vont montré qu'ils sont indépendants', *Saigon-Dimanche*, 22 April 1928.
82. Thompson, *French Indo-China*, p. 311; also H. Ardin, 'Tribune Eléctorale', *Tribune Indochinoise* [reprinted from *Saigon-Republicain*], 13 October 1926.
83. 'Après le Divorce Outrey – De Lachevrotière', *Saigon-Dimanche*, 28 April 1932.

him'.[84] This dispute, coupled with the effects of the Depression, appears to have finally convinced French Indian voters that Cochinchina's politicians 'only smiled at them in front of the ballot box'.[85]

An article in *Saigon-Dimanche* in 1928 expressed the new tone of scepticism among the French Indian electorate:

> We know that Mr. Ernest Outrey owes a good part of his popularity to voters originating from French India … The loyal friendship of these courageous men has been exploited by him during the election period. He then forgets about them just as he forgets about the other voters.[86]

By the 1930s, *Saigon-Dimanche* was publishing articles voicing the profound frustration of the Indian renouncers with the myth of their venality at the ballot box. Cochinchina's politicians made hollow declarations of support, always just prior to election day, but had done nothing of substance for the Indian electorate. The newspaper conveyed deep disillusion with the unwillingness of politicians to act specifically to address the plight of Indians in the lowest positions in the administration. The French citizenship of lower-ranking functionaries had never been fully recognised (see Chapter Five) and with the economic crisis their situation had become increasingly insecure.

In the lead-up to the Deputy election of 1932, editor Raoul Vernier of the *Saigon-Dimanche* made an attempt to redeem Indian French citizens from the 'tenacious and stupid legend' of their electoral venality. An electoral candidate had been put the question, 'Who subsidises your fund for the French of India?', which the journalist took to mean, 'Who gives you money to buy the votes of the French Indians?' Vernier sought to establish that the French of India voted independently like anyone else. This claim was more convincing in the 1930s than it could have been prior to the great loss of Indian faith in Outrey:

> Let's put an end to this comedy, which has gone on far too long, let's stop it once and for all! … There are exceptions, we will freely admit it. We will freely admit that some twenty or so of the most wretched French Indians, for whom the elections are manna from heaven, vote venally (a fault which one finds equally among the French from the Metropole and the French of

---

84. Thompson, *French Indo-China*, p. 311.
85. 'Considérations pré-électorales d'un Français de l'Inde', reprinted from *L'Alerte* in *Indochine-Inde* (formerly *Saigon-Dimanche*), 22 March 1936.
86. 'M. Outrey n'a pas payé sa dette aux électeurs français originaires de l'Inde', *Saigon-Dimanche*, 20 April 1928.

Indochina). But almost unanimously the French of India vote according to their conscience and understand the seriousness of their act when they go to the ballot box.[87]

Outrey survived and secured yet another term, but by the late thirties scepticism had turned to extreme pessimism for some Indians. One renouncer spoke of the 'state of misery' in which many Indian renouncers in Cochinchina found themselves. He blamed local politicians, 'with Mr. de Lachevrotière at their head', who 'prolong this state of pauperism to exploit it at the moment of the elections'. 'The legislative elections will take place soon', he bemoaned, 'and we will hear nothing but jokes in bad taste addressed to a category of French citizens; the French of India.'[88]

Although Cochinchina's Indian voters had discredited him by the 1930s, Outrey's legacy, as much as his vision of himself, lives on in Pondicherry. A house in the French quarter bears the name 'Villa Ernest Outrey' above its front entrance. The present occupant is the son of a French Indian magistrate, Henri Saint-Jacques (whose efforts to gain a concession were discussed in Chapter Three). The magistrate admired Outrey for his defence of renouncers' rights in Cochinchina, and when he retired to Pondicherry he named the house he built there after the 'perennial Deputy'. Saint-Jacques wrote to Outrey to inform him of his new namesake; Outrey graciously accepted the compliment by despatching to Pondicherry a marble bust of himself. In 2002 Saint-Jacques' son pointed to an alcove in the wall of the reception room of the same house. 'That was the place', he said, 'where we kept my father's bust of Ernest Outrey.' He lamented the unfortunate sale of the statue some years ago, which has left the niche now empty. Yet the legend of the Indian voter memorialised in the not-so-solid presence of Deputy Ernest Outrey is somehow entirely fitting.[89]

Conclusion

Journalist Virginia Thompson described the electoral imbalance between Indians and peoples native to Cochinchina as 'a practical joke

---

87. R. Vernier, 'Les Français de l'Inde ne sont pas à acheter: encore la tenace et stupide légende', *Saigon-Dimanche*, 17 April 1932.
88. 'Considérations pré-électorales d'un Français de l'Inde', reprinted from *L'Alerte* in *Indochine-Inde* (formerly *Saigon-Dimanche*), 22 March 1936.
89. Interview with Antoine Saint-Jacques, Pondicherry, January 2002.

Plate 12: The 'Villa Ernest Outrey', Pondicherry. Photograph by N. Pairaudeau, January 2002.

unwittingly perpetuated by the French Revolution'.[90] Commenting on the state of electoral franchise in France's colonies in 1914, the writer Pierre Mille similarly observed that 'all the electoral legislation of our colonies is made up of inconsistencies and really incredible idiocies'. In Algeria, he noted, citizenship was extended *en bloc* to the Jews in 1870, and they were thereby given suffrage, but not to the Arabs, who were thus unable to vote. Whereas in Cochinchina:

> only the whites can vote; the indigenous Annamites, the most intelligent among our native subjects, have no political rights. But '*Malabars*' from our French Establishments in India may go to Cochinchina with their statutes

---

90. Thompson, *French Indo-China*, p. 172.

and as a result may take part in elections: an important minority who, most of the time, determine the success of the candidate.

If a 'negro from Senegal' went to France or India, he continued, he could not vote. But an Indian could vote in Senegal or in France. 'Why? No one can ever explain.'[91]

This chaper has offered an explanation for Mille's conundrum, if only a partial one. The renouncers of Cochinchina held their French masters to account on the vague promise that France's republican values, and French citizenship, might extend seamlessly through the overseas empire. Their efforts did not bear fruit for non-renouncers. But renouncers earned their right to vote on par with Europeans throughout the French Empire. Ironically, it was only at home in French India that they continued to vote in separate electoral colleges. However, their continuing need of powerful people to help defend their rights as citizens in French Cochinchina, and weaknesses in the political system of the colony, made them particularly malleable in the hands of certain politicians. Many of these politicians are admirable at first glance. They ardently defended the political rights of colonised peoples; they promoted notions of citizenship free of race. Yet their motives were questionable, and their hold over the Indian electorate was finally broken towards the end of the 1920s.

The battle of Indian French citizens for their status to be upheld in Cochinchina was fully justified in terms of the principles upon which the Republic claimed to be founded. It certainly served the French Deputies well. But the tremendous strain it placed on the colonial social order did little, as we shall see, to serve the immediate interests of French authorities in the colony in their day-to-day struggles to assert their hold on power.

---

91. Pierre Mille, 'Élections coloniales', *La France d'Outre Mer*, 14 May 1914.

CHAPTER FIVE

COLONIAL CITIZENSHIP AND CONTRACTUAL PRIVILEGES

Beginning from the 1880s, numerous conflicts arose in Cochinchina over the contractual terms of renouncers employed within the administration. These conflicts were mainly over whether Indian employees were entitled to benefits otherwise reserved for Europeans. No legal challenge was made after 1901 to renouncers' recognized right to vote as French citizens in Cochinchinese elections, but the contractual disputes continued well beyond that date.

In these disputes, Indian employees posed different types of threats to the social order depending on whether they were employed in upper- and middle-ranking positions, or filled subordinate posts. The upper- and middle-ranking employees threatened the colonial budget and its ability to pay for the generous benefits accorded to Frenchmen of metropolitan origin. With their high levels of French education and their assured handling of French culture, society, and law, the Indians could generally defend their position within the administration on the occasions it was challenged. The more educated and more savvy of the French Indians were able to exploit the divisions between legislators in the Metropole, who ardently defended republican principles, and more pragmatic colonial administrators. They knew they stood a better chance of securing their legal rights as citizens if they could bring their plight to the attention of their elected representatives in the French parliament and of other metropolitan authorities, and they could argue their case in law. Yet they were also adept at engaging with the French rationale used to justify European privilege in the colonies. They could hold their own in debates grounded in ideas derived from the developing (if dubious) social, environmental, and race sciences, which emphasised the need to offset the physical and moral fatigue induced in Europeans by expatriation. Debates along these lines usually arose with officials based in the colony rather than in the Metropole. As expatriates themselves, educated Indians could be taken seriously when they put forward ideas about the dangers to which their service in Cochinchina exposed them, even if they did not always win arguments in this vein. Colonial authorities were less convinced, however, by appeals from Indian employees in the lower ranks for working conditions and contractual terms which reflected their citizenship status. Such requests were politically problematic when the Indians worked alongside Vietnamese employees; for this reason some Indian renouncers employed by the colonial administration never received contractual privileges which matched their French citizenship.

OTHER BOUNDARIES OF RULE

The maintenance of a superior status for Europeans, and thereby of European prestige, has been studied for French Indochina, as elsewhere in Southeast Asia, primarily in relation to concubinage and Eurasian mixed-race populations. From the latter half of the nineteenth century, European fears of a growing population with mixed European and 'native' blood were instrumental in establishing 'boundaries of rule' which separated the colonised from their colonisers, and thereby preserved the privilege, prestige, and power of the latter.[1] Efforts to establish a firm and clear divide between the colonial 'masters' and those they ruled over become evident from around the 1890s. From this period, colonial authorities began to police the private lives of European men in Indochina; campaigns were mounted to discourage concubinage and to send European women to the colonies to improve the gender balance and foster the formation of stable European families; and children of mixed race became a source of anxiety, a subject of study and a target of colonial policy.[2]

Yet debates over the political rights of Indians in Cochinchina and their status within the Cochinchinese administration reveal that the

---

1. The seminal work is Ann Laura Stoler's *Carnal Knowledge and Imperial Power: Race and the Intimate in Colonial Rule*, Berkeley: University of California Press, 2002). Saada's *Les enfants de la colonie* is particularly valuable for its close attention to the role of colonial law in shaping and reshaping social boundaries.
2. Marie-Paule Ha, 'French Women and the Empire', in *France and "Indochina", Cultural Representations*, Kathryn Robson and Jennifer Lee, (eds), London: Lexington Books, 2005, p. 107; Saada, 'Les enfants de la colonie', p. 14; Christina Firpo, 'Crises of Whiteness and Empire in Colonial Indochina: The removal of Abandoned Eurasian Children from the Vietnamese Milieu, 1856–1954', *Journal of Social History*, 43, 3, 2010, 587–613, p. 587.

business of racial boundary-raising in colonial societies had broader dimensions which merit further consideration. Around the same period, a wider set of concerns prompted administrative and legal measures aimed at producing a greater distance, in private life as in public function, between Europeans in the colony and the Asian populations, both indigenous and foreign. Suddenly from the 1880s, a Cochinchina which had been open to all comers began to question whether French Indians should be allowed to vote in Cochinchina – even though they had been quietly doing so for over a decade. It questioned whether Asians hired by the colonial administration should be allowed to enjoy contractual privileges otherwise reserved for Europeans; Indians, *tagals* from the Philippines, Malays, and *métis* had all been so employed from the moment an administration had been formed under the Admirals. *Métis* and foreign Asians were required to seek French naturalisation in order to continue to be entitled to European legal status at work. Indians originating from the French possessions and employed as 'Europeans' in the administration were for their part required to renounce their indigenous personal status if they wanted to retain their 'European' contractual status.

In order to naturalise, *métis* and foreign Asian employees made use of the same 1881 decree introduced for the indigenous *Annamites* of Cochinchina, a decree which was itself a means of firming up colonial social boundaries by severely limiting the number of local people who could accede to citizenship. Regulations which allowed colonial peoples to accede to citizenship – narrowing from voluntary modes of 'renunciation' in the old colonies to more restrictive decrees on naturalisation in the new – were instruments which served to legislate where the 'boundaries of rule' were drawn. Saada has noted that it was at the time when new regulations on concubinage were being introduced that the accession of colonised peoples to citizenship begin to attach to themes of preserving the 'dignity ' and 'prestige' of the coloniser. Legal commentator Alfred Girault captured the transition from renunciation to naturalisation: 'It cannot suffice that the native aspires to be treated as a European: it is also required that we judge him worthy of being considered one of us.'[3]

This shift from accepting and even encouraging the mingling of 'natives' and Europeans and the placement of non-Europeans in European

---

3. Girault quoted in Saada, 'Citoyens et sujets de l'Empire Français', p. 4.

roles, to deep anxiety over the same practices and interactions, was a phenomenon experienced globally across European colonial settings. This rather sudden change in European thinking about its relationship towards the peoples it had colonised can be understood as a signal of the advent of new modes of state power. In the late nineteenth century France's presence in Cochinchina moved from military to civilian administration; in the wider Indochinese peninsula it moved from conquest to economic *mise en valeur*, and from an age of private European 'pioneer' entrepreneurs forging direct commercial links and personal relationships to an era of colonial bureaucrats. These men were 'placed at a safe distance from the *indigène*', because their business, notably taxation, relied on a 'relationship to local populations far more vertical in nature'.[4] The greater depth of this change and the wider range of its impacts can become lost in the tremendous surge of interest in intimate relationships between European men and colonised women, and the social and political consequences of such unions.

French authorities in Cochinchina used popular versions of the emerging 'sciences' of race and climate to justify why Indians in the administration did not need to be treated on par with their European colleagues.[5] The demarcation of 'boundaries of rule' in the French Empire, however, was never consistently or exclusively racial. A complex web of motives beyond a desire to draw a racial line between white Frenchmen and colonised peoples was used to negotiate and renegotiate the boundaries of rule. Fiscal concerns, nativist anxieties, and legal constraints all contributed to the shaping of these boundaries. Arguments between French Indians and the Cochinchinese administration over Indians' rights to contractual privileges provide a valuable schema of how 'racial' factors fed into the reasoning used over time to justify European privilege in French Cochinchina. They also demonstrate, however, a French imperial context in which the rule of law could become a powerful instrument in the hands of colonised people. Arguments over whether the Cochinchinese climate was more morally and physically degenerat-

---

4. Gregor Muller, *Colonial Cambodia's 'Bad Frenchmen': The rise of French rule and the life of Thomas Caraman, 1840–1887,* London: Routledge, 2006, p. 10.
5. On the rise of race and climate science in France, see William Schneider, 'Towards the Improvement of the Human Race: the History of Eugenics in France', *Journal of Modern History*, 54, 1982, 269–291. Stoler discusses its wider application in late nineteenth and early twentieth century colonial societies: see Stoler, *Carnal Knowledge*, pp. 61–67.

ing to Indian or metropolitan staff never reached any firm conclusions. Rather, it was through the French courts that Indian renouncers established that, as citizens, their contractual rights could not be denied to them on account of their 'race'. Thus from the late nineteenth century, while colonial authorities began to question on the grounds of race the privileges granted to non-Europeans, these same authorities could be obliged to uphold these privileges if they were proved to be legally founded in citizenship.

The Pension funds affair: 'Asian' agents on 'European' terms

Indians were hired on European terms and wages in the Cochinchinese administration even before the process of renunciation had been given official recognition in French India (in September 1881). Their right to pay and privileges at 'European' levels, like their right to vote, was never questioned in the early days, presumably because they possessed skills and qualities which the French administration urgently needed.

Indians first began to protest that these privileges were under attack from the early 1880s. Unlike later petitions, early complaints were not based on claims that renouncers' contractual terms did not match their citizenship status. Most of the petitioners at this point had yet to renounce their personal status. Rather the Indians complained that privileges freely accorded to them as employees with 'European' status were now being taken away. Their claims prompted French authorities to oblige all non-European employees who held 'European' positions (including Indians, mixed-blood *créoles* from France's other overseas possessions, and some Malays and Japanese) to obtain legal proof of their European status.

The trigger for the first Indian complaints about their contractual privileges in Cochinchina was a very generous pension fund established in the 1870s for employees classified as 'Europeans'. Financed by the local budget, it entitled each functionary to tens of thousands of francs after twelve years' service, described by the principal analyst of French colonial law as a 'small fortune'.[6] It also protected wives and families, who could receive payments if the employee should die before serving out his twelve years. The pension was justified as compensation for hardship.

---

6. Girault, *Principes*, p. 123.

As one Indian public servant described it, the fund served 'to recognise by an extraordinary allocation the sacrifices of all kinds imposed upon agents of the local service in Cochinchina who must make their careers in this colony, and notably the risks they run to their health'.[7]

Initially reserved for those working within the Department of Native Affairs, the pension was extended to other categories of public servant in 1876. It continued to be only those agents classed as 'European' though who were eligible for the benefits. The pension was again extended in May of 1881, this time to lower-ranking functionaries, or 'inferior agents' (*agents inférieurs*). But this category of employees included those in positions classified as 'European' as well as those classified as 'native'. Thus in an effort, it seems, to make clear that those employed on 'native' terms were excluded, an article stipulated that 'agents of Asian origin' were not eligible.[8]

This more restrictive policy, however, was introduced in the same month as the law on naturalisation in Cochinchina (May 1881). Although no document explicitly says so, this new decree too may well have motivated the restriction on 'Asian agents'. With *Annamites* now able to obtain the status of citizens, Cochinchina's chief administrators may have felt it necessary to state that some (expensive) privileges were reserved only for 'real' Europeans, and were justified by the particular hardships they endured – as Europeans – in Cochinchina's climate and environment.

It could be taken as a simple oversight that the authors of the decree failed to notice that many Indian employees, technically 'of Asian origin', were already employed, and had in some cases been employed for many years, as 'European' agents. Their access to the pension fund had not until now been questioned. However, authorities acted upon the ambiguous wording of the decree to deny the pension to their Indian employees. The controversy then called into question other 'European' privileges these intermediaries had quietly enjoyed.

Not long after the offending changes to the pension fund had been made public, Indians employed in the administration 'on European terms' petitioned the Minister of Colonies to protest againsst their exclusion.

---

7. VNA2 SL 2582 Liquidation de compte de prévoyance de M. Adicéam, comptable du 2e classe, 1888: 'Mémoire tendant à l'admission des Indiens agents au service locale en Cochinchine, au bénéfice du compte de prévoyance', signed Adicéam, 3 March 1888.
8. Ibid.

Their petition has not survived, but a related letter from the Governor of Cochinchina to his superior in Paris lays out reasons for rejecting the Indians' assertions. It draws on ideas current at the time about the propensity of different 'races' to adapt to new physical environments. Special provisions were not required for Indian functionaries serving in Cochinchina, he claimed, because the climate into which they were being introduced presented no danger to them: 'The situation of Pondicherry and Saigon with respect to latitude and climate' was 'almost identical'. The Indians retained a 'material way of life which does not differ in any visible way between the two countries'. By contrast (and displaying a slippage from environmental adaptation to racial determinism characteristic of this 'science'), 'the *créoles* from other colonies live like the Europeans' and merited 'European' treatment because 'they have the same needs'.[9]

The Governor's pseudo-scientific claims were supported by a paternalistic defence of the rights of *Annamites* against the undue privileges of Indians. 'If the Indians are reputed to be French citizens', the Governor argued, 'the *Annamites* are our subjects and also have a right to our beneficence.' Rather than being excluded from (French) privilege, the category of Indians who benefited from European salaries was already overly privileged. 'In effect, Indians do not spend more than *Annamites*. An [Indian] employee of the first category whose annual income is from 800 to 1,000 francs does not have any more expenses than a native agent at 760 piastres.' This idea, that the Indians' situation was comparable not to that of Europeans but to that of the indigenous Cochinchinese exposed the more salient risks underlying the affair, which were political as well as fiscal. The problem was not so much the Governor's claim that *Annamite* and Indian lifestyles were comparable, as the risk that the *Annamites* themselves might make these comparisons:

> If we grant payments from the pension fund to [Indians] already two or three times better paid than the natives and who do not contribute as they do to municipal and public charges and who do not participate in paying taxes, there would be no reason to refuse the same benefit to the latter.[10]

---

9. VNA2 SL 2362 Compte de Prévoyance: concession du compte de prévoyance aux fonctionnaires et employés originaires des Établissements français de l'Inde: GCCH to MMC, 27 October 1882.
10. Ibid.

The Governor's mention of taxation points to one of French Cochinchina's inherent weaknesses and one of its great injustices. Fiscal shortfalls were of continual concern in a colony always pressed to be economically self-sufficient. Its indigenous people paid in heavy taxation for the privileges enjoyed by those brought in to rule over them. 'European' functionaries, Indians included, who did not pay these taxes, drew their generous pensions and other benefits from the pockets of *Annamite* taxpayers. Yet if the Governor did not spell this out, the Minister of Colonies firmly grasped the immediate risks implied. In his reply to Cochinchina's Governor he agreed that 'to admit [Indian agents] to the benefit of the pension fund would lead, logically, to inviting native agents to participate, and would result for the colony in a considerable and unjustifiable expense'.[11]

One Indian employee to question this decision was Mr. Cherubin Guanadicam Adicéam. Adicéam was among the first young recruits from Pondicherry to work in the developing administration in Saigon, arriving there in 1868 to fill a clerical post with the Department of the Interior. He was employed from the beginning on European contractual terms. In 1885 he requested the liquidation of his pension fund from the administration after seventeen years of consecutive service. His application was rejected on the basis that he was classed, by virtue of the decision of May 1881, as a functionary 'of Asian origin'.[12]

Adicéam's challenge to the administration is of note because of the strategy it demonstrates, and the style and force of his arguments. These factors are all telling of his French cultural competence. He possessed a sophisticated understanding of French administrative and political procedure. His rhetorical skills were sharp too; they enabled him, once he had reached an attentive and sufficiently influential audience, to undermine the reasoning of those who opposed him. He relied on the backing of superiors in Saigon, who were clearly supportive of his work, to pass his petitions up through the administrative hierarchy. He then hired a lawyer from Paris, 'to enlighten the Department on the situation of the Indians' and to address his claims 'through hierarchical channels to the

---

11. VNA2 SL 2362: MMC to GCCH, 9 March 1888.
12. It is not certain whether Cherubin Guanadicam is the same Adicéam referred to in Chapter Four – names have been misspelt in some sources – but it is very likely.

Minister of the Navy and Colonies' in order to 'incite an interpretation of the ... said decree'.[13]

In a lengthy memorandum, Adicéam subverted arguments forward by the Governor of Cochinchina some years earlier. In so doing, he demonstrated how colonised people, as much as their colonial masters, bought into popular versions of prevalent social theories and could shape these ideas to their own purposes. Adicéam implicitly accepted the Governor's proposition that the physical environment from which colonial functionaries originated had a bearing on how well they fared in the Cochinchinese climate. He also accepted the notion that the privileges enjoyed by Europeans in the colonies were intended to cushion them from the risks to which they were exposed. However, he cleverly placed the expatriated Indians on a similar footing to that of their European colleagues serving overseas by claiming that India's climate could in no way be equated with that of Cochinchina:

> The Governor of Cochinchina put forward the opinion that the climate of Pondicherry offered the same insalubrious character as that of Cochinchina and that the acclimatisation of the Indians to this latter colony posed no danger ... These judgements are erroneous, and it is certain that from the study of medical reports of the two colonies that the two climates are completely different. It is in effect no secret that Pondicherry, which enjoys a dry, albeit hot climate, is a clean city. We may not say as much of Cochinchina.[14]

Not only did Indians, like Europeans, suffer the physical effects of Cochinchina's climate and environment. From a cultural perspective, Adicéam argued, the Indians' indigenous habits were different (and, he implied, cleaner) than those of the Vietnamese. To the Governor's claim that 'the eating habits of Indians were not costly', Adicéam replied: 'On the contrary, the Indian diet, inexpensive in India, must be the same in Indochina as that of the Europeans due to the risk of intestinal problems that do not spare anyone not belonging to the yellow race.' The expatriate Indians' cultivation of European habits ('the agents of the local administration, although Indian, all dress themselves and their families included in European dress') was used by Adicéam to bolster

---

13. VNA2 SL 2582 Liquidation de compte de prévoyance de M. Adicéam, comptable du 2e classe, 1888: Adicéam to Director of Local Services, 6 October 1888.

14. Ibid.: 'Mémoire tendant à l'admission des Indiens agents au service locale en Cochinchine, au bénéfice du compte de prévoyance', author Adicéam, 3 March 1888.

his claim that the administration's Indian employees deserved European privileges.[15]

Adicéam had renounced his personal status on 5 November 1881, not two months after the decree had been issued in French India. Yet he did not rely on legal claims to citizenship to argue that he qualified for French privileges. He drew instead on a more ambiguous piece of legislation. He interpreted the presidential order of 1871, which distinguished peoples to whom the *Annamite* legal code applied from those subject to French legislation, as proof that Indians had been legally ruled in Cochinchina to be more like the French than the *Annamites*. The decree itself was grounded in the idea that some ethnic groups had assimilated more than others to the 'indigenous' Vietnamese (relative newcomers to the southern delta) because these groups had resided in Cochinchina prior to French rule; by extension, they were the more easily assimilable 'races'. This reasoning was faulty on several counts. Adicéam was quite willing to use it though, to place other Asians among the 'Asian agents'. Those who were intended to be included under the term 'Asian agents', he maintained, were only the 'Annamites, Chinese, Malays and Cambodians', who were already 'acclimatised or are easily acclimatised, having lived in the Colony prior to the French occupation.'[16]

Adicéam closed his petition by claiming the root of the problem was an error in wording on the part of lawmakers. Indians were not meant to be included in the term 'agents of Asian origin', but given the 'presence of a large number of Asians of diverse nationalities' who could be placed in the category of those assimilated to the 'natives', 'the writer preferred to use a generic expression in which the literal sense surpassed his thinking'. Although both parties dressed their arguments in the social theory of the day, his opponent's racist undertones were not lost on Adicéam. He concluded: 'It is regrettable that the French administration enters into the examination of the skin colour of its agents, in order to resolve a financial problem.'[17]

Adicéam's argument won over the recently appointed Minister of the Navy and Colonies, who determined that the pension fund should have

---

15. VNA2 SL 2582.: 'Mémoire tendant à l'admission des Indiens agents au service locale en Cochinchine, au bénéfice du compte de prévoyance', author Adicéam, 3 March 1888.
16. Ibid.: Note from Head of Service, 9 March 1888.
17. Ibid.: 'Mémoire tendant à l'admission des Indiens agents au service locale en Cochinchine, au bénéfice du compte de prévoyance', author Adicéam, 3 March 1888.

properly been 'reserved for certain categories of French functionaries, without distinction of origin': 'Agents in the local service who originate from French India therefore, although "Asian" in the literal sense of the word, should be considered to have access to the pension fund.'[18]

This decision was clear enough, but a muddle followed. Indochina's administrators, particularly those at higher levels, were remarkably slow in recognising and understanding the ways in which race and legal status were beginning to intersect in the colony. A letter Adicéam wrote two months later indicated that the decision had now been made public, and that he was aware the matter had been decided in his favour. He expressed frustration though that the Cochinchinese authorities had yet to act. For its part, the Cochinchinese administration had been slowed by its own interpretation of the ministerial orders. The circular it issued to all departments stated that 'Indians without distinction of origin, as well as other Asians not properly belonging to Indochina' were now entitled to the pension fund. Replies to a request to all of these local departments to draw up lists of eligible Indians reveal how departmental heads took it upon themselves to interpret these orders. Without exception, they carefully excluded any Indian employed 'on native terms' (*à titre indigène*). Some higher level administrators did not even seem aware that some Indians were hired on 'native' terms and others under 'European' contracts; this reflects the informality with which European privileges were granted to non-Europeans in the early days of colonial rule in Cochinchina. When the Treasury reported as 'nil' the number of Indians in its employ, for example, it was noted in the Cochinchinese Governor's office 'and yet there are Indians who are tax inspectors'. The situation confounded the Colonial Council to the extent that it suspended pay-outs from the pension fund to Indians until a solution could be reached. The Governor General wrote to Paris seeking clarification in terms which suggest that authorities in Saigon, as much as their leader in Hanoi, really had no idea what was intended by the Minister of Colonies' earlier instructions. The Governor carefully worded his inquiry, betraying both caution about all possible interpretations and anxieties about fiscal pressure. The Governor pressed the Minister to 'examine please whether there is reason to be concerned, as the commission thinks there is, about the size of the expense that

---

18. Ibid.: MMC to GCCH, 21 August 1888.

would entail the payment of the pension fund to all Indians holding the title of employee on European terms. If your response is in the negative, please advise us as to whether Indians serving "on Asian terms" should also be eligible.'[19]

This affair made problematic the privileges some Indian employees enjoyed within the administration. It revealed a further troubling distinction between different Indians within the service, but it also drew attention to similar problems posed by non-European and *métis* employees. Having asked about the proposed status of Indians in his letter to the Minister, the Governor General went on to inquire whether he should include in the benefits of the pension other Asians who were not of Indochinese origin, such as 'Malays, Japanese, [and] Tagals'. Similar to the Indians, they occupied, 'some European jobs', and they had never been asked for legal proof of their 'European' status. Several Cochinchinese *métis* were in the same position:

> There are also several *métis* of French men and *Annamite* women; some of them, legally recognised by their fathers, are eligible without question for the pension, whereas two others whom their fathers have neglected to recognise have been excluded ... both serve as agents on European terms. As the appearance and attitude of each of them does not reveal anything of their semi-Asian origin, they both insist upon being put in possession of their dues from the pension fund.[20]

Any pretension on the part of Chinese employees to privileged status was more easily dismissed. 'I exclude the Chinese', he added, 'who can be assimilated with the natives of the colony.'[21]

The Minister's reply stated that his intention was to permit only French Indians employed in Cochinchina on the same level as Europeans, and not those hired 'on Asian terms', to access the pension fund. His message did not reach Hanoi, however, until mid-April, by which time the fund in its entirety (rather than just the Indian drain on it) had been judged an excessive strain on local finances, and a 'general liquidation' had been declared.[22]

---

19. VNA2 SL 2582: Adicéam to Director of Local Services, 6 October 1888; VNA2 SL 2362 Compte de Prévoyance: concession du compte de prévoyance aux fonctionnaires et employés originaires des Établissements français de l'Inde: undated circular (late August 1888); 'Note', 5 November 1888; GGI to MMC, 29 January 1889.
20. VNA2 SL 2362: GGI to MMC, 29 January 1889.
21. Ibid.: GGI to MMC, 29 January 1889.
22. Ibid.: MMC to GGI, 1 April 1889; Girault, Principes, p. 124.

In the course of resolving Indian claims on the pension fund, the Cochinchinese administration began to require that any Indian working on 'European' terms should show proof that he had renounced in order to justify his contractual privileges. With the first general pay-out from the fund in April 1889, Indians employed in the administration on 'European terms', such as the lighthouse guards Michel Samy, Joseph Gézegabel, and Emmanuel Lazare, were simply granted the sums due to them.[23] A year later, however, the Pension Fund commission refused to make payments to Indians from the fund unless they could provide proof of renunciation. François Dourressamy, employed in the Public Works Department, had taken the trouble to arrange a proxy to renounce for him in Karikal in February of 1889. However, he was not granted his four thousand francs in pension (under the new surname Marius) until this act of renunciation could be produced.[24] Other Indian employees resented this new requirement, perceiving that renunciation was being forced upon them. Lighthouse guardian Lambarre and accountant Rattinam objected that they had been suspended from their work until they could provide acts of renunciation:

> These employees, who do not want to renounce their status, told me that these documents were not previously requested in similar circumstances from many of their compatriots and that it had been sufficient only to prove that they were natives of the French Establishments in India. They protested against the decision taken today with regard to them ... that imposes on them a renunciation, a measure that was not taken with respect to their predecessors.[25]

Other non-European employees engaged 'on European terms' also began to be asked for legal proof of status, in their cases of naturalisation.[26] Some, like the Filipino Ciriaco Villaruel, reacted similarly to Lambarre and Rattinam. Villaruel indicated that naturalisation, now presented to him as a necessity, was not something he had ever actively sought:

---

23. VNA2 Goucoch 2413 Liquidation des comptes de prévoyance de MM. Brun, Samy, Joseph, Lazare, 1889.
24. VNA2 SL 2415 Liquidation des comptes de prévoyance de ... M. Marius, indien renonçant sous le nom Dourressamy (François), commis auxiliaire des travaux publics, M. Villaruel, 1890: 'Analyse de l'affaire', 20 May 1890.
25. VNA2 SL 2412 Liquidation des comptes de prévoyance de ... Rattinam (Indien) commis aux travaux publics, Lambarre (Indien) gardien de phare, Hakiko, conducteur de 3ᵉ classe des travaux publics (Japonais naturalisé) 1889–1890: Director of Public Works to GCCH, 22 May 1890.
26. VNA2 Goucoch 2413 and VNA2 SL 2412 (above) include cases of Japanese employees naturalised as Frenchmen.

> Despite my lack of naturalisation, I find, by virtue of my settling here which goes back twenty-four years, that I have adopted Cochinchina as my second home ... I must admit ... that I have never aimed to be naturalised. With little knowledge of the law, and working always far from Saigon, I came to know only recently that this formality was necessary.[27]

No regulation exists which marks firmly this change in policy. However, another reference dating from 1890 indicates that renunciation had become necessary for those contracted on 'European' terms to hold their posts. Appavou, a government warehouse employee in Saigon, mentioned in a petition to the Minister of Colonies in 1890 that his renunciation was 'indispensable ... to the exercise of my employment for which it is one of the conditions stipulated by the Government'.[28]

The pension funds affair resulted in the rationalisation of contractual privileges within the Cochinchinese administration. Renunciation became compulsory for Indian employees, as did naturalisation for their Asian peers, if they wanted to maintain the European contractual privileges they had already been granted. We have become accustomed to understanding that the acquisition of rights and privileges follows on from a change in legal status. Here though, the reverse was true. Cochinchina's 'Asian' functionaries enjoyed 'European' privileges in their employment in the 1860s and 1870s; with the introduction of legal instruments allowing access to the rights of citizens in 1881, they were then obliged to secure proof that they legally held these rights in order to retain the privileges they already enjoyed.

The pension funds affair by no means put to rest debate over 'European' benefits within the administration. Local authorities made attempts to undermine the European privileges of some of its Indian employees, while Indians hired on 'native terms' now began too to seek better contractual conditions for themselves.

Troubles with 'native status'

It became necessary by about 1890 for all Indians employed on European contractual terms within the Cochinchinese administration to 'regularise' their situation by renouncing their personal status. Yet by the start

---

27. VNA2 SL 2415 Liquidation des comptes de prévoyance de ... M. Marius, indien renonçant sous le nom Dourressamy (François), commis auxiliaire des travaux publics, M. Villaruel, 1890: Ciriaco Villaruel to GCCH, 25 January 1890.
28. Appavou, *Absurde Renonciation*, p. 7.

of the twentieth century *all* Indian functionaries, be they employed on 'European' or on 'native' terms, had chosen to renounce. Additionally, some administrators within the Cochinchinese local service had changed the terms of their Indian employees' contracts to 'native' ones where they felt their European privileges were not merited. Problems arose from both situations, centred on complaints from Indians that as French citizens they should not be subject to 'native' terms of employment.

In the 1900s two groups of Indian employees protested against the terms of their treatment within the Cochinchinese administration. The first group consisted of postmen of Indian origin who continued to be contracted on 'native' terms even though they had all renounced and were thus French citizens. The second group was made up of Indian tax inspectors (*porteurs de contraintes*). Again, all had renounced. The tax inspectors' positions were previously classified as 'European', but had been downgraded to 'native' contractual status as soon as the Indians were hired.

Both of these contractual disputes took place shortly after the French Supreme Court ruled (1901) that renouncers could participate on par with metropolitan Frenchmen in Cochinchinese elections. When at that point Cochinchinese Deputy François Deloncle stepped up to defend the Indian postmen, it was within a context where they had been legally recognised at the highest level as French citizens, and had also just had their rights confirmed as voters who made up a significant proportion of the Cochinchinese electorate. Despite this context, Deloncle was remarkably timid in his appeal and only partially effective. He appeared to lack conviction that these men, who were clearly not of the 'educated classes', had any claim to the privileged status of Frenchmen other than their basic loyalty to France.

In early 1903, Deputy Deloncle wrote to bring the 'miserable' and 'precarious' situation of Indian postmen in Saigon to the attention of the Governor General of Indochina. A recent reorganisation of the postal service, he noted, had made no mention of the eleven Indians employed there. He asked that they be given privileges closer to those enjoyed by European employees, rather than the native entitlements which they received. The postal service did not employ any Europeans as postmen, with whose situation new terms for the Indian postmen might be equated. However, Deloncle's request included some of the basic benefits enjoyed by employees under 'European' contract. These included a salary fixed in French francs, the right to administrative leave after three years of service, rights to travel in a higher class and to be admitted to better hospitals, and access to a pension.[29]

Deloncle did not support his request by emphasising the postmen's legal status as citizens. Instead, he pressed arguments about their greater loyalty, compared to the Vietnamese, to the French cause. With the growth of Saigon, it was desirable to expand the number of Indian postmen. Only they were capable of ensuring 'the security of correspondence and professional discretion', while Cochinchinese employees were not. He cited an incident which took place in Sóc Trăng in 1901, in which a Vietnamese postman passed a letter from the Public Prosecutor to a third party before delivering it to the lawyer to whom it was addressed. 'This could most certainly never have taken place with an Indian postman,' the Deputy insisted. 'The Indian postman, upheld by a strong sense of duty, and envisioning the penalties to which he would be exposed, would never transgress the obligations of his work.'[30]

The Governor General did not agree. Instead, he insisted that cultural similarities between the Indians and the *Annamites* made the Cochinchinese environment less physically taxing for the Indians than it was for Europeans. The postmen's request for longer leave he dismissed on the grounds that 'the way of life of these employees is essentially the same as that of the *Annamites*'. Furthermore, there was no need for the Indian employees to be paid in francs as the piastre was stable. Granting such a request risked similar demands from the Vietnamese employees, who, like the Indian postmen, received a salary in piastres.[31]

The political crux of the issue was that privileges extended to Indian employees 'would not fail to be noticed by the natives presently serving in the diverse services of Indochina'. The risk of bringing injustice to the *Annamites* by favouring the Indians was a theme which had been raised before. The same worry was expressed during the pension funds affair; in the postmen's case, the concern was more immediate. Unlike Adicéam and other Indians employed on 'European' terms, the Indian

---

29. ANOM GGI 4073 Au sujet de la situation des postiers Hindous à Saigon 1903: Deputy Deloncle to GGI, 2 January 1903.
30. Ibid.
31. ANOM GGI 4073: GGI to Deputy Deloncle, 3 April 1903.

postmen worked alongside Vietnamese colleagues, who were employed under the same 'native' terms to do precisely the same work.[32] The fear of problems arising when one group of postmen was favoured over another was therefore very real.

While Cochinchina's administrative heads found it difficult to justify the granting of European privileges to Indians employed in the lower 'native' ranks of the service, they took opportunities where they could to downgrade the status of Indians employed as 'Europeans'. Deputy Deloncle had achieved only partial success with his claim on behalf of the postmen, but he was called again in 1906 to defend the interests of the three Indian tax collectors (*porteurs de contraintes* Marie Dessaints, Gnanamouttou Lannes and Gnanapregassame Dessaints), employed by the Treasury. Acting on a petition sent to him by the men, Deloncle called on their behalf for the repeal of a decision of 1894 which had changed their employment status from 'European' to 'native'. The reasoning used to justify the change was that Europeans had initially occupied the three tax collectors' posts. When the Europeans were replaced by three Indians, the terms of employment were altered accordingly, even though all three men were renouncers and therefore French citizens.[33]

The tax inspectors' affair shows how status problems were created in the administration even as attempts were made to resolve them. These problems were not merely caused by the 'Asian origins' of the Indian employees. They stemmed equally from the fact that 'European' employees were invested with the power to oversee Vietnamese subordinates, and in some cases to press charges against Europeans. Indians working in higher- and middle-ranking posts had usually achieved superior levels of French education and displayed higher levels of French acculturation. In these cases their inferiors usually accepted their authority as 'Europeans' because they dressed and behaved like Frenchmen. As Deputy Deloncle pointed out in a later petition, such men usually found that '[their] quality as French citizens [was never] … contested'.[34]

---

32. See ANOM GGI 17248 Au sujet des agents de police indiens citoyens français de la ville de Saigon, 1910: 'French citizens of Indian origin' to Deputy Deloncle, 11 April 1907.
33. ANOM GGI 3761 Situation des porteurs de contraintes originaires de l'Inde Française 1906: Deputy Deloncle to GGI, 17 May 1906.
34. ANOM GGI 17248 Au sujet des agents de police indiens citoyens français de la ville de Saigon, 1910: 'French citizens of Indian origin' to Deputy Deloncle, 11 April 1907.

Lower-ranking 'European' positions, however, similarly required postholders to oversee Vietnamese or act against Europeans, but the same levels of education were not expected. The Franco-Tamil press would term such employees in the 1920s the *petits fonctionnaires*, the lesser functionaries; one commentator in the early 1930s called them the 'European bureaucratic proletariat'.[35] The lower ranks of policemen, bailiffs, and the tax inspectors concerned here were all in this category. The 'European' status of other subordinate administrative posts (such as prison guards and lighthouse keepers) was grounded in little more than the need for political loyalty among these employees. Their utility as intermediaries, and European hesitation to take up such posts, meant that Indians tended to carve out niches of employment in these lower status 'European' positions. At the same time, their presence created difficulties for the French administration. Indians hired to such posts did not necessarily possess the levels of French cultural competence which might have offset the fact that they were not of European origin, and their authority was not always respected, either by Europeans or by local people. As a consequence, the rights of this group of Indian employees to European privileges were more regularly called into question. On the other hand, their weaker knowledge of their rights in law compared to their better educated cousins made it easier for French officialdom to relegate them to 'native' status.

Changing 'European' status to 'native' status, though, created problems of its own. The Indian tax inspectors, as Deloncle claimed, had 'the power to press charges even against Europeans'. When French authorities decided that these relatively humble employees did not deserve European privileges, they created an awkward situation in which people classed as 'natives' had powers over Europeans. Deloncle made use of this conundrum to make his case for the Indians. If the Indian tax inspectors were permitted to have powers over Europeans, 'is it not', he wrote, 'because, like them, they are part of the electorate? In that case why this anomaly… which classes them in the category of natives?'[36]

Deloncle's support for the tax inspectors went somewhat farther than his defence of the postmen in that it included at least some reference to their legal claim as citizens. His handling of the details of their

---

35. Jean Suignard, *Les Services Civils de l'Indochine*, Paris: Larose, 1931, p. 154; 'Les interventions de M. Ernest Outrey', *Réveil Saigonnais*, 5 May 1924.
36. ANOM GGI 3761 Situation des porteurs de contraintes originaires de l'Inde Française 1906: Deputy Deloncle to GGI, 17 May 1906.

contractual demands, however, is telling of the timid way in which he approached the defence of men who were less well assimilated and certainly not of the 'educated classes'.

Deloncle's own underlying conviction that the tax inspectors were not equal to their metropolitan counterparts, even though they were French citizens, emerges in his bid to the Governor General on their behalf. His request was based, like the Governor's handling of the complaint, on now familiar ideas of the Indians' ability, relative to Europeans, to acclimatise in Cochinchina. Using this reasoning, Deloncle negotiated a compromise which effectively created an intermediate level of privilege for the Indian tax inspectors.

Deloncle requested benefits on the tax inspectors' behalf that approached but were not equal to those of their European colleagues. Deloncle claimed they could not make ends meet with their existing wage, but he argued only that their wages, paid in local piastres since 1894, should be fixed once again in French francs. As 'native' employees, the tax inspectors had been treated at *Chợ Quán*, the Vietnamese hospital in Cholon, where they had, in Deloncle's words, experienced 'moral suffering'. His request to have them admitted to military hospitals would have seen them treated alongside a lower class of Europeans. The only privilege requested on par with metropolitan Frenchmen was to shorten their length of service to three years, because the six years they currently had to serve were 'long days for a foreigner in the colony'. 'This is what contributes', he claimed, 'to the high rate of mortality of Indians in the colony.' He also requested access for them to a non-native pension.[37]

The Governor General allowed the tax inspectors to be paid in francs and even granted them a small raise. As he stated himself, since they were only three claimants he could be generous. They were accepted into the same military hospitals used by soldiers, sailors and other subordinate French agents. But they were only granted a local pension and their request for more frequent leave was rejected on the basis that they could last longer in the Cochinchinese climate than Europeans. 'These three agents from French India certainly do not need to leave as frequently as functionaries coming from France. The climate for them is less new and less dangerous.'[38]

---

37. Ibid.
38. ANOM GGI 3761: 'Note' [n.d.].

Colonial authorities found it easier to dismiss the claims of Indian French citizens employed as functionaries who had lower levels of education and lower social standing than elite Indian recruits, and who were perhaps less articulate, less confident, and less persistent when they challenged the administration. Neither postmen nor tax collectors, nor some other groups of Indian employees who were among the *petits fonctionnaires* of the Cochinchinese administration, were ever given contracts which fully recognised their French citizenship. Some such men however, found better-placed renouncers willing to help them champion their causes. The campaign to defend Saigon's Indian policemen demonstrates how a wider community of renouncers participated in an organised, high profile, and highly effective campaign to right injustices against Indian policemen within the municipal police service.

The campaign to defend Saigon's Indian policemen

The most forceful and successful campaign Indian renouncers led in defence of their rights as citizens within Cochinchina's administration was a protest against changes in the terms of employment of Saigon's Indian policemen. This time Indians organised themselves and publicised their grievances beyond the confines of the police force. A wider community of Indians in Saigon, which crossed class, educational, and professional boundaries, took complaints to high offices in Paris, where they managed to raise the debate above local-level arguments about acclimatisation. Styling themselves Cochinchina's 'Indian colony', they emerged not only as defenders of Saigon's policemen, but as colonial defenders of the Republic, pressing French legislators to recognise their citizenship as a universally applicable right.

In January 1907, policemen employed in the Saigon police force protested against a move by a new municipal government in the city to deprive the fifty-seven Indian agents in the force, all of them renouncers, of privileges due to them as French citizens. This marked the nadir of administrative manoeuvres to create categories of Indian agents increasingly separate from and inferior to their European colleagues. The reason for their discontent went back to 1897, when ranks within Saigon's municipal police force were formally organised for the first time. Indians had begun their employment at that time in a 'superior cadre', reserved exclusively for Indians. That cadre consisted of three subordinate ranks (classes five, six, and seven). The arrangement gave them the status of mere trainees at the beginning of their careers, but nonetheless provided them with some European privileges and permitted them to be promoted in time to proper 'European' ranks (classes one through four). But then, in November 1906, a decision aimed at creating a completely separate 'Indian cadre' was drafted. This would have excluded them from European privileges and would have prevented them from being promoted into European ranks. It was never implemented; renouncers were later to claim that this was because of concerns within the municipal government that it would infringe upon the Indian policemen's citizenship rights.[39]

The Indian policemen's objections of January 1907 arose when a new municipal government attempted, some weeks after it had been initially rejected, to re-introduce the 'Indian cadre' proposed in the decree of November 1906. By 20 January 1907, when they were called in to sign their payslips under the new conditions, the Indian policemen had already hired a lawyer. On his advice they proceeded to sign the slips, adding 'commitment not binding' (*sous toutes reserves*). A week later the municipal government made the minor concession of changing 'Indian cadre' to 'special superior cadre'. This was no more than a cosmetic change, and a poor effort, a laughable one even, to reassure the Indian policemen that they were not being classified on the basis of their origins. The proposed contractual arrangements remained unchanged; they still prevented the Indian employees from obtaining 'European' status. The payslips were returned to the Indian policemen with orders to cross out the offending sentence, write 'barred three words nul and void', and sign again. They refused to do so. As a result, their pay was withheld and the most senior Indian agent, sub-brigadier Saint Louis, was demoted for insubordination and brought before an inquiry.[40]

In April, by which time the Indian policemen had continued to work without pay for three months, a group of 'French citizens of Indian origin resident in Cochinchina' wrote to their Deputy François Deloncle

---

39. ANOM GGI 17248 Au sujet des agents de police indiens citoyens français de la ville de Saigon, 1910: Municipal Commissioner Duranton to GCCH, 10 November 1907; in the same file, Pamphlet, 'La Question des Agents de Police originaires de l'Inde française à Saigon', 'Avis', Minister of Colonies – *Comité Consultatif des Contentieux*, 30 March 1908.
40. ANOM GGI 17248 Au sujet des agents de police indiens citoyens français de la ville de Saigon, 1910.

to protest at the situation. Their letter laid out in strictly legal terms the cause of their complaint. Their renunciation, the petitioners maintained, constituted 'a form of naturalisation'. To prove its applicability in Cochinchina, they quoted legal commentator Arthur Girault on the Supreme Court of Appeal's decision to recognise the right of renouncers resident in Cochinchina 'to be registered on the electoral lists alongside other citizens'. The court had already acknowledged there was no such thing as 'an Indian form of [French] nationality... which conferred lesser rights'.[41]

The 'French citizens of Indian origin' went on to launch a bold attack on Saigon's Mayor and President of the Municipal Commission, Duranton, whom they held responsible for the offending decree. They condemned his 'mediocrity' and 'abuses of authority'. 'This functionary', as they described him, had 'not failed to make a mark in his new position by fantastical whims and acts of unparalleled high-handedness'. They berated him for his ignorance of metropolitan legislation and for his naivety in thinking that as 'a mere local administrator' he could 'with a stroke of his pen briskly take away the quality of citizen from a population of men who have been long-accustomed to this idea that they belong to the great French family'. The petitioners extended their criticism to imply that Duranton's incompetence was born of too long a stay in the colony (he had long served in the residence in Hue prior to his transfer to Cochinchina). They warned that 'political liberties' and republican values – much like the robust physical health enjoyed in Europe – could degenerate under tropical colonial conditions, and that a watchful metropolitan eye needed to be kept on these cherished values.[42]

Deputy Deloncle did not immediately respond to the Indians' petition. So three signatories of the April petition (Hilaire, Arokiam, and Madet) sent an urgent telegram to him and two other high-level parties (the Governor General of Indochina and the Minister of Colonies in Paris). 'President of Municipal Commission continues to vex Indian colony in Cochinchina', it read. 'Appeal Justice Minister against abuse of power.'[43]

41. ANOM GGI 17248 Au sujet des agents de police indiens citoyens français de la ville de Saigon, 1910: 'French citizens of Indian origin' to Deputy Deloncle, 11 April 1907.
42. Ibid.
43. ANOM GGI 17248: Telegram Hilaire, Arokiam, Madet to GGI, MMC, Deputy Deloncle, 22 May 1907.

COLONIAL CITIZENSHIP AND CONTRACTUAL PRIVILEGES

This message prompted the Deputy to action. He did not merely plead, as he had done in the past, for sympathy for the plight of his Indian electorate. Although he followed rather than led the petitioners in their campaign, he now defended their case solely on the grounds of the legal rights they had acquired. He forwarded the Indians' April petition to the Minister of Colonies. In a letter to the same Minister he described the renouncers as 'French citizens'. Any difference between them and their French colleagues, he insisted, was:

> an anachronistic distinction based on a difference of colour and origin, which denies the privileges they have acquired and ignores the principle of the incontestable equality of the rights of citizens enjoying their full civil and political rights and fulfilling their military service.[44]

Calling for the Minister to intervene, Deloncle stated hopefully that 'The municipal authorities of Saigon will understand once you notify them that the respect for the equality of citizens before the law is the first responsibility of any French administration.'[45]

The Indian signatories of the petition and telegram were not policemen themselves, but Indian renouncers employed outside the administration in Saigon. Mr. Hilaire was a businessman, and the others were employees of various French firms in the city. The President of the Municipal Commission was clearly deeply irritated at Indians outside the administration taking the affair into their hands. Duranton initially professed to be unaware of the cause of their complaint when he was called to respond to the telegram:

> I have been unable to trace any affair concerning from near or far the named Hilaire, Arokiam and Madit [sic] … I add that these protestors do not belong to the municipal personnel and I do not at all recall having received from them the least claim or verbal communication.[46]

He then admitted, disingenuously, that it might 'have something to do with the measures taken to reorganise the municipal personnel and with matters concerning the police agents originating from India.'[47]

---

44. The latter claim was premature. Citizens residing in the French establishments in India would not be obliged to serve in the French military until a year later, in 1908. Ibid.: Deputy CCH to MMC, 21 May 1907.
45. Ibid.
46. ANOM GGI 17248: President Municipal Commission to GCCH, 24 May 1907.
47. Ibid.

Duranton's reasoning with regard to Saigon's police force was typical of local-level justification for refusing 'European' status to renouncer employees. Echoing previous administrative conflicts, it was based on his assessment of how well the men could withstand the trials of the tropical Cochinchinese climate. Of the fifty-seven Indian policemen only seven leaves of absence for convalescence were recorded on the books. Duranton took this as 'indisputable evidence' of their ability to 'support the climate' and to 'live here as they do at home'. Thus rather than the standard European entitlement (three years' service followed by six months' leave) he insisted Indian policemen should work for five years before being given leave. This was the Commissioner's own innovation, produced from his assessment of countries which he felt to be the hygienic and climactic equivalents of Indochina. It was in part borrowed from a regulation intended for 'personnel born in the French possessions of the Indian Ocean' and serving outside their place of origin. From this regulation Duranton surmised: 'I estimate that Indochina can be considered to be just as healthy, or just as unhealthy, as Madagascar and other countries included in this category.'[48]

Duranton claimed that the Indians' physical ability to acclimatise enabled them to work easily in Cochinchina, but otherwise he maintained that for cultural and indeed racial reasons they did not make good policemen. Thus while their physical aptitude was cause to deprive them of European privileges, so too was their supposed moral and intellectual ineptitude. The Indian agents did not speak Vietnamese, he complained, and therefore provided 'an even worse service than their *Annamite* colleagues'. The preponderance of Indians in positions of some authority (the force consisted of ninety-six non-Vietnamese agents, fifty-seven of whom were Indian, and a corps of 160 Vietnamese subordinates) made the whole Saigonese force 'utterly hopeless' in Duranton's estimation. In one assessment he judged them as no less than racially unfit for the role of policing:

> The Indian does not possess, in either moral or physical terms, any of the qualities necessary to assure a police service. Timid and meek of nature,

---

48. ANOM GGI 17248: President Municipal Commission to GCCH, 24 May 1907; also President Saigon Municipal Commission to GCCH, 7 July 1907. It is not clear whether the Indian Ocean regulation distinguished between those of European and non-European origin.

without energy, completely devoid of any spirit of discipline and besides too black, these agents are in no way qualified to exercise their duties.[49]

There is no hint, though, throughout Duranton's lengthy assessment of the 'deficiencies' of Indian policemen (all of whom would have been ethnically Tamil), that a 'martial races' ideology in any way influenced his attitudes. This is in contrast to its prevalence in the thinking of so many British colonial officials, both in British India and more widely in the British Empire in the same period.[50]

In Duranton's view the Indians' meek character, and indeed their very 'blackness', accounted for their lack of authority over either the Europeans or the 'native population' in the city. Another French official in Saigon, Central Police Commissioner Belland, described interactions between the Indian policemen and the public which suggested that notions of racial superiority prevented Indian policemen from being taken seriously. These attitudes came not only from Europeans but also from indigenous Cochinchinese residents. The European population was 'absolutely impervious to any intervention by Indian agents in the disputes which arise daily between themselves and the native population; they can accept even less [Indian] intervention in disputes between Europeans.'[51] Belland depicted Indian attempts to wield authority over Cochinchinese natives as equally ineffectual. He also captured a racial charge in these interactions:

> The native population, both *Annamite* and Chinese, professes a profound disdain for the Indian race, which they consider to be absolutely inferior; they are generally hostile to all interventions by Indian agents and object to any observation they pass. The natives frequently contest the sincerity of reports that [Indian] agents are called to file during their service, especially when these pertain to questions of hygiene and salubrity.[52]

That Chinese and Vietnamese could take umbrage at Indian policemen's assessments of their levels of cleanliness only confirms what Adicéam's correspondence suggested earlier. It was not only Europeans, but a

---

49. Ibid.: President Municipal Commission to GCCH, 24 May 1907.
50. Metcalf, *Imperial Connections*, esp. pp. 71–78.
51. ANOM FM Indo NF 221/1774 La création du cadre spéciale supérieur par le Maire de Saigon M. Duranton, pour les Français d'origine indienne 1907: Central Commissioner to President of Municipal Commission, 12 September 1907 [quoted in Nadia Leconte, 'La migration des Pondichériens', pp. 120–121].
52. Ibid.: Central Commissioner to President of Municipal Commission, 12 September 1907.

wider swathe of colonial society which borrowed from environmental 'science' and social theory to forge ideas about its own position in the colonial social order.

While Police Commissioner Belland captured the racial dynamics of relations between Indian policemen in Saigon and their public, his reports on individual police agents reinforce Duranton's view of the moral inadequacies of the Indian character. In service reports for Saigon's policemen for the year 1907, as Nadia Leconte has described in her assessment of this affair, 'of a total of thirty-four agents classed as "superior special cadre" only nine satisfied their superiors'.[53] The Indian agents were consistently described as 'mediocre', 'worthless', 'apathetic', and 'inebriated'. Some were reproached for poor intelligence, while others were reported to be using their cunning to avoid punishment. The label 'Indian agent' stood alone in some reports to indicate a lack of aptitude. Even the more positive reports read half-heartedly. Belland judged agent Louis to be 'an Indian agent for whom I have neither good nor bad to say. An agent without great value'. Jean Belvindrassamy was 'a reasonably good agent, though lacking in zeal'. Agent Thiroux's 'professional worth is equal or superior to that of the best of his colleagues', but:

> He has done nothing to my knowledge more than the others. He is the same as the majority of the Indians, beneath the duties he is assigned. Charged 25th June last with tackling a horse which had broken its foot, he handled the task so badly and so slowly that he did not put the injured beast out of its suffering until two hours later, and after having shot it five times in the head.[54]

In the preceding six months, Duranton affirmed, of twenty-nine disciplinary punishments meted out to police agents, the vast majority of those disciplined were Indians.[55]

Yet prejudice, rather than incompetence, could equally account for the inordinately high number of punishments given to Indians. A further petition from the group of Indian French citizens sought to correct the view that the Indian police force was inept. Instead, it blamed 'prejudices of colour and race' within the administration. The petitioners responded to Duranton's assessment, which in their words 'did not cease to find

---

53. Leconte, 'La migration des Pondichériens', p.122.
54. ANOM FM Indo NF 221/1774 La création du cadre spéciale supérieur par le Maire de Saigon M. Duranton, pour les Français d'origine indienne 1907: Relevé des notes obtenues par les agents de cadre spécial supérieur de la Police Municipale pendant l'annee 1907.
55. Ibid.

faults and defects with the Indians', by providing an account going back to 1887 of services rendered and acts of courage by Indian policemen. The list of twelve Indian policemen included Lamartine who had 'discovered a gambling house' and 'speaks very good Vietnamese'; it also featured Enoch 'who had stopped a bolting horse attached to a carriage in which there was a European woman on her own'.[56]

In this new petition, the Indian renouncers now referred to themselves as the 'Indian colony' (*colonie indienne*, or *colonie hindoue*). This title underlined their quality not as 'natives' but as Frenchmen, albeit of Indian origin, acting alongside other French colonisers. This 'Indian colony', moreover, now sought to defend its reputation not only within the administration, but to the wider public. The account of the good deeds of Indian policemen appeared again as an article in the local French-language press, with Hilaire credited as its author.[57]

The theme of Indian French citizens used to manipulate electoral politics, familiar from the previous chapter, is present too in this affair. In the same petition, the Indians claimed Central Commissioner Belland's poor assessments of the Indian policemen were produced for electoral reasons:

> It is quite curious to find that this same Commissioner had previously furnished laudatory reports on the very Indian agents whom he disparages today and treats as incapable, for the simple reason that they did not want to cede, at the last election, to administrative pressure.[58]

The clear suggestion was that Belland had pressed his Indian employees to vote for a particular candidate. Dismayed when they did not comply, he turned against them. Belland's reports also contained references to electoral politics; he maintained though that many of the Indian agents he claimed were incompetent had retained their jobs in return for their votes. The Indian agent Roch was fired in 1904, for being on duty 'in a state of absolute drunkenness, acting eccentrically and threatening passers-by with his sabre which he had unsheathed'. Despite this he was hired again in 1906, 'for electoral reasons, along with many other

---

56. ANOM GGI 17248 Au sujet des agents de police indiens citoyens français de la ville de Saigon, 1910: Hilaire, Madet et al. to MMC, 18 June 1907.
57. Ibid.: Pamphlet entitled 'Ce qui se passe au Colonies, les Immortels principes!: La question des Indiens Citoyens Français en Cochinchine'.
58. Ibid.: Hilaire, Madet et al. to MMC, 18 June 1907.

Indians'.[59] In the same vein, Duranton claimed that the 'special cadre' created for Indian police agents back in 1897 was instituted as 'a measure of good politics and for electoral reasons'; it was intended to please the Indians, and retain their votes, by avoiding the terms 'native' or 'Asian' for their rank.[60]

Municipal Commission President Duranton held the highest-ranking of the Indian policemen responsible for his colleagues' collective insubordination in January 1907 when they refused to sign their payslips. Sub-brigadier Saint Louis was reprimanded and demoted by Duranton in March of 1907. The legality of this decision continued to be questioned though by Duranton's superiors. In August 1907 Saint Louis was still 'in service on the pavements' rather than carrying out his desk duties as a head of station and in league with European colleagues of his rank.[61] To settle the disagreement with his own superiors, Duranton brought Saint Louis before a hearing of the Municipal Commission. It was this hearing which brought the Indian policemen's dispute to a head.

Duranton was later accused of having arranged the inquiry as a means to lend an air of legality to his earlier arbitrary decision. Although the Commission concluded the hearing by exonerating its President, the Saint Louis inquiry ultimately worked in the Indians' favour.[62] It provided a platform for the policemen to present the legal basis for their complaint. And it gave the affair further publicity, rather than containing it within administrative bounds as Duranton had hoped.

Early in the proceedings, the metropolitan lawyer hired to advise the Indian policemen spoke forcefully in their defence. 'French citizens', he declared, 'cannot be divided into two categories.' Joyeux, a dissenting member of the Commission, was another articulate defender of the Indians' cause. He questioned the legality not only of Saint Louis' demotion, but of the decree itself (January 1907) which sparked the affair by creating a 'special superior cadre'. All Municipal decrees required

---

59. ANOM FM Indo NF 221/1774 La création du cadre spéciale supérieur par le Maire de Saigon M. Duranton, pour les Français d'origine indienne 1907: Relevé des notes obtenues par les agents de cadre spéciale supérieur de la Police Municipale pendant l'année 1907.
60. ANOM GGI 17248 Au sujet des agents de police indiens citoyens français de la ville de Saigon, 1910: President Municipal Commission to GCCH, 10 November 1907.
61. VNA2 Goucoch 1A.17/092 (12) Au sujet du brigadier Saint Louis 1907: Verbal Record [procès-verbale], 2 August 1907.
62. Ibid.: Note 'Administrator fulfilling the function of joint inspector' to GCCH, 24 September 1907.

approval by the Governor of the colony and this had not taken place. He also spoke out against the Municipal Commission's disregard for the Indians' French citizenship:

> [The Indian policemen] have been called to cast their vote in the ballot box, and to participate in the public life of the country, and they find themselves suddenly relegated to a special category. We say to them: 'You are Indians and you will remain Indian, that is to say in an absolutely inferior class; you will not be allowed to take our superior positions.' And they are to accept this without uttering a word?[63]

For their part, hostile members of the Commission continued to be disturbed that the affair had reached beyond the confines of the administration. They drilled Saint Louis with questions. Had he addressed himself to newspapers, local societies, or the League of Human Rights? Had he written to friends or colleagues in France about the matter? All of these charges he denied. Their lines of inquiry prompted dissenter Joyeux to accuse his colleagues of colonial provincialism, and to suggest – returning to a familiar theme – that their intellectual and moral fitness had degenerated from too long a stay in the colony.[64]

Despite the spirited defence of his case, Saint Louis' demotion was approved by the Commission by a majority of five votes to three. These votes reveal Vietnamese participation in the inquiry in an interesting way. Two of the five votes against Saint Louis were cast by Vietnamese members of the Municipal Council. One of them was none other than Huỳnh Tịnh (Paulus) Của, among the best-known Francophile Vietnamese intellectuals of the time; neither he nor his Vietnamese colleague was a French citizen. This prompted the 'Indian colony', in a memorandum sent to the Minister of Colonies following the vote, to complain that as 'mere French subjects' the Vietnamese councillors were 'not competent to understand questions involving the civic rights of a certain category of citizens'.[65] There is no record of any Vietnamese response to this challenge. Paulus Của is known though to have agreed with the stance of Pétrus Ky, another noted Francophile intellectual,

---

63. Ibid.: Verbal Record [*procès-verbale*], 2 August 1907.
64. Ibid.
65. ANOM GGI 17248 Au sujet des agents de police indiens citoyens français de la ville de Saigon, 1910: Pamphlet, 'La Question des Agents de Police', p. 5.

against taking French citizenship: 'Remain Annamites since we are born Annamites; I do not see any utility in being naturalised.'[66]

The vote against Saint Louis only made the 'Indian colony' of Saigon more unified in their outrage, and more vocal. A weighty pamphlet by the 'renounced Indians of Saigon' was published some days after the Saint Louis decision. It was sent to the incoming Lieutenant Governor of Cochinchina, Louis-Alphonse Bonhoure, to inform him of the situation, and was distributed publicly. The pamphlet included an 'exposé of the facts' to date, and cuttings from the local French press on the affair. Indian French citizens of high standing in both Saigon and Pondicherry lent their support. Just days after the Municipal Commission's ruling, Ra. Soccalingam, the banker and president of the Syndicate of the Frenchmen of India (*Syndicat des Français de l'Inde*), wrote to the Lieutenant Governor asking him to re-examine Saint Louis' case and the offending decree, and to 'join his efforts with those of the Deputy of the colony, Deloncle, to protect [Indian French citizens'] rights'. By September, Louis Rassendren was writing letters as the representative of the 'renouncers of Pondicherry' to protest to the Minister of Colonies and to the Indian Deputy and Senators in Paris.[67]

This persistent campaign prompted the Minister of Colonies to seek judgement from the Colonial Administrative Tribunal in Paris (*Comité Consultatif des Contentieux*). In March 1908, the Tribunal ruled in the Indians' favour, stating unequivocally that 'the Indian renouncer acquires *ipso facto* by the fact of his renunciation' the 'quality of French citizen'. This status was not fixed to locality. A renouncer could exercise these rights:

> wherever he wishes, as shown notably [with regard to their electoral rights] for the Indian renouncers established in Cochinchina ... as a consequence the Indian renouncers, French citizens, have the same access to posts, the same administrative aptitudes as those of French origin, and have the right to be subject ... to the same regulations.

---

66. Osborne, *French Presence*, p. 128.
67. Rassendren assumed the role of leader of the renunciation movement in Pondicherry following the death of Laporte. References in this paragraph: VNA2 Goucoch 1A.17/092 (12): President Syndicate Frenchmen of India to GCCH, 7 August 1907; ANOM GGI 17248 Au sujet des agents de police indiens citoyens français de la ville de Saigon, 1910: Pamphlet 'Ce qui se passe au Colonies'; ANOM FM Indo NF 221/1774 La création du cadre spéciale supérieur par le Maire de Saigon M. Duranton, pour les Français d'origine indienne 1907.

The ruling reached to the root of the renouncers' difficulties with regard to their civil and political rights in Cochinchina. While the Metropole had the power to change the terms of the law, it stated, local governments did not:

> Acts emanating from metropolitan agencies invested with legislative powers in colonial matters … can alter the principle of civil and political equality granted to Indian renouncers by the legal prescriptions of the decree of 21 September 1881. By contrast, decisions emanating from local authorities cannot call these [legislative] decisions into question at the risk of violating the law.[68]

Just over a week later, the Governor General in Hanoi received a telegram which informed him of the ruling and instructed him to revoke the 'superior special cadre' instituted by Duranton for Saigon's policemen. The caution the Governor General deployed indicates just how heated and politically fractious the issue had become. He did not immediately annul the offending cadre; rather, he asked the Lieutenant Governor of the Colony (now Ernest Outrey) for his views as to 'how this measure might be applied without provoking protests, and with as much consideration as possible for the position of Duranton'. In the meantime, the Minister of Colonies fed suggestions to Duranton to help him to cope with his 'Indian police force' now the law insisted they must be 'treated on the same equal footing as their European colleagues'. 'If the service of the Indian agents does not satisfy him, he should not recruit them in future or should not give promotions to those who are not as yet in the upper ranks and who do not appear to him to be capable of reaching them.' Not long before the new decision was finally enforced, the 'Indian Colony' sent an urgent plea to the Governor General. The Minister's order to abolish the 'superior special cadre' had arrived in Saigon four months earlier; the delay in carrying out the order was 'provoking great emotion' among them. Finally, Duranton's offending decision was replaced. The new one eliminated the 'special superior cadre' and placed Indian policemen within the ranks of European personnel.[69]

---

68. References and quotes in this paragraph: ANOM GGI 17248 Au sujet des agents de police indiens citoyens français de la ville de Saigon, 1910: Pamphlet, 'La Question des Agents de Police' (Minister of Colonies to Senator India, 29 April 1908; 'Avis. MMC to *Comité Consultatif des Contentieux*, 30 March 1908').

69. ANOM GGI 17248 Au sujet des agents de police indiens citoyens français de la ville de Saigon, 1910: Colonial Administrative Tribunal to GGI, 9 April 1908; and in the same

This was an important legal victory for the renouncers in Cochinchina. It recognised that their civil and political rights were applicable throughout the French Empire, and could be altered through legislation in France but not by colonial authorities. Despite this victory, the Minister of Colonies' passing advice to Duranton – to avoid hiring or promoting Indians if he judged their capacity to be lacking – was taken up by French administrators wishing to suppress the role of Indian French citizens in Cochinchina, as a primary means to circumvent the legal obstacles placed in their way.

THE PERSISTENCE OF INDIANS AS 'NATIVE CADRES'

Disputes between Indian employees and their superiors did not grind to a halt in the years that followed, but the nature of Indian exclusion changed. There was a rise post-World War One in the number of Indians employed in some middle-level positions in the administration, particularly the judicial service. Yet in the more problematic lower-level 'European' ranks, Cochinchina's local administration deliberately refrained from hiring Indians or promoting those already employed there. These were clearly efforts to side-step metropolitan orders to comply with the Republic's rule of law, and indicate that the struggle between metropolitan principles and colonial pragmatics by no means abated with the new emphasis on the law.[70] Local authorities never fully accepted that the less educated of their Indian employees had the right to European terms and privileges, and they continued to employ, or even downgrade, certain Indian agents to 'native' contractual terms. By the 1920s, however, the wider context had vastly changed. Vietnamese reformers had begun to demand that 'European' classes of employment be open to Vietnamese employees. Shortly thereafter, the economic crisis eliminated many jobs altogether, and pushed the principled question of Indian functionaries' citizenship far to one side. Their priorities changed from defending their legal rights and privileges to the much more fundamental question of staying in work and putting food on the table.

---

file, Telegram GGI to GCCH, 9 April 1908; Minister of Colonies to GGI, 28 April 1908; Telegram Indian Colony to GGI, 20 July 1908.

70. For Governor General Klubowski's attempts to keep Indians out of the Cochinchinese administration circa 1910, see ANOM GGI 17248 Au sujet des agents de police indiens citoyens français de la ville de Saigon, 1910: 'Indian Colony' to GGI, 30 September 1910; Telegram MMC to GGI, 25 October 1910; Telegram GGI to MMC 26 October 1910; Telegram GGI to Lt GCCH 24 October 1910; and Telegram Lt GCCH to GGI 25 October 1910.

An Indian petition issued at the end of the First World War brought to light the administrative practices both of side-stepping and flouting the law to exclude Indian employees. By now Ernest Outrey had been elected Cochinchina's Deputy, and he read the Indians' statement before the Chamber in Paris:

> [As Indian French citizens] we come up incessantly against the indifference and occasional bad faith of many representatives of authority. These sentiments are expressed as a systematic rejection of the majority of our requests for work in the public administration of the colony and hurtful allusions to our origin.[71]

Lending his support, Outrey remarked to Governor General Albert Sarraut:

> Numerous Frenchmen of India have for some time been excluded from public positions and many of them are only admitted to serve on Asian terms, even though they are French citizens...they protest against this exclusion and demand to be treated on the same footing as other French citizens resident in Indochina.[72]

In his response, Sarraut boldly sanctioned the idea that Indian French citizens were not to be treated as full citizens unless they could display outward signs of French cultural assimilation. Sarraut's proposals amount to a fascinating attempt to apply new criteria for citizenship to the Indian renouncers, in keeping with Cochinchina's regime of naturalisation rather than Pondicherry's process of renunciation, even though the Indians were already French citizens. He maintained that differing levels of education (and by implication, manners and behaviour) were acceptable criteria for determining contractual arrangements for Indians employed in the administration. Pointing to the example of two Indian clerks who had recently been hired on 'European' terms, with benefits 'in perfect equality' with those of other French citizens, he insisted that those Indian French citizens who were 'in the educated classes, and of course with the same qualification, diploma, or knowledge' as French from the Metropole 'always benefited in Indochina from a treatment based on principles of the strictest equality' with their European peers. The exclusion of Indians not possessed of 'a sufficiently high level of culture or professional instruction' was justified in his

---

71. ANOM FM Indo NF 329 La situation des travailleurs Indous en Indochine 1919: Chamber of Deputies Parliamentary report 3rd session, 27 March 1919.
72. VNA1 C.01/443 Recrutement des citoyens français originaires de l'Inde résidant en Indochine 1919.

view. He admitted that some Indians were employed as Asian cadres, but this was because they were 'agents almost completely illiterate and who, despite their quality of French citizen, cannot for reasons of their insufficiency be admitted to serve on the same level as European agents'. Moreover, most were aware of and accepted this situation. He cited the example of Mr. Gnanadican, employed in Annam on the railways on 'Asian terms'. Described as 'illiterate' and 'incapable', although honest, 'Mr. Gnanadican appears to be happy with his present situation and does not aspire to an equality of treatment that he knows he does not merit.'[73]

Indian employees whose superiors did not deem them sufficiently cultivated or educated were kept within the lower 'European' cadres, or moved, if the opportunity arose, out of those ranks altogether. In 1923 Deputy Outrey brought a complaint before the Minister of Colonies on behalf of Saigon's older Indian policemen (in the lowest 'European' ranks of the service) who were being bypassed for promotion by younger European employees. In the same period, Indian interpreters in the judicial service, although all renounced, were still being hired as native cadres. Five Indian renouncers serving as ticket inspectors for the railways and originally hired on European terms, were downgraded in 1924 to native salaries, although they continued to have leave entitlements 'on European terms'. Another problem revealed at this time was the practice of keeping Indian employees in temporary employment for long periods of time. When lighthouse keeper Mr. L. died in 1929 at his post at Can Gioc, he had served thirty consecutive years (since 1899) at the same lighthouse as a day-labourer (*à titre journalier*). Although the terms of his hire were ostensibly 'European' he had served the full thirty years without paid leave or pension.[74]

The Cochinchinese administration continued to disregard the citizenship rights of its lower-ranking French Indian employees, but after the turn of the twentieth century renouncers employed in higher

---

73. ANOM FM Indo NF 329 La situation des travailleurs Indous en Indochine 1919: GGI to Minister Colonies, 7 September 1919.
74. ANOM FM Indo NF 158 Rapport du Gouverneur Général de l'Indochine au ministre des colonies sur le statut personnel accordé aux diverses catégories d'étrangers en Indochine 1908: Deputy Outrey to MMC, 18 October 1923; 'Les interventions de M. Ernest Outrey', *Réveil Saigonnais*, 5 May 1924; 'Une injustice à réparer', *Réveil Saigonnais*, 25 February 1924; 'Défendons les deshérités: De grâce qu'on régularise la situation des gardiens de phare', *Saigon-Dimanche*, 18 August 1929.

administrative classes registered no complaints about their own contractual terms. Better-educated Indian cadres, in better positions, remained relatively secure in their employment. They would undoubtedly have been fully aware of the tribunal decision of 1908 re-affirming their citizenship rights, and possibly felt that the legal ruling gave them more security. There were no further campaigns to match the scale of the one mounted in defence of Saigon's Indian policemen in 1907–1908, or to reflect the level of solidarity of its supporting 'Indian colony'. This is not to say that there was no further outcry. Rather, protest in the 1920s and 1930s consisted of short press campaigns run by the Franco-Tamil newspapers. Articles denouncing the poor treatment of Indian *petit fonctionnaires* in the Cochinchinese service arose invariably around the time of elections. They were frequently linked to the 'Interventions of Ernest Outrey', a heading which one paper used regularly for articles of this nature. Yet little if any substantial progress appears to have been made through these campaigns. If anything the condition of Indian employees worsened, providing support for the growing opinion among Indian voters that their Deputy's motives were purely self-serving.

Articles published in the Franco-Tamil press in the 1920s and early 1930s in support of Cochinchina's Indian *petit fonctionnaires* demonstrate how debates over Indian contractual terms in this period were less about citizenship rights and more about survival in the face of growing Vietnamese discontent and deepening economic crisis. While the policeman campaigning in 1907–1908 were opposed to the categories of 'Indian cadre' and 'special cadre', the lowest-ranking of Indian functionaries now found refuge in such classifications.

A key part of Governor General Varenne's administrative reform from 1925 was to admit more Vietnamese into the public service, beginning with the lowest 'European' ranks of the administration. It included, too, the tidying up of those 'native' ranks in which Indians had been habitually employed. It is seldom noted though that Indians and other Frenchmen of colonial origin felt the greatest impact of these reforms.[75] Indian postmen were particularly affected. They had not been completely satisfied when in 1917 a 'special cadre' was established in Cochinchina for them expressly; much like the Indian policemen's

---

75. See L. Pargloire, 'Les cadres subalternes de fonctionnaires français', *Saigon-Dimanche*, 9 December, 1934.

'special superior cadre' a decade earlier, it created a category of Indian French citizens separate from the ranks of proper 'European' employees. Within the sweep of Varenne's reforms, however, the 'special cadre' of Indian postmen was 'to be dissolved through a process of extinction', as a bureaucrat elegantly put it. The administration stopped hiring Indian postmen, and the eleven Indians already employed within the cadre were to stay there until they retired or died; all were already deemed too old to be promoted to higher 'European' positions.[76]

Following the announced 'extinction' of their cadre, both the *Saigon-Dimanche* and the *Réveil Saigonnais* ran articles supporting the Indian postmen. Under headlines such as 'Why letters get lost in the post in Saigon', these articles compared unreliable Vietnamese postmen of questionable morals to Indians dedicated to the service and to France. The *Réveil Saigonnais* questioned in an earlier article why Indians who were recognised as French citizens were not always hired as French cadres in Cochinchina after all the years of struggle. But soon both Franco-Tamil newspapers recognised that a more practical strategy in the face of government determination to increase indigenous Cochinchinese employment was to defend those jobs reserved exclusively for Indians.[77] Cochinchina's French administration eventually declared, in December of 1928, that the cadre of Indian postmen would be re-established, as a '*Hindou* cadre'. The relevant decision declared that salaries were to be paid in Indochinese piastres and leave payments disbursed in rupees.[78] To the Franco-Tamil press, it was a triumph. Renouncers in Cochinchina had long defended their equality before the law with metropolitan French citizens. Yet neither newspaper commented on the fact that now, in 1928, they were commending the formation of exclusive categories for Indian functionaries, and seeking to protect them as closed shops which hired Indians exclusively. It was even a triumph in comparison to

---

76. 'La question des facteurs indiens', *Réveil Saigonnais*, 12 August 1925. This pre-dates by some months the actual arrival in Indochina of Governor General Varenne, although he would have just assumed the post in Paris by this date.
77. 'Défendons nos facteurs. Les facteurs indiens rendent de réels services à l'Administration', *Réveil Saigonnais*, 23 May 1928; 'Comment les lettres se perdent à Saigon', *Saigon-Dimanche*, 8 July 1928.
78. 'Le statut des facteurs hindous', *Saigon-Dimanche*, 16 December 1928; See also 'Le cadre des collecteurs de marchés', *Réveil Saigonnais*, 24 August 1925. The new '*Hindou cadre*' for postmen was never established in the end, to renoucer dismay. See 'Va-t-on renvoyer des facteurs français de l'Inde?', *Saigon-Dimanche*, 16 April 1932.

the situation four years later. One of the administration's first responses to the economic crisis was to now reduce, rather than reform, the lowest administrative ranks, and Indians in the postal service were among the first employees to be laid off.[79]

Conclusion

These debates show that Indians in the administration were not mere servants of French interests during their sojourn in Indochina. They also put pressure to bear on 'Greater France' to serve them as its citizens. Through these debates, Indians with French citizenship played a role in determining where the lines demarcating the 'boundaries of rule' were to be drawn. France's extension of citizenship to certain colonised people meant the law could determine who was entitled to European privileges and who was not. But this chapter has shown that although the law could establish these boundaries in principle, racial justifications could shift the boundaries in practice, and the law could never quite provide the 'last word' on the colonial citizens' status. Indian renouncers relied on French law to secure their claims as citizens. While they achieved remarkable success, local level authorities nonetheless managed to undermine some of the Indians' rights as citizen-employees using reasoning drawn from race and climate 'science'.

Elite renouncers were generally successful in securing the benefits which they claimed were their due as French citizens, while renouncers at the lower end of the social scale, and with positions of lower status, were less fortunate. Their cases together show the 'boundaries of rule' from another angle. They were not firmly plotted, but were drawn and redrawn, by French rulers but also by colonial citizens and indigenous subjects as conditions changed. Indian French citizens' own idea of their place in the Cochinchinese social order shifted. It is symptomatic of the ways in which the political landscape had changed that the disadvantaged class of renouncers could by the 1920s embrace contractual arrangements which they had vehemently rejected twenty years' earlier.

Local French administrators habitually referred to the risk of offending the *Annamites* as cause to deny contractual privileges to the Indians.

---

79. 'Va-t-on renvoyer des facteurs français de l'Inde?', *Saigon-Dimanche*, 16 April 1932; 'Et voici maintenant celui du licenciement de plusieurs facteurs des P.T.T. Français de l'Inde.' *Saigon-Dimanche*, 4 June 1932.

Yet we do not know what the local population of Saigon made of the renouncers' many conspicuous displays of their privilege in the period up until the 1900s. Unfortunately, there are no first-hand Vietnamese analyses of the Indians' curt dismissal of distinguished scholar Paulus Của as a mere French subject unfit to pass judgement on Indian French citizens such as themselves. Nor, for that matter, are there any Vietnamese accounts of the spectacle of Saigon's Indian renouncers shouting victoriously from their 'Malabar' carriages following the legislative election of 1888. By no means can we conclude from this, however, that there was no Vietnamese reaction. Vietnamese responses to the privileges of Indian French citizens in Cochinchina only emerged in a public and organised way in the context of calls for constitutional reform post-World War One. This occurred several decades after the Indian renouncers had so intensely debated and finally secured their own electoral representation and citizenship rights on Cochinchinese soil.

CHAPTER SIX

VIETNAMESE ENGAGEMENT WITH INDIAN MIGRANTS

Although Indian renouncers resident in Cochinchina very publicly asserted their rights as French citizens, it was not until the mid-1900s that first-hand Vietnamese accounts of the Indian presence began to appear. Vietnamese comment did not consist solely of criticism of the renouncer presence, by any means, even though by the 1920s such critiques came to hold a firm place in the catalogue of Vietnamese reactions. Vietnamese attacked with equal vigour the wealth acquired by overseas Indian traders and landowners, the Chettiar hold on the money market, and the relationships formed between some Indian men and local women. These latter relations, and more novel kinship ties such as dubious recognitions of paternity, produced particularly strong (and racially charged) reactions. Strong anti-Indian reactions at the prospect of kinship, however, did not prevent mixed unions from being formed, nor did they prevent both Vietnamese and resident Indians from sharing harmoniously in some of their religious and popular beliefs.

Vietnamese responses to the Indian presence in Indochina include both intellectual critiques of the Indian presence and grassroots reactions based on ground-level encounters. Understanding them necessitates casting a wide net, examining Vietnamese reactions both to the Indian renouncers and to the wider overseas Indian presence. Some renouncers were among those engaged in the activities under attack. Even when they weren't, Vietnamese responses to these activities, particularly by the late 1920s, came to colour the ways in which all Indians, including renouncers, were viewed.

The Vietnamese comment on Indian migrants appeared with the emergence in the south of the very first French-educated 'modernist intellectuals' who began to challenge the colonial order and garner support for their causes through the press. Once they had established channels to communicate their messages publicly, this southern non-communist elite made regular comment on the Indian presence in Cochinchina. These criticisms reflect southern intellectuals' distinct agendas for reform; the critiques are as notable for what they choose to ignore at any given time as for what they seize upon and attack. The reactions of the earliest commentators (1900s) stand out as much for their attack on Indian economic dominance as they do for their complete lack of interest in renouncer efforts to secure contractual privileges in the Cochinchinese administration, even though those debates were at their height at the time. Similarly, while the exercise of renounced Indians' citizenship rights on Vietnamese soil was used by Vietnamese reformers post-World War One as solid proof of the need for constitutional reforms in Cochinchina, neither the Constitutionalists of this period, nor the earlier reformers, showed much concern for the power wielded by Indian moneylenders. This runs counter to the popular notion that resentment of the Chettiars was an ongoing phenomenon not tied to any specific period, and was virtually the only Vietnamese reaction to the Indian presence.

Incidents in the 1920s and 1930s, in which some Vietnamese physically attacked Indian interests in Cochinchina (and also in Annam), reflected the spilling over of pre-existing ground-level tensions between Indian shopkeepers, tax farmers, and petty traders, and the local people with whom they regularly came into contact. This went hand in hand with the rise of a broader-based, more radical, and more violent form of anti-colonialism. The Vietnamese outcry over Chettiar loan foreclosure during the economic crisis of the late 1920s only added through the 1930s to growing anti-Indian antagonism. Very few renouncers, if any, directly incurred mob violence and few were practising moneylenders, but the racial nature of the attacks meant renounced Indians were increasingly included, in Vietnamese perceptions, in a single problematic overseas Indian community.

The complaints that Vietnamese journalist-reformers regularly published about the power and privileges of Indian intermediaries in Indochina, as well as the grassroots relationships between the local peoples of Cochinchina and overseas Indians, are all virtually unknown in historical analyses, and shed new light on the colonial history of southern Vietnam. Indian migrants added to the complexity of local people's ground-level experiences of colonialism, and 'Indian questions' formed an integral part of demands for reform by members of the southern intellectual elite in the early twentieth century.

'Native' constructions of racial hierarchy

While colonial citizenship was one defining characteristic of the French Empire, another closely connected feature was its reputation for producing non-racial, colour-blind colonial societies.[1] On the face of it, Indian French citizens' successful appeals to the force of law to defend social and political equality free of race support the claim of a colour-blind French Empire. Yet as the previous two chapters have demonstrated, racial thinking was embedded in local-level officials' questioning of French Indian status in Cochinchina in the first place. French Indians were arriving in Cochinchina at a time when the developing colonial society there was being shaped in a more racialised way than older parts of the French Empire. This new colonial order was shaped by measures such as naturalisation decrees which placed controls on the process of 'native' assimilation, and regulations aimed at restricting intimate relationships between Europeans and local people. The new order conflicted with republican principles dictating that citizenship was a political right founded in law and not one flowing from race. Metropolitan authorities continued, from a distance, to hold to republican principles and the rule of law, but Cochinchinese authorities readily employed racial reasoning and attendant theories of acclimatisation to justify why Europeans required special treatment. They worked racialised thinking into local-level regulations in order to override instructions from the centre, feeling they better understood the realities of colonial life and its unwritten racial 'laws'.

Although they were able to secure their rights to citizenship in Cochinchina, and enjoy its advantages there, expatriate Indians did not entirely overturn a social structure that otherwise became based on the notion of a racial hierarchy dominated by Europeans. They did, however, disrupt this new 'ideal' and contribute to a more complex, if embattled, social reality. The presence in Indochina of colonised people with French citizenship created a social structure which was partially,

---

1. Sue Peabody and Tyler Stovall, 'Introduction: Race, France, Histories', in Sue Peabody and Tyler Stovall, (eds), *The Color of Liberty: Histories of Race in France*, Durham and London: Duke University Press, 2003, p. 1.

but not entirely, racially-based. It reflected simultaneously a racial order and a legal order; but it reflected too the yawning gap within the legal order between the citizens' rights so freely available to Indians from the French possessions, and the lack of rights for the vast majority of Indochinese.

A Vietnamese academic recalled the complex social hierarchy governing the cities of Vietnamese Indochina when he was growing up in Hanoi in the 1930s and 1940s. The structure he described placed the metropolitan French firmly at the top. Other French citizens, including the Indian renouncers, came directly below, followed by Europeans of non-French origin. The Vietnamese educated elite followed on, then Chinese and Indian merchants and traders. Finally, ranked at the lowest point were, in his description, the 'normal' Vietnamese.[2] In this schema, the educated Vietnamese elite could not advance in their own country above another colonised people (the Indian French citizens), much less the metropolitan French.

If French colonial society was not as colour-blind as it is made out to be, nor was racial thinking the sole preserve of Europeans. When squeezed by budget constraints, or worried about how the *Annamites* might react to Indian privileges, the French authorities in Cochinchina could construct complex arguments over degrees of French versus Indian 'racial' adaption to the Cochinchinese climate and their consequences for pay levels and home leave entitlements. Yet Chapter Five has showed how Indian French citizens engaged just as actively in these debates and bought into ways of thinking along racial lines, even if only to claim a better place for themselves within a racially constructed society. Distinctive Vietnamese views existed too, about a rightful social order and the role of race in shaping it. A racialised Vietnamese version of the social order placed the 'black' Tamils firmly beneath the Vietnamese. This way of thinking is evident in racially charged conflicts between the common Vietnamese man (and often woman) and migrants Indians. Vietnamese commentators who expressed their opposition to the Indian presence in racial terms seemed to resent colonial interference in a purer and more proper racial order. Relationships were nonetheless forged between Vietnamese women and Indian men, but they were often harshly condemned in Vietnamese sources.

---

2. Conversation with Dr. Nguyễn Đức Nhuận, Paris, May 2004.

Although racially-based prejudice existed, it was not a constant source of tension in relations between Vietnamese and Indians in Cochinchina. Indeed much of the present chapter concerns economic and political tensions rather than racial ones. The point rather is that engagements between Vietnamese and Indians (as between Indians and French colonial authorities) took place in a society which had become increasingly racialised. There were specific times and places where Vietnamese deployed racial reasoning to portray the Indian presence as unjust or unwanted. Vietnamese reformist elites in the south in the 1920s were not completely free of racial reactions to local Indians, but their criticisms adopted racial overtones most markedly when they sought a broader base of support. Racially charged responses to Indians were at their height during the economic crisis of the 1930s. And as Chapter Eight will later show, the same feelings had apparently disappeared entirely among the Viet Minh in the late 1940s, as they aimed (with limited success) to fashion Indochina's resident Indians as global partners in their nationalist struggle.

Gilbert Chiếu : 'Hit the *Chệc* and expel the *Chà*!'

The *Minh Tân* ('New Light') was the first of three reform-minded, non-communist movements implanted in the south prior to the emergence of the Communist party as the dominant political force in the 1930s. Its founder and leader, Gilbert Trần Chánh Chiếu, was typical of the strong personalities who headed these movements, and served as journalists and editors as well as political leaders.

The *Minh Tân* movement emerged in early twentieth-century Cochinchina, in the account of southern scholar Sơn Nam, with the rise of a new class of landowner which thrived under Governor General Paul Doumer's policies of expansion in the Mekong Delta. These landowners acquired generous land concessions which they worked through tenant farmers, and found capital readily available through the Chettiars or the French banks. They were hostile to the advantages and protection given to Chinese and Indian traders by the colonial regime, but were themselves reliant on colonial power to manage their tenants. They thus sought through constitutional means to reform the situation and to undermine the foreign monopoly by building up a force to compete with them.[3]

---

3. Sơn Nam, *Đất Gia Định - Bến Nghé Xưa và Người Sài Gòn* [Gia Định Soil; Old Bến Nghé; People of Saigon], Ho Chi Minh City: Nhà Xuất Bản Trẻ, 2004, pp. 392–393.

Gilbert Trần Chánh Chiếu was a wealthy Rạch Giá landowner, a teacher and interpreter within the French administration, and one of the few Vietnamese of his time to be granted French citizenship. He formed the *Minh Tân* movement after meeting the *Duy Tân* leader Phan Bội Châu in the course of the latter's trip to gather support in the south. Inspired by the *Duy Tân* movement's goal of establishing a constitutional monarchy with Japanese support, Chiếu set up *Minh Tân* as a clandestine southern branch. The *Minh Tân* movement provided financial support for southern youths to study in Japan, but hid this secretive political activity behind a public programme of modernisation disseminated through Gilbert Chiếu's journalism. In 1906 Chiếu acquired editorial control of the newspaper *Nông Cổ Mín Đàm* (Discussions on Commerce and Agriculture), which ran under his editorship until 1907. He founded another, *Lục Tỉnh Tân Văn* (News of the Six Provinces), in late 1907, which he edited until November 1908. The medium of publication for both newspapers was *quốc ngữ*, the romanised Vietnamese script which was just beginning to come into wider use.

Both of Gilbert Chiếu's newspapers extolled modernist agendas. Their readerships were made up primarily of the new rising class of landowners and businessmen, who were exhorted to be progressive in their thinking and actions. Both newspapers urged compatriots 'to reproach themselves and to reject behaviours and manners not fitting with the times'.[4] In business dealings, they were called on to be patriotic, and to oppose Chinese and Indian economic domination. The newspapers published slogans encouraging readers to seize power from the overseas migrants, and laid out detailed plans to mount enterprises which could contribute to the cause. The *Minh Tân* established a hotel which, while it competed with Chinese business, also served as the headquarters of the movement and as a meeting place for supporters when stopping in Saigon. Another *Minh Tân*-run hotel doubled as the editorial office of the *Lục Tỉnh Tân Văn*, and a third operated as a secret meeting place for collecting funds. A soap factory in Mỹ Tho was set up as a model of a Vietnamese joint-stock enterprise. The movement's activities were vibrant, but they were brought to an abrupt halt in 1908, when the

---

4. Sơn Nam, *Phong Trào Duy Tân ở Bắc Trung Nam, Miền Nam Đầu Thế Kỷ XX - Thiên Địa Hội và Cuộc Minh Tân* [The Duy Tân movement in the North, Centre and South and The South in the Twentieth Century; The Heaven and Earth Society and The Minh Tân Organisation], Ho Chi Minh City: Nhà Xuất Bản Trẻ, 2003, p. 39.

anti-government activities of the movement were exposed and Gilbert Chiếu was arrested.[5]

Pierre Brocheux maintains that Gilbert Chiếu and the *Minh Tân* movement have been relegated to the periphery by Vietnamese nationalist historians.[6] The fact that issues of neither *Lục Tỉnh Tân Văn* nor *Nông Cổ Mín Đàm* published during Gilbert Chiếu's editorship were to be found in Vietnam or France during the time of my research lends support to this view. I rely here on articles reprinted by Sơn Nam from *Lục Tỉnh Tân Văn*, and found in his studies of the *Duy Tân* and *Minh Tân* movements. I also make the assumption that his selection of articles is, as he claims, 'representative of all economic, cultural, and political topics at the time'. He identifies three types of articles: those consisting of general calls to support the *Minh Tân*, those criticising corrupted or outdated practices, and articles directly addressing domestic and world politics.[7]

For Gilbert Chiếu and advocates of his movement, Indian questions were more than an add-on to their attempts to break the Chinese monopoly. They were, in their own right, a source of contention and a subject of debate. Of the eighty-two articles and excerpts from *Lục Tỉnh Tân Văn* reprinted in Sơn Nam's two volumes, eight make reference to Indian economic dominance alongside that of the Chinese, and a further four directly address issues related to the activities of Indian businessmen in Cochinchina.

Indian migrants, frequently referred to as *Chà* or *Chà Và* in the newspaper's columns, were included in many of *Lục Tỉnh Tân Văn*'s slogans exhorting readers to seize power from the overseas Chinese: 'Send *Quan Công* to his country and Buddha back to India!', 'Hit the *Chệc* and expel the *Chà*!'[8] The meaning of the term *Chà Và*, employed in the nineteenth

---

5. This description is compiled from various sources including David Marr, *Vietnamese Anti-Colonialism, 1885–1925*, Berkeley: University of California, 1971, p. 144; Philippe M.F. Peycam, *The Birth of Vietnamese Political Journalism: Saigon, 1916–1930*, New York: Columbia University Press, 2012, pp. 55–58; Sơn Nam, *Phong Trào Duy Tân ở Bắc Trung Nam*, pp. 35–39, pp. 220–224; Sơn Nam, *Bến Nghé Xưa*, pp. 391–407; Ralph Smith, The Development of Opposition to French Rule in Southern Vietnam 1880–1940', *Past and Present*, 54, 1972, pp. 94–129, 102–104; Pierre Brocheux, 'Note Sur Gilbert Chiếu (1867–1919), Citoyen Français et Patriote Vietnamien', *Approches Asie*, 11, 1991, pp. 72–81.
6. Brocheux, 'Note Sur Gilbert Chiếu', p. 72.
7. Sơn Nam, *Cuộc Minh Tân*, pp. 225–226.
8. Slogans as quoted in Sơn Nam, *Bến Nghé Xưa*, p. 396. General Quan Công (Guan Yu) was a third century Chinese military hero, brought into the Taoist pantheon of tutelary gods. See

century to identify Javanese traders in southern Vietnam, was expanded with new migrant influxes under French rule to include not only Javanese but Malays, Bawean (from the island of Bawean, near Madura in Java), and Indian migrants.[9] As explained by a southern Vietnamese linguist, the perceived proximity in physical appearance of all of these groups led to the term being used more broadly.[10] The *Chệc* (or *Chệt*) was a racial slur ('Chink') applied to overseas Chinese.[11]

The *Chà* to whom the newspaper referred were the traders, shopkeepers, and tax farmers situated in the towns and along the waterways of the Mekong Delta. They would mainly have been South Indian Muslims. The use in the Vietnamese press of another term, *Bảy* (or *Bảy Chà*), to refer to the objects of their criticism also suggests that the main targets were Muslim. *Bảy*, literally the number 'seven' in Vietnamese, is still in occasional use by southern Vietnamese to refer to people of Indian origin, but its source remains obscure.[12] An explanation ventured by a Tamil-speaking Indo-Vietnamese was that *Bảy* derived from the Tamil *Bhai*, a polite addressive form used specifically for Muslims. It became corrupted and took on a derogatory tone in Vietnamese, while its meaning became broader, referring to any Indian migrant irrespective of his faith.[13]

There was some hostility present in the articles in *Lục Tỉnh Tân Văn* that addressed Indian economic dominance in Cochinchina. This was relatively restrained, however, in favour of reasoned analysis and studied descriptions of how the Chinese and Indians managed to secure their hold on the economy. More often than not, it was the Vietnamese who were rebuked for permitting the foreigners to make profits at their expense.

Some articles, in their criticism of Vietnamese attitudes, went so far as to express admiration for foreign businessmen. A piece of September 1908, signed by 'Cang', claimed the Vietnamese preference for doing

---

Philip Taylor, *Goddess on the Rise: Pilgrimage and Popular Religion in Vietnam*, Honolulu: University of *Hawai'i Press*, 2004, p. 3.

9. On Bawean in southern Vietnam see M. Stokhof, 'Javanese in Hồ Chí Minh City today'.
10. Interview with Dr. Lý Tùng Hiếu, Southern Institute of Social Sciences, Ho Chi Minh City, 2 March 2005.
11. Goscha, 'Widening the Colonial Encounter', p. 1203.
12. Interviews with linguist Dr. Lý Tùng Hiếu, HCMC, March 2005; historian Dr. Nguyễn Đình Đầu, HCMC, February 2005; Mr. Nguyễn Tạo Ngô, Hanoi, February 2005.
13. Discussions with Mr. Atmanadene Audemar, HCMC, March 2005.

business with the Chinese and Indians was understandable. These foreigners, the author argued, refrained from social snobbery, whereas their few Vietnamese competitors looked down arrogantly on their customers, especially those 'coming in from the paddy fields'. 'If you continue to make a lot of hoo-ha and the foreigners quietly make profits, whose fault is it?', the author asked.[14]

Nguyễn Thị Phải, writing from Thủ Dầu Một in January 1908, had harsher words for those Indians who collected market and ferry taxes. Phải, who claimed to be a female market vendor, described the way in which the Indian tax farmers demanded fees higher than the official ceiling set by French authorities. They then beat people who refused to pay, and paid off village officials to keep them quiet. Yet while she condemned Indians for these actions, she also judged the Vietnamese for their complicity: 'If we let the *Chà Và* get away with it, how shameful is that for the Vietnamese people?' This shame, Phải implied, was heightened because Vietnamese men were failing in their duty to prevent their own women from being abused by foreign men.[15]

Sơn Nam asserts that *Lục Tỉnh Tân Văn*'s attacks on the Chinese and the Indians were not racist.[16] For those articles that set themselves the task of understanding the workings of foreign Asian businesses in order to better compete with them, this is true. The absence of racial judgement about the Indian presence in Cochinchina in the majority of these articles underlines the fact that these are considered, intellectual responses to the foreign Asian presence in the colony. Some articles do demonstrate the existence of baser prejudices against Indians in Cochinchinese society; one example is examined in the last section of this chapter. However, these newspapers did not generally resort to such attacks themselves. One article which illustrates this, published near to the Lunar New Year of 1908, criticised the extravagant spending of employees of Chinese and Indian businesses, pointing out the huge economic gap between the foreign businessmen and local people. The author refers to an Indian as *Bảy Chà*, but then confirms that it is an insulting expression by remarking: 'If I called him that [to his face] I would

---

14. Cang, [no title given], *Lục Tỉnh Tân Văn* 44, September 1908, p. 6, [excerpted in Sơn Nam, *Miền Nam*, p. 265].
15. Nguyễn Thị Phải, [no title given], *LTTV* 11, January 1908, p. 6, [excerpted in Sơn Nam, *Miền Nam*, p. 248].
16. Sơn Nam, *Miền Nam*, p. 226.

be scared he would hit me so hard I'd see stars' (lit. 'see my mother', *kêu vậy sợ oật ní nẹ*).¹⁷

Gilbert Chiếu is credited with turning both *Nông Cổ Mín Đàm* and *Lục Tỉnh Tân Văn* into anti-colonial newspapers. Both lost their political edge when they came under the control of subsequent owners and editors, who were more moderate or more loyal to the French. Sơn Nam's account of Gilbert Chiếu's downfall suggests that Chiếu was betrayed by his supporters. Once French authorities arrested Chiếu, many of his former associates took cover under the claim that they were not anti-French or anti-government, but merely donating funds to support new enterprises.¹⁸

Once the anti-colonial movement behind the publication of *Lục Tỉnh Tân Văn* was curtailed, the newspaper's more anti-French views were reined in. This did not prevent the paper, however, from continuing to publish articles critical of the foreign Asian business presence in Cochinchina. This included the campaign in which the paper is known to have played a key role – the Chinese boycott of 1919. It is striking in the post-Gilbert Chiếu *Lục Tỉnh Tân Văn* that the paper not only continued to produce many articles which decried Indian (and Chinese) economic dominance, but also began to patently appeal to baser prejudices. Between 1910 and 1919, the newspaper regularly reported Indian migrants' involvement in both petty misdemeanour and serious crime. Although presented as straight news items, many of these reports employed derogatory terms for their subjects, and aimed to capitalise on popular sentiments. The distinctions made in these articles between Indians who were French or British, Tamil or *Bombay*, citizens or subjects, were minor. The overseas Indians were collectively *Chà*, and were equally uncivilised, lascivious, and dishonest, either robbing local people or being robbed themselves because of their excessive wealth.¹⁹

When Gilbert Chiếu criticised overseas Indian business, his critique included the modest number of Indian French citizens who were

---

17. I am grateful to Nguyễn Tạo Ngô for this translation. 'Ng. H. H.', [no title given], *LTTV* 14, February 1908, p. 9–10 [excerpted in Sơn Nam, *Miền Nam*, p. 254].
18. Sơn Nam, *Bến Nghé Xưa*, p. 401.
19. See for example, 'Chà-Và ăn cướp [*Chà Và* Robber]', *LTTV*, 6 November 1913; 'Bịnh Mao-Ếch [An Epidemic Disease]', *LTTV*, 13 November, 1913; Một Vụ ăn cướp To [A Big Robbery]', *LTTV*, 1 November 1917; 'Chà-và Làm Ngan [*Chà Và* Misdeeds]', *LTTV*, 25 August 1913.

engaged in such activities. He never attacked the privileges which renouncers enjoyed in Cochinchina because of their French citizenship. This is puzzling when we recall that Chiếu had been naturalised as a French citizen, and was himself a cadre in the colonial administration prior to the establishment of the *Minh Tân* movement. It is more of a mystery when we consider that the short period during which Gilbert Chiếu's newspapers conveyed their calls for reform began not long after renouncers had finally secured their voting rights in Cochinchina. Moreover, it coincided with the Indian policemen's affair, the battle renouncers fought over their citizenship rights in the colony which was the most publicised. Yet these events and their significance were apparently of no interest to the *Minh Tân* press. This indifference is consistent, however, with historians' observations that the Vietnamese did not necessarily consider French naturalisation to be a privilege worth seeking prior to World War One, and that before the rise of the Constitutionalist Party they showed a 'total lack of interest' in native representation.[20] Equally consistent, as the next section shows, is the strong reaction of the reform-minded southern elite to the presence and privileges of Indian French citizens in Cochinchina after the First World War. Gilbert Chiếu's other area of silence, the Chettiar presence, is a question explored later in this chapter.

THE CONSTITUTIONALISTS AND NGUYEN AN NINH: 'LA QUESTION INDIENNE'

It was not until the emergence of the Constitutionalist Party in Cochinchina that there was active Vietnamese criticism of the privileges of Indian French citizens resident in Cochinchina. The advocates and leaders of the Constitutionalist Party were businessmen, landlords, civil servants, and teachers of southern Vietnam who made up a newly-assertive, French-educated bourgeoisie. The newly acquired wealth of many within this group, and their western education, united them in the conviction that their increasingly powerful contribution to social and economic progress entitled them as a class to a leadership role.[21] Rather than national independence, they sought political reform. The main

---

20. On early Vietnamese attitudes towards naturalisation see Osborne, *French Presence*, pp. 126–129; On 'native' representation, Tai, 'The Politics of Compromise', p. 373.
21. Hue-Tam Ho Tai, *Radicalism and the Origins of the Vietnamese Revolution*, Cambridge, Mass.: Harvard University Press, 1992, pp. 40–41.

pillars of their programme were fourfold: the expansion of education; the modernisation of local government and the abolition of the remains of the mandarinal system; the creation of a truly representative council or parliament based on a wide indigenous electoral franchise; and the reform of the naturalisation decrees to enable the Vietnamese (at least those they deemed to be sufficiently well-educated and forward-thinking) to have a more easy access to French citizenship.[22]

The Constitutionalist Party emerged in the context of Governor General Albert Sarraut's policy of 'Franco-Vietnamese collaboration'. Goscha provides an intriguing and very relevant reading of Sarraut's policy in relation to state migration strategies within Indochinese borders. He examines contests over belonging between Indochina's main ethnic groups, contending that discontent originated in the ways the French drew boundaries and managed movement within the larger Union. The new boundaries drawn under French rule forced the Lao, Cambodian, and Vietnamese peoples to coexist within a shared colonial space. France purposefully neglected to reunite the three parts of the former ethnic Vietnamese territory, divided through France's piecemeal conquest beginning in Cochinchina. At the same time, and as part of the strategy of 'Franco-Vietnamese collaboration', French rule facilitated the movement of Vietnamese trade, labour, and administrative assistance into Laos and Cambodia. It denied the ethnic Vietnamese a unified colonial territory, while it created outlets for their 'vitality' and 'ambition' by nurturing longstanding Vietnamese expansionist urges westward. Goscha does not include Indian migrants in his analysis of the flows of different ethnic groups across Indochina's internal borders, but French Indians, particularly as employees of the colonial state, can fit neatly into this picture. In Cochinchina, in the capital of the Government General in Hanoi, and in other French-run cities where France used Indians to run the middle and lower levels of government, it denied Vietnamese a full role in public life, in much the same way as it used the Vietnamese in Laos and Cambodia.[23]

Albert Sarraut's encouragement, within the framework of 'Franco-Vietnamese collaboration', of westernised elite participation in the

---

22. See Smith 'Bui Quang Chieu and the Constitutionalist Party', p. 135; Ralph Smith, *Vietnam and the West*, Ithaca, New York: Cornell University Press, 1971, p. 93.
23. See Goscha, 'Widening the Colonial Encounter'; also Goscha, *Going Indochinese: Contesting Concepts of Space and Place in French Indochina*, Copenhagen: NIAS Press, 2012.

press and publishing has been read as a conscious political strategy of engendering public debate in order to suppress more radical nationalist reactions.[24] Newspapers associated with the Constitutionalists took advantage of relatively lenient censorship laws governing the French (as opposed to *quốc ngữ*) language press from the 1920s by publishing in French. At least at their inception, these papers enjoyed direct French state support. The *Tribune Indigène* (1917–1925) was subsidised by Sarraut, who also selected Bùi Quang Chiêu as its editor.[25] Chiêu continued as editor to the newspaper's successor, the *Tribune Indochinoise* (1926–1942). Although Chiêu's detractors derided his conservatism, his newspaper became sufficiently intimidating to the colonial regime that in 1919 Cochinchina's Governor Georges Maspéro, less liberal than Sarraut, attempted to dilute the threat by supporting the establishment of a second 'moderate' newspaper. This was the *Echo Annamite*, with Nguyễn Phan Long appointed as its director. Although it began with a similar conservative political stance, the *Echo Annamite* nonetheless quickly became more critical than the *Tribune Indigène*.[26]

Bùi Quang Chiêu (1873–1945) was the effective leader of the Constitutionalist movement. A French citizen, he was educated at the *École Coloniale* in Paris in the late 1890s and entered the colonial bureaucracy upon his return. He was also one of the most prominent landowners in Cantho.[27] Nguyễn Phan Long was an employee of the customs service, who had occasionally written articles for the *Tribune Indigène*.[28]

Although Constitutionalist politics have been much analysed, nowhere has it been remarked how the Constitutionalists' class aspirations, their interest in reform within the French system, and their demands for native political representation were conveyed in part through criticism of the privileges of the Indian French citizens in Cochinchina. Moreover, although the Constitutionalists eventually disassociated themselves from more extremist views such as those put forward by Nguyễn An Ninh, his newspaper *La Cloche Fêlée* [The Cracked Bell] published ar-

---

24. Peycam, *The Birth of Vietnamese Political Journalism*, pp. 40–43.
25. Tai, 'The Politics of Compromise', pp. 379–380.
26. Tai, *Radicalism*, p. 45.
27. Smith 'Bui Quang Chieu and the Constitutionalist Party', p. 133.
28. Tai, *Radicalism*, p. 45.

ticles on the topic of renouncer involvement in Cochinchinese politics which closely echoed the objections of the Constitutionalists.

Articles questioning the political powers and legal privileges Indian French citizens enjoyed in Cochinchina began to appear intermittently in the *Tribune Indigène* following Governor General Maurice Long's 1922 reorganisation of the Colonial Council. This reorganisation responded in part to Constitutionalists' demands for better 'native' representation. Through these reforms, the number of Vietnamese representatives on the Colonial Council was increased to ten, and the Vietnamese electorate was expanded from 1,500 to 20,000. As Ralph Smith has commented, these numbers were still small compared to the total population of three million Vietnamese in Cochinchina at the time.[29] However, a remaining and just as pressing concern for the Vietnamese elite was the power of French citizens of Indian origin to decide the outcome of legislative and Colonial Council elections in the colony.

The undue influence of Indian renouncers on the political destiny of the colony was the main theme of an article entitled 'La question indienne', which appeared in the *Tribune Indigène* in December of 1922. The problem was expressed as the 'relative numeric weakness of the French grouping and the exclusion of the indigenous element'. The size of the 'French' electoral college, the article noted, was some 2,000 citizens. Among them, 350 were naturalised Vietnamese, 700 were renounced Indians, and 1,000 were French from the Metropole. But of the metropolitan French, 'half are absent from the colony and of the other half, a good number abstain or are unable to vote on the day'. Given that their votes, it claimed, were open to the highest bidder, Indians with French citizenship became the 'uncontested arbitrators' of any election.[30]

The problem of Indian political privileges in Cochinchina continued to be raised in the pages of the *Tribune Indigène*, and its successor the *Tribune Indochinoise*, at virtually every legislative and Colonial Council election throughout the 1920s. These complaints were joined by critiques, often more forceful ones, in the Constitutionalist-associated *Echo Annamite*.

The *Echo Annamite* was more thorough than Bùi Quang Chiêu's newspapers in its criticism of Indian privileges in Cochinchina, at-

---

29. Smith, 'Bui Quang Chieu and the Constitutionalist Party', p. 137.
30. 'La question indienne', *Tribune Indigène*, 30 December 1922.

tacking not only the political status of Indian French citizens, but the way in which their citizenship was acquired. Two years before the *Tribune Indigène* had begun its critique in 1922 of the renouncer role in Cochinchinese politics, the *Echo Annamite* was already publishing articles which spoke of the ease with which Indians could obtain French citizenship and compared this to the paltry number of naturalised Vietnamese in Cochinchina:

> After sixty years of French domination, there are in Cochinchina at most 250 naturalised *Annamites* against 500 to 600 Indians [with French citizenship]. And [the naturalised *Annamites*] are still thought to be too many for the tranquillity of the country![31]

Although in previous decades the Vietnamese were uninterested in French naturalisation, the First World War brought about a change in attitudes. Many Vietnamese now favoured naturalisation as the just reward for their loyalty and support – be it financial or in military service – during the years of conflict. In the catalogue of reforms compiled and presented to incoming Governor General Varenne in late 1925, the Constitutionalists now claimed to be 'deeply interested' in the question. In addition to the 'political, legal, and administrative privileges' which naturalisation conferred, it also acted as a barometer of the 'liberal intentions of the French government towards the French people'. This 'Wish List of the Vietnamese People', serialised in the *Echo Annamite*, again used the citizenship of Indians from the French possessions to demonstrate how far French 'liberal intentions' towards the Vietnamese fell short. The 'Wish List' compared the 'simple formality' of renunciation enjoyed by Indians with the lengthy and complicated procedures by which the Vietnamese were required to apply for, much less be granted, the status of citizens. The regime of naturalisation in Cochinchina had resulted in a mere three hundred Vietnamese obtaining citizenship by 1925, out of a total of three million inhabitants.[32]

If France's intentions towards the *Annamites* fell short, however, its liberal extension of citizenship to Indians resulted in Cochinchina in a system far removed from the Republic's principles of equality. The 'great

---

31. 'La naturalisation française', *Echo Annamite*, 24 April 1920.
32. The 'Wish List' was serialised in the *Echo Annamite* from 28 November to 4 December 1925. I have used here the English translations as published in Truong Buu Lam (ed.), *Colonialism Experienced, Vietnamese Writings on Colonialism 1900–1931*, Ann Arbor: University of Michigan Press, 2003, pp. 208–227. Quotes in this paragraph pp. 218–220.

influx of Indian immigrants arriving in the Cochinchinese colony', as the *Echo Annamite* stated in its 'Wish List of the Vietnamese People', 'constitutes an important block that overlaps with the European contingent to dominate the electorate in Cochinchina'. 'Under the protection of Republican France', it pointed out:

> Three different races live together in Asia. [Their] political power is in inverse proportion to their number ... the electorate of Cochinchina for the legislative election consists of three thousand voters, for whom two thousand are Europeans, seven hundred are Indians and three hundred are naturalised Vietnamese; the latter are supposed to represent a population of three million.[33]

Those voters with the most power, the *Echo Annamite* claimed, had the least commitment to the colony. Moreover, those who financed the whole structure had no voice at all:

> Of the three ethnic groups that form the electorate, the European component is made up of a majority of civil servants who never think of settling down in this colony ... The Indians have always looked at Indochina as a colony of transit. As for the three million Vietnamese who are riveted to their land and who provide all the revenues for the budgets, they have no say in the matter.[34]

Indian and French functionaries were a further focus of attack. The 'Wish List' underlined the need to cut subordinate positions in the administration filled by French and Indians in order to create more positions for qualified Vietnamese while avoiding an 'over-inflation of civil servants'.[35]

The *Echo Annamite*'s attack on Indian voters was taken up again in the lead-up to local elections in 1927. In one article Nguyễn Phan Long accused Édouard Marquis, the politically-involved editor of the Franco-Tamil *Réveil Saigonnais*, of trying to fashion for himself a role in local Cochinchinese politics akin to that of the Pondicherry leader Henri Gaebelé. Gaebelé had secured a monopoly on French Indian seats in the French Senate and National Assembly through political manipulation. Nguyễn Phan Long wrote of Marquis:

> The Indians are free to do what they want in their own country. In this country, which is ours, a legal fiction allows them to presume they have the rights of the conqueror over us. It is completely unjust that the natives must tolerate

---

33. 'Wish List' in Truong, *Colonialism Experienced*, p. 220.
34. Ibid.
35. Ibid., p. 221.

such an abnormal situation which is so prejudiced against them, because of Indian intrusion into elections where the natives are themselves excluded.[36]

Such attitudes clearly created some concern amongst French authorities as this article was included as a clipping in the Security Services' 'Press Review' for 1927.

The Constitutionalist Party eventually distanced itself from the more extreme anti-colonial views of Nguyễn An Ninh. He was the main figure at the head of a 'new younger generation of French-educated Vietnamese who were impatient for change' and who were willing to support violence to bring it about.[37] Yet during its intermittent publication from 1923 to 1926, Ninh's *Cloche Fêlée* took a similar stance to the Constitutionalists on Indians with French citizenship and their domination of Cochinchina's electoral college. His newspaper's political critique of French colonial power was more pointed than those seen in Constitutionalist-related publications.

In the legislative election of 1924, the 'perennial Deputy' Ernest Outrey was re-elected as the representative of Cochinchina in the French National Assembly.[38] The *Cloche Fêlée* attributed his continued ability to win to a system which allowed French politicians to manipulate the supposed venality of Indian voters:

> [Outrey] is once again pompously called *Deputy of Cochinchina,* that is the representative of almost four million human beings … He cannot deny he owes his position in Parliament to the French … of India, of Corsica, of Réunion … [he was] elected by the majority of an electoral college of 300 voters, foreigners living nearly all at the expense of Princess Cochinchina …
>
> No one can deny just how heavily the mass of the French … of India weighs in the legislative elections, these black Frenchmen, these *pariahs* whose mentality Mr. Outrey knows only too well, this category of voters whose interests are not here but in Pondicherry … These *Hindous* sent here by the French administration to lend weight to the prestige of the dominators and to the official candidates, up until now have nevertheless shown themselves worthy of the role reserved for them.
>
> No one can deny that success is assured to the candidate for the deputation who speaks this language to an electoral college composed primarily of

---

36. ANOM FM/5 SLOTFOM 14 Revue de la Presse Indochinoise 1927: Nguyễn Phan Long, 'La France laissera-a-t-elle les Indiens faire de la Cochinchine ce qu'ils ont fait de l'Inde française?', *Echo Annamite*, 25 March 1927. I am grateful to Sarah Womack for alerting me to the censor's digest at the Aix archives.
37. Smith, 'Bui Quang Chieu and the Constitutionalist Party', p. 142.
38. The phrase is Virginia Thompson's: Thompson, *French Indo-China*, p. 311.

functionaries: 'Vote for me and I promise to prevent the *Annamites* from acceding to the citizenship rights that you enjoy and that would permit them to take the places that you occupy.'[39]

The *Cloche Fêlée* also permitted itself to publish harsher, more racially-based judgements of Indian migrants than the Constitutionalist newspapers. An article in the *Cloche Fêlée* dated from 1925 suggested that the Vietnamese had no admiration for the French Indians' struggle to secure equality with the French. To Vietnamese reformers, the legal gains made by renouncers resident in Cochinchina simply made a mockery of the *mission civilisatrice:*

> Following a survey … it has been found that French civil servants in Indochina send annually to their families in the Metropole some 60 million francs in total … the least police agent, white or black, earns, from his start in the honourable corporation, 300 piastres per month courtesy of *Annamite* taxpayers. … These gentlemen, the European civil servants – whether they be snow white, *café au lait* or raven black – have come here, be assured, to civilise the savage *Annamites*… It is fair that the latest barefoot newcomer from France or Pondicherry should have his aperitif at noon and in the evening. Where do we fit into all of this? What is to become of the prestige of the conqueror? And what purpose is served by the colonies?[40]

By the late 1920s, the *Echo Annamite* began to publish articles which took a similar approach. In a 1927 article a certain Le-Lac-Tho claimed that the Indian French citizens brought to Cochinchina 'no element and no quality susceptible of civilising the *Annamites*'. They were, as the title of the article stated, a 'Fourth Colour', added to the three colours of the French flag. This colour, 'black':

> extends like an ink stain; it invades the administration where, in subordinate positions it represents a growing number of French who are 'too brown', who sometimes have *Annamites* under their orders and towards whom they can claim no moral or intellectual superiority, indeed the reverse. They cannot and do not want to be anything other than functionaries living as parasites in this country.[41]

The Constitutionalists have been referred to as a 'bourgeois elite', in contrast to more radical voices demanding change, beginning with the emergence of Nguyễn An Ninh. They have been berated for not

---

39. 'Le Sens de l'Election de M. Outrey', *Cloche Fêlée*, 19 May 1924.
40. 'La solde des fonctionnaires européens d'Indochine', *Cloche Fêlée*, 24 December 1925.
41. Le-Lac-Tho, 'La quatrième couleur', *Echo Annamite*, 5 April 1927.

being sufficiently radical and the accusation of colonial collaboration, levelled at them in their time, has remained with them to the present. Yet Bùi Quang Chiêu, despite himself, was a pivotal figure in the turn to a radical anti-colonial struggle for independence, and the failure of the French colonial government to address the moderate demands of the Constitutionalists itself paved the way for a more radical politics. The same French unwillingness to address Constitutionalist demands in turn invited the Vietnamese elite reformers to make unfavourable comparisons with aspects of British rule on the Indian subcontinent which they felt to be more progressive.

By mid-1925 the Constitutionalists' moderate cause, which had yet to receive any adequate French response, began to be outpaced by events, and by late 1926 the party had lost much of its relevance. In June of that year, Phan Bội Châu, the foremost political exile and intellectual of an earlier generation, was arrested and tried in Hanoi. This was followed in late March 1926 by the Saigon arrest of Nguyễn An Ninh. A day later the death of another returned political exile, Phan Chu Trinh, was announced in Saigon. Bùi Quang Chiêu was returning from talks in Paris as these latter events unfolded. Docking in Saigon port the day after news had come of Phan Chu Trinh's death, the Constitutionalist leader was greeted by Saigonese crowds from all walks of life, from housewives to high school children. They expected him to now take up leadership of a more broad-based and radical cause; they pressed him to take forward their plans for mass demonstrations in the form of public expressions of mourning for Phan Chu Trinh. He failed to assume this leadership role. These events pressed a younger generation of dissenters to take the political lead. Discontent with French rule now reached more widely across Vietnamese society, and was set on a more radical, anti-colonial path. The relevance of Constitutionalist concerns, such as parity between themselves and other more privileged colonised peoples, was rapidly and sharply diminished.[42]

The radical turn of 1925–26 was a crucial point in Vietnam's political history, but the consequences of French unwillingness to enfranchise the bourgeois elite in relation to this turn have received less attention than they deserve. Bùi Quang Chiêu claimed that the French had made a fatal error in failing to register Constitutionalist criticisms of Indian political,

---

42. For a detailed account of this crucial period see Tai, *Radicalism*, pp.140–157.

legal and administrative privileges in Cochinchina, and in refusing to grant any real concessions – other than subsidised newspapers – to his modernised, elite and Francophile sector of Vietnamese society. By the latter half of 1926, as Vietnamese Indochina became crippled by strikes and protests, the Constitutionalists' tone became cynical and despondent. A Bùi Quang Chiêu editorial of August 1926 reads:

> In the French electoral college, faced with ethnic French and French Indian elements, the naturalised citizens constitute such a derisory minority that we can affirm that their action on the election of the Deputy and the Colonial councillors is nil.[43]

Bùi Quang Chiêu continued to publish articles berating the French colonial state for keeping educated Vietnamese 'virtually excluded from the public life of the country'.[44] 'What emerges as a great danger,' he wrote in September of 1926, appearing to foretell the radical turn in Cochinchinese politics without acknowledging that it had already happened, 'is to keep these westernised *Annamites* distanced from the public life of their country, to treat them as *pariahs* in their own country'.[45]

The reference to Indian outcasts was not accidental. In his writings in the latter half of the 1920s, Bùi Quang Chiêu increasingly compared France's denial of colonial social and political recognition to the progress he observed in British India, where limited measures of local self-government had been introduced starting in the 1860s.[46] Indeed, in contrast to their harsh criticism of (French) Indian migrants in Indochina, both Bùi Quang Chiêu *and* Nguyễn An Ninh kept a close watch on nationalist currents in India, and looked to the Indian National Congress as a model for their aspirations. Ralph Smith has noted that:

> The comparison with British India is not so unreasonable as the events in Vietnam since 1945 might lead one to suppose; it was one which the Constitutionalists themselves made, for one of their principal sources of inspiration during the 1920s was the career of Gandhi.[47]

---

43. 'Le Conseil Colonial', *Tribune Indochinoise*, 23 August 1926.
44. Ibid.
45. 'Propos d'un Annamite au sujet d'une motion', *La Tribune Indochinoise*, 10 September 1926.
46. See Sugata Bose and Ayesha Jalal, *Modern South Asia: History, Culture, Political Economy*, London and New York: Routledge, 1998, pp. 104–105. Bùi Quang Chiêu's optimism about the aims and effects of these forms of political franchise was not necessarily shared either by his Indian contemporaries or later scholars of South Asia. See *inter alia* Anil Seal, 'Imperialism and Nationalism in India', *Modern Asian Studies*, 7, 3, 1973, 321–347.
47. Smith 'Bui Quang Chieu and the Constitutionalist Party', p. 148.

Both Bùi Quang Chiêu and Nguyễn An Ninh observed political developments and regularly published articles on India. Both men took an avid interest in the writings of the politically engaged Bengali poet, philosopher, and Nobel Prize Laureate, Rabindranath Tagore. When historian Kalidas Nag spoke in Saigon in 1924 (standing in for Tagore who was obliged to postpone his visit), Ninh's presence was noted by the Secret Service.[48] When Tagore finally did visit, in June 1929, it was at Bùi Quang Chiêu's invitation (Chapter Seven).[49] Bùi Quang Chiêu established ties with the Indian Congress Party in 1927, and was invited to its annual conference in Calcutta in January of 1929.[50] His published travelogue of this journey provides a fascinating account of his impressions of Indian nationalist politics and the complex changes in his thinking as his political career declined under attack from more radical quarters.[51] Ralph Smith maintains that had the French lent greater support to the Constitutionalists, Chiêu could have gone on to form a party 'comparable to the Indian Congress Party, smaller in scale but capable of uniting into a single movement the majority of the colony's moderate politicians.'[52]

Newspaper reports at the time indicate that the Vietnamese Constitutionalists rubbed shoulders with resident members of the renouncer elite at 'Indian' events in Saigon, such as Tagore's visit. There is evidence, too, that some of the more independent-minded Indian residents in Saigon were politically aligned at some points with Bùi Quang Chiêu. During the municipal elections of 1919, for example, when the Constitutionalists really emerged as a serious political force, but before their concerns about Indian political influence had been voiced, two Pondicherry candidates, Sinnaya and Isidore, ran for office alongside Chiêu on the list of the socialist Monin.[53] Along with Chiêu, they had to accept Monin's defeat. However, at least one comment by Nguyễn

---

48. ANOM GGI 65474 Rapport Annuel Contrôle des immigrants asiatiques 1923–1924: Milieux Indiens.
49. Smith, 'Bui Quang Chieu and the Constitutionalist Party', p. 148.
50. Peycam, *The Birth of Vietnamese Political Journalism*, p. 123.
51. An article published as this manuscript was going to press provides a valuable and detailed analysis of this journey and its wider context. See Agathe Larcher and Kareem James Abu-Zeid, 'Bùi Quang Chiêu in Calcutta (1928): The Broken Mirror of Vietnamese and Indian Nationalism', *Journal of Vietnamese Studies*, 9, 4, 2014, 67–114.
52. Smith, *Vietnam and the West*, pp. 94–95.
53. 'Résultats élections municipales', *Réveil Saigonnais*, 31 December 1919; on Monin see Tai, 'The Politics of Compromise', pp. 387–388.

An Ninh suggests that his interest in developments in British India only heightened his scorn for what he perceived as the hypocrisy of French Indians on Vietnamese soil: 'Already indifferent to the fate of India itself, [they] cannot think of the unfortunate destiny of another subjugated Asian race.'[54]

The Indian presence in Cochinchina provides a new perspective on the politics of the colony in this period. The Vietnamese elite felt that Indian renouncers, as successful colonial citizens, were blocking the advancement of their own bourgeois class. Held back by their French masters from social and political franchise in ways French Indians were not, Vietnamese reformers of the 1920s were simultaneously all too aware of how their counterparts in British India were being granted an albeit carefully measured say in political life. These were powers that their own French masters denied to them, even as they espoused republican egalitarianism and applied it, however imperfectly, to French Indians.

Grassroots responses and increasingly troubled relations

While the educated elite of Cochinchina engaged in debates over the privileges and power of some Indian residents of the colony, more fundamental tensions existed between local people at the grassroots level and the Indian migrants with whom they came into contact. The record of poor relations and scattered confrontations between overseas Indians and local Cochinchinese in the first decades of the twentieth century reveals more raw and in many ways more troubled engagements than the relatively measured responses of members of the intellectual elite. In the 1920s and 1930s, these tensions spilled over into incidents of violence, some of which, according to French security officials, bore the stamp of communist organisation. They were also channelled into particularly harsh criticisms of Indian moneylenders with the onset of the Great Depression.

Anti-Indian feeling at grassroots level stemmed from specific types of contact between the local Cochinchinese and overseas Indians. Some of the most fraught relations were between Indian tax farmers and local people who sold their produce in rural markets, or moored their boats at landings. This animosity was born in part of Vietnamese dislike for

---

54. 'Le Sens de l'Election de M. Outrey', *Cloche Fêlée*, 19 May 1924.

the French institution of tax farming, and in part of their dislike for the Indians hired to undertake the task. It did not help matters that some tax farmers were liable to abuse their positions by charging higher dues than the posted rates and resorting to physical violence against those who would not pay.[55] Brocheux's work on the Mekong Delta, although it does not refer to violence, similarly mentions that itinerant peddlers and market traders were hounded by Indian tax collectors at markets and ferry crossings.[56] The Vietnamese response, both to the colonial institution and the less-than-honest tax farmer, was to hurl verbal abuse.

When Cochinchinese villagers refused to recognise the legality of an Indian tax farm, as they did on several occasions, the tax farmer was faced with the immediate problem of collecting his dues. However, he generally managed to pass the problem on to the state, by refusing to pay his contracted sum, and, in some cases, by taking legal action against the villagers. Through these actions, tax farmers and villagers together created potentially more serious threats to social order and French colonial authority. In this equation, the most troubling effects the tax farmer finally had to endure were the villagers' ongoing campaigns to insult him. In 1918, the tax farmer So Mouttayah brought a case against the notables of the village of Phước Tân in Biên Hoà province, for refusing to recognise the extent of his farm over mooring and loading along the quay. Central among So Mouttayah's complaints to the provincial administration was that the villagers 'incite[d] the boatmen and carters to direct indecent gestures to me'.[57] In 1925, a tax farmer of markets in the vicinity of Cantho by the name of Yaccoumsah (Yakum Sahib) was jailed for withholding his revenues from the French authorities – revenues he had been unable to collect in the markets. As a British subject, the law of *indigénat* had been incorrectly applied to his sentence. In Yaccoumsah's appeal for his release, one of his most pressing concerns was that he had had to suffer the taunts of Vietnamese prisoners working the *corvée* alongside him.[58]

---

55. Nguyễn Thị Phải, [no title given], *LTTV* 11, January 1908, p. 6, [excerpted in Sơn Nam, *Miền Nam*, p. 248].
56. Brocheux, *Mekong Delta*, pp. 87–88.
57. VNA2 GD 3397 Plainte de M. So Mouttayah contre les exigences des notables du village de Phuoc Tan (Biên Hòa) 1918: So Mouttayah to Administrator Biên Hòa, 3 January 1918.
58. VNA2 GD 445 Peine administrative infligée par le Chef de la province de Cantho contre M. Yaccoumsah, indien sujet anglais 1925.

If shows of organised resistance to tax farms remained limited, the pouring forth of verbal abuse was a more constant response. Indian migrants engaged in tax farming had close market-level contact with local people. Nevertheless, many did not readily speak Vietnamese. One of Vietnam's former prime ministers, who grew up in Vĩnh Long before the Second World War, remembers female market traders hurling insults at Indian tax farmers. Satisfied at being able to vent their frustrations, the market vendors he claimed were secure in the knowledge that the tax farmers (who just put out their hands and asked for their money) did not understand the full extent of the women's invective.[59]

Shouting abuse at Tamil tax farmers might be explained as a way of indirectly venting one's frustrations at French colonial rule. Other rumours, taunts, and forms of verbal abuse were more specifically directed at the Indian migrants. Hanoi is more rife than Saigon with memories of teasing Indian merchants as a childhood game. The Indian merchant community was smaller in Hanoi than Saigon; the equation perhaps was that childhood bravado came in inverse proportion to the size of the foreign population able to give chase. One Hanoi author admits to playing a game specifically devised to anger the city's Indian Muslims. As a child growing up in Hanoi's old quarter, he and his friends found endless amusement in 'showing the pig's ears' to Muslims gathered at the Tamil mosque. This activity consisted of young boys grasping two handfuls of the cloth from their shirts and waving them at the merchants, who would run after them, incensed, in hot pursuit.[60] A poem recalled by another Hanoian is widely remembered by people of his generation who grew up in the city in the 1930s and 1940s. It is infused with disrespect for Indian migrants, some of whom ran cake shops in the city:

> Ông Tây đen
> Nằm trong cái bồ
> Đánh cái rắm
> Thành bánh ga tô!
>
> Black Westerner sat
> In a basket to bake

---

59. Conversation with Võ Văn Kiệt, Hanoi, September 2005.
60. Nguyễn Mạnh Cường and Nguyễn Minh Ngọc, *Người Chăm (Những Nghiên Cứu Bước Đầu)* [The Cham (Initial Studies)], Hanoi: Nhà Xuất Bản Khoa Học Xã Hội, 2003, pp. 5–6. I am grateful to Andrew Hardy for bringing this reference to my attention. Also, discussion with Professors Lê Thi and Đặng Phong, Tam Đảo, September 2008.

VIETNAMESE ENGAGEMENT WITH INDIAN MIGRANTS

> Let out a fart
> And out came a cake!⁶¹

The term *Tây đen*, or 'Black Westerner', was used for Indian migrants, as well as the small number of Africans who found their way to Indochina through engagement in the French army. *Tây đen* conveyed the gap, in some Vietnamese perceptions, between the privileges these foreigners enjoyed, and the low place they should have 'rightfully' occupied in a racially ordered social hierarchy.

It might be delving too far for present purposes into questions of psychology to try to establish whether the children who deployed these taunts and poems with such delight drew their inspiration in any way from the attitudes of their parents. An advertisement which appeared in Saigon's *Lục Tỉnh Tân Văn* in 1914, however, demonstrates that adults in the south could display sentiments they held for Indian milk sellers more consciously (see Plate 8). These bad feelings could even be turned to commercial purposes. The advertisement, which promoted a French brand of milk, depicted a Vietnamese woman-servant at the gate of a wealthy villa. She shouts at a man dressed humbly in a *dhoti* holding two milk bottles. The caption reads:

> You little *Chà Và*, where have you come from? Why don't you go away. Your milk smells like old goat. Our household only buys *La Petite Fermière* milk. Run off now, or you're dead!⁶²

Vietnamese antagonism towards Indian emigrants was thus deployed by a French company to market tinned milk to a Vietnamese clientele. Vietnamese disdain for the humble Tamil milkman continued into the 1930s. In 1931, the Franco-Tamil *Saigon-Dimanche* printed a refutation of the 'idiotic rumour' prevalent in Cochinchina that Indian milkmen 'milked their cows and goats with their mouths'.⁶³

In the record of ground-level animosity that Vietnamese held for resident Indians, little trace can be found of the money-lending Chettiars prior to the Great Depression. This is surprising taken the long record of French concern over the usurious rates the Indian 'parasites' supposedly

---

61. Discussion with Professor Đặng Phong, Hanoi, Spring 2002; Discussion with Professors Lê Thi and Đặng Phong, Tam Đảo, 2 September 2008.
62. *LTTV*, 26 February 1914. I am grateful to Erica Peters for drawing this advertisement to my attention. See also Erica J. Peters, *Appetites and Aspirations in Vietnam: Food and Drink in the Long Nineteenth Century*, Lanham: Rowman and Littlefield, 2012, 190–195.
63. 'Taper sur les pauvres hindoues est si facile!', *Saigon-Dimanche*, 6 December 1931.

demanded.⁶⁴ It is surprising too that Chettiars were never the subject of concerted attack by Saigon's non-communist reformist press. It is particularly puzzling in the case of Gilbert Chiếu, not only because of his commitment to fighting foreign economic domination, but because it was the Chettiars who oversaw his downfall. At the sudden end of his political and journalistic career, at the time of his arrest, all of Gilbert Chieu's land was mortgaged and he was indebted in large part to a 'Souna Parra Ana Sirra Soupramanianchetty'.⁶⁵

The reasons for a subdued Vietnamese response to the Indian moneylenders, before 1929, are too complex to delve into in detail here, but probably relate to the composition of the Chettiar client base and the nature of lending itself. The Chettiars' rural clients at the beginning of the twentieth century were primarily the better-off land-owning class who benefited from the availability of Chettiar credit to finance agricultural and extra-agricultural activities, as well as to on-lend to landless peasants.⁶⁶ As long as the Mekong Delta economy was buoyant and the frontier expanding, the Chettiars' wealthy landowning clients had little objection to make. This was as relevant to supporters of the *Minh Tân* movement as it was to landowners among the intellectual elite of the 1920s.

Popular Vietnamese responses to Indian migrants in their midst did not directly concern Indians who were French citizens, except to the extent that a limited number of Indian traders, tax farmers, and (possibly) milkmen were renouncers. On one level, however, all Indians, regardless of distinctions of religion or place of origin, were included in Vietnamese invectives against the *Chà*. It was not until anti-Indian feeling turned to physical violence that renouncers based in Cochinchina began to grasp this. A series of anti-Indian incidents which turned violent occurred in various parts of Vietnamese Indochina in the 1920s and 1930s. They were reported and analysed in the small but active Franco-Tamil press, which represented above all the interests of renouncers. These newspapers also debated with the Vietnamese and metropolitan French presses over the facts of the incidents and the conclusions to be drawn from

---

64. See for example Mathieu, *Les Prêts Usuaires*.
65. Brocheux, 'Note Sur Gilbert Chiêu', p. 73.
66. Accounts of this type of credit relationship are described in Ngô Vĩnh Long, *Before the Revolution*, pp. 84–97; Phan Trung Nghĩa, *Công tử Bạc Liêu*, p. 27; P. de Feyssal, *L'Endettement agraire en Cochinchine: Rapport d'ensemble au gouverneur général de l'Indochine*, Hanoi: Impr. d'Extrême-Orient, 1933.

them. For each incident there were conflicting versions of events, making it difficult to establish what really took place in each case. Running through all of the events though, was a consistent pattern. An Indian shopkeeper was accused of brutality against a Vietnamese customer, leading to violent attacks on Indian shops and in some cases anti-Indian boycotts. The customer subject to the initial Indian attack was invariably a member of Vietnamese society considered to be particularly vulnerable, and thus in need of the wider society's protection. The reports of these incidents provide a further context in which to understand the responses of the Vietnamese to the Indian migrants in their midst.

The first incident took place in Saigon in 1925. Labelled the 'Bombay boycott', it began with a *fracas* in one of the 'Bombay' shops on Catinat Street, which was more correctly one in a row of shops on that street owned and run by the Sindhi trading network. A Vietnamese woman was accused of stealing an umbrella from the shop. She claimed in her defence to have purchased it at a neighbouring 'Bombay' shop. An Indian employee of the shop then hit the woman with the purportedly stolen item, breaking it in two. The horror of this action was emphasised in the *Echo Annamite* by the fact that, as the wife of a functionary, the injured woman was highly respectable. The same newspapers which had called some years' earlier for the anti-Chinese boycott of 1919 (the *Trung Lập Báo* and the *Lục Tỉnh Tân Văn*), now exhorted Vietnamese women to stay away from the Indian shops. The boycott lasted two weeks, after which the *Trung Lập Báo* backed down. It asked its readers to find 'pity for the compatriots of Gandhi' and 'respect for French merchants' who had objected that, as suppliers to the Sindhis, they too were being affected by the boycott. Public posters continued though to urge people to protest. The *Echo Annamite* had refrained from participation in the boycott itself, but now claimed that the *Trung Lập Báo* had given in too soon to the 'foreigners who have forgotten the pure and simple civility which they owe to us and to our women in exchange for the generous hospitality which is given to them'.[67]

In June 1928 two anti-Indian incidents occurred within days of each other, one in the town of Vinh in Annam, the other in the *rue Viénot* in Saigon. Both featured events similar to those which led up to the 'Bombay boycott'. In the *Réveil Saigonnais* telling of the story, the Vinh

---

67. 'Boycottage', *Echo Annamite*, 22 September 1925.

trouble occurred at an Indian shop which was crowded on market day in early June. An Indian employee spotted a young man stealing cloth; he caught the thief and slapped him. The thief, who was clubfooted, fell and hit his head. This action outraged the customers in the busy shop. A crowd began to throw bricks and stones at the shop, and at two other Indian-owned premises on the street. The *gendarmes*, unable to control the situation, called in the militia to clear the street. The Indian shops remained closed for three days under militia guard. When they opened again, the shopkeepers were threatened by menacing visitors: 'They ... came into the shops demanding to be sold "black khaki", and if that was not produced they would have "red khaki".' Such was the tension, the newspaper claimed, that the Indian merchants packed up their shops and left the town shortly afterwards.[68]

The *rue Viénot* incident took place a few weeks' later in a Saigon street known for its Indian cloth merchants. The Franco-Tamil *Saigon-Dimanche* reported that a man by the name of Pham Van Hai attempted to steal bobbins from 'Abdoulkadare and Company'. An Indian employee threw a shoe to stop him, but the shoe hit the thief in the eye, inflicting a serious injury. To avenge Hai's injuries, a Vietnamese mob mounted an attack on the shop, described as a 'veritable battle', some days later.[69]

In August 1936 a confrontation took place at the Amiral Roze Street Temple in Saigon dedicated to the Hindu goddess Mariamman, between the '*Bengali*' guard stationed to watch the temple and two young Vietnamese girls. Tensions between the two communities again played out in remarkably similar ways. The Vietnamese press, according to *Indochine-Inde*, ran a series of hysterical but conflicting headlines: 'An Indian after having [indecently] stroked a young *Annamite* girl, then hit her violently'; 'At the Black Lady pagoda in Saigon an Indian tried to rape a 13-year old girl'; 'The Indians of the pagoda in Amiral Roze Street hit two young girls'; 'A young girl was brutalised by the Indians'. In the version of events reported by *Indochine-Inde* itself, when the guard had asked the girls not to bring the babies they were carrying into the shrine, they had yelled abuse at him. He threw them out of the temple whereupon they continued to cause a scandal and invent stories. The Amiral Roze affair led

---

68. 'Une curieuse coincidence. L'affaire de la rue Viénot', *Réveil Saigonnais*, 27 June 1928.
69. 'Des Annamites agressent un marchand musulman', *Saigon-Dimanche*, 29 June 1928; and 'Antagonisme de races? Des annamites agressent un marchand musulman pour se venger de la brutalité commise par celui et contre l'un d'eux', *Réveil Saigonnais*, 25 June 1928.

to Vietnamese calls for a boycott on all Hindu temples in the city, though it is unclear whether this boycott was actually carried out.[70]

Yet another incident occurred with a similar narrative in the imperial city of Hue, in Annam, in 1937. According to French Security reports, a Vietnamese woman caught stealing from a 'Bombay' shop had then attracted passers-by, shouting that she had been abused by the shop's manager. A crowd gathered and threw stones at the shop. In the days that followed a more organised group of some 2,000 students gathered to shout 'Expel the *Bombay*, useless to society!' The students also sent a telegram to the Governor General, pleading: 'Please intervene immediately, huge demonstration amassed Hue against *Hindou* brutalities towards *Annamite* women.' Posters appeared inciting the population to boycott the 'Bombay' stores: 'We must end all our relations with the Bombay store. They come here only to beg in an indirect way and to live off the blood of the people of Annam. Despite this, they dare to look for trouble. For our honour and for that of future generations we must expel them from the territory of Hue, cutting all relations with them.' French security agents claimed the group of Vietnamese communists around the Saigon newspaper *La Lutte* were behind the demonstrations.[71]

Collectively, these incidents show how tensions between Indians and the local community could turn to open conflict. Chettiar loan foreclosure with the onset of the economic depression in 1929–1930 further soured Vietnamese relations with resident Indians. Vietnamese responses to the Chettiar presence were relatively subdued prior to the economic crisis, but the Indian moneylenders were vilified thereafter. A 1929 newspaper cartoon depicts a Chetty 'monster' squeezing the life from a Vietnamese borrower.[72] A 1937 petition from a group describing themselves as 'native modest-earners of Indochina' (*gagne-petits indigènes de l'Indochine*) to the French Minister of Colonies, displayed disdain for the 'coloured lenders' who 'make a profession of sucking human blood':

---

70. 'A propos d'un incident qui se serait produit à la pagoda de la rue Amiral Roze', *Indochine-Inde*, 30 August 1936.
71. ANOM GGI 65457 Notes mensuelles Sûreté Annam, 1937; On *La Lutte* see Philippe Devillers, *Histoire du Viêtnam de 1940 à 1952*, Paris: Éditions du Seuil, 1952, pp. 67–69.
72. Cartoon from *La Presse Indochinoise*, 20 September 1929, reprinted in Nasir Abdoule-Carime, 'Les communautés indiennes en Indochine', Association d'échanges et de Formation pour les Études Khmères, http://aefek.free.fr/iso_album/vidy.pdf, 2003.

'throughout Indochina, in every language of the Union they are called 'vampires', which proves their voracity and their ferocious appetite.'[73]

The most troubled incidents between Vietnamese and Indian migrants at grassroots level appear as tales of accusation and bitter counter-accusation. The animosity in these stories in undeniable. Yet it is tempered by evidence in other spheres of more peaceable interactions.

Religious accommodation

Vietnamese in the French colonial period accommodated Indian religious practices in numerous ways; evidence exists equally of Indians expressing interest in indigenous Indochinese religious practices.

Whatever the truth of events that spurred the confrontation between local Vietnamese and overseas Indians at Saigon's Amiral Roze Street Temple in 1936, the conflict occurred within a context of religious syncretism. It is significant that when the altercation between the two Vietnamese girls and a 'Bengali' guard occurred, the girls were not passing by a place marked off as 'foreign' to them. Rather, they were about to enter the temple, most probably with the intention of praying to the overseas Indians' Hindu goddess.

It was at this temple in central Saigon, dedicated to the goddess Mariamman, that the most lively interactions occurred between local Cochinchinese and overseas Indians. As already mentioned, it is not clear if the boycott called by Vietnamese protesters on the temple actually took place. If it had, it would have deprived many Saigonese of an opportunity for prayer. All the city's Hindu temples were experiencing at the time a 'rising popularity' with Vietnamese worshippers.[74] The Mariamman temple had become particularly popular, both with Vietnamese and ethnic Khmer. In south India, Mariamman was portrayed as a 'dark' and sinister goddess, with powers to increase or stem the spread of smallpox as she saw fit. Vietnamese in Cochinchina understood her as the Indian embodiment of a local deity, the 'Black Lady' (*Bà Đen*) of their own popular religious belief.[75] Yet the Vietnamese 'Black

---

73. VNA2 GD 2990 Chettys, Dossier de principe 1937.
74. 'A propos d'un incident qui se serait produit à la pagode de la rue Amiral Roze', *Indochine-Inde*, 30 August 1936. The worship of Mariamman as a local goddess has survived, and is being vigorously revived in the present day.
75. Nguyễn Phương Thảo, 'Văn hón dân gian miền Nam Việt Nam [The Culture of Worship in the South of Vietnam]', [no publisher or place of publication given], 1997, p. 214.

Lady' was herself a goddess derived from the Vietnamese adoption in the lower Mekong region of Khmer deities (accounting for the interest of Khmer worshippers in the Mariamman temple). The Khmer deities were in turn absorbed from a Hindu pantheon brought to the region in ancient times when commercial and cultural exchanges with India were said to have created a 'Greater India' through Southeast Asia.[76] The link between *Bà Đen* and the Indian Hindu deity thus had deeper historical implications; these came full circle with the establishment of Hindu shrines by Indian migrants in late-nineteenth century colonial Saigon. As the next chapter shows, Indians in interwar Saigon tapped into these common cultural roots when they glorified the architects of 'Greater India' as their ancient migrant forebears.

Local Cochinchinese were also attracted to the spiritual beliefs of other migrant Indians. Tamil Muslims in Cantho erected a shrine in the nineteenth century over the gravesite of a Muslim 'saint', Bava Bilal. This shrine still stands in Cantho's Muslim cemetery. Although little historical documentation exists about Bava Bilal, Indo-Vietnamese informants claim he was an Arab or Indian merchant who gained extraordinary powers upon his death. The shrine was frequented not only by Tamils, but by Cham Muslims and Vietnamese devotees. Similar to the *keramat* of the Malay world, the site was considered by all of these parties to possess a strong spiritual power. Individual devotees visited his grave to invoke Bava Bilal's assistance, while up until the 1970s an annual festival attracted pilgrims from across the Mekong Delta seeking to benefit from his powers. These practices survive in the present, albeit in limited form.[77]

Indians, for their part, participated in local forms of devotion. Chettiars and other Tamil businessmen gave generous donations to the mausoleum of General Lê Văn Duyệt to fund its restoration in the late 1930s. Lê Văn Duyệt (1764–1832) served as Emperor Gia Long's viceroy in the south, before the region came under centralised control. His mausoleum stands

---

76. On Vietnamese absorption and adaptation of Khmer deities, see L. Malleret, 'Cochinchine, terre inconnue', *Bulletin de la Societé des Études Indochinoises,* 18, 3, 1943, 9–26; L. Malleret, *L'Archéologie du delta du Mékong,* Paris: École Française d'Extrême Orient, 1959. See also Thảo, 'Văn hón dân gian', pp. 185, 214, and Taylor, *Goddess on the Rise,* pp. 3, 82.
77. Interviews with Mr. Nhi, caretaker of Cantho cemetery, and descendants of the Meydine family, Cantho and HCMC, April 2005. On Malay *keramat*, see Sumit Mandal, 'Popular Sites of Prayer, Transoceanic Migration, and Cultural Diversity: Exploring the significance of keramat in Southeast Asia', *Modern Asian Studies,* 46, 2, 2012, 355–372.

near to Bà Chiểu market on the outskirts of Ho Chi Minh City. Tamil reverence for Lê Văn Duyệt was in keeping with that of Chinese migrants who propitiated the spirit of the general in the belief that in his death, as in his life, he continued to support their enterprises. One of the most generous donations, inscribed on a tablet in the mausoleum, came from the landowner and banker Appapoulé.[78]

Finally, works which chronicle the 'miracles' witnessed at the Catholic pilgrimage site of La Vang in Annam include mention of Indian Catholics. Those pilgrims who travelled to La Vang, and upon whom the Virgin was said to have bestowed favours in the 1920s included two Indians, Lesage and Sandjivy. Their names both suggest that they were renouncers.[79]

REACTIONS TO THE PROSPECT OF KINSHIP

The prospect of kinship with Indians stirred some of the deepest-rooted Vietnamese objections to the Indian presence. Suggestions of conjugal relations between Vietnamese women and Indian men drew the strongest reactions of a specifically racial nature (unions between Indian women and local men, the record indicates, were non-existent). These reactions indicate that some Vietnamese saw themselves as racially superior to the Indians, and to the darker-skinned Tamils in particular. Such prejudices nevertheless did not prevent mixed unions and other types of kinship ties from being formed.

Pierre Brocheux has maintained that Indian migrants were less well-accepted than Chinese immigrants within Cochinchinese society because, unlike the Chinese, 'they lacked the kinship relations that might have offset the indignities suffered by the Vietnamese as a result of the Chettys' money-lending activities and economic exploitation.'[80] When we examine in detail Vietnamese responses to unions with Indians, however, we find firstly that kinship ties, even though they were far less frequent than Vietnamese–Chinese unions, did indeed exist, and secondly that these ties aggravated, rather than offset, Vietnamese antagonisms towards Indians in Cochinchina. This was particularly so

---

78. Taylor, *Goddess on the Rise*, pp. 77–78. See also Bùi Thị Ngọc Trang, *Lăng Tả Quân Lê Văn Duyệt*, HCM City: Nhà Xuất Bản Tổng Hợp, 2004. I am grateful to Philip Taylor for bringing to my attention the tablets in the mausoleum listing its benefactors. Appapoulé is pictured in Plate 14.

79. No author given, Mẹ Maria Lệnh Cho Ta Dùng Phương Pháp Cứu Rỗi Là Lần Hạt Mân Côi, www.dongcong.net/MeMaria/ThangManCoi/12.htm.

80. Brocheux, *Mekong Delta*, pp. 102–103.

when Indians attempted to go outside the tolerable norms established for such unions.

The prevalence of mixed unions between Indians (or at least Tamils) and local Cochinchinese (or at least Vietnamese) was probably linked to two factors. For some migrants more than others, the possibility of marrying a 'customary' choice of partner became more restricted by the sojourn overseas. The importance of marrying within one's own circle was also more important for some groups of overseas Tamils than for others. Adherence to caste and clan distinguished legitimate from illegitimate unions more firmly for some migrants than for others. Catholic renouncers from the elite (that is, those originating from high caste backgrounds, even if they had, in principle, renounced their caste labels) rarely took local partners and it was considered to be something of a scandal when they did. Instead, they preferred marriages within clans or between allied clans, even when these marriages were so close as to be inadmissible, strictly speaking, according the French Civil Code which they had legally embraced.[81] These marriage practices were facilitated by the benefits of free passage and paid leave which many of the Catholic elite enjoyed in their positions within the Cochinchinese administration.

Similarly, Nattukottai Chettiar marriages to local women were virtually unheard of. 'Legitimate' marriage in Chettiar terms occurred strictly within the caste and between its nine clans, requiring the receipt of a garland from one of the nine clan temples. These practices guaranteed that any union outside of the caste would not be recognised within it. As particularly fervent caste Hindus, the bounds of possible partners were probably also regulated by notions of purity. Chettiars sometimes took long-term partners in Cochinchina, but some claim this was infrequent, in part because their stints as agents overseas were not open-ended but strictly regulated in 3-year cycles.[82]

South Indian Muslim migrants made up one group that regularly formed mixed unions with local women in Indochina. The better-off among them often practised 'double marriages', marrying once at home in India and taking another partner or partners in Indochina. Because

---

81. Interviews in Pondicherry, October and November 2004.
82. S. Muthiah et al., *Chettiar Heritage*, pp. 152–155; Discussion with Mrs. Meenakshi Meyappan, Karaikkudi, September 2004; Interview with R.M. Krishnanchettiar, Tiruchchirapalli, September 2004.

Islamic law recognised polygamy, they could legitimately contract second marriages, although this is not to say the merchants always sought for these unions to be legally recognised. Indochinese wives or partners, who were frequently traders themselves, played a role in the merchants' commercial strategies. The offspring from these unions helped to establish a Muslim community in Indochina, while periods of sojourn in India allowed male children to be immersed in their paternal heritage and to learn the other side of the family trade.[83]

While the wealth of some Muslim traders meant they could afford to maintain two households, other Indians formed local relationships because they were men of modest means. This included employees of Indian businesses, and soldiers stationed in Indochina. The latter often stayed on past their military term to work in the administration or commercial enterprises.

Tax farming too, often generated mixed unions, as it provided an opportunity for Indians collecting taxes to strike up relationships with Vietnamese market vendors and other local women. Despite prejudices which Vietnamese freely expressed against such unions, the women, usually from poorer backgrounds, often saw the relationship as the path to an easier future.[84]

A civil case which was heard in the courts of Tourane in 1905 provides a good measure of the behavioural boundaries and the appropriate social contexts for unions between Indian men and Vietnamese women. It does so by recounting what happened when one Tamil trader, apparently obsessed with a young Vietnamese woman, went utterly against these norms.

In 1904, Aboubakare, a Tamil merchant based in Tourane, attempted to press adultery charges against his 'wife', claiming she had taken up with another man. His ostensible wife, Nguyen Thi Den, was a young woman of eighteen, a tobacco seller and the daughter of a relatively wealthy man who held the tax farm for the city's slaughterhouse. Aboubakare claimed to have married her in July 1904.

In their testimonies in the court transcripts, Nguyen Thi Den and her family insisted that she had never been married to Aboubakare.

---

83. Interviews and discussion with Mumtaz Alam, HCMC, January-February 1997; Abdul Gaffour, Pondicherry, January 2002 and October 2004; Tony Bui, Pondicherry, October 2004.

84. Conversation with historian Dr. Đào Hùng, Hanoi, July 2006.

They made it clear they would have opposed such a union. The father told the court how Aboubakare, having trouble with his associates, had come to ask for help. Den's father had permitted him to stay in a building adjacent to the family house for two months. But then, 'Having learned that Aboubakare was telling everyone (Chinese and *Annamite*) that I had given him my daughter in marriage, I chased him from my premises, not wanting this rumour, which I considered to be scandalous, to last any longer.' He added, 'I would anyway be opposed to such a union because I consider this Indian to be a savage.' In her testimony his daughter spoke in similar terms: 'I would never consent to take Aboubakare for a husband because I find him too black.'[85]

Aboubakare's claim failed to hold up in court. He had no marriage papers to prove it, and his 'wife' maintained that in May of the same year she had married someone else, a young Vietnamese man by the name of Le Van Thai. Aboubakare then changed tack, accusing Den and her mother of defamation. He claimed the mother, Lam Thi Hue had appeared outside his door, a dog in hand, yelling: 'I brought this dog for Aboubakare to f…. because he doesn't have a wife!' 'This scandalous scene', it was noted in the court records, 'drew a considerable crowd in front of the shop.' The following day, Aboubakare claimed, Den herself appeared outside his house screaming: 'F… your father, your mother, your family!'[86]

Whether these scenes of obscenity, and pure rage, actually occurred cannot be firmly established by the court records. The parents' fury at Aboubakare's advances on their daughter, however, is well evidenced elsewhere. According to Nguyen Thi Den's father, sometime after he had been chased from the house, Aboubakare returned accompanied by four Vietnamese women carrying plates of betel nuts. 'Asking them what this visit signified', the father related, 'they said they had come to ask, on behalf of Aboubakare, for my daughter's hand in marriage.' The father's testimony was corroborated by two of the women commissioned to enact Aboubakare's version of a Vietnamese betrothal. Den's mother, according to one of the betel-carriers 'flew into a violent rage, took a

---

85. VNA1 Tribunal de Paix de Tourane G.5 No 81. Plainte civile entre Lam Thi Hue, Nguyen Thi Den and Aboubakare au sujet de diffamation à Tourane 1905: Commissariat de la police, plainte contre Aboubakare, 27 May 1905.
86. Ibid.: Bailiff's report, 3 June 1905.

broom and chased Aboubakare away. Feeling ashamed, I left Hue's property immediately along with the three other women.'[87]

In his conclusion, the judge reasoned that Aboubakare, obsessed with the young woman, had tried in his own way to charm her and her family into an agreement of marriage. When his charms could not carry him, he resorted to intimidation to prove she was his wife. Aboubakare had stayed long in the country, the judge resolved, and should have known of the prevailing norms, of 'the racial antagonism existing between his race and the *Annamite* race, and that a native who is better-off would never consent to give his daughter's hand in marriage to a *Malabar*'.[88]

One article which appeared in Gilbert Chieu's *Lục Tỉnh Tân Văn* is an exception to the otherwise tempered responses to Indian economic dominance found in that newspaper. It provides another example of the racially-based horror embedded in the popular imagination of the period at the prospect of a *Chà* son-in-law. It describes the author's visit to an acquaintance in a rural town. Upon his arrival, the acquaintance announced that he had arranged for his daughter to be married and encouraged the author to stay the night in order to meet the prospective son-in-law. Greeted in the morning by the sight of what he refers to as a *'thằng Chà Và'* seated in a chair, he took him for a trader come to sell cloth. The use of *thằng*, the classifier for boys, is demeaning in this context. The author describes the Indian as 'the devil of thunder manifest on earth' (*thiên lôi giáng thế*). Discovering the Indian was the prospective son-in-law, he exhorted readers not to follow this model. 'It is better to marry [your daughter] to a poor Annamese', the article concluded, 'rather than to a *Chà Và* with wealth.'[89]

Vietnamese resistance to the greater integration of Tamils into society persisted through the 1920s and up into living memory. It weighed in the murder in February of 1923 of Francisque, an Indian soldier of the 11th infantry stationed in Saigon. He was attacked and killed following an argument between the neighbour and the *congaie* (concubine) with whom he lived in the quarter of Dakao. Typically for the republican stance of the newspaper, an editorial in the Franco-Tamil *Réveil Saigonnais* insisted that colour should not enter into the question of the murder of a French

---

87. VNA1 G.5 81: Commissariat de la police, plainte contre Aboubakare, 27 May 1905.
88. Ibid.: Judge's conclusions, n.d.
89. Thiên-hồ, 'Chàng Rể Chà', *LTTV* 34, p. 9 [reprinted in Sơn Nam, *Miền Nam*, pp. 287–288].

soldier: 'Indochina is French territory. In the shadow of its flag, men of all colours stand guard.' Nonetheless the paper acknowledged: 'It occurs to us that this attack can be explained by the hatred that *Annamites* hold for black and brown soldiers.'[90]

If the example above demonstrates how prejudices played out in the poorer classes of society, the more privileged were not unaffected by such attitudes. An historian who grew up in Hue in the 1940s described how his mother's maid, from a very poor background, received an offer of marriage from a Tamil cloth trader, Issoup. His mother considered this an excellent prospect for a simple girl. She encouraged the relationship and went so far as to organise the wedding. The match improved the former maid's economic condition considerably. She kept in contact with her former employers, and her husband Issoup occasionally invited them to dinner. As a young boy the Hue historian accompanied his mother on these visits, and developed through them a taste for curry. His father, however, would never demean himself to accept the Tamil's invitations: 'Indians were badly regarded, and he was an intellectual. The Vietnamese looked down on the Indians [at that time], considering them to be black.'[91]

I have spoken so far of the prejudices provoked by relationships created through marriage. But kinship between Indians and Vietnamese was created not only by conjugal ties. In 1935, an ex-soldier living in Hanoi, who went by the name of Paul Louis Mariapragassam, applied for French naturalisation. Investigating his application, French authorities concluded that he was the same person as Nguyen Dinh Luy. According to their records, Paul Louis, or Luy, had arranged in 1921 for Karikalais and French citizen Amaladassou Mariapragassam to officially 'recognise' him and register him as a son. Mariapragassam charged 200 piastres for the service. One hundred piastres was paid up front, but the remainder was never collected as 'the Indian died that November'. As a French citizen, Paul Louis then earned four times his previous salary.

The process of 'recognition' (*reconnaissance*) was the faculty in French law allowing men to declare paternity of children born out of wedlock. It was used in Indochina primarily by French men wishing

---

90. 'Un crime à Saigon. Le soldat Francisque tombe sous les coups d'une vengeance', *Réveil Saigonnais*, 6 February 1923; 'Le Crime de Dakao', *Réveil Saigonnais*, 26 March 1923.
91. Conversation with historian Dr. Đào Hùng, Hanoi, 10 July 2006.

to confer French citizenship on their *métis* offspring. The legal provision was occasionally abused by Europeans selling their paternity to Vietnamese desiring French citizenship.[92] Indians from the French possessions were well-placed similarly to engineer 'false recognitions', as they could obtain French citizenship easily, and voluntarily, through renunciation. Amaladassou Mariapragassam was probably not the only one so tempted. This offsets the picture of racial prejudice described so far, to the extent that it demonstrates that Indians and Vietnamese, even if they were 'cheating the system', collaborated in some contexts to their mutual benefit.

Paul Louis' file states that 'physically, he has all the traits common to the *Annamite* race'. It also contains the detail that he was rejected by his family because he had taken steps to be 'recognised as French by a *Malabar'*. He should have taken over the care of his family altar, it was noted, but was chased out by the family who would not accept that someone now 'Indian', and related to an Indian, could carry out the role of honouring the ancestors.

Paul Luy's other manipulations of the French legal system put similarly in doubt the real identities of his five children. They were named in the document as Jeanne, Anne, Jules, Valle, and Lanne, and also used the surname Mariapragassam. Paul Louis' application for naturalisation was prompted by his loss of the French citizenship Amaladassou Mariapragassam had falsely bestowed upon him; the ruse of his false recognition had only been discovered when he had himself fraudulently adopted two people who he claimed to be 'children', but who were no longer minors, presumably with the intention of passing his citizenship on to them. He was stripped of his own citizenship when this second fraud was discovered.

It is fitting that Paul Louis Mariapragassam's application for naturalisation was reviewed by an Indian French citizen. The two words at the bottom of Paul Louis' application ('Noted, Ratinassamy') were pencilled by Louis Ratinassamy, senior official in Hanoi's Registration Bureau. It is a shame that Ratinassamy left no further trace of his views on this affair. His signature on this document, however, shows that renouncers

---

92. Stoler analyses European anxieties created by the practice of 'false recognition' (*fausse reconnaissance*): Stoler, *Carnal Knowledge*, pp. 91–96; Saada describes legal controls introduced in the French colonies in attempts to eradicate it, controls which ran counter to metropolitan law: Saada, *Les Enfants*, pp. 137–163.

were engaged in serving French interests in Indochina to the very extent that they were part of the bureaucracy monitoring Vietnamese applications for naturalisation.[93]

Conclusion

Vietnamese reacted to the Indian presence in a variety of contexts, and in a number of different ways, but all reflect how Indian emigrants influenced the Vietnamese experience of French colonialism. Early reformers such as Gilbert Chiểu resented the riches made by Indian and Chinese businessmen in the south, but aimed to copy them in order to capitalise themselves on the gains the foreign entrepreneurs had made in the course of French expansion. The French-educated elite of the 1920s expressed frustration at the privileges and powers enjoyed by Indian French citizens in Cochinchina. The privileges willingly accorded on Cochinchinese soil to renounced Indians in the face of their own similar but unfulfilled demands made a mockery in their eyes of the notion of a *mission civilisatrice* and of genuine government support for 'native' progress. Anti-Indian feeling at grassroots level stemmed from specific types of contact between local Cochinchinese and Indians working in the colony in a variety of occupations. Indian contacts with local people were not confined to tense interactions in commercial or administrative spheres. Happier exchanges existed in the context of religious belief, while harsh Vietnamese judgements of inter-ethnic relationships also formed part of the varied catalogue of grassroots reactions. These were the most racially charged reactions to the Indian presence. All of these interactions took place within a society which was a racialised one. Racial resentments did not form the backbone of Vietnamese engagements with Indian migrants, but were expressed at specific times in response to specific pressures.

The heightened atmosphere of animosity between Vietnamese and overseas Indians from the late 1920s and through the 1930s left little room for distinctions to be made between one overseas Indian and another. As a part of their wider reaction to Vietnamese anti-colonialism, renouncers became increasingly aware of this slippage. They began

---

93. All references to this affair from VNA1 D.89 3329 Au sujet de la demande de naturalisation française formulée par Mariapragassam (Paul, Louis) ex-militaire, domiciliée à Hanoi 1935–1936: Report Inspector Méchard of Security Services to Mobile Judiciary Police Commissioner, 18 April 1935.

to recognise that their reputation was linked to that of the Muslim traders, the Chettiar moneylenders and other overseas Indians in the colony. Despite daily contacts within Saigon's Tamil community, Indian French citizens had previously set themselves apart from these groups. Vietnamese criticisms levelled against the Indian presence in the 1920s and 1930s led Indian French citizens to sense that they were viewed as part of the 'problem'. The attempts of Indian renouncers and their supporters to counter this view is the subject of the chapter which follows. In the present chapter, Vietnamese engagements with Indians in daily life were shown to expose racial ideas in their rawer forms; the following chapter also demonstrates how European race theory was eagerly adopted and adapted in the interwar period by Vietnamese and other non-European commentators, including the Indians, to project ideas of themselves as dynamic and forward-looking peoples.

CHAPTER SEVEN

RAISING THE INDIAN PUBLIC PROFILE

By the 1910s, Indian renouncers had gained recognition in Cochinchina of their rights as French citizens. This was a legal triumph, despite the efforts of colonial authorities during the First World War to prevent the spouses and families of Indian soldiers from receiving wartime allocations at 'French' rates.[1] Yet in the interwar period, the Indian French citizens of Cochinchina began to face some uncomfortable realities. Some of this discomfort was created by virtue of the very position they had fought so vehemently to defend in the late 1880s and early 1900s. The public sector became less secure as a niche of employment for Indians French citizens, even though the 1920s was otherwise a decade of prosperity. A new class of French-educated Vietnamese, their rise fostered by Governor General Sarraut's policy of 'Franco-Vietnamese collaboration', now competed with the French Indians for jobs.[2] Members of this same class, Vietnamese 'bourgeois' moderates led by the Constitutionalist Party, began to question openly the participation of Indian French citizens in the political and administrative life of Cochinchina, as the preceding chapter has shown. Reforms of the administration by the succeeding Governor General Varenne further threatened Indian employment and in particular the positions of Indian functionaries employed at the lowest levels.[3] By the 1930s, the increasing radicalisation of Vietnamese anti-colonial politics along with the effects of the global economic depression hardened local attitudes towards Indian French citizens as well as other migrants from India.

1. See Jennifer Anne Boittin, Christina Firpo, and Emily Musil Church, 'Hierarchies of Race and Gender in the French Colonial Empire, 1914–1946', *Historical Reflections,* 37, 1, 2011, 60–90, p. 67.
2. Agathe Larcher, 'La voie étroite des réformes coloniales et la 'collaboration franco-annamite' (1917–1928)', *Revue française d'histoire d'outre mer,* 82, 309, 1995, 387–420.
3. See 'La question des facteurs indiens', *Réveil Saigonnais,* 12 August 1925; Édouard Marquis, 'Le Problème Hindou', *Réveil Saigonnais,* 18 November 1924; Édouard Marquis, 'Lettre ouverte à mes compatriotes', *Réveil Saigonnais,* 15 May 1929.

Renouncers reacted to these interwar pressures with conscious efforts to raise their own public profile and to thereby lend purpose to their presence in Cochinchina. These ideas were generated from locally-based social organisations, and by the small but vibrant Franco-Tamil press. In the 1920s, their press and their associational life brought together all French citizens of Indian origin, both renounced Indians and the Indo-French, as the *Français de l'Inde*, the French of India. In their efforts to raise the '*hindou* profile' in Cochinchina, the *Français de l'Inde* put forward notions of themselves as modern, dynamic, and forward-looking. They depicted themselves as a people with both a future in Indochina, and a meaningful presence there which was deeply rooted in the past. During this period they conceived of themselves less as people with French citizenship at the forefront of their identities, and began more to see themselves as part of a larger 'Indian' social unit whose good name they needed first to rescue, then nurture and protect in order to ensure their continued survival in Indochina. And even as they were engaged in Saigon in these profile-raising exercises, they were caught up in internal conflicts played out through their social organisations.

The Indian French citizens of Cochinchina, and the wider group of expatriate *Français de l'Inde*, shaped a vision of themselves in the 1920s and 1930s as established residents deserving of a rightful place in the colony. This vision was directed outwards to an audience of Europeans, French-educated Vietnamese, and other cosmopolitan residents of the colony. It was grounded in the conviction that their French citizenship should be a cosmopolitan one, free from geographical limitations or racial prejudices. Yet as their internal disagreements show, and their shift to include the wider Indian community in their profile-raising indicates, their commitment to achieving and exercising full French citizenship within the French Empire came to be overtaken by other social and political priorities.

Southeast Asia's cosmopolitan heyday

Cultures of print and cultures of association flourished throughout Southeast Asia, and indeed throughout the world, from the late nineteenth century. Unprecedented mobility across Asia from the late nineteenth century produced 'multiple layers of sociability' within colonial societies, and contributed to the vitality of public cultures in Southeast

Asia and around the Indian Ocean Rim.[4] The activity of periodical presses, philanthropic societies, and recreational clubs was intensified in the interwar years, which witnessed a 'near simultaneous engagement across the world with the norms and forms of public life'.[5]

An equally vibrant public culture developed in Vietnam's cities in the interwar period. Hanoi and Saigon experienced a massive increase in periodical publication. An educated urban class eagerly embraced the modern age and fostered a spirit of civic awakening by forming societies and sports clubs. The new print technologies encouraged Buddhist and Confucian revivalist movements. In Saigon a culture of political journalism thrived alongside the development of a public popular culture.[6]

Less is known about how the cultural heterogeneity of Vietnamese cities, and particularly Saigon, helped to shape the terms of public debates. Vietnamese reformers in 1920s Saigon used the renouncers' French citizenship to press home arguments for the extension of their own participation in the public life of the colony. The debates which jointly engaged Saigon's moderate reformers and Indian French citizens in the pages of the Saigonese press show that Saigon's political journalism was not purely Vietnamese, but was shaped by a wider range of participants. Yet while they were locked in political rivalry, the Franco-Tamil press at the same time shared with its Vietnamese counterpart an outward-looking, cosmopolitan vision. It pursued with the same enthusiasm ideas of modernity and progress, a belief in the power of science, and the possibilities of advancing as a 'race' and a civilisation. Indian French citizens, as reflected in their Saigonese expatriate newspapers, were interested in questions of how to live and behave in the modern world, of the role of women in society, of the raising of children, of hygiene, and of sport. Talk of 'unity' and 'solidarity' framed much of their discussion.

French Indians in Saigon used this shared vision of modern self-advancement to counter the sense that their place in Indochina, and that of other Indians, was increasingly under scrutiny. The universalist

---

4. Harper, 'Globalism and the Pursuit of Authenticity', p. 261.
5. Andrew Arsan et al., 'Editorial – the roots of global civil society and the interwar moment', p. 160.
6. Peter Zinoman, 'Vũ Trọng Phụng's *Dumb Luck* and the nature of Vietnamese Modernism', introduction to Vũ Trọng Phụng, *Dumb Luck*, Ann Arbor: University of Michigan Press, 2002; Shawn McHale, *Print and Power: Confucianism, Communism & Buddhism in the making of modern Vietnam, 1920–45*, Honolulu: University of Hawaii Press, 2004; Tai, 'The Politics of Compromise'; Peycam, *The Birth of Vietnamese Political Journalism*.

and pan-Asian ideas of unity and civilisation they presented to inter-war Saigon did not persuade their intended readership. Yet Indian French citizens' failed attempts to convince the Vietnamese bourgeoisie that Indian residents were the rightful inheritors of Greater India's legacy in Indochina, and the tensions hanging in the air as an audience of Vietnamese Constitutionalists and resident Indians sat listening to Rabindranath Tagore on his visit to Saigon in 1929, should not detract from interwar Saigon's position as a vibrant inter-ethnic and cosmopolitain space in which a rich array of ideas were proposed and discussed.

INSTRUMENTS OF THE PUBLIC SPHERE: THE PRESS AND ASSOCIATIONAL LIFE

Locally-based social organisations, and a small but active Franco-Tamil press were two closely-linked vehicles of French Indian public expression in colonial Saigon. Both appeared from the 1900s. One of the earliest Indian associations on record, the *Syndicat des Français de l'Inde,* played a role in protesting against the treatment of Saigon's Indian policeman; it was probably formed, at least in part, for the purpose of strengthening the Indians' defence in debates over their citizenship. The first Franco-Tamil newspaper was less obviously established for the purpose of lobbying; it became a force pulling Indian French citizens into Saigon's public sphere through later circumstances. The activities of both associations and newspapers intensified in the inter-war period. From the 1920s they became instruments crucial in defending the interests of French citizens of Indian origin (renouncers as well as Indo-French). They became the channels through which French Indians made claims to a rightful place within French Indochina, for themselves and later for expatriate Indians more widely.

Between the turn of the twentieth century and the outbreak of World War Two, no less than fourteen social organisations were founded in Cochinchina catering solely to expatriate Indians originating from the French *comptoirs*. Most of these organisations were registered as mutual aid societies, but among them were also friendly societies (*amicales*) and sporting clubs.[7] The overwhelming majority were based in Saigon.

---

7. Six such organisations saw the light from 1903 to 1910, including the *Société de Secours Mutuels des Indiens en Cochinchine,* the *Syndicat des Français de l'Inde,* the *Amicale des Français de l'Inde,* the *Libérale de l'Inde,* the *Association Sportive Hindoue* and the *Mutuelle de Karikal.* The first mention of the *Union Amicale Indo-Française* dates to 1919, and from 1922 through

While these organisations were frequently short-lived, one of the earliest registered, the *Amicale des Français de l'Inde* ('Friendly Association of the French of India'), was still active in 1958. For the interwar period at least, none ever boasted a membership higher than about 200 members.[8]

It is not possible to confirm in all cases, but most Indian associations formed prior to the 1920s required their members to be French citizens. Surviving membership lists show that several societies had a majority of members who were renouncers (about three quarters) and a smaller number of Indo-French members. By the late 1920s, these societies were less concerned about whether their members actually held French citizenship; although Indian French citizens remained in the majority, French subjects were now admitted to some organisations.

Mutual associations in Cochinchina were formed within a French legal framework. Like the metropolitan models they were modelled on, they provided to members a financial and moral safety net. They were legally bound to remain both apolitical and secular, although the Indian societies did not adhere strictly to either stipulation. The Cochinchinese societies were financed through membership fees, a portion of takings from a 'Mutual lottery' and funds raised through charity fêtes. The stated aim of most of the Indian mutual societies was to prevent destitution among compatriots resident in Cochinchina; the earliest such societies were formed in the 1900s, at a time when a surge of renouncers arriving eager for posts in the Cochinchinese administration had begun to exceed the number of vacant positions. The impact of the 1930s Depression revived the role of the societies in mutual assistance; one of the main reasons for the 1934 merger of the *Mutualité Hindoue* and the *Mutuelle des Indo-Français Employés de Commerce et d'Industrie* was better to protect compatriots who were 'no longer able to make ends meet with their reduced salaries' or were 'out on the street'.[9]

---

to 1934 seven more associations were founded (*Solidarité, Union Progressiste Hindou, Mutualité Hindoue, Mutuelle des Indo-Français Employés de Commerce et d'Industrie, Mutuelle Hindoue de la Cochinchine*, the *Société Hindou-Sport de Saigon*, and the *Jeunesse Florissante de Pondichéry*).

8. VNA2 GD 2997 Mutuelle Hindoue de la Cochinchine, 1935: Annual Bulletin of the Mutuelle Hindoue 1935.

9. On mutual societies in France see Paul Dutton, *Origins of the French Welfare State: The Struggle for Social Reform in France, 1914–1947*, Cambridge: Cambridge University Press, 2002. See also Erica J. Peters, 'Resistance, Rivalries and Restaurants: Vietnamese Workers in Interwar France', *Journal of Vietnamese Studies*, 2, 1, 2007, 109–143, p. 139.

Some of the first Indian social organisations were led by respected French citizens within Tamil business circles. Louis Sinnaya, a legal clerk, entrepreneur, and later a publisher in both Saigon and Pondicherry, was the founding president of the *Société de Secours Mutuels des Indiens en Cochinchine*. Behind the *Syndicat des Français de l'Inde* was the banker and landowner Ra. Soccalingam. Other renouncers created themselves through their very involvement with associations. Neither man had a particularly remarkable career in Cochinchina, but Symphorien Lami and Lourdes Nadin both made their names through their work with associations. Both were duly awarded, among other accolades, with the 'Bronze Medal for Mutuality' in 1935.[10]

As the Franco-Tamil press developed in Saigon, Indian publicists too began to play prominent roles in the establishment of social organisations. From its outset, the society *Solidarité* received support and publicity from Édouard Marquis at the *Réveil Saigonnais*. Raoul Vernier of the *Saigon-Dimanche* attempted to form one organisation to unite French citizens of 'colonial' origin employed in Saigon. He founded another (the *Mutuelle des Indo-Français Employés de Commerce et d'Industrie*) to protest at the exclusion of Indians from its European equivalent. While these publicists were instrumental in the founding of some Indian social organisations, they provided sustenance for many others by publishing the proceedings of meetings and conferences.[11]

Édouard Marquis and Raoul Vernier were the leading figures behind Saigon's Franco-Tamil newspapers. Two French-language publications, the *Réveil Saigonnais* (1907–1929) and the *Saigon-Dimanche* (1927–1935) served as mouthpieces for the interests and ideas of Indians residing in Indochina. The latter newspaper changed names twice; it re-

---

10. References for the preceding paragraphs are as follows: VNA2 Goucoch IB.24/0215 Sociétés 1902–1909 ... Syndicat des Français de l'Inde, 1907; no author, *La Mutualité Hindoue: Statuts*, Saigon: Imprimerie Nguyen-Kha, 1932; ANOM GGI 2276 Rapatriement des Indigents provenant de l'Inde, de la Réunion et de la Corse, 1908; VNA2 Goucoch IB.24/0810 Sociétés ... Société Indo-Française de la Cochinchine; VNA2 GD2997 Mutuelle Hindoue de la Cochinchine, 1935; VNA2 GD2998 Mutuelle des Indo-Français Employés de Commerce et d'Industrie, 1934; VNA2 Goucoch IB.24/0213 Sociétés 1902–1911 ... Association Sportive Hindoue; No author, *La Mutuelle Hindoue de Cochinchine, Société de Secours Mutuels, Statuts*, Saigon: Imprimerie Joseph Viet, 1935; VNA2 SL 4585 Demande de réhabilitation formuléé par M. SINNAYA (Louis) demeurant à Saigon 1902; Pourouchotam Tamby, *British raj et swaraj*, Pondicherry: L. Sinnaya Press, 1918.

11. 'Un banquet', *Réveil Saigonnais*, 9 June 1923; R.V., 'A ceux qu'on ne défend pas: Employés de commerce Français de l'Inde groupez-vous!', *Saigon-Dimanche*, 18 September 1927.

Plate 13: Recipients of the 'Bronze Medal for Mutuality', Symphorien Lami and Lourdes Nadin. *Bulletin of the Mutuelle Hindoue*, 1935. Courtesy Vietnamese National Archive Number Two, Ho Chi Minh City.

appeared as *Indochine-Inde* (1936–1937) and then, in Tamil, as *Indōṣin-Indiyā* (1939–1941). It was joined by two short-lived publications: the Tamil-language newspaper *Saigon Vartamany* (1928) and the French-language magazine *L'Inde Illustrée* (April 1933–September 1934). No copies of *Saigon Vartamany* have survived in public holdings.[12]

The *Réveil Saigonnais* was the longest-running of Saigon's Franco-Tamil newspapers. From the outset it had connections with the French possessions in India. Its founder and owner, the widow Rose Quaintenne, was a French woman of metropolitan origin, who had come to Saigon from Pondicherry with her husband, Victor Quaintenne. A

---

12. Historian Hue-Tam Ho Tai mentions that Camille Delivar's *Temps d'Asie* was a similar Franco-Tamil newspaper and that Marquis was a pseudonym for Devilars. Yet while *Temps d'Asie* may have sympathised with Indian causes, it was not a Franco-Tamil newspaper to the extent of being run by Pondicherry journalists. The paper-trail of Marquis' life-history, and photographs of him in the *Réveil Saigonnais,* indicate that the Devilar connection was perhaps a wild rumour at the time, but one which can't be substantiated (Tai, *Radicalism*, p. 123). On *Saigon Vartamany* and editor S. Samou see 'Un confrère tamoul', *Saigon-Dimanche*, 26 August 1928; VNA2 Goucoch IB.24/0213: calling card of S. Samou; 'Amicale des Français de l'Inde, banquet d'au revoir', *Réveil Saigonnais*, 25 June 1910.

local councillor, he had led Pondicherry's *Parti Français*, and was an avid defender of the renouncers against the supposed electoral and political manipulations of Mayor Chanemougan. Defying the 'rigorous norms' ruling the lives of European women in the colonies, Rose remained in Saigon with her three children when her husband died, and built for herself a respectable career. She worked on de Lachevrotière's *Opinion* and may have established as many as three Vietnamese newspapers before founding the *Réveil Saigonnais*.[13]

Although the *Réveil Saigonnais* did not state outright its defence of renouncer interests until the 1920s, it published articles and put forward views prior to the First World War which were clearly intended to attract a readership of French-speaking Indians and to appeal to renouncer politics. The newspaper covered political debates in French India, and published editorials defending renouncers against Chanemougan's views. It put forward views on the British presence in India which compared British oppression unfavourably with a French policy of assimilation in its Indian *comptoirs*, a position which sat comfortably with Indian French citizens and French colonialists alike. The *Réveil* also ran articles promoting social progress in India and the abandonment of 'outdated' customs.[14]

From around 1910 the *Réveil Saigonnais* began to forge links with emerging Indian social organisations. Notices submitted by the associations announcing upcoming meetings or covering events held in honour of prominent members attest to this. The newspaper also began to facilitate the involvement of Indian French citizens in Cochinchinese electoral politics by publishing pieces underlining then Deputy Deloncle's commitment to renounced Indians' interests in Cochinchina.[15]

---

13. On Quaintenne's activities in Pondicherry and Saigon see Weber, *Pondichéry*, pp. 221, 258, 264, 268; Édouard Marquis, 'A nos Abonnés et Lecteurs', *Réveil Saigonnais*, 31 December 1921; Peycam, *The Birth of Vietnamese Political Journalism*, p. 112; On the 'rigorous norms' ruling the lives of single European women in the colonies see Stoler's *Carnal Knowledge*, p. 61. The 'colonial widow...the editor of a major Saigon daily', cited by Stoler as the rare exception to the rule was undoubtedly Quaintenne herself.

14. Rose Quaintenne, 'Chanemougan est un Sénateur au crampon', *Réveil Saigonnais*, 26 May 1908; Rose Quaintenne, 'Les soulèvements de l'Inde', *Réveil Saigonnais*, 20 August 1910; 'L'émancipation des veuves hindoues', *Réveil Saigonnais*, 17 September 1910.

15. Examples include 'Amicale des Français de l'Inde, banquet d'au revoir', *Réveil Saigonnais*, 25 June 1910; 'Un lien Pondichéry-Inde' *Réveil Saigonnais*, 2 February 1910; Rose Quaintenne, 'Banquet donné par M. Ra. Soccalingam en l'honneur de M. François Deloncle', *Réveil Saigonnais*, 16 April 1910.

When Rose Quaintenne died suddenly in 1921, Édouard Marquis assumed provisional direction of the newspaper, becoming its fully-fledged editor not long afterwards. He was by his own description a 'native of Pondicherry', and was probably of mixed Indian and French parentage. Trained as a doctor in India, his desire to enlist during the First World War had brought him to Cochinchina where he was employed on military convoys, tending to the health of Vietnamese workers transported between Saigon and Marseille. He was subsequently employed as a medical officer on the prison island of Poulo Condore. Dissatisfied at his inability to advance (his Pondicherry medical qualification was not fully recognised in Cochinchina), Marquis put aside medicine in 1921. He worked briefly in the Saigon Public Library, but soon found a place for himself in journalism.[16]

Rose Quaintenne's funeral in December of 1921 was both a tribute to her attachment to French India and a marker of the direction the newspaper was more firmly to take. A eulogy was delivered by the businessman Xavier de Condappa on behalf of the *Amicale des Français de l'Inde*. She 'never hid her sympathy for us', he declared, 'her last lines, even, were devoted to the defence of the French of India'. Édouard Marquis penned her obituary, and took charge; he cannot have been employed for more than six months with the *Réveil* at the time.[17]

With Marquis at the helm, the *Réveil Saigonnais* made its affinities with the French Indians much more evident and began to show signs that it had a large and loyal following. From 1922 it routinely printed stories defending the interests in the colony of French citizens of Indian origin. It ran regular columns with news from the French Establishments, published analyses of nationalism in British India, and printed articles which advocated 'progress' in India. Announcements of the births, deaths, and marriages of renouncers and Indo-French alike dominated the 'classifieds' section of the newspaper. Some of these events had taken place in Indochina, others in India. Under Marquis it was responsible for

---

16. 'Mes chers compatriotes', *Réveil Saigonnais*, 17 April 1929; ANOM GGI 33987 M. Marquis (Édouard) engagé comme Agent sanitaire contractuel à Saigon-Cholon, 1925 [sic]: Marquis to GGI, 10 October 1921 and in the same file, Note Cabinet GGI to Secretary General, 8 August 1921.
17. Édouard Marquis, 'A nos abonnés et lecteurs: Obsèques de notre Directrice', *Réveil Saigonnais*, 31 December 1921.

the creation of one Indian mutual association, *Solidarité*.[18] It also became deeply involved in political lobbying, following local and legislative elections and promoting the career of Ernest Outrey in his heyday as Cochinchina's Deputy. 'The interventions of Ernest Outrey' on behalf of Cochinchina's Indian French citizens were published faithfully, and most notably around the time of legislative elections. Outrey was close to the newspaper in more ways than one, having himself acted as editor for a brief interim in late 1921.

The *Réveil's* involvement in political lobbying reached its logical conclusion in May 1929 when Édouard Marquis ran for a seat on the Municipal council. His platform was the defence of the *colonie hindoue* or more precisely the Indian *petits fonctionnaires* who stood to lose their positions through Varenne's policy of opening the ranks of 'French' cadres to non-naturalised Vietnamese. Marquis' defeat at the polls, as well as the bleak financial outlook, undoubtedly both contributed to the demise of the *Réveil Saigonnais* a month later, in June of 1929.[19]

Saigon's French Indians were not left, however, without a newspaper of their own. The *Saigon-Dimanche* had appeared on the scene in July of 1927, two years before the *Réveil Saigonnais* ceased publication. It was edited by Raoul Ramraja Vernier, a Saigon-born French citizen of Indian origin. Vernier ran a printing press (Imprimerie R. Vernier) while publishing the paper. He was replaced during his occasional absences from the country by another French Indian, Samy Abraham. Abraham had abandoned his training in law to follow his ambitions as a journalist and writer of fiction.[20]

The *Saigon-Dimanche* did not initially aim to be either a political newspaper or an 'Indian' one. 'There are published in Saigon', its inaugural editorial claimed, 'too many newspapers which call themselves political, unfortunately of a politics which is often miserable and prone to envy and hatred.' The *Saigon-Dimanche* meant instead to be 'a good

---

18. 'Un banquet', *Réveil Saigonnais*, 9 June 1923.
19. 'Élections municipales du 5 mai 1929', *Réveil Saigonnais*, 14 April 1929; Édouard Marquis, 'Lettre ouverte à mes compatriotes', *Réveil Saigonnais*, 15 May 1929; 'A nos lecteurs', *Réveil Saigonnais*, 27 June 1929.
20. Advertisement for 'Imprimerie R. Vernier', *Saigon-Dimanche*, 19 March 1932; 'Hindoue Tamoule Djana Sangam, Amicale Hindoue', *Indochine-Inde*, 8 March 1936; Raoul Vernier, 'Dernier appel à mes compatriotes', *Saigon-Dimanche*, 30 April 1933; 'Une oeuvre de M. Samy Abraham', *Saigon-Dimanche*, 30 November 1930.

recreational and relaxing periodical with the aim only of distracting you a moment without stirring your bile.'[21]

Yet just over a month into its publication the *Saigon-Dimanche* gave up any pretensions of avoiding political journalism. Under the heading, 'Colonials Let's Defend Ourselves', Raoul Vernier called upon 'The French of Réunion, of Martinique, of Guadeloupe, of Algeria, and India … as well as the French of Indochina', to defend their rights as French citizens of colonial origin. The position of these 'real colonials', he claimed, in Cochinchina's administration, in its commerce, and in its industry, was threatened by people newly arrived from Europe, many of whom were not even from France. Colonial citizens 'who through our families have a long colonial past behind us … who were born in these lands and who have lived here if not our entire lives, at least a good part of them' understood the culture and language of the colony and were acclimatised to the conditions: 'so much so that our country is less France than the colony we have seen born and grow'. Vernier stressed the French citizenship of the 'real colonials' and called upon them to form a society to defend their position in Indochina.[22]

Despite the bold call for 'intercolonial solidarity', the *Saigon-Dimanche* did not continue as the voice of a broader band of Saigon's colonial citizens. It quickly found itself taken up instead with the full-time defence of causes which were expressly Indian. Once it had decided to commit itself to political comment and to focus on an Indian readership, the *Saigon-Dimanche* was even more willing than Marquis' *Réveil Saigonnais* to show itself as the voice of Indian French citizens in Saigon. It began by covering the same ground as the *Réveil*, with reports and analyses from British and French India and by its support for Saigon's Indian social organisations; but it showed a greater sense of purpose, was more critically engaged, and came to make very effective use of focused press campaigns.

Saigon-Dimanche was also more forcefully involved in local politics than the *Réveil*. It ended the practice whereby Cochinchinese Deputies used the Franco-Tamil press to court the Indian electorate, by leading a charge of Indian voters disillusioned in the late 1920s by their long-standing supporter, Deputy Ernest Outrey. This was coupled with

---

21. 'Notre programme', *Saigon-Dimanche*, 3 July 1927.
22. R. Vernier, 'Coloniaux Défendons-Nous', *Saigon-Dimanche*, 7 August 1927.

a press campaign, to 'fight to the death the odious legend' of Indian electoral venality.[23]

While *Saigon-Dimanche* did not follow slavishly the 'interventions' of the colonial Deputy in the manner of the *Réveil*, it continued to use political channels to lobby for the welfare of Indian French citizens in Cochinchina. Like Marquis before him, Vernier ran for the municipal council, seeking to continue his 'action' in favour of his 'compatriots the *Français de l'Inde*' by putting himself forward as a councillor in the election of May 1933. Unlike Marquis, he won a seat. The message of thanks he penned to his supporters reads like a declaration of the death of the Deputy as the manipulator of the Indian vote. Claiming to his readership to be the 'first of your kind' to serve as a councillor in the Saigon municipality (the term of Douressamy-Naiker in the late 1880s was by then long forgotten), he claimed that the Mayor elect (Marc Casati on whose list Vernier ran) would now 'compensate for the deficiencies and the silence' of Deputy Outrey by coming to the defence of Saigon's resident Indian French citizens. Although there is no record of any action on the part of Casati in this regard, Vernier's words show how the relationship between Deputy and Indian voters had irrevocably changed.[24]

The *Saigon-Dimanche* was not only more strident than the *Réveil* in its efforts to present itself as spokesman for the *Français de l'Inde* in Cochinchina. It was also more willing to show itself as a more broadly 'Indian' newspaper, depicting and appealing to an Indian expatriate community made up not only of renounced Indians, or Indians from the French possessions, but of overseas Indians of all creeds. A regular feature was a listing of all Indian places of worship in Saigon and Cholon. The newspaper took a greater interest than its competitor in the numerous Indian visitors, many of them politically-minded figures, who were beginning to pass through Saigon in this period and who were eager to impart their views to their compatriots overseas. It also came to the defence of Indians who did not necessarily have any connection or bear

---

23. 'M. Outrey n'a pas payé sa dette aux électeurs français originaires de l'Inde', *Saigon-Dimanche*, 20 April 1928; R. Vernier, 'M. Outrey, les Français de l'Inde ne meritent pas l'affront que vous leur faites!', *Saigon-Dimanche*, 21 April 1932; Raoul Vernier, 'Dernier appel', *Saigon-Dimanche*, 30 April 1933.

24. 'Notre Programme', *Saigon-Dimanche*, 3 July 1927; Raoul Vernier, Appel aux amis de *Saigon-Dimanche* et à mes compatriotes', *Saigon-Dimanche*, 24 April 1933; ANOM FM Indo AF53: Laurans to Sen EFI, 15 March 1888; Raoul Vernier, 'Mes remerciements', *Saigon-Dimanche*, 7 May 1933.

any loyalty to France and its empire. An Indian, or more often specifically Tamil, cultural allegiance was openly displayed in notices advertising everything from the latest Tamil music just arrived at Saigon's largest department store, to troupes of visiting Tamil performers, to local Indian restaurants and suppliers of curry powders, chutneys, and palm toddy. The newspaper's first relaunch in the late 1930s as *Indochine-Inde* confirmed its decidedly more Indian perspective, while its later shift to publication in Tamil made clear that its Indian interests represented those more precisely of the expatriate majority in Cochinchina, the ethnic Tamils. The close interlinking of Indian social organisations and the Franco-Tamil press proved crucial in Indian French citizens' interwar efforts to 'raise the Indian profile' in Cochinchina.

Modern men, historical purpose

In one respect the *Français de l'Inde* in Cochinchina in the interwar years were no different from their moderate and modernist Vietnamese counterparts, or from educated urban 'progressives' elsewhere in Southeast

Plate 14: Advertisement for the Indian supplier 'Au Comptoir Hindou'. *Indochine-Inde*, 1932. Courtesy General Sciences Library, Ho Chi Minh City.

Plate 15: Announcement of a Tamil film screening in Saigon. *Indochine-Inde*, 5 July 1936. Courtesy General Sciences Library, Ho Chi Minh City.

Asia in this period, in their eagerness to portray themselves as a dynamic, forward-looking, and unified group. The messages Saigon's French Indians put across were undoubtedly intended to assure French authorities that they were respectable, modern men worthy of their trust; but they were also attempts to find common ground with Cochinchina's own growing moderate and modern middle class, and to smooth over existing tensions.

Like other self-consciously modern peoples of the period, French citizens of Indian origin actively sought to improve the calibre of their youth both intellectually and physically. This they did through activities ranging from vocational training, to discussions and conferences on subjects such as hygiene and childrearing, to organising sports teams and tournaments.[25] Characteristic of modernist ideas at the time, they very consciously subscribed to the idea that progressive colonised peoples

---

25. For examples see *La Mutualité Hindoue: Société d'entre-aide et de protection fondée à Saigon le 6 mai 1928*, Saigon: Imprimerie Nguyen Kha, 1932; VNA2 GD 2997 Mutuelle Hindoue de la Cochinchine, 1935: Statutes of *Mutualité Hindoue*, 1932; 'Mutualité Hindoue', *Saigon-Dimanche*, 1 June 1930; VNA2 GD 2998 Mutuelle des Indo-Français Employés de Commerce et d'Industrie, 1934: Statuts 1931.

were engaged, indeed had a duty to engage, in a contest to better themselves. This element of their thinking emerges clearly in exhortations to participate in competitive sport. A 1931 article in *Saigon-Dimanche* urged 'all young *Français de l'Inde* who are no less worthy of their race than the Metropolitans, the *Annamites,* or the Chinese of their own' to 'found a *hindou* Sporting Union!'[26] A similar attitude can be found in reports of the achievements of Indian sportsmen, both abroad and at home. Indochinese tennis star James Samuel, of Pondicherry stock, was gleefully reported to have 'crushed' his French opponent in the 1933 Tonkin interclub final; aviator Avadiayappachettiar, visiting Saigon in 1933, was lauded as 'a magnificent example of modern *hindou* youth: evolved, educated, and courageous. Indifferent to none of civilisation's technical progresses, he knows how to adapt to everything.'[27]

Similarly, local renouncers perceived to have succeeded in the colony were honoured through banquets and other events, usually hosted by Indian social organisations. Lengthy accounts of these occasions were written up in the Franco-Tamil press. A banquet held in July 1923 for the entrepreneur Xavier de Condappa and the *colon* Mouttou is one example; a *champagne d'honneur* in honour of the Civil Service Administrator Mr. Samy is another.[28]

A further way in which the French Indians sought to secure their future in the colony was to elevate their past. They did not have to look far back into history to find reason to claim a rightful position within the colonial project. But – better still – they eagerly seized upon new French historical and archaeological evidence from Indochina to find justification for their own presence reaching back to antiquity.

From the 1920s French citizens of Indian origin in Cochinchina increasingly began to make public reference to the pioneering colonial

---

26. 'Pourquoi ne Fonderiez-vous pas une « Union Sportive Hindoue »', *Saigon-Dimanche*, 18 October 1931.
27. 'Soiree musicale pour J. Samuel', *Saigon-Dimanche,* 11 October 1932; 'Championnat Interclub du Tonkin. Le T.C. est champion, mais Saumont est écrasé par Samuel', *Saigon-Dimanche*, 26 March 1933; 'Aviateur Hindou Avadiayappachettiar arrivé à Saigon', *Saigon-Dimanche*, 24 December 1933.
28. 'Un banquet', *Réveil Saigonnais*, 9 July 1923; 'On fête un partant', *Réveil Saigonnais*, 27 August 1923; See also 'Un grand philanthrope hindou M. Xavier de Condappa', *Saigon-Dimanche*, 15 February 1931; VNA2 GD 2997 Mutuelle Hindoue de la Cochinchine, 1935: Annual Bulletin 1935.

spirit established by their forebears. It was one of the central points made by Édouard Marquis at a *Solidarité* banquet held in 1923:

> In this grandiose monument that France has built in this country, our ancestors have carried their stone... soldiers and functionaries of the hour, they have silently paid their tribute to French sovereignty. They died alongside our brothers from the Metropole. *This cannot be forgotten.*

The Indian French citizens of the 1920s had inherited a loyal commitment to strive to develop French Indochina. 'Following their example', Marquis continued, 'we bring our own modest contribution to the sublime work of France in this country. We have only one wish:to work for the greatness of France.'[29]

Saigon-Dimanche made similar claims that the French Indians had earned their right to remain in Cochinchina. In the course of defending Indians barred from a French mutual association, the newspaper claimed:

> The insalubrious beginnings of the colony took the lives of many valiant pioneers. Dysentery ... caused ravages greater than those brought by *Annamite* bullets. The French of India were called to hold subordinate positions that no European could fill. And their services were appreciated at their proper worth. Endemic illnesses did not spare them. Many of them fell on this soil that they helped to make French.[30]

The notion that Indian migrants had contributed to the conquest and the French colonisation of Cochinchina was not new. It had been used in the past, notably by European defenders of the renouncers' electoral rights in Cochinchina, and by renouncers themselves in their campaign on behalf of Saigon's Indian policemen.[31] The novelty in the 1920s was that the Indian French citizens now asserted this claim not only to a French colonial audience, but to a public which included educated Vietnamese. It is doubtful that the more radical Vietnamese of the late 1920s were in any way persuaded by Indian migrants eager to demonstrate their role as joint architects of French colonialism. Although Indian French citizens' claims to the right of conquest in

---

29. 'Un banquet', *Réveil Saigonnais*, 9 July 1923.
30. Raoul Vernier, 'Ceux qu'on ne défend pas', *Saigon-Dimanche*, 7 August 1929.
31. See H. Ternisien, 'La Question Électorale en Cochinchine', Supplement of *Journal d'Outre Mer*, 21 February 1888; ANOM FM Indo NF 329 La situation des travailleurs Indous en Indochine 1919: Chamber of Deputies Parliamentary report 3rd session 27 March 1919; ANOM GGI 17248 Au sujet des agents de police indiens citoyens français de la ville de Saigon, 1910: Pamphlet 'Ce qui se passe au Colonies', p. 4.

Indochina might not have been accepted in more radical quarters, such claims were not rejected out of hand by the more moderate Vietnamese thinkers of the time. Their own calls for reform, after all, did not necessarily lie outside the bounds of empire:

> Do [the Vietnamese] not have the right to question [the Indians] who constitute a political and administrative oligarchy in their country and do not offer the moral and intellectual guarantees that one would expect generally of those who aspire to occupy the first positions in a well-organised society? The French are here by their 'right of conquest'; but next to this right...they make a more respectable claim on the natives by bringing to them the fruits of a long civilisation built on several centuries of work and study. We bend before this superiority without relinquishing the hope that we will...by studying our educators...rise to the level of Europeans.[32]

The *Tribune Indigène* suggested that the Vietnamese could accept the French right of conquest because the French had also brought the 'fruits' of their (implicitly admirable) civilisation. The Indians, by contrast, had come with no 'moral' or 'intellectual guarantees' and no such civilisation. The French of India presented themselves as 'sons of the conquest' in the 1920s not merely to stir their own pride or appeal solely to French patriotism. They participated in an ongoing, if politically conservative, discussion with moderate, non-communist Vietnamese over the meaning of colonisation and the progress of civilisation, which both parties took seriously at the time.

As if in direct response to the *Tribune Indigène*, Indian French citizens seized upon the idea of 'Greater India', and quite literally upon its scholars, as they passed through Saigon en route to Angkor and other points of archeological interest. The notion of Greater India, as historical anthropologist Susan Bayly has described it, was an interwar interpretation of much older Indian political, commercial, and cultural exchanges with Southeast Asia as 'a great Pan-Asian mission of overseas cultural diffusion in ancient times'. It was conceived in the 1920s by Indian social scientists drawn to the early twentieth-century scholarship of French and Dutch Indologists, epigraphists, and archaeologists working in Southeast Asia. European studies of Southeast Asia's artistic and architectural splendours (which Europe's colonial presence in the region had given its scholars the licence to undertake) emphasised the influence of early, expansion-

---

32. 'La Question Indienne', *La Tribune Indigène*, 6 December 1922.

ist, Indian kingdoms on Southeast Asia's ancient civilisations.³³ As the Indologist Georges Coedès stated, Indian thinkers discovered in this new scholarship a long-forgotten past:

> It is a curious thing; India quickly forgot that its culture had spread to the East and the Southeast over such vast areas. Indian scholars were unaware of this until very recently. It took a small group of them, who had learned French and Dutch and undertaken studies... in the Universities of Paris and Leiden to discover, in our works and those of our colleagues in Holland and Java, the history of what they now call, with a legitimate pride, 'Greater India'.³⁴

But beyond this sense of rediscovery, the appeal of the European findings for the Indian scholars and their supporters lay in the way in which studies of this ancient past could be shaped to resonate with the present. They posed a satisfying challenge to the idea, received mainly through British imperialist thinkers, of India as a minor player in world history, a 'domain of timeless, ahistorical essences, and fixed territorial units successively conquered by the irresistible forces of "Aryan", "Muhammedan" and European civilisation'. The Indian scholars' India-centred interpretations of the works of Greater India thinkers emphasised the 'centrality of their forebears in the engendering of high culture in other lands'. India was not timeless and unchanging, but dynamic and expansive. Its peoples were not defeated, but harboured a 'genius' for civilising others, having indeed been colonisers themselves.³⁵ Their form of imperialism, moreover, had been 'peaceful and benevolent... a unique thing in the history of mankind'.³⁶

It comes as little surprise that Indians residing in Indochina in the early twentieth century should have come into contact with ideas of Greater India and found much there that appealed to them. With Saigon as their central node, Indochina's Indian communities were at the crossroads for access to Angkor in the Cambodian heartland, to the Cham monuments of central Vietnam, and to the sites of Funan and Oc Eo in the Mekong Delta. By placing themselves within the ranks of those who had brought French civilisation to Cochinchina, French Indians had already begun to develop a view of themselves as a 'supra-local civilising force', albeit

---

33. Bayly, 'Imagining "Greater India": French and Indian Visions of Colonialism in the Indic Mode', *Modern Asian Studies*, 38, 3, 2004, 703–744, p. 708.
34. G. Coedès, *Les États hindouisés d'Indochine et d'Indonésie*, Paris: de Boccard, 1989 [1948], p. 4.
35. Bayly, 'Imagining "Greater India"', pp. 710–711, 716, 720–721.
36. 'SVK' quoted in Bayly 'Imagining "Greater India"', p. 712.

one wedded to French colonialism.³⁷ Greater Indianists' challenge to Anglo-Saxon imperialist thinking sat comfortably with the conservative politics of most Indian French citizens. They remained loyal to France as an imperial power but were relatively free in their criticism of British colonialism in the Indian subcontinent. The 'peaceful' and 'benevolent' ancient Indian colonising force of Greater Indianists' perceptions was expressed in terms which mirrored French colonialist views of their own 'respectful' civilising mission.³⁸ This point would not have been lost on Indochina's Indian French citizens, who largely endorsed the *mission civilisatrice* despite their battles with Cochinchinese authorities to ensure its principles, in their regard, were respected.

It is not surprising either that the *Réveil Saigonnais*, with its links to French India, should have come across Sylvain Lévi, a French Indologist much admired by Greater Indianists. In July of 1923 the *Réveil* published an article by Lévi in which he traced French contributions to Indology from the late nineteenth century. The French conquest of Indochina, he maintained, had opened up avenues vital to the study of ancient Indian overseas expansion. The discovery by Étienne Aymonier (the self-trained archaeologist and scholar of Champa) of a vast epigraphic literature proved that 'Indochina received its civilisation from India; the literature, the sacred language, the teachings, the arts of India flourished there from the first centuries of the Christian era.' 'Attention was swiftly drawn', Lévi continued, 'to the role of India in the civilisation of the Far East and its place in the ensemble of human civilisation.'³⁹

The article for the *Réveil* served a dual purpose. On the surface it merely enlightened readers about the development of French scholarship in Asia. On a more profound level it invited Indian expatriate readers to feel a sense of belonging with a far greater historical depth than one that began with the French conquest. Renouncers and other Frenchmen of Indian origin could go further and reconcile the two historical narratives. They could claim as their legacy the civilising energies of the ancient Indians, while asserting that the French colonialism to which they were loyal was an avenue through which this ancient force could be revitalised. If France, as Lévi emphasised in closing his article,

---

37. Bayly, 'Imagining "Greater India"', p. 706.
38. Ibid., p. 714.
39. Sylvain Lévi, 'Indianisme', *Réveil Saigonnais*, 19 July 1923.

could 'recall with a legitimate pride' the part played by French scholars in uncovering Southeast Asia's ancient ties to India, the French Indians in Indochina could claim both traditions and both forms of 'genius' as their own.

French Indians received their opportunity to claim publicly the legacy of Greater India with the arrival in Saigon of an unexpected visitor. The anticipated arrival, in July of 1924, of the Bengali poet and Nobel Prize Laureate Rabindranath Tagore prompted a call in the *Réveil Saigonnais* for Saigon's expatriate Indians to show respect for their esteemed compatriot, and to demonstrate to the rest of the colony the success that their people could achieve, by receiving him in a fitting manner. This plea for a proper reception for Tagore was perhaps the first time a call for '*hindou*' unity in the Franco-Tamil press was explicitly intended to include more than the narrow group of renounced Indians and the small coterie of Indo-French who joined them. 'This is the moment, more than ever', the article proclaimed, 'to forget all personal animosity, to make a clean slate of all prejudices of caste or religion and to unite ourselves and give [Tagore] a sumptuous reception…Let's show him that we are proud of him. Let's give him the proof of our unity and allow the poet to carry home an excellent impression of the Indian colony of Saigon.'[40] In practice too preparations for Tagore's arrival were carried out by a committee representative of all of the Indian interests in the colony. A meeting held some weeks later to prepare for Tagore's arrival at Saigon's 'Chettiar temple' was attended by twenty-one members of a provisional reception committee, including 'four Chettys, two Muslims, four Indian French subjects, four Bombay merchants, four Hindus, and three Parsis'. The committee was headed by a renouncer.[41] The Indian community pledged nearly 5,000 piastres towards the cost of a lavish reception. The event was to include a pavilion to receive the poet at the port. A cortège, including two decorated elephants, was to take him in procession, 'preceded by music', up Catinat Street, Saigon's main avenue. Preparations were made for a visit to the ruins at Angkor.[42]

---

40. Un Hindou, 'Un appel aux Hindous!', *Réveil Saigonnais*, 2 June 1924.
41. ANOM GGI 65474 Rapport Annuel Contrôle des immigrants asiatiques 1923–1924: Milieux indiennes.
42. 'Pour Recevoir Tagore', *Réveil Saigonnais*, 1 July 1924.

In the event, matters required Tagore's swift return to Calcutta and he was unable to stop in Saigon. One member of his party did stop, instructed to carry Tagore's message of apology to those awaiting his arrival. This person was the historian and Greater India thinker Kalidas Nag, who had studied in Paris under Sylvain Lévi. Although there is no record of whether he was treated, in place of Tagore, to the planned elephant procession, there is ample proof that his visit injected further enthusiasm among Saigon's French Indians for the idea of a Greater India.[43]

Among the Greater India thinkers, Nag most consciously signalled in his overseas visits that contemporary Indian expatriates were the 'future agents of an Indian-led mission of pan-Asian cultural renewal', and his sojourn in Saigon is clear evidence of this.[44] He actively sought contact with expatriate Indians during his stay. He resided in Saigon in the French quarter, at the villa of a Louis Annoussamy. A notice placed in the *Réveil Saigonnais* announced that he would receive visitors there at fixed times every morning and afternoon.[45]

Nag was interviewed by Édouard Marquis at the *Réveil* shortly after his arrival. In the interview he voiced the idea of ancient India's peaceful moral conquest:

> This civilisation did not seek military conquest or economic invasion. It focused on the intellectual domain: it was a great and beautiful idea of fraternity and of peace which spread throughout the countries and peoples. The genius of India propagated itself beyond its frontiers and reunited in a cluster the peoples of the Far East.[46]

Nag swiftly projected this vision on to the present, and into the future, by pointing to expatriate Indians as the agents with the potential to perpetuate this force. 'Everywhere we see the strong imprint of Indian thought. And I reckon that the Indian colony is sufficiently large that its youth can orient itself towards this thought.' Self-improvement was the key:

> It requires that the Indians of Saigon shake off all apathy, and devote themselves to intellectual work. Certainly, not everyone is capable of it. But the new generation must be able to show to [other] peoples that it orients itself

---

43. 'Un savant hindou à Saigon', *Réveil Saigonnais*, 17 July 1924.
44. Bayly, 'Imagining "Greater India"', p. 729.
45. 'Un savant hindou à Saigon', *Réveil Saigonnais*, 17 July 1924; VNA2 GD 1346: Annoussamy to GCCH, 22 May 1924.
46. Édouard Marquis, 'Le savant hindou Nag à Saigon', *Réveil Saigonnais*, 22 July 1924.

towards the Light, towards Knowledge, towards Beauty. It will find there excellent nourishment for the intellect.[47]

Clearly noting that Saigon's expatriate community were already caught up in a campaign of self-improvement, Nag remarked that their 'efforts lean in this direction'.[48]

In the course of his visit, Nag intended to tour Angkor and the Cham sites of Annam to study the epigraphy. His other main purpose was to strengthen cooperation between French scientists from the *École Française d'Extrême Orient* (France's Hanoi-based centre of scholarly learning in the Far East) and Indian scholars of Sanskrit and Pali. His call for *rapprochement* was seized upon by Marquis and interpreted as a merger of the 'genius' of Greater India with 'French genius'. From his interview with Nag, Marquis concluded: 'If there are two thoughts called to complete each other, they are surely Latin thought and Indian thought. The affinity which exists between them is remarkable.' 'The *École Française d'Extrême Orient*', he expounded, 'holds high a torch where scholars of the Far East must come and warm themselves. This is the flame of French Genius.' The high esteem in which Dr. Nag clearly held French science allowed Marquis, in his article, to produce quotes from Nag expounding French virtues in support of his own thesis. 'The French archaeologists', Nag had asserted, 'are remarkable. It is France which has created archaeology.' Marquis reiterated Nag's call for 'intellectual *rapprochement*' between France (in Indochina) and India by reworking it into one which extolled French genius while not forgetting that Indochina owed its civilisation to India. The two narratives of benevolent imperialism were brought together. It was implied, in the process, that the Indians of Indochina (at least those loyal to France) had rightful claims over both: 'The role of France in the Far East has never been to enslave the people. Like India, France has sought a moral conquest. Now, she may be forcefully aided by Indian thought in her ideals of Goodness and Justice.'[49]

The use of the notion of Greater India to elevate their own presence in Indochina continued to appeal to the French Indians, but there was less appetite for displaying this view in public by the late 1920s.

---

47. Édouard Marquis, 'Le savant hindou Nag à Saigon', *Réveil Saigonnais*, 22 July 1924.
48. Ibid.
49. Ibid.

Cochinchina's ethnic Vietnamese majority had never identified with the peoples and cultures properly indigenous to the south; claims to a pan-Asian brotherhood with its roots in the ancient heritage of Greater India were problematic as a means to convince the Vietnamese of the Indians' rightful place in the colony. And Vietnamese politics had shifted to more radical forms.

When Rabindranath Tagore eventually did visit Saigon, in June of 1929, he delivered a lyrical speech which positioned him as a present-day bearer of the force of Greater India:

> I look across the centuries and I see the vision of a life that has left its mark on this land, and which runs still through my veins. I come to you with the memory of an encounter, an encounter which awoke the soul of this country to direct it on a new path of achievement, with all of its richness in Arts and Ideas. This age is now mute…all that remains is its shell which stretches out in magnificent ruins. The heart of India beat, in times past under [this] sunny sky…it lived its dreams in Beauty and sowed its thought in view of a rich monsoon of Culture in this foreign land. I feel that this distant India has come in me to visit once again…I am a messenger of the past. I am standing at your door, and I seek a place in your heart. I ask you to recognise me, even today when this story has been erased and the lamp has been put out.[50]

On this occasion, unlike Kalidas Nag's visit five years' earlier, neither of Saigon's Franco-Tamil newspapers took the opportunity to work Tagore's words into extended articles about the glorious legacy which overseas Indians had inherited under the French flag. Tagore's speech was delivered to a mixed audience which included the Vietnamese reformers Bùi Quang Chiêu and Dương Văn Giáo. His visit had been organised by a more formal 'Franco-Indian Annamite' committee, with Chiêu as its president.[51] Tagore's speech in this context risked being interpreted, in its exaltation of the 'lost' Indian contribution of the past, as an effort to diminish levels of culture and civilisation in modern Indochina. The *Saigon-Dimanche* printed the speech in full but was nonetheless quick to provide an interpretation favourable to harmony between the peoples of Indochina. In his coverage of the event Samy Abraham hastily commended the 'excellent soirée where all races forgot themselves and communed in the idea of Fraternity', and concluded, 'We would be fail-

---

50. S.A., 'L'arrivée du poète Tagore, un des sommets de la pensée humaine', *Saigon-Dimanche*, 26 June 1929.
51. 'Réception à Saigon de Rabindranath Tagore', *Réveil Saigonnais*, 17 June 1929.

ing in our duty if we did not express here our heartfelt gratitude to the French and *Annamites* who put aside all racial sentiments and received our poet Rabindranath Tagore in such a dignified manner.'[52] The *Réveil Saigonnais* allowed itself a minimal indulgence in Greater India glory. It published the brief greetings delivered by Pondicherry lawyer Xavier at a reception held for Tagore at Saigon's main Chettiar temple. There Xavier thanked Tagore for reminding 'French Cochinchina, so hospitable to my compatriots', of its 'noble filiation, its Indian origin'. The *Réveil*, however, did not publish any of Tagore's speech.[53]

CALLS FOR UNITY AND EPISODES OF DISCORD

In their drive to advance themselves in Indochina, Indian French citizens were preoccupied not only with claiming a position within the wider society, but also with demonstrating their own internal unity. They were aware that 'for us to gain esteem and to march in perfect accord with all the others, it is necessary first of all to be grouped and united ourselves'.[54]

Most of the social organisations established in Saigon by the *Français de l'Inde* included among their main goals 'unity', 'social union', or 'solidarity', and used their numerous gatherings to elaborate on this theme. *Solidarité's* banquet of July 1923 included a lengthy treatise on unity.[55] The same theme ran through an event held a month later to fête the departure for Pondicherry of an esteemed member.[56] 'Social union' was the subject of not one but two talks hosted in the summer of 1929 by the *Mutualité Hindoue*. The first was conducted by a *Mutualité* member, while the second was delivered by the society's honorary patron and president of the Saigon Chamber of Commerce, Mr. Darles. Darles' appointment suggests that the French Indians did not always keep good company when seeking the patronage of men in power. As a Provincial Resident in Tonkin, Darles had previously earned the title of 'the butcher of Thái Nguyên' for his many acts of 'capricious despotism', notably dur-

---

52. S.A., 'L'arrivée du poète Tagore, un des sommets de la pensée humaine', *Saigon-Dimanche*, 26 June 1929.
53. 'Tagore est rentrée chez lui. Une réception à la pagode des chettys', *Réveil Saigonnais*, 23 June 1929. For a detailed account of Tagore's 1929 visit, and a reading of his reception in colonial and post-colonial Vietnam see Phạm Phương Chi , 'The Rise and the Fall of Rabindranath Tagore in Vietnam', unpublished MA thesis, University of California at Riverside, 2012.
54. 'Un banquet', *Réveil Saigonnais*, 9 July 1923.
55. Ibid.
56. 'On fête un partant', *Réveil Saigonnais*, 27 August 1923.

ing the 1917 prison revolt.[57] Despite his deep unsuitability as a moral guide, his talk on the topic of unity, according to the *Saigon-Dimanche*, was 'loudly applauded'.[58]

Although unity featured as an important element in the French Indians' programme to better themselves, it was their weakness rather than their strength. Even as they entered the public arena to demonstrate their potential for advancement to the rest of Cochinchina, they were dogged by internal divisions. One of the main sources of discord, but not the only one, was a distinction Indian French citizens claimed to have set aside long ago, the distinction of caste.

The first overt reference to conflict among French Indians occurred at the *Solidarité* banquet honoring two prominent members of the community, de Condappa and Mouttou. This was held in July of 1923, prior to the departure of both men on leave to India. The reticence of some of the speech-makers at the banquet to speak directly of the 'retrograde' problem of caste prejudice suggests the subject continued to cause discomfort. Two of the four speakers suggested that the very reason the society was founded was to address problems of caste prejudice within the community, but they seemed loath to admit this. The president of the association, Bonjean, referred to 'a grievous spectacle of coteries' which had formed within the community and a problem of 'clans' which had 'risen up and torn each other apart'. *Solidarité's* leaders, he claimed, had gone 'from door to door' in an effort to make peace and 'to call for a union in the spirit and of the heart'. The second speaker, Mouttou, shied away from any specific mention of conflict, saying only that 'in the first days of our arrival in the colony' (he had been there thirty years) each man had struggled for himself, and now was the time to come together for a common purpose. De Condappa was more bold, openly naming caste differences as the cause of the discord that continued to divide expatriate renouncers. He declared he would fight for the 'defence of the interests of the Indian Colony (*la colonie Indienne*)', but that he would only do so in return for a union which 'abandons all notions of caste'

---

57. Darles' unsavoury character is described in detail in Zinoman, *Colonial Bastille,* pp. 191–196. Quotes here from Zinoman, *Colonial Bastille,* p. 191, and Tai, *Radicalism,* p. 118, respectively.
58. 'Une Conférence', *Saigon-Dimanche,* 28 July 1929; 'Une remarquable conférence de M. Darles', *Saigon-Dimanche,* 1 September, 1929.

and which 'banish[es] from our society the social prejudices so strongly rooted in India, but which have no place here'.⁵⁹

De Condappa's stern reproach was not nearly as well-received, however, as the final speech, by Édouard Marquis. Marquis downplayed the persistent rivalries, flattering his audience instead with the brighter proposal that the French of India were riding the crest of the most progressive wave of social reform in India. He won enthusiastic applause from the one hundred *Solidarité* members in attendance by moving rapidly beyond talk of internal discord, and instead depicting Saigon's Indian French citizens as agents caught up in an exciting Indian moment of change:

> India, asleep under the British yoke, has begun to awaken ... The same thought, the same pride, animates this people of the most diverse castes. Thus the barriers of prejudice, peoples' habits and customs, are falling away. Muslims, Hindus, Catholics, children of all castes are uniting ... India is beginning to think. She is manifesting her willingness to act ... something is changing over there. India is thinking [applause]. India is throwing off her lethargy and has found her conscience by ... the finest revolution that the country can achieve: the abolition of caste and class [repeated applause].⁶⁰

Marquis urged the two honoured members to carry to India the message that in Cochinchina 'the children of India seek solidarity, they are trying to unite'.⁶¹

Social reform in India was a process both more difficult and more complex than Marquis suggested, and his call to unity, confined to expatriate Indians with French citizenship and French loyalties, was clearly not intended to bring together all expatriate Indians regardless of caste or creed. His point however, was not to dwell on details but to rouse his audience with the stirring notion that their own drive for unity reached across to a larger movement in India whose meaning was more profound. Moreover, it was the very benevolence of French rule which the French of India had to thank for their social advancement. British rule in the subcontinent, Marquis argued, was marked by brutality. He stopped short of claiming that the British presence had served to strengthen social prejudice, but it had done nothing to alleviate it and had induced 'lethargy'. By contrast, the French presence in Pondicherry

---

59. All quotes from 'Un banquet', *Réveil Saigonnais*, 9 July 1923.
60. Ibid.
61. Ibid.

and the other French Establishments was a positive force serving to address social inequality. In a later article Marquis wrote of the 'happy evolution' Indians had undergone under French administration. This was undoubtedly a reference in part to their access to French citizenship.[62] Unlike the unhappy lot of Indians under British rule, French rule in both India and Indochina had brought 'French peace'. 'Here, well-being and joyous smiles circulate on your faces. In the shadow of this French flag which you love profoundly unfolds the most loyal and peaceful existence possible.'[63] The enthusiastic applause which greeted Marquis' *Soldarité* speech might indicate that, stirred by the suggestion of social revolution, the French Indians temporarily forgot their quarrels.

The notion that Cochinchina's French Indians were aligned with a 'social revolution' in India might be expected to have raised concern among the French authorities in Cochinchina that they were similarly sympathetic to Indian nationalism. After all, French security forces feared the spread of subversive ideas and kept a watchful eye on Indochina's numerous Indian visitors in the 1920s.[64] Yet Marquis' line of argument – attacking British policy in India in order to legitimate the French approach in the subcontinent – was widely accepted. It did not call his loyalty into question. If Marquis did any disservice to Indian French citizens, it was in emphasising how far France had gone in reducing social and political inequalities in India, in contrast to its poor record on the same scores with the Vietnamese. This can have done little to convince thinking Vietnamese, however moderate their views, that they held anything in common with the Frenchmen of India.

Marquis' words sought to sweep away rather than address the discord within the ranks of Indian French citizens, and indeed accusations of caste-based prejudices did not go away. Rivalries which erupted both within and between three mutual societies in the late 1920s and early 1930s were centred on accusations of caste-based exclusion. But they did not remain solely about caste. The disputes also reflected divisions

---

62. Édouard Marquis, 'Un movement social', *Saigon-Dimanche*, 20 November 1932.
63. 'Un banquet', *Réveil Saigonnais*, 9 July 1923.
64. See ANOM GGI 65474 Rapport Annuel Contrôle des immigrants asiatiques 1923–1924: Milieux Indiens; ANOM GGI 65475 Service de la Sûreté Cochinchine Rapport Annuel 1924–26: Service de la sûreté rapport annuel 1er juillet 1926 à 1er juillet 1927. Tome II Ch VII Les Indiens; ANOM GGI 65476 Service de sûreté, Rapports annuels: Service de la Sûreté, Rapport Annuel de Commissariat spécial pour la port de Saigon-Cholon (1927–1928): Action Indienne.

in French Indian political allegiances since 1929, with some Indian voters continuing to remain loyal to their Deputy Outrey while others sought more independent political paths. Some Indian French citizens were beginning to express the view that their attachment to India was stronger than their attachment to France. Divisions within the group also surfaced in disagreements about what was being spent by the social organisations and to whose benefit. In general, the less educated, less securely employed French Indians felt they were suffering the effects of the Depression more keenly than their more privileged compatriots. In their view, their more securely employed rivals continued to allow themselves the luxury of banquets, honours, high-minded speeches, and other more frivolous 'profile raising' social occasions, while the 'underprivileged' faced unemployment. Class divisions paralleled, albeit imperfectly, underlying caste origins which probably meant many people continued to perceive of caste discrimination as the core of the problem.[65]

Despite the two talks on 'social union' hosted by the *Mutualité Hindoue* in the summer and autumn of 1929, before the year was out the Governor of Cochinchina had received lengthy complaints from Indians claiming they had been barred from joining that very association. The central accusation in the first complaint was that the members of the society were 'all casted' and anyone who was not of caste (*non casté*, of *pariah* status) was prevented from joining. This correspondent further claimed that the 'clan' controlling the mutual association had offered financial support to 'the anti-French of French India'. It was this accusation of political involvement, and a separate petition maintaining that the *Mutualité Hindoue* was a front for an 'electoral group' in the hands of unnamed local politicians, which prompted French authorities to send a French security agent to monitor the group's meetings.[66]

The report issued by the *Sûreté* agent failed to expose any political activity within the *Mutualité*, seditionist or otherwise. The society's president, however, was forced to accept as members those he had pre-

---

65. VNA2 GD 2997 Mutuelle Hindoue de la Cochinchine, 1935; VNA2 GD 2998 Mutuelle des Français de l'Inde Employés de Commerce et d'Industrie 1934.
66. VNA2 GD 2997 Mutuelle Hindoue de la Cochinchine, 1935: subfolder 'Mutualité Hindoue', Belconde to GCCH, 29 October 1929, and in the same subfolder, *Français de l'Inde* to GCCH, 31 October 1929.

viously turned away.⁶⁷ In an announcement printed shortly thereafter in the pages of the *Saigon-Dimanche*, the *Mutualité Hindoue* outlined procedures for sponsoring new members designed 'to avoid unjustified criticisms'.⁶⁸ This gesture suggested the association might become more transparent in selecting its members. The president however in a speech made on the occasion of the *Mutualité's* anniversary denied any decisions had been made on the basis of caste. He made no apologies for wanting to limit membership to 'a group of right-thinking [*bien pensant*] men [rather than] a disorganised crowd'.⁶⁹ French security now considered the problem solved. It appears though to have only created a society which fed for a time on antagonism, as it held vocal members of rival camps under one roof. The minutes of the 1930 Annual General meeting of the *Mutualité* Hindoue, which were submitted to the Municipality, record accusations and counter-accusations before reporting that the meeting 'suddenly became stormy [obliging] the president to bring [it] to a close'.⁷⁰

Another Indian mutual association was created in the midst of this discord. The *Mutuelle des Indo-Français Employés de Commerce et d'Industrie de la Cochinchine* was founded in 1931. It was formed with the backing of the *Saigon-Dimanche* as a response to the 'French Mutual Association for Employees of Commerce', which had refused to accept French citizens of Indian origin as members. It was drawn right from its inception into the rivalries between Indian French citizens in Saigon. These rivalries then continued both internally within each of the mutual associations, and across them. The Cochinchinese government was alerted in a curious letter from 'a sincere group of French Indian employees of commerce', apparently all members of the *Mutualité Hindoue*, that disagreement was rife within the small group which had formed to create the new association and it would 'not work'.⁷¹

---

67. VNA2 GD 2997 Mutuelle Hindoue de la Cochinchine, 1935: subfolder 'Mutualité Hindoue', Sûreté to GCCH, 13 November 1929, and Note confidentiel pour le GCCH re Mutualité Hindoue, 4 November 1929.
68. 'Mutualité Hindoue', *Saigon-Dimanche*, 1 June 1930.
69. 'À la *Mutualité Hindoue*', *Saigon-Dimanche*, 15 September 1929.
70. VNA2 GD 2997 Mutuelle Hindoue de la Cochinchine, 1935: subfolder 'Mutualité Hindoue', Minutes of Annual General Meeting, 10 August 1930.
71. Raoul Vernier, 'Ceux qu'on ne défend pas', *Saigon-Dimanche*, 7 August 1927; VNA2 GD 2998 Mutuelle des Indo-Français Employés de Commerce et d'Industrie, 1934: Sincere group of French Indian employees of commerce to Chief of 1ˢᵗ Bureau, 23 May 1931.

Indeed, it did not take long for differences among the new society's 150 members to rise to the surface. In May 1934, the society's accountants were withdrawn from their positions following disagreements over the statutes. The founding president had already complained to the Governor General about caste prejudices operating within the association. In July he invited a police agent to attend the Annual General Meeting. At that meeting, the president's opponents issued a 'summary of regrettable incidents' outlining 'mistakes' he had made by bringing 'caste affairs' within the society to government attention. When certain members demanded the policeman in attendance should leave, the president resigned, proclaiming as he did so the suspension of all activities of the society to await the government's arbitration.[72]

By order of the president of Saigon's Civil Tribunal, an extraordinary general meeting of the *Mutuelle des Indo-Français Employés de Commerce et d'Industrie* was held in September of 1934. As at the previous meeting, an outsider had been invited to observe on behalf of government. The minutes of this meeting named the observer as Mr. E. Marius, Security Inspector, an Indian French citizen himself, although not a member of the *Mutuelle*; his presence provides another indication of just how far Indian French citizens were embedded in the Cochinchinese state. This meeting witnessed a rash of resignations and re-resignations of those who had already resigned but been persuaded back for the extraordinary meeting. These re-shuffles satisfied Inspector Marius that the meeting had 'put an end to the dissensions that opposed the previous Committee and the majority of members'.[73]

Despite the quarrels between and within these two mutual societies, members of the two organisations began from 1933 to envisage a merger, their purpose being to better come to the aid of French Indians affected by the economic crisis.[74] The negotiation of the merger was again fraught with disagreement, and now hard economic times brought class differences to the surface. One group, speaking on behalf of the *Mutuelle Indo-Français*,

---

72. VNA2 GD 2998: Note Police to GCCH, 11 August 1931, and in the same file, Minutes of Annual General Meeting, 22 July 1934 and Assemblée Générale 22 July 1934.
73. Ibid.: Procès-verbal de l'assemblée générale 2 September 1934, and in the same file Police service to GCCH, 6 September 1934.
74. Ibid.: 'Moral report', in Minutes of Annual General Meeting, 22 July 1934; VNA2 GD 2997 Mutuelle Hindoue de la Cochinchine, 1935: Bulletin de la Mutuelle Hindoue, 'procès-verbal', 17 November 1934, p. 24.

maintained that wage-earners in the private sector were hardest hit. The new merged association, it claimed, should be created uniquely to protect the 'Indian proletariat'. 'The possessing class (landowners and those assimilated to them) and the favoured class (the functionaries) must give to the unfortunate class (the employees of commerce and the unemployed) without asking for anything in return.' Anything less was 'exploitation':

> Thus a functionary who has his existence guaranteed, who has free medical care, reduced tariffs in hospital, paid holidays every three years, and a pension at the end of his career, has the right to dispute the few meagre benefits conceded to an unfortunate employee of commerce who has nothing but his miserable salary for him and his family to live on.[75]

The notion that financial assistance from mutual funds should go solely to this 'unfortunate class' caused a 'storm of protest' from the leaders of the *Mutualité Hindoue*, who claimed that all who contributed their monthly fee, regardless of their position, had the right to pay-outs from the society.[76]

These two unhappy associations did merge, in November 1934, to form the Mutuelle Hindoue de la Cochinchine. Members of both societies could be commended for their persistence. Even as the vote for the merger took place, accusations continued to fly of caste exclusion and the domination of the underprivileged by the better-educated and more financially secure; petty clashes of personality continued to be aired. Discontent continued, with complaints that a 'spirit of caste' as well as a current of nationalism were infecting the new organisation. The latter accusation stemmed from the fact that the man chosen to be the head of the merged association was a French subject and not a French citizen. He was one who, moreover, had the 'audacity' to declare himself 'an Indian first and foremost'. Some members continued to suggest people were being barred from the society because of their caste background. They objected too that mutual society funds were being lavished on some members (an expensive funeral wreath for one, a costly banquet for others), while the cost of some members' medical bills had not been properly reimbursed.[77]

---

75. VNA2 GD 2998: 'Moral report', in Minutes of Annual General Meeting, 22 July 1934.
76. Ibid.
77. VNA2 GD 2997 Mutuelle Hindoue de la Cochinchine, 1935: Bulletin de la Mutuelle Hindoue, 'procès-verbal', 17 November 1934, and in the same file Faife and Belconde to GCCH 8 February 1935, and 'procès-verbal' 12 April 1935.

French authorities evidently remained concerned at discontent within the new association. They continued to send agents to report on the society's meetings. Following the General Assembly in December 1935, French security reported that 'no question of politics' had been raised at the meeting. In a handwritten note in this file an unidentified French official claimed 'this fusion should have never taken place, it is the union of the carp and the hare (*pariahs* and the casted). See what we can do about it.'[78]

Ultimately, though, French authorities did little to attempt to heal the social divisions within the group of Indian French citizens. Some of the high-caste, better-educated renouncers made genuine attempts to seek reconciliation, but many of these attempts were so high-minded as to be ineffectual. One example is provided in a speech given by Mr. J. Antoine, an active committee member in all three of the Indian associations founded from the late 1920s and otherwise lauded as a member who fought tirelessly to quell discord among French Indians. In a speech delivered to the *Mutuelle Hindoue* in December of 1935 he quoted Montesquieu, Aristotle, Theocritus, and Napoleon Bonaparte among others, to demonstrate how all of these great men favoured man's solidarity with man. He looked to 'the mysterious Indies' and in particular to one of the bas-reliefs at Angkor depicting a scene between Krishna and Shiva, to provide an example of how 'the divinities preached solidarity long before Victor Hugo'. 'All our compatriots, sons of the same soil which is the hearth of humanity and the cradle of civilisation', he declared, 'must show themselves to be worthy of their ancestors. No more personal quarrels, no more uncontrolled passions, no more sectarian spirit.'[79] Despite his reiteration of unifying Greater India themes, he may only have alienated many of those with whom he sought to connect by his European cultural erudition and his references to India and Indochina as exotic cultural landscapes, even though both would have been familiar to the audience he was addressing.

Divisions that appeared within the group of Indian French citizens in Indochina with the onset of the Depression signalled that renunciation no longer carried the force it once did to bind them together. The idea that Indian renouncers had put aside caste distinctions in accepting

---

78. VNA2 GD 2997: Director of Security to GCCH 23 December 1935; in the same file, handwritten note, sender and receiver both illegible, circa November 1935.
79. Ibid.: Annual Bulletin of the *Mutuelle Hindoue* 1935.

French citizenship had proven to be tenuous at best. They no longer rallied around the single political figure of the Cochinchinese deputy, and some among them had even begun to question whether their loyalty to France was steadfast. A growing sense of belonging to a wider overseas Indian community now became a necessary response to the political situation in the Vietnamese territories.

Necessary solidarities

One aspect of the Indian renouncers' changing view of themselves which emerged most strongly from the late 1920s was their sense that, whether they themselves felt that way or not, they were viewed by the Vietnamese public as belonging to a wider group of overseas Indians.

From the early days of French colonization, Indian French citizens and other Tamil expatriates interacted on many levels in daily life, especially in the urban contexts of Saigon and Cholon. There were also occasions in the 1920s when Indian French citizens came together socially with the wider Indian community to welcome esteemed Indian visitors, visitors all groups were happy to claim as their own. Yet despite this openness on one level, and despite the calls by Indian social organisations for 'solidarity' and social change, Indian renouncers and the small group of Indo-French who joined them remained closed within their own mutualist circles throughout much of the 1920s and into the 1930s. The *Français de l'Inde* paid little attention to signs that an interest in Indian social and political reform was developing among other migrant Indians in Indochina. The *Réveil Saigonnais* largely ignored the presence of several Indian social and political reformers who visited Saigon in the 1920s, although these visitors met other members of the Indian expatriate community, amongst whom they held conferences or raised money for social causes.[80] Nor did French Indians' calls for unity in this period ever fully include expatriate Indians outside of their own narrow grouping.

French Indians began to identify with overseas Indians outside the bounds of their own small group once more aggressive forms of Vietnamese anti-colonialism and economic crisis produced more forthright Vietnamese

---

80. See ANOM GGI 65474 Rapport Annuel Contrôle des immigrants asiatiques 1923–1924: Milieux Indiens; ANOM GGI 65475 Service de la Sûreté Cochinchine Rapport Annuel 1924–26: Service de la sûreté rapport annuel 1ᵉʳ juillet 1926 à 1ᵉʳ juillet 1927. Tome II Ch VII Les Indiens; ANOM GGI 65476 Service de sûreté, Rapports annuels: Service de la Sûreté, Rapport Annuel de Commissariat spécial pour la port de Saigon-Cholon (1927–1928): Action Indienne.

objections to the Indian presence in the colony. They were disturbed by incidents of violence – quickly contained but nonetheless ugly – which took place between Indian cloth merchants and Vietnamese in the lead-up to the economic crisis. French Indians were troubled too by attacks on the Chettiar moneylenders, who were blamed for aggravating the crisis when it hit. Although those under attack were mainly British Indians who could be held to be different from their French counterparts, the attacks against them were strongly racial in nature. Regardless of their differences, they concluded, Chettiar or Muslim actions in Cochinchina affected how all Indians were viewed in the colony. They took it upon themselves, albeit paternalistically at times, sometimes to monitor the behaviour, and at other times come to the defence of other Indian immigrants.

This new concern to oversee the behaviour of other Indian migrants is evident in the *Réveil Saigonnais'* reaction to the 1928 Viénot Street incident discussed in Chapter Six. The *Réveil* deplored the Vietnamese mobs who attacked the Indian shop, but reserved most of its indignation for the Indian employee's 'act of brutality' when he caused serious injury to the Vietnamese thief. The merchants, described emphatically as 'British subjects' and 'Muslims', were patently positioned outside the circles of the *Français de l'Inde*. They were condemned in terms which reiterated French and Vietnamese criticisms of the presence of Foreign Asians in the colony:

> The cloth merchants, all British subjects, must not forget that they have come here to do business with the Vietnamese population...The *Annamite* does not tolerate violence from the rare Frenchman. For even greater reason, he does not accept it from Muslims who come here to enrich themselves at the expense of Cochinchina.[81]

The actions of (British) Muslim merchants reflected badly on Indians from the French possessions in the colony precisely because their work (and thus their identities in Vietnamese eyes) overlapped in areas such as tax farming.

> The Indian French citizens and subjects who have come up against the Muslims as competitors for various public contracts do not want to have to put up with reprisals or even the distrust and resentment of the natives towards them because of [the actions of] British subjects.[82]

---

81. 'Antagonisme de races?', *Réveil Saigonnais*, 25 June 1928.
82. Ibid.

The *Réveil* now extended its programme of self-improvement beyond its own small group of French citizens of Indian origin. It sounded a warning to both Vietnamese and [Muslim] Indians that it was their duty as 'Asian races' to strive to better themselves. If the Vietnamese continued to engage in mob behaviour, they risked 'remaining in comparison to the European races in a state of undeniable inferiority'. While Europeans had their disagreements, they resolved them not on the street but 'through the legal system'. The article criticised a 'susceptibility' in Asians 'that the European races do not have':

> The Asians proceed differently. In India, Muslims and Hindus have killed each other for futilities; recently in Tonkin, Chinese and *Annamites* have fought openly over a quarrel between two individuals. And here *Annamites* and Muslims fight for a bobbin of thread.[83]

Asians must improve themselves, the *Réveil* urged; 'there must not be an antagonism between races'. Cultural influence was expressed now in terms other than the one-sided 'genius' brought from one place to another. Racial discord 'cannot exist between Asians who have affinities of religion, of civilisation, such as the Chinese, *Annamites, Hindou*, Malay, etc.'[84]

At the instigation of the businessman Léon Prouchandy, the *Saigon-Dimanche* launched a 'Clothing Crusade' in 1933 with the support of the short-lived Franco-Tamil magazine, *L'Inde Illustrée*. The purpose of the 'Crusade' was to secure better treatment for all Indians in the colony by encouraging expatriate Indian residents to 'modernise' their appearance. It shared with the *Réveil,* in its reaction some years earlier to the Viénot Street affair, the goal of improving the standing of all migrant Indians, but the approach of *Saigon-Dimanche* differed considerably. The *Réveil* had maintained a careful distance between its readership and the cloth merchants, whom it referred to as 'British subjects' and 'Muslims', but never as fellow Indians. The *Saigon-Dimanche* adopted a more amicable approach to the Muslims and Chettiars, both of them groups who continued in Cochinchina to retain many aspects of Indian dress and towards whom the campaign was directed.

In articles published to launch the campaign, Raoul Vernier lamented the fact that 'too many expatriate compatriots' continued to wear 'incommodious' national garb. The appearance of 'backwardness' conveyed by

---

83. Ibid.
84. Ibid.

'floating cloths and chignons', he argued, did not help to foster respect for Indians overseas. He observed a worldwide trend in which 'more and more, people are tending to unify their clothing following the ethic of Western civilisation'. The early adoption by the Japanese of 'Western clothes and manners' had been a key to their success in the modern world. Pointing out that Chettiars and Muslims in Hanoi, 'and even in Annam we have heard', all donned Western dress 'with the exception of a fez or cap', the *Saigon-Dimanche* expressed the hope that their brothers in Cochinchina would soon do likewise.

While the *Réveil* warned Muslim merchants that their behaviour reflected more widely on the Indian expatriate community, here the *Saigon-Dimanche* attempted to put forward friendly advice to its compatriots on how they could make themselves 'better considered…by the Europeans as much as by the natives'. Referring to the animosity that had grown between the communities in this period, relations would 'become more cordial and less humiliating for some people, as has happened to them so many times in Saigon'. It might not be necessary to adopt Western dress at home, but living in a distant land they must do everything so that 'their dignified demeanour, their honourable way of life, earn them the esteem of the inhabitants'. The adoption of Western dress would consequently not only protect their interest but also 'the general interest of all Indians'.[85]

The 1930s saw a more general shift towards Western dress on the part of overseas Indians in Southeast Asia.[86] Saigon's 'Clothing Crusade' of 1933 might be credited with some part at least in bringing about this change. The *Inde Illustrée* published studio photographs of some of Saigon's most prominent Indian businessmen in suits and hats, waistcoat and spats, to encourage more widespread adoption.[87] Just over a month after its launch, and following assurances that its advice was intended in a friendly vein, the *Saigon-Dimanche* claimed triumphantly that its call

---

85. Raoul Vernier, 'Une croisade vestimentaire', *Saigon-Dimanche*, 3 September, 1933; R.V., 'A propos de la réforme vestimentaire des hindous. Une mise au point nécessaire', *Saigon-Dimanche*, 24 September 1933.
86. See for example Muthiah et al., *Chettiar Heritage*, p. 268.
87. 'Une Importante réforme chez les Hindous de Cochinchine', *L'Inde Illustrée*, March 1933; 'Chez les Indous de Cochinchine', *L'Inde Illustrée*, April 1933.

Plate 16. Monsieur Appapoulé, banker, promoting the 1933 'Clothing Crusade'. *L'Inde Illustrée*, March 1933. Courtesy General Sciences Library, Ho Chi Minh City.

had been heard: 'We hear from a good source that the Chettiars have decided to adopt European dress.'[88]

Efforts on the part of French Indians to maintain the prestige of a wider 'Indian colony' in Cochinchina are evident too, in an extended campaign in the *Saigon-Dimanche* in the 1930s in support of the Chettiar moneylenders. In the preceding decade the *Réveil Saigonnais* had rarely made reference to the Chettiar presence in Cochinchina, save to reiterate common French and Vietnamese views about Chettiar 'usurers' as a 'terrible social evil', or to post notices announcing the annual *Thaipusam* chariot procession held at the main Chettiar temple.[89] As soon as the Chettiar moneylenders began to be blamed for aggravating the economic crisis, however, *Saigon-Dimanche* took the unpopular step of coming

88. R.V., 'A propos de la réforme vestimentaire des hindous. Une mise au point nécessaire', *Saigon-Dimanche*, 24 September 1933; 'Une campagne qui porte ses fruits', *Saigon-Dimanche*, 15 October 1933.

89. 'Les prêts d'honneur', *Réveil Saigonnais*, 23 April 1923; For example, 'Fête des chettys', *Réveil Saigonnais*, 18 January 1929.

to their defence. It was the only Saigon newspaper to do so, and while fighting off claims that he was in the pay of the 'black barons', its editor Raoul Vernier kept up this defence through the 1930s.

Vernier's purpose was to debunk the many myths which he saw as being ever more elaborately built up around the Chettiars as the crisis deepened. To the accusation that the Chettiars were 'Black Shylocks' who charged high rates of interest, Vernier replied that they lent on the basis of moral rather than material guarantees (something the European banks would never do) and this was why their loans were valued by so many people in need. To charges that the Chettiars drained Indochina of its capital, he pointed to the eighty million piastres they had invested in the country and the five hundred thousand piastres they paid annually in trading licences in Cochinchina. Against claims that they were 'pitiless' in their haste to foreclose on loans (and that their underlying aim was thus to obtain land cheaply), Vernier reminded his readers that previous to the crisis the Chettiars had held a reputation for being particularly accommodating with extending terms of repayment. Their interest, he maintained, lay not in pursuing their debtors at the first opportunity, but in prolonging loans, the better to collect interest. Moreover, the Chettiars were not alone in seizing assets. Credit unions and building societies under the control of the Bank of Indochina had undertaken as many land seizures as the Chettiars, yet they alone had born the brunt of public anger and state sanction. 'Deport the Directors of the Bank of Indochina', Vernier clamoured, once Chettiar expulsions began in late 1932. And why, he asked in early 1933 when the remaining Chettiar bankers were asked to discount their outstanding credits by fifty to sixty percent, had the Bank of Indochina not been asked to do the same?[90]

---

90. See Raoul Vernier, 'Haro sur les Chettys! Ceux qu'on accuse de tous les maux', *Saigon-Dimanche*, 31 May 1931; Raoul Vernier, 'Haro sur les Chettys! On expulse les Chettys pour permettre à la Banque d'Indochine et à ses filiales de créer en ce pays un monopole de crédit', *Saigon-Dimanche*, 26 March 1933; Raoul Vernier, 'Haro sur les Chettys! Pourquoi certains quotidiens attaquent les banquiers hindous', *Saigon-Dimanche*, 13 September 1931; Raoul Vernier, 'Haro sur les Chettys! Lesquels on tout de même investis 80 millions de piastres en ce pays', *Saigon-Dimanche*, 27 September 1931; Raoul Vernier, 'Haro sur les Chettys! Les banquiers hindous n'ont pas intérêt à accarper les terres des Annamites', *Saigon-Dimanche*, 7 July 1931; 'La paille et la poutre: Réponse à l'Opinion', *Saigon-Dimanche*, 19 March 1933; Raoul Vernier, 'À propos de l'expulsion inique d'un banquier hindou: M. Soccalingamchettiar', *Saigon-Dimanche*, 9 October 1921; Raoul Vernier, 'Haro sur les Chettys! On veut obliger les Chettys à rabattre 50 à 60% de leurs créances', *Saigon-Dimanche*, 5 March 1933.

Vernier's defence of the Chettiars was based on a rare but solid understanding of their economic role in Cochinchina. This was reinforced by arguments aimed at establishing the longstanding and rightful place of Chettiars in the colony. Like their renouncer compatriots, the Chettiars had 'come to Indochina…in the heroic time of its settlement'.[91] They were already extending credit to expand rice cultivation in the Mekong Delta before metropolitan capitalists had yet gained sufficient confidence to invest.[92] When Bùi Quang Chiêu made a speech in which he accused the Indian moneylenders of exporting massive amounts of capital to India, Vernier replied: 'But Mr. Bùi Quang Chiêu, you know quite well that it was in large part thanks to these Chettys that rice paddies could be cultivated.'[93]

Vernier's defence of the Chettiar moneylenders exposed the anxieties created for all Indians in the colony by the treatment of the Chettiars during the Depression. 'I am compelled to say', he wrote, 'that I defend the Chettiars because they are Indians and, because of this, my compatriots. And also because if the *Impartial* and the *Opinion* have attacked them, *it is precisely because they are Indians*' [his italics].[94] The low esteem in which the Vietnamese held the Chettiars, he feared, extended to bad feelings for overseas Indians in general.

While the first half of the 1930s saw the French Indians of Cochinchina locked in internal disputes within their mutual associations, by the end of the 1930s most other 'caste and creeds' among the overseas Indians had formed similar associations. These associations were modelled on French Indian ones, but they were also influenced by Indian visitors to Cochinchina urging them to unite, and to defend their increasingly beleaguered interests in the colony.

In 1931, at the height of public outcry against them, the Chettiars created the 'Indochinese Association of Nattukottai Chettiars'. This association, through annual reports and other missives, transmitted to the government the wishes and concerns of the bankers and aimed to draw

---

91. 'La paille et la poutre: Réponse à l'Opinion', *Saigon-Dimanche*, 19 March 1933.
92. Raoul Vernier, 'Haro! Comment les chettys loin d'être une plaie sont au contraire d'une grande aide pour le gouvernment', *Saigon-Dimanche*, 27 December 1931; Raoul Vernier, 'Haro sur les chettys. Pourquoi certains quotidiens attaquent les banquiers hindous', *Saigon-Dimanche*, 13 September 1931.
93. Raoul Vernier, 'Haro. Une réponse à M. Bùi Quang Chiêu ', *Saigon-Dimanche*, 25 October 1931.
94. Ibid.

greater public attention to their acts of philanthropy in Cochinchina.[95] An association for those of Hindu faith, the *Hindoue Tamoule Djana Sangam*, followed in 1936. Its president was the wealthy businessman Katthéappathévar, who by the 1920s had begun to contribute to charitable causes in the colony. For members who were renouncers, such as former *Saigon-Dimanche* editor Raoul Ramradja Vernier, the creation of this society marked an identity shift, with religious belonging acknowledged in a way it had not been before. Several members were employees of Chettiar banks, but the Chettiars themselves, albeit Hindu, preferred it seems to remain within their own association.[96] Finally, Tamil Muslims attempted to form a similar modern organisation which could defend their interests in the colony and bolster their image in the eyes of the local population. It is unclear though whether such an organisation actually saw the light of day. In late 1936 the *Indochine-Inde* printed a letter from 'a Muslim subscriber' who asked why 'the leaders of the Tamil Muslim colony of Cochinchina do not take the initiative to create a fellowship society for Muslim compatriots'. The 'Catholics, Hindus and Chettiars' already had associations they could join, he pointed out, and the Muslims were the only 'element' of the overseas Indian community which did not have a society of its own.[97] By the 'Catholics' we may understand that he meant the Indian French citizens. The two categories of 'renouncer' and 'Catholic' very closely overlapped, but by describing them in this way he revealed that for some other Indians their religious identity stood out over their secular citizenship.

When Pragasam, lawyer and ex-member of the Legislative Assembly of British India, came to Saigon in 1929 he proposed an All-India Association for Indochina. He urged expatriate Indians that a union between them without distinction of caste or religion was necessary if they were to earn the respect of the *Annamites* and the French. Although neither Chettiars nor other expatriate Indians answered his call in the full spirit in which it was intended, one French observer claimed this visit influenced the Chettiar decision to form an association. The prominent banker Annamalaichetty, who visited Saigon in the same year, brought

---

95. VNA2 GD 2994 Demande de capacité juridique présenter par l'Association Indochinoise des Nattukottai Chettiars 1940: Annual reports, 1938–1940.
96. 'Hindoue Tamoule Djana Sangam, Amicale Hindoue', *Indochine-Inde*, 8 March 1936.
97. 'Pour un amicale des Musulmans tamouls', *Indochine-Inde*, 20 September 1936.

a similar message. Annamalaichetty spoke to local Chettiars of the need for solidarity between them and proposed they form an association through which to more easily present their causes to government. Similarly, the South Indian Muslim expatriate community was encouraged by a visiting preacher to form its own association.[98]

French citizens of Indian origin began to identify more closely with other Indian expatriates from the late 1930s. They did so by monitoring and defending the behaviour of all overseas Indians, out of recognition that their fate was tied to that of Indian migrants other than themselves. Although French Indians extended their efforts to 'raise the Indian profile' beyond their own limited horizons, and their Indian compatriots also began to recognise the need to defend actively their interests in the colony, none of these groups in the 1930s was as yet prepared to join in a single united effort to do so. For Indian French citizens, the pursuit of closer ties with other groups within the Indian expatriate community placed new emphasis on other forms of allegiance and belonging aside from the French citizenship which had been the focus of their energies in Cochinchina until that time.

Conclusion

With the end of the First World War, Vietnamese political moderates became critical of privileges enjoyed by renounced Indians in Cochinchina, and began themselves to demand political representation and a better position within the French system. In response to these criticisms, Indian French citizens and the wider group of *Français de l'Inde* developed visions of themselves as noble contributors to colonialism in Cochinchina. They put forward an image of themselves as respectable modern men, full of potential for advancement whose ancestors had played a just role in Cochinchina reaching far back into its past. Even as they did so, however, these Frenchmen of India began to be involved in internal disputes, with rival groups questioning how and for whom 'advancement' was to proceed.

---

98. VNA2 GD 2994 Demande de capacité juridique présenter par l'Association Indochinoise des Nattukottai Chettiars 1940: note Commissaire ports of Saigon-Cholon to Head of Security, 11 October, 1930. It is likely the visiting Muslim preacher was Mavoulana Check-Fariksaid, described in Sûreté files as an 'Arab' who resided and preached at the main Saigon mosque from 1925 to 1926. ANOM GGI 65475 Service de la Sûreté Cochinchine Rapport Annuel 1924–26: Service de la Sûreté rapport annuel 1er juillet 1926 à 1er juillet 1927. Tome II Ch, VII Les Indiens.

By the late 1920s increasingly radicalised Vietnamese anti-colonialists superseded the moderate Constitutionalists. Indians with French citizenship, and Indian expatriates generally, faced more racially charged criticisms of their presence and purpose in the colony. These criticisms were intensified as the effects of the global depression of the 1930s were felt in Cochinchina. In response, the French of India used the position they had established for themselves within Saigon's public sphere to monitor and defend the behaviour of the colony's wider community of overseas Indians. The lead they took in defending their own interests in the colony was actively followed too by other overseas Indian groups. By the 1930s the Indian French citizens were joined in their efforts to establish modern social organisations to represent their interests in the colony by Chettiars, Hindus, and Tamil Muslims resident in the colony, all striving to do the same. Yet the interwar decades, with their rising tensions, their profile raising, and their internal disputes, arguably loosened for Indian renouncers the bonds of French citizenship that had tied them together during half a century's sojourn in Indochina.

What followed from the end of the 1930s, along with widespread conflict, was nearly two decades of political and social repositioning for the Indian French citizens of Indochina. Opportunities for urban interethnic intellectual exchange were much diminished with the outbreak of the Second World War, as the territories of Indochina became drawn into a global conflict. Indochina's Indian French citizens no longer declared their allegiances on a public stage. Instead, and often merely to survive the war, they exploited the gap between an idealised colonial society compartmentalised into race, ethnicity, and economic niche (a 'plural society'), and the ground level reality of connections across these lines. Vietnamese thinking towards the Indian presence briefly took a less hostile turn, in the early stages of the French Indochina conflict, when the Viet Minh coalition for national independence attempted to garner Indian migrant support. While the Viet Minh did not win the sympathy of all overseas Indians, France's defeat at Dien Bien Phu forced it to give up not only Vietnam but also French India, meaning that the Indian French citizens had once again to seek new ways of belonging, and a new form of citizenship.

CHAPTER EIGHT

DIASPORIC DILEMMAS

A photograph which remains in the possession of a Pondicherry family shows Hanoi's Indian community posed outside an art-deco building in the city's French commercial district. Indian nationalist leader Jawaharlal Nehru, in a three-piece suit, stands at the centre of the photograph. It was taken in August of 1939, when the Indian nationalist leader alighted briefly at Saigon and Hanoi en route to Chungking.[1] The people in the photograph represent respectable members of the various groups making up Hanoi's Indian community at the time. Just over half of the group consists of men dressed in white tropical European-cut suits, the uniform of French functionaries and employees of European companies. The Muslim merchants are distinguished from their confrères by their fashionable 'Turki' caps, in a nod to Turkey's modernist developments.[2]

Whether they hailed from India's British or French Empires, Hanoi's Indian residents appear rather pleased to be standing so close to one of India's great nationalist leaders. Nehru and the Indian National Congress continued at that time to view the welfare of Indians overseas as 'an extension of the anti-imperialist struggle'.[3] The dominant position of India's French citizens on Indian nationalist questions was a seemingly contradictory one – it featured ardent anti-colonialism towards British India, coupled with intense pride in the French Empire and their own French citizenship. Nonetheless, and indeed because of these very contradictions, this is as perfect a picture as one might find, in August 1939, of patriotic pride within the Indian diaspora.

Yet this photograph was taken on the brink of enormous shifts in the geopolitical landscape in both South and Southeast Asia. The Second

---

1. VNA2 GD 2994 Demande de capacité juridique presenter par l'Association Indochinois des Nattukottai Chettiars 1940: Traduction du Rapport Annuel de la Neuvième Année de l'Association Indochinois des Nattukottai Chettiars, présenté à l'approbation de l'Assemblée Générale le 28 janvier 1940.
2. Interview with Said family, Pondicherry, November, 2004.
3. Lal et al. *Encyclopedia of the Indian Diaspora*, p. 83.

Plate 17: Hanoi's Indian community posed with Nehru, August 1939. Courtesy of Maurice Sinnas, Pondicherry.

World War, the First Indochina conflict, and the role of the French defeat at Dien Bien Phu in 1954 in deciding the fate of French India as well as the future of French Indochina, all presented Indian French citizens with a particularly complex web of political allegiances to negotiate.

Negotiating nationalisms

Across Southeast Asia in 1929–30, as the economy contracted and jobs became scarce, local attitudes changed and migrant populations emerged among indigenous Asians as a political problem. The Second World War 'accentuated and exaggerated the dilemmas of political affiliation that diasporas faced' in Japanese-occupied Southeast Asia. At the war's end, long-standing diasporas were subject to new states' assertions of their territoriality. Across the post-colonial states of Southeast Asia, citizenship and national belonging became tied to territory and to ethnic uniformity. New nation-states, new borders, and new restrictions on movement created both new forms of displacement, and new forms of immobility. Migrant communities of long standing found the long distance circuits which had sustained them now disrupted. They were forced to choose between returning to their 'ethnic homeland' or settling in newly formed nations which marginalised them because of their migrant origins.[4]

The situation of Indian French citizens in Indochina within the period from the 1930s through to the emergence of the post-colonial states fits into some of these more general prescriptions, but with key differences. Firstly, we might question, given their French citizenship, whether they should be considered an 'Asian' diaspora at all. And, while wider hostilities against Asian migrants arose in Southeast Asia with the onset of the Great Depression, Indian French citizens were already the subject of Vietnamese reformist hostilities in the early 1920s. Finally, Indochina was spared many of the horrors endured elsewhere in Southeast Asia during the Second World War, but it experienced an intense and complex wartime occupation which put particular pressures on French Indian residents.

French capitulation to the Nazis lent its own particular twist to Indian French citizens' experiences of the Second World War. They did not fit into Vichy France's programme of traditionalist renewal in either its French or Indochinese iterations, and Pondicherry's backing of the Free French made French Indians in Indochina politically suspect. Vichy repression was counterbalanced to some extent by Japan's pan-Asianism, until the Japanese coup of March 1945 made the French citizenship of the 'renouncers' a life-threatening liability. With appeals from the Indian nationalist Subash Chandra Bose added to this equation, the Second World War presented Indian French citizens with multiple tests of allegiance. Once French forces reasserted control in Indochina in the wake of the Japanese surrender, and Vietnam then entered into a violent fight for its independence, Indian French citizens found themselves vilified from Vietnamese quarters, as colonial Frenchmen and imperial collaborators. Violent attacks by Saigonese mobs in September 1945 brought home a sense that they belonged to the past and not to the more promising future; so too did the Vietnamese victory in 1954 at Dien Bien Phu. Yet for a short spell in between, the Viet Minh used an internationalist approach in their national struggle, seeking to gain support

---

4. This overview is drawn from Amrith, *Migration and Diaspora in Modern Asia*, Chapters 3 and 4; Cribb and Narangoa, 'Orphans of Empire'; and Engseng Ho, *The Graves of Tarim*, Chapter 10.

from Indochina's resident Indians (including Indian French citizens) as allies in their fight for independence from colonial rule.

Many Asian migrants, in the post-independence period, found they were not able to move as freely within the region as they once had done. Indochina's Indian French citizens were not quite so restricted. They had been influential in negotiations over a new status for the peoples of French Indian origin following French India's merger with the post–1947 Republic of India. This new status enabled them to embark on new circuits of mobility. If they elected, as many Indian renouncers did, to retain French citizenship rather than adopt Indian nationality, they could move freely between France and India and reside as French citizens in the former French possessions in India. This arrangement was one of many possible post-colonial alternatives which were forgotten as the global momentum for decolonisation accelerated, and a model of independent territorial nation-states became a natural and inevitable norm.[5]

DE GAULLE'S PONDICHERRY, PÉTAIN'S SAIGON

For Indian French citizens residing in Indochina, the first significant political shift to shape their experience of the Second World War was the French capitulation to the Nazis in Europe, and its consequences for the French Empire in Asia.

Indochina recognised the Vichy government with little delay, in June of 1940, following the French signing of the Armistice with Germany. In India, however, capitulation in Europe revealed the vulnerability of the small tracts of French Indian territory, and the extent of their reliance on British India for trade and communications. Pondicherry's Governor Louis Bonvin managed for several months to maintain the practical necessity of friendly relations with British India, initially with the approval of the new French government at Vichy. The situation was strained, however, and eventually untenable. Strongly encouraged – pressured even – by the British Indian government, Bonvin came out in support of General Charles de Gaulle in early September 1940.[6] Bonvin was sentenced to death for breaking with Vichy; his sentence was passed at

---

5. See Frederick Cooper, 'Possibility and Constraint: African Independence in Historical Perspective', *Journal of African History*, 49, 2009, 167–196, p. 168.

6. Gouvernment des Établissements français dans l'Inde, *Livre Jaune de l'Inde Française: Recueil des correspondences échangées avec la France, l'Indochine et l'Inde Britannique pendant la période du 24 mai 1940 au 1er octobre 1940*, Pondichéry: Imprimerie du Gouvernement, 1940.

the nearest base in Asia of Petain's authoritarian government, which was in Saigon.[7]

The political shift in French India had immediate practical consequences for French Indians residing in Indochina; it severed communications with home for the duration of the war. 'We didn't come back to Pondicherry at that time,' stated one French Indian woman who was an adolescent at the outbreak of the war and living in Saigon with her family. 'There was no communication. From time to time the Red Cross sent us messages, enquiries about lost persons or reports that family was well. But that was it.'[8] French India remained an important point of contact for French Indians in Indochina, and thus the suspension of home leave, the cutting of direct communications with Pondicherry, and not least the blocking of monetary remittances to India were abrupt changes in their lives.

The thirst of overseas Indians for news from Pondicherry and Karikal fed the mistrust of Vichy officials. Despite bans in Vichy Indochina on receiving broadcasts from French India, French Indians readily 'listened with the radio turned down very low' to news from Pondicherry.[9] The residents of Pondicherry were similarly eager to know what was happening in Saigon. Until at least late 1941 Saigon's Vichy broadcasts could be listened to, unobstructed, from Pondicherry. An astounded British consular official reported: 'News from Saigon is still allowed in public, and in one of the most frequented parts of the sea front, a loudspeaker attracts a large crowd whenever the Saigon station is broadcasting.' Bonvin's government did nothing to block the Saigon broadcasts, and transcripts of the same Vichy transmissions were published in the *Journal Officiel* of the French Establishments. It was only General de Gaulle's alarm at the latter discovery that prompted French authorities to curtail the enemy broadcasts. The same British agent remarked, 'The General would probably be even more astonished if he saw the crowds that flock to listen to these broadcasts and suck in every word.'[10]

Vichy's Indochina-based officials harboured suspicions that Indian French citizens resident there sympathised with the Gaullist cause.

---

7. Annasse, *Les comptoirs français dans l'Inde*, p. 140.
8. Interview with Mrs. Amélie Marius Le Prince, Pondicherry, November 2004.
9. Ibid.
10. BL IOR/L/PS/12/545 EXT 4589/41 News Broadcasts by the Saigon Wireless 6 Aug 1941–18 October 1941, Extract from report on local events, dated 31 May 1941.

These suspicions, for the most part, were justified. Pondicherry authors in accounts of their war-time experiences in Indochina maintain that most French Indians were supporters of the Free French cause, even if few of them were actively involved in the resistance.[11] As the next section shows, Indian French citizens' treatment under the Vichy regime in Indochina gave them little cause to embrace its doctrines.

INDIAN EXPERIENCES OF VICHY'S 'NATIONAL REVOLUTION'

In France, Marshal Philippe Pétain's authoritarian Vichy government put in place an ideological programme of 'National Revolution'. Its aims were to promote traditional values, exclude 'undesirables' including Jews and foreigners, and despite its name to reverse many of the changes in society and government brought about by the French Revolution. Traditionalist rather than fascist, and intent on establishing 'moral order', the Vichy regime replaced the republican slogan, *Liberté, Fraternité, Égalité*, with its own: 'Work, Family, Homeland' (*Travail, Famille, Patrie*).[12] The implementation of this programme in Indochina took contradictory turns. Not only was this plan projected through the lens of French Empire. It was also carried out under the watchful eye of Japanese forces, who secured an uneasy relationship with the French authorities when they entered Indochina and stationed troops there from September 1940. The Japanese entry into Indochina presented a serious challenge to European authority in Indochina. Japan maintained its challenge to French rule not only through its military presence – it assumed control of military instalments, airbases, and ports, while the administration continued to be Vichy-run – but through a programme of wartime propaganda, similar to Vichy's but with a message of anti-colonial pan-Asian solidarity, of 'Asia for Asians'.[13]

Some of Vichy's metropolitan social policies were simply extended to Indochina, but with consequences which undermined France's tenuous position there. Laws put forward in France banning Jews from holding a number of professions were implemented in Indochina. The colonial

---

11. Marius, 'Les Pondichériens dans l'administration coloniale de l'Indochine', p. 394; also Prosper Dairien. '9 Mars 1945...Septembre 1946 et les Français et les Français de l'Inde', *Le Trait d'Union*, August 1995.
12. Roger Price, *A Concise History of France*, Cambridge: Cambridge University Press, 1993, pp. 253–255.
13. Philippe Devillers, *Histoire du Vietnam de 1940 à 1952*, Paris: Éditions du Seuil, 1952, pp. 82–85.

state sought further to purge itself of other individuals it perceived to be an internal threat, including Gaullists and Freemasons. In France, these measures were bullying and extremist and carried tragic consequences. When implemented in Indochina, they effectively targeted members of the colonial commercial and administrative elite and amounted to an internal attack on French colonial power at a time of deep concern over nationalist dissent within the local population. Indochina's Vichy Governor General, Admiral Jean Decoux, applied these social policies but not without raising frequent objections to them. By sacking key military officers and trusted administrators, he argued, not to mention forcing Jews out of businesses which then moved into Japanese hands, the measures eroded French Indochina's security and morale when it was most in need of stability.[14]

While Vichy practised persecution within its own privileged colonial ranks, it extended and nurtured indigenous forms of 'National Revolution' amongst the peoples of Indochina. Doctrines of traditionalism, anti-modernism, and paternalism were adapted to local conditions. Indochina's Vichy-led 'National Revolutions' aimed to foster attachment to France, build federalism, and encourage nationalist pride in each of the *pays* of the Union, particularly among youth. This was a *nationality* policy, intended to counter both indigenous nationalist threats and competing Japanese wartime propaganda.[15]

The Indian French citizens, with their control of certain areas of the civil administration, their electoral privileges, European salaries, dress, and manners, were the very emblem in Indochina of colonial republicanism. They might have been expected to become neat scapegoats, like the Jews of Europe, for society's ills, and thus targets for Vichyist racial and political persecution. Indian French citizens were indeed marginalised under Vichy, but they did not fare as badly as they might have done. The Japanese programme of 'Asia for Asians' and Japanese support for Subhas Chandra Bose's Indian National Army (INA) in its fight against British and Allied forces elsewhere in Southeast Asia both helped to protect local Indians from Vichy excesses. Indian French citizens got away with

---

14. Eric Jennings, *Vichy in the Tropics: Pétain's Nationalist Revolution in Madagascar, Guadaloupe and Indochina, 1940–1944*, Stanford: Stanford University Press, 2001, pp. 143–144, 147.
15. Anne Raffin, *Youth Mobilization in Vichy Indochina and Its Legacies: 1940 to 1970*, New York: Lexington Books, 2005, p. 66.

expressing views for which metropolitan Frenchmen in Indochina were sometimes more harshly punished.

This is not to say that the Vichy administration was content with the citizenship status of French Indians. It did indeed attempt to strip them of their rights. 'During the war', maintained one retired Saigon policeman, speaking from his Pondicherry home, 'the Vichy government put all of the French Indians into the category of 'Asian cadre.'[16] Although no single legal sanction appears to have been imposed, those working for the colonial administration had their European status withdrawn through the Vichy authorities' judicious use of a number of different regulations. One Indian French citizen serving in the customs department in Saigon was removed from his post using a local decree which cited the anti-Semitic and racist Vichy ordinance of 27 September 1940.[17] In a move which harkened back to the renouncers' Pension Funds affair of 1881, French Indian functionaries were deprived, on the basis of their 'Asian origin', of hardship bonuses reserved for employees classed as 'European'. The decree which regulated this decision, dated February 1942, was applied by the civil administration, but ignored by the military. Pondicherry commentator Arthur Annasse read this as evidence that the well-being and co-operation of the French Army's many soldiers of Indian origin was worth the risk of defying Vichyist social policies.[18]

It was not only Indians working for the colonial state whose status was challenged under the Vichy administration in Indochina, but also those Indians employed in the French private sector. One case suggests Indochina's social hierarchy became more strictly racial under Vichy, and French colonials in Indochina became much more liable to place the Indians' 'racial' origin before their citizenship status. Mr André Marius Le Prince, a French citizen of Indian origin, had managed the Ariault pasta factory in Saigon through the 1930s. 'They made everything,' reported his daughter. 'Little shells, macaronis, little ABCDs, little stars, there was everything. And it was very well made, it was very good... made *à la française*.' When its owner became ill, Marius Le Prince

---

16. Interview with Mr. Antoine Samy, Pondicherry, January 2002.
17. Prosper Dairien. '9 Mars 1945...Septembre 1946 et les Français et les Français de l'Inde', *Le Trait d'Union*, August 1995.
18. The offending decree was not revoked until February 1949. Annasse, *Les comptoirs français dans l'Inde*, p. 143.

managed the factory single-handedly. The business changed hands in 1940, after the ailing owner was repatriated to France and shortly after the Vichy-backed administration took power in Indochina. Under new ownership, Marius Le Prince was tapped for his knowledge of factory management, and then promptly dismissed. An Indian manager, his daughter explained, did not fit with the new times: 'It was at the time that Germany occupied France, the time of collaboration. So we were very *mal vu* [badly seen] in Indochina.'[19]

Although Vichy applied exclusionist policies to the Indian French citizens of Indochina, sometimes they were able to use Vichy doctrine to their own advantage. Marius Le Prince was a father of six when he was laid off from the Ariault pasta factory in Saigon:

> He was a *père de famille nombreuse* ['father of a large family'] … there was a slogan at the time, *Travail Famille Patrie*, the slogan of Pétain. So he wrote to [the Cochinchinese administration] and he said, *voilà*, I am in this situation, please give me work. I am unemployed with six children and I am suffering greatly.[20]

As a result of his efforts he was assigned as a storeman for the railways, albeit as an 'Asian cadre'.

The French Indians of Indochina were thus affected by policies of exclusion under Vichy, but they were also treated with caution by its authorities. They were able at times to publicly voice their discontent with some of the decisions of Decoux's government, evidence of Vichy's (relative) lenience towards them.

Arthur Annasse's memoir carries an account of how he helped a group of French Indians organise a march through Saigon to the central radio station, in order to listen to a broadcast by General de Gaulle. Annasse gives no date for the march, but his account suggests the broadcast may have been de Gaulle's address from London on the 18 of June 1940, the speech which founded the French Resistance. Although the marchers were harassed by the authorities along their route, they were nonetheless permitted to listen to the broadcast. Annasse did not escape punishment for his involvment in this march. He records that he was sent home on 'extended leave' as a result, but took up his post again in

---

19. Interview with Mrs. Amélie Marius Le Prince, Pondicherry, November 2004.
20. Ibid.

1941.²¹ In 1942 the *Amicale des Français de l'Inde* organised a public demonstration against the French Indians' demotion to the status of 'Asian cadre'.²² Annasse wrote to the Governor General to object to the same decree, and quotes Decoux's haughty reply: 'It is barely conceivable that a functionary only just entered into the ranks of permanent cadres of the administration should presume to undertake a critique of the decisions of the government he serves.' Annasse was eventually withdrawn from his position at the Mỹ Tho Tribunal, 'due to my constant opposition to [Decoux's] government'. His uncle, serving as president of the Rạch Giá tribunal, was similarly removed from his post for challenging Decoux's authority.²³ While Vichy chose to punish these French Indians for their opposition, their punishments appear lenient in contrast to other cases. For example, a Frenchman of metropolitan origin, cited in Jennings' history of Vichy in the French Empire, was handed down a sentence of five years' hard labour in Indochina for merely voicing in private his support for the Free French.²⁴

While uncooperative Indians under Vichy were (relatively lightly) punished, it does not appear that all French Indians were committed Gaullists firmly opposed to Marshal Petain's government. Papers from the French Foreign Affairs archive show that French Indians based in Bangkok made generous donations to the Vichy cause, several of them 'accompanied by touching words addressed to France and the Marshal'.²⁵ The president of the *Mutuelle Hindoue de la Cochinchine* too, transmitted through the Minister of Colonies a message of goodwill to the Marshal. He asked the Minister to express the 'untiring loyalty' of the association's members 'to the Venerable Marshal Pétain as well as his Government of the French State'. French Indians in Indochina, the message continued, spoke both for themselves and for 'their compatriots residing in India who because of the...forced influence of the English enclave are deprived of all communication with the Metropole

---

21. Annasse, *Les comptoirs français dans l'Inde*, pp. 141–142.
22. This was probably a protest against the February 1942 decree. See Marius, 'Les Pondichériens dans l'Administration de l'Indochine', p. 394.
23. Annasse, *Les comptoirs français dans l'Inde*, p. 143.
24. Jennings, *Vichy in the Tropics*, p. 143.
25. Archives du Ministère des Affaires Etrangères (hereafter AMAE) Guerre 1939–1945 Vichy Asie Serie E 437–438: Telegram French Embassy Bangkok to Minister of Navy and Colonies, 4 June 1942.

and Indochina'. They sought through their message to 'recognise in the Victor of Verdun a worthy leader, saviour of France and of her Empire'.²⁶ The Minister of Colonies for his part contacted the (Vichy-run) French Consul in Bangkok expressing his hope that the small number of French Indians residing in that city would be able to pass information 'about the present situation in the Establishments' on to the Consul in Siam.²⁷ We do not know whether the same proposal was put to French Indians in Indochina.

Indochina's Vichy government was distrustful of the French Indians once Pondicherry went over to the Gaullist camp. They were subjected by its administration to actions intended to marginalise them and exclude them from posts and privileges which, as French citizens, they had previously been entitled to hold. Yet Vichy did not deal as harshly as it might have done with men who, as colonial citizens, stood for republicanism rather than Pétainist 'National Revolution'. It even attempted to use those based in Southeast Asia – at least a handful of French Indian residents of Bangkok – as informers to transmit information from French India. Japan's relationship with French Indians in Indochina, although it had different characteristics, was similarly two-sided.

Indochina's Indians, Japanese pan-Asianism, and the Indian Independence League

If French Indians were generally *mal vu* by Vichy authorities, they were 'more or less *bien vu*' (well-regarded) by the Japanese forces occupying Indochina, a sentiment which extended to British Indian migrants.²⁸ When Japanese forces pushed into southern Indochina in July of 1941, British Indians resident there had expected to be treated as the enemy, but this did not come about.²⁹ Instead, Japanese at high levels of authority in Indochina made efforts to cultivate overseas Indians as potential

---

26. AMAE Guerre 1939–1945 Vichy-Asie, Serie E 242 Établissements français dans l'Inde: dossier général 29 July 1940–27 March 1944: Telegram Decoux to Minister of Colonies, n.d.
27. Ibid.: Telegram Minister of Colonies to French Embassy Bangkok, 30 June 1942.
28. Quote from Mr. Antoine André, interviewed Reddiar Palayam, Pondicherry, August 2004.
29. This expectation was in part prompted by the treatment of Britons of European origin. Under Decoux's civil administration, they had their property confiscated and their employment terminated in December of 1941, followed in early 1942 by confinement or arrest and internment by the Japanese military. British National Archives (hereafter TNA) WO 203/6217 Indians in Siam and French Indo-china, 4 Mar 1946–2 May 1946: 'Report on the condition of Indians in French Indochina (Secret)' by M.S. Aney, January 1946; TNA FO 916/491: 'Sequestre', Hanoi, 15 Dec 1941, and in the same file 'Arrêté retirant l'autorisation

partners in Japan's pan-Asian project of 'East Asian Co-Prosperity'. Indian French citizens and other Indians from the French possessions were included in this project, at least until the Japanese adopted a harder line in the spring of 1945 which brought the pro-French sympathies of some of these Indians into clearer view. The immediate Japanese task with respect to Indians in Indochina was to secure their commitment to Subash Chandra Bose's efforts; but Indian French citizens who remember the war recall that Japanese soldiers at ground level identified with the wider Indian national cause. The Japanese 'gave a lot of liberty to the Indians. They didn't bother us. As we were Indian, they would say "Gandhi", they knew Mahatma Gandhi and they left us in peace.'[30]

Japanese efforts to draw Indians to the pan-Asian cause were nonetheless hampered, as they were across Southeast Asia, by the Japanese tendency to mete out harsh and humiliating treatment to the very people they sought to convert.[31] Pondicherry's retirees retain vivid memories of the Japanese in wartime Saigon:

> Once when I was with a classmate … we were in front of his door, talking to each other, and I don't know what he said to me but I started laughing. There were two commandants with bayonets passing by. They thought I was making fun of them. So they came back with their bayonets. We ran inside and shut the door, but I left my bicycle outside. They knocked over the bicycle, kicked it with their boots, destroyed it and left … If we had been there they would have shot us.[32]

With the Liberation of France in the summer of 1944, the already tense relationship in Indochina between the French civil administration and its Japanese military counterpart became only more so. Japan began to fear the French administration which, no longer tied to Vichy, began to refuse orders and make contact with the Allies and secret forces; the Japanese military administration felt particularly vulnerable following the humiliating Japanese defeat in Burma. On the 9 March 1945, Japanese Ambassador Shunichi Matsumoto took action, presenting Decoux with

---

d'exercer le commerce de la banque aux personnes physiques et morales de nationalité anglaises' signed Decoux 13 Dec 1941.
30. Interview with Mr. Antoine André, Reddiar Palayam, Pondicherry, August 2004.
31. On Japanese face slapping in Indochina and elsewhere in Southeast Asia, see Christopher Bayly and Tim Harper, *Forgotten Armies: The Fall of British Asia, 1941–1945,* London: Allen Lane, 2004, p. 234; also Susan Bayly, *Asian Voices in a Postcolonial Age, Vietnam, India and Beyond,* Cambridge: Cambridge University Press, 2007, p. 142.
32. Interview with Mr. Alfred Sinnas, Pondicherry, October 2004.

an ultimatum to disarm French troops. This was the trigger for a coup in which Japanese forces overturned French authority and seized full control of Indochina. In the violence of that evening and the following day, and during the Allied bombardments which followed in the months afterwards, French authorities and employees of the French colonial administration were interned, injured or killed by Japanese forces.[33] Indian employees of the French administration were the victims of this violence along with their metropolitan and Vietnamese colleagues. Indian French citizens now found that the long-standing tendency of the Indochinese public to mistake them for non-French Indians provided an essential cover. They used the ambiguous ties between their place of origin, their citizenship, and their possible political allegiances to help them survive this turbulent period. On many occasions, posing as 'Bombay' traders or seeking refuge among Indians less suspect than themselves undoubtedly saved their lives.

First-hand French Indian accounts of the weeks following the March coup invariably feature details about how they deployed 'Indian-ness' as protection against Japanese exactions. An Indian soldier in the French Army in Hanoi, seriously wounded on the night of 9 March, was saved by his sister when she pleaded with the Japanese colonel in charge, 'Let me take care of him … I am Indian.' Her son is now retired and living in the Pondicherry village dubbed 'little Saigon'. He related how his father, a police officer, used the same strategy of 'Indianising' himself during the March coup:

> He took off his uniform at that time and said, 'I am a merchant.' He could not admit that he worked for the French. We, the *Pondichériens*, did not say that we had French nationality; we behaved as if we were Indian. And they didn't bother us too much. We could buy rice and we could eat. If we had been French, we would have been interned.[34]

Similarly, a French Indian functionary in Phnom Penh was urged to stay put at his place of work after an Allied air raid, rather than attempt to reach and rescue his injured brother. The threat was not the risk of further Allied bombing: it was the white suit he was wearing which would 'get him killed'.

---

33. For a detailed history of this period, see David Marr, *Vietnam 1945: The Quest for Power*, Berkeley: University of California Press, 1995.
34. Interview with Mr. Antoine André, Reddiar Palayam, Pondicherry, 30 August 2004.

Indian-ness provided cover not only for French Indians. The family of the same Phnom Penh-based functionary gave refuge in this period to the young son of a French high functionary and his wife. The couple brought the boy to the Pondicherry family, in hopes that in an Indian household, he would remain undisturbed.[35]

In yet another account, one of the few Pondicherry French citizens who participated actively in the resistance went undercover with his family as soon as the Japanese took power. For several weeks they moved between the homes of Saigon's *Bombay* merchants where, easily mistaken for a family of traders, they could remain relatively unnoticed. The father's miscalculation – he returned home in mid-June, assuming the Japanese had lost interest in him – saw him immediately arrested by the *Kempeitai*. During his internment, the Japanese military police pressured him to redirect his sympathies. They tried, without success, to persuade him to rally the Indian French citizens round the cause of Subash Chandra Bose.[36]

During the Second World War, Japan promoted the cause of the Indian nationalist Subash Chandra Bose, to mount and sustain the Indian National Army (INA) to fight the British in Southeast Asia in a projected onward advance into India. In Indochina, Bose's followers attempted with Japanese assistance to set up branches of the Indian Independence League (IIL), the funding body of this movement. These efforts were delayed by French objections; the Vichy administration denied their approval on the grounds that regulations prohibited the formation of politically-motivated social organisations. Under Japanese pressure, however, a 'Saigon Indian Association' was established in 1943 and served as a thinly-disguised cover for the IIL. Another all-Indian association formed in wartime, Hanoi's 'Association of Indians in Indochina', openly displayed Indian nationalist as well as Japanese sympathies.[37]

---

35. Interview Mrs. Amélie Marius Le Prince, Pondicherry, November 2004.
36. Discussion with Claude Marius, Pondicherry, September 2012. See also his account of his father's wartime experiences in Marius, 'Les Pondichériens dans l'administration coloniale de l'Indochine', pp. 394–395.
37. TNA WO 203/6217 Indians in Siam and French Indo-china, 4 Mar 1946–2 May 1946: 'Report on the condition of Indians in French Indochina (Secret)' by M.S. Aney, January 1946; AMAE Guerre 1939–1945 Vichy E Asie 281 Telegram GGI to French Foreign Ministry, 29 January 1942; VNA1 D.62 2932 A.s. demande d'authorisation de former une association dénommée 'Association des Indiens en Indochine', formulée par Mohamed Abdullah, domicilié à Hanoi. 1942–1945; ANOM RST 4217 Renseignements sur

The Saigon Indian Association actively urged local Indians to make contributions to the INA. The IIL was insistent in its demands for dues from the local Indian communities, and it became increasingly coercive after the Japanese coup. Records show the IIL was not popular among Indochina's Indians. Decoux wrote to the Minister of Colonies in 1944: 'The majority of Indians [oppose] with the force of inertia the solicitations of which they are the object.' A post-war report by the Indian Government agent Aney stated: 'The Indians remained far from enthusiastic and their activities were strictly confined to conventional meetings and compulsory subscriptions to the movement.'[38]

With the Japanese takeover, the Saigon Indian Association 'did away with its mask', coming out openly as a branch of the IIL, and the Hanoi 'Association of Indians in Indochina' formed closer ties with its Saigon affiliate.[39] This coincided with a broader reorganisation of the IIL taking place across Southeast Asia. The INA retreat from Burma prompted Bose to reassemble his civil administration at Bangkok in June of 1945. At the same time he relocated two ministers of his *Azad Hind* ('Free India') government-in-exile to Indochina. They were charged with reorganising the IIL there, in hopes of revitalising and reviving the movement's flagging operations.[40] The Indochinese IIL branches now began to pursue their fund-raising efforts with greater zeal, coupled with increased impatience. The account by a local Chettiar agent of his encounters with the IIL ('Azad Ministers as well as local League leaders

---

l'Association de Indiens étrangers en Indochine et sur les commerçants indiens 1943: Res sup Tonkin to GGI 26 Jan 1946.

38. M.S. Aney was an Indian Government agent assigned to report on the post-war welfare of Indian communities in Southeast Asia in early 1946. TNA WO203/6217 Indians in Siam and French Indo-china, 4 Mar 1946–2 May 1946: 'Report on the condition of Indians in French Indochina (Secret)' by M.S. Aney, January 1946; AMAE Guerre 1939–1945: Vichy Asie Sûreté 242: Établissements française des Indes dossier: Secret telegram GGI to Ministry of Colonies Vichy, 27 March 1944.

39. TNA WO203/6217 Indians in Siam and French Indo-china, 4 Mar 1946–2 May 1946: 'Report on the condition of Indians in French Indochina (Secret)' by M.S. Aney, January 1946.

40. Bose's Minister of Finance, Major-General Chatterji, had stood poised prior to the defeat at Imphal to assume responsibility for the civil administration of liberated Indian territories. He was now assigned to the IIL at Saigon, and the Minister of State Sahay, to Hanoi. See TNA FO 959/2 Indian community F.I.C. 1945–1946; Sugata Bose, *His Majesty's Opponent: Subhas Chandra Bose and India's Struggle Against Empire*, New Delhi: Allen Lane, 2011, p. 296.

were thundering on at us repeatedly') reveals the growing desperation within Bose's cause.[41]

The IIL became increasingly heavy-handed. With the help of their Japanese allies, they freely threatened to jail members of the local Indian community who refused to cooperate and to confiscate their assets. In early July the Japanese military arrested and imprisoned J.M. Abdul Aziz, the younger of the Ishmael brothers who was now the most prominent Indian merchant in Saigon. According to the post-war report penned by the Chettiar agent Ramassamy, Aziz was arrested 'at the instigation of the League' for non-payment to the IIL. His imprisonment appears to have had the desired effect. Reports circulated within the Indian communities that Aziz was 'being submitted to cruel treatments'. These other Indians, 'in panic, expedit[ed] payment of exactions'.[42]

Indian French citizens were less relentlessly targeted by IIL fundraisers than other overseas Indians. Associations whose members were made up of Indian French citizens do not appear to have been directly solicited for funds. There is evidence nonetheless that some French Indians, citizens as well as subjects, participated in IIL and INA activities. These activities were monitored by Decoux's government and were clearly of concern to it. In two secret telegrams between Saigon and the Minister of Colonies at Vichy in early 1944, Decoux gave the Minister the names of five French Indians resident in Saigon, three of them citizens, who had joined the INA.[43] A wealthy Saigon-based Pondicherry businessman, who was a French citizen but not dependent on the French for his position, was an early supporter of Bose's national movement, and a willing and generous contributor to its war fund. According to family accounts, his large house in Saigon was used by the IIL as its Secretariat. He was arrested, imprisoned, and tortured following the Japanese surrender, an experience which broke him mentally. His departure from

---

41. TNA FO 959/2 Indian Community in French Indochina 1945–46: Ra. Ramassamy Chettiar to Major General Commanding the Allied Forces in South Indochina, 23 Nov 1945.
42. Ibid. Later French papers, which concern Aziz's nomination for the *Légion d'Honneur*, make a somewhat different claim, that he was 'jailed and tortured by the Japanese who knew of his Francophile sympathies and thought him to be an agent working in the service of France'. ANOM HCI 250/728 Minorités Ethniques Cambodgiens et Chams, 1954, Activités Indiennes et Pakistanaises (1951).
43. AMAE Guerre 1939–1945: Vichy Asie Sûreté 242: Établissements françaises des Indes dossier: Secret telegrams GGI to Ministry of Colonies Vichy, 9 January 1944 and 27 March 1944.

the French Indian status quo – one of his own sons was interned by the Japanese – soured his relationship with the community in ways which may have contributed afterwards to the harsh treatment against him.[44]

Aside from these few examples it is difficult to gauge levels of sympathy among Indian French citizens in Indochina for Bose's cause. Certainly the IIL's heavy-handedness, particularly after March 1945, was off-putting and intimidating for those directly approached for contributions. Post-war judgements now weigh heavily though on how actors targeted by multiple appeals to their political allegiance in 1940s Saigon are prepared to present themselves today. The political causes in question were complex and entangled, and these actors' commitments were no doubt less clear at the time than they are now with hind-sight made out to be. A Pondicherry man who was in war-time Saigon as a youth shouted when interviewed in 2004, 'That Chandra Bose! A national hero?! *Non*! He was a criminal for supporting Hitler and the Nazis!' He then referred to a recent, condemning, article he had read in *Paris Match* about the INA leader. Yet the same man retains a vivid memory of Bose speaking from the balcony of Saigon's Majestic Hotel. And although he may be less comfortable with INA politics now, Bose was clearly an acceptable figure within his wider family circle in wartime Indochina. When he took me to meet his cousin, who had also been in Saigon, he made no comment at my interest in a picture hanging on a wall in her house. The picture was finely embroidered, using a technique still popular in Vietnam. It was a triple portrait of Gandhi, Nehru, and Bose and had been purchased, his cousin confirmed, in 1940s Saigon.

THE 20TH INDIAN DIVISION IN SAIGON: GLOBAL REPERCUSSIONS, DIASPORIC CONNECTIONS

Following the Japanese surrender on 15 August 1945, British forces were tasked with restoring law and order in the southern half of Vietnamese Indochina. British use of Indian Army divisions in this deployment (as well as in a similar operation on Java) drew international condemnation for its suggestion that one colonised people was being used against another at a moment when nationalist groups were declaring independence. The use of Indian troops also made its mark on how Indians resident in Cochinchina, be they French citizens or British subjects,

---
44. Interview with family member, Pondicherry 2004.

loyal or otherwise to their respective colonial masters, experienced the end of the Second World War and their almost immediate immersion thereafter in the first Indochina conflict.

The 20th Indian Division, headed by the British General Douglas Gracey, arrived in Saigon in early September 1945. Gracey's remit was to receive the Japanese surrender below the 16th parallel, to locate and evacuate Allied prisoners of war, and to maintain law and order. Ho Chi Minh had just declared independence, and the birth of the Democratic Republic of Viet-Nam, in Hanoi's Ba Dinh Square on 2 September, a claim unrecognised by European imperial powers. In this sensitive environment, Chief of Southeast Asia Command Admiral Lord Louis Mountbatten and Indian Viceroy Lord Wavell both voiced concerns in their official correspondence that Britain could be seen to be facilitating Indochina's return to French hands, and using colonial troops to suppress a nationalist movement. In the days after Gracey's arrival in Saigon, local Viet Minh leaders found their supporters targeted, attacked, and arrested by the 20th Indian Division; they quickly concluded from Gracey's actions that restoring French power was exactly what he aimed to do, and they took the use of another colonised people against them as a deep affront. Indian nationalist leaders Jawaharlal Nehru and Vallabhbhai Patel both raised objections in public against the use of Indian troops in Indochina and Java. It was their increasingly influential voices, as India stood poised at the brink of independence, which prompted Viceroy Wavell finally to push for the withdrawal of Indian troops.[45]

To counter British attacks on them, the Viet Minh aimed to undermine the Indian soldiers' loyalty by appealing to their sympathies as fellow victims of colonial aggression. Viet Minh nationalists picked up and re-transmitted news broadcasts from as far away as San Francisco which criticised the British deployment of Indian troops. They managed to make contact with remaining INA and IIL members still being held at Japanese headquarters in Saigon, who assisted them with a propaganda campaign. The handbills they produced urged Indians troops to recognise the Viet Minh as allies in the anti-colonial struggle:

---

45. Marc Jason Gilbert, 'Persuading the Enemy', in Wynn Wilcox, (ed.), *Vietnam and the West, New Approaches,* Ithaca: Cornell Southeast Asia Program Publications, 2010, 107–142, pp. 121, 127; Christopher Bayly and Tim Harper, *Forgotten Wars: The End of Britain's Asian Empire,* London: Penguin, 2008, p. 155.

Indian Soldiers! The Indian people are shedding much blood for freedom, why do you shed blood for your own enemies: the colonisers? You must back your countrymen by fighting against all imperialists and colonisators [sic]. Indian and Vietnam are in the same situation. Their people help each other in their struggle against the oppressors. British and French. Indian-Viet Namese friendship for ever![46]

The Viet Minh propaganda campaign is important not only for the way it illuminates the complex interactions between political players on the ground in Saigon in the turbulent period which followed the Japanese surrender. In a close study of this campaign and Gracey's reaction to it, the historian Marc Jason Gilbert argues that it influenced the shape and timing of the events of 23 September in ways which have not previously been recognised. On 23 September 1945, Gracey ordered the rearming of French prisoners of war and Japanese soldiers at the behest of the French Republic's Commissioner for Cochinchina, General Jean Cédile. France regained control on that day in a bitter and violent *coup de force*. Yet Gilbert's study of Gracey's correspondence demonstrates that the British General was motivated in his actions not just by French pressures but by Indian political considerations. Gracey learned of the Viet Minh handbills through French channels from around 20 September and became alarmed by their connections to the INA. The leaflets, Gilbert maintains, 'served to stiffen British determination to hand Indochina back to the French as quickly as possible'. One of the reasons Gracey repeatedly cited thereafter to justify the actions he took on the 23 September was 'a sheet published in English aimed at subverting British troops against the French'.[47]

In the two days that followed, from 24 to 25 September, mass Vietnamese unrest in response to the French and French-led violence saw up to 150 Europeans, Eurasians, and Indians brutally abused and killed in Saigon.[48] Vietnamese violence was directed in part against locally resident Indians, in response to the role played by Indian soldiers in the French coup. It was revenge for the actions of Indian troops of the British 20th Division, but also for those of French Indian soldiers, who were also

---

46. Quoted in Gilbert, 'Persuading the Enemy', pp. 122–125.
47. Christopher E. Goscha, *Historical Dictionary of the Indochina War (1945–1954), An International and Interdisciplinary Approach*, Copenhagen: NIAS Press, 2011, p. 92; Gilbert, 'Persuading the Enemy', pp. 127–128.
48. Devillers, *Histoire du Vietnam, de 1940 à 1952*, p. 160.

involved on the day.[49] The Polish journalist Germaine Krull was at the Saigon Municipality, which the Viet Minh had made their seat of government in the south, on the morning of 23 September. There, she identified the French troops forcibly removing Viet Minh representatives as soldiers of the 11th RIC, the Saigon-based French division so popular with Indian French citizens.[50] When they recounted the events of late September 1945 to the Indian Government agent Aney in mid-January 1946, Saigon Indians said they were convinced that 'the use of Indian troops and the employment of Indians in the French police turned the *Annamites* against them'. Local Indians reported that six Indians had been killed and another 70 kidnapped during the violence; by the time of Aney's visit in early 1946 only 16 people had been returned to safety.[51]

Among those Indians who disappeared in late September 1945 was Antoine Ratinassamy. Ratinassamy was the son of Louis Ratinassamy, a long-standing employee of the Office of Registration and Stamp Duty and one of Hanoi's prominent Indian French citizens. Antoine Ratinassamy was born and raised in Hanoi and fluent in Vietnamese. He had posed to be photographed with Nehru alongside other members of Hanoi's Indian community in 1939.[52] By 1945 he was a brigadier in the Hanoi police force. Three years after Antoine's disappearance, his father wrote a summary of everything known to him about the seizure and detention of his son, in a final plea to French authorities to assist in his return. The document serves as a reminder of how Viet Minh networks extended far beyond the bounds of French Indochina, just as it shows how Louis Ratinassamy relied on the equally transnational movements of Indian merchants to gather what information he could about his son's fate.

Antoine Ratinassamy was taken by the Viet Minh on the road between Saigon and Gò Vấp (in the Saigon suburbs) on 25 September 1945, two

---

49. Bayly and Harper, *Forgotten Wars*, p. 165.
50. Krull's account was reprinted post-war, without commentary, in the Pondicherry-based *Trait d'Union*. It is a haunting addition to the pages of a newspaper whose adjacent columns contained bids to secure the welfare in Indochina of Indian French citizens during the decolonisation of India and Indochina. Germaine Krull, 'Reportage sur l'Indochine', *Trait d'Union*, May 1947.
51. TNA WO 203/6217 Indians in Siam and French Indo-china, 4 Mar 1946–2 May 1946: 'Report on the condition of Indians in French Indochina (Secret)' by M.S. Aney, January 1946.
52. See Plate 17, page 274. He is in the back row, directly above his mother, who stands to the immediate right of Nehru. His sister Simone Sinnas is to Nehru's left, and the little girl in the front row is her daughter, and Antoine's niece.

days after French troops had been set upon the Vietnamese population in the south, and in the midst of the violent Vietnamese retaliation. He was visiting Saigon off-duty, and in civilian dress. His father's account of the kidnapping relates that Ratinassamy attempted to save himself, as so many French Indians had done since the Japanese seizure of power in March, by claiming he was a 'Bombay' merchant. His true identity as a French police officer was revealed after several days, and thereafter he was mistreated (*maltraité*) for four to five months. Eventually, he encountered several of his Vietnamese classmates from Hanoi's prestigious *Lycée Albert Sarraut*, who had joined the Viet Minh. 'Mostly to save his life', Louis Ratinassamy relates, Antoine 'consented to work with them.'

In the years immediately following his kidnap, Ratinassamy's family continued to gather information about his condition and to record sightings of him. Details concerning his well-being and his location were channelled to the family from merchants, political activists, and hostages released from Viet Minh captivity, some of whom reported that Ratinassamy had assisted their escape. From these various parties, Louis Ratinassamy learned that Antoine was 'for some time the keeper of a cow herd', and 'during this time … he succeeded in helping some people to escape (Eurasians and Indians)'. He was spotted several times in Bangkok in early 1948, at the Chittapong Pagoda, 'by an Indian from Phnom Penh who was visiting this city'. A former Cambodian nationalist leader reported having seen him at the home of a Mr. Quang, the head of the Viet Minh in Bangkok. Louis Ratinassamy continued to update the document with information received through his various networks. In an undated note in the margin he has written: '[seen] 10 months [ago] at the Bangkok Market in the company of 3 or 4 VM [Viet Minh] by an Indian from Phnom Penh who was passing through'. A final annotation at the bottom of the page reads: 'According to the latest information to be found in the province of Nghệ An or Thanh Hóa (North Annam) with 4 or 5 Indians, 10 November 1948'.[53]

Ratinassamy was taken by the Viet Minh against his will, but whether he willingly chose to remain with them is a question that is not clearly answered through his father's detailed plea. Louis Ratinassamy claimed

---

53. 'RATINASSAMY, Antoine – Indien français', request dated 23 September 1948, private family papers of Mr. Maurice Sinnas, Pondicherry. See also Natasha Pairaudeau and Chi Pham Phuong, 'The Indian Dimension', at http://www.endofempire.asia/0924.2-indochinas-indian-dimension/.

that Antoine tried to escape four or five times. He insists Antoine 'would be considered by the Viet Minh as a dangerous man due to his situation in the French Police force and his perfect knowledge of the Tonkinese language', and that he was 'currently closely watched by the Viet Minh'. His close surveillance might explain why, posed as a cow herd in an open field or visiting a public temple in Bangkok he might be too afraid to flee. By the time of later sightings of him, it might be understood he was remaining willingly with the Viet Minh. His father's final request, to ask the Siamese authorities 'to arrest him in order to extract him from the grip of the Viet Minh', could suggest either.

Ratinassamy's case captures the ambiguity of political allegiances in a tense and uncertain time. It also demonstrates just how fluid, when needs be, migrant identity could be.[54] Here we see the colonial French citizen posed as a Bombay merchant to protect himself from the gaze of Vietnamese nationalist forces; as a humble and inconspicuous cow herd; then as the invisible migrant, blending into the cosmopolitan melée at a Bangkok temple. His family, in the end, were not sure which side he was on, whether he stayed with the Viet Minh out of fear or choice; only that he never came back.

Colonial intermediaries, national misfits

Between the end of the Second World War and the beginning of the Franco-Vietnamese war for Vietnam's independence, there was no peace. Indeed levels of violence increased and insecurity became a part of everyday life for all Indochinese, its Indian residents included. On the wider global stage, Western attitudes towards colonisation had shifted, just as Vietnamese attitudes towards other Asians, and India's attitude towards its countrymen overseas, were reshaped. A tangled mass of questions hung over the overseas Indians of Indochina, Indian French citizens included, concerning their legal status, their national and imperial allegiances, and their sense of belonging. For Indians from the French possessions, another decade would pass, and the colonial empire that sustained them would unravel, before these questions would begin to be answered.

---

54. Ratinassamy's post-September 1945 existence bears comparison with the 'fluidity of the social world' inhabited by other Southeast Asian radicals, the ethnically ambiguous Lai Teck and the Malay Shamsuddin Salleh. Bayly and Harper, *Forgotten Armies*, p. 55.

The situation in Saigon had deteriorated into violence by late September 1945. In Hanoi too, where the Japanese surrender was overseen by Kuomintang General Chiang Kai-shek and his troops, there was tension and disorder. Louis Ratinassamy wrote a lengthy declaration to the Hanoi police, days before his son was kidnapped, stating that on 8 September five *Annamites* had burst into his house with knives and revolvers. The intruders had gagged and tied him and his three servants, and had stolen away with 12,000 piastres worth of money and valuables.[55] A Pondicherry-born merchant who was a young man at the time observed that after 1946 all Indians in Hanoi began to move closer together for protection; 'it was more tense with the Vietnamese from then on'.[56]

The Viet Minh attack on French forces in Hanoi on the evening of 19 December 1946 is generally considered in historical accounts as the starting point of the First Indochina War. A much less well-known incident, undoubtedly because it does not belong to the nationalist history but is part of the transcript of the messy transnational margins of decolonisation, is the 'Kewelram' or 'Palace of Silks' Affair. This French attack against Indian merchants was nonetheless one of the first acts of violence at the outbreak of the 'Battle for Hanoi'.

Early in the morning of 20 December 1946 three Indian merchants were shot at the 'Palace of Silks', the premises of the Sindhi merchant Kewelram, on the rue Paul Bert in Central Hanoi.[57] A report of the incident was filed by a British agent of the Interim Government of India, formed in September of that year to oversee India's transition to independence. The report reads as follows:

> On the morning of December the 20th last, a French captain and two or three French soldiers broke into Atmaram's shop as the result of an allegation that there had been shooting from the roof. A Viet Minh flag was found in one of the drawers and, without any proper inquiry being made, and despite the fact that the deceased exhibited British identity papers, Atmaram, Hardasmal and Jaidev were shot dead in the courtyard. The other two Indian nationals present were, on the intervention of a French civilian, permitted to leave unharmed. No fire arms were found in the building; nor was there any evidence, such as empty cartridges, that firing had in fact taken place from any part of

---

55. 'Déclaration au sujet d'un vol à mains armées commis chez M. Louis Ratinassamy au No. 5 Rue Capitaine Brusseaux à Hanoi', private family papers of Mr. Maurice Sinnas, Pondicherry.
56. Interview with Mr. Abdoul-Gaffour, Pondicherry, September 2004.
57. The rue Paul Bert is now Tràng Tiến Street.

the building. It is then alleged that, after the shooting, the soldiers proceeded systematically to loot the shop and to remove everything of value in lorries.⁵⁸

Kewelram was not present on the premises at the time of the shootings, but his brother (Atmaram) was one of the three men killed, and the looted premises included his family apartment.

The incident prompted the Indian government, on behalf of the families concerned, to request from France an inquiry and compensation for the deaths and material losses. French unwillingness to settle on the large sums of money requested by the wealthy merchant families affected delayed the resolution of the case. Another factor which slowed negotiations was Kewelram's proven involvement in the IIL, a circumstance which may have fuelled the brutality and haste with which the French soldiers had responded.⁵⁹ The main delay in resolving the 'Palace of Silks Affair' though was the Indian Partition and the desperate exodus it triggered across new borders. It threw into doubt the legal identities of the victims and their families, and French authorities seized upon this doubt as a tactic of negotiation and delay.

The Interim Government of India presented an initial request to the French authorities for compensation for the victims of the Kewelram affair in January of 1947. India's new Minister of External Affairs then transferred the dossier to his Pakistani counterpart in October of 1947, on the grounds that, given their Sindhi origins, the victims' proper homeland was in Pakistan. In March of 1948 responsibility for the case was transferred back to India, 'as the persons concerned have migrated from Pakistan to India.'⁶⁰

---

58. AMAE ASIE OCEANIE 1944–1945 INDE 109, 'Hindous en France Possessions françaises, Indochine 1 avril 1950–31 mai 1951 E.67.2': Joint secretary to Govt of India in the External Affairs Department to Consul General for France at Calcutta, 1 February 1947.

59. VNA1 D.62 2932 A.s. demande d'autorisation de former une association dénommée 'Association des Indiens en Indochine', formulée par Mohamed Abdullah, domicilié à Hanoi. 1942–1945; AMAE OCEANIE 1944–1955 INDE 109 Hindous en France Possessions Françaises, INDOCHINE 1 avril 1950–31 mai 1951: Minister of External Affairs Government of India to French Ambassador, 15 September 1948.

60. TNA FO 959/15 Hanoi – Fate of Indians 1948: Joint Secretary to the Government of India in the External Affairs department to French Consul Calcutta, 18 January 1947; in the same file Under Secretary Govt of India Ministry of External and Commonwealth Affairs to Secretary to Government of Pakistan Ministry of Foreign Affairs and Commonwealth Relations, 28 October 1947; AMAE OCEANIE 1944–1955 INDE 109 Hindous en France Possessions Françaises, INDOCHINE 1 avril 1950–31 mai 1951: Minister of External Affairs and Commonwealth Relations, New Delhi, to Ambassador of France, New Delhi, 5 March 1948.

French authorities blamed the Indian and Pakistani governments for holding up the process. Yet they too undermined the claim by confounding efforts to establish the legal identities and nationalities of the victims and the claimants. When the case returned to the desk of the Indian government in the autumn of 1948, France's Ambassador in New Delhi, Daniel Lévi, continued to press the Indian government for definitions of 'the respective nationalities of Indians and Pakistanis residing overseas'. In correspondence with his French colleagues he explored whether 'the nationality argument can play (*peu jouer*) in our favour', by suggesting that the victims at the Palace of Silks, who died in Hanoi before Partition, should be considered in death to be legally Pakistani and should remain Pakistani even if their relatives had opted to become Indian. Effectively, Levi sought to construct a bureaucratic boundary to separate the surviving family members in India from the supposed legal home of their dead relatives in Pakistan. In spite of his tactics, the French government eventually agreed, in 1953, to pay compensation to the families, albeit far less than the nearly 4 million rupees they had requested.[61]

French diplomacy handled emerging Pakistani and Indian nationalities as entities whose lack of legal clarity could be played to advantage. This begs the question of how seriously French authorities took the new French citizenship which had been extended to all peoples throughout France's colonial possessions some months' earlier. France's new postwar constitution vastly broadened the scope of French colonial citizenship, with a law which French West African deputies (and notably its namesake, the Senegalese lawyer, deputy, and *orginaire* Lamine Guèye) fought hard to push through.[62] The *Loi Lamine-Guèye*, introduced in May of 1946, granted blanket citizenship to all subjects of the French Empire. Moreover, it gave them that much-sought-after form of citizenship, the right to exercise political franchise while retaining indigenous personal status.[63] Citizenship became a cornerstone of the new structure for France's possessions overseas. The 'French Empire' was replaced

---

61. AMAE OCEANIE 1944–1955 INDE 109: French Ambassador India to Minister of Foreign Affairs Paris 12 August 1948; and in the same file, Minister of External and Commonwealth Affairs New Delhi to French Ambassador Delhi 22 October 1948, and French Ambassador New Delhi to Minister Foreign Affairs Paris, 28 October 1948.
62. Cooper, 'Possibility and Constraint', p. 175
63. Aldrich, *Greater France,* pp. 280–282.

later that year by the 'French Union', a federation of autonomous states with continued ties to France.

Within French West Africa, promises made under the Lamine-Guèye law provided a driving motor for labour movements to make claims to social and political equality for citizens within a federated Union.[64] In Indochina, by contrast, the 'French Union' was arguably used by French negotiators to sideline the Viet Minh by introducing an administration in Cochinchina favourable to continued French influence, a process which paved the way to open conflict in December of 1946. The blanket extension of French citizenship meant little in practice in late 1946 when nearly three quarters of southern Vietnamese territory was under Viet Minh control.[65] And for those whose colonial citizenship had been long-standing, such as the Indian French citizens, this new French citizenship was seen, if not always as political expediency, at least as a form of citizenship lesser than their own.

In early 1947, only a month after the murders at the Palace of Silks, fighting broke out between the Viet Minh and the French in Hanoi, putting the city's old quarter area of '36 streets' under siege. Indian cloth merchants whose shops lined the *rue du sucre* and *rue de la soie* were among those trapped inside the perimeter. On 24 January, the entire community of Indian merchants in the '*Annamite* district' of Hanoi, amounting to 180 persons, was evacuated from this part of the city. Newsreel footage of the evacuation shows Indian merchants in Turki caps emerging from the old quarter alongside elderly Vietnamese women with betel-stained teeth.[66]

Despite the success of the evacuation, at least seven Indians were killed during the Hanoi hostilities and another 33 reported missing and in Viet Minh hands. This brought the number of Indians detained in Viet Minh custody to over 100. It included those taken from Saigon in late September 1945 and another group of 40 Indians who had been caught up in fighting

---

64. Cooper, 'Possibility and Constraint', p. 175.
65. Martin Thomas, with Bob Moore and L.J. Butler, *Crises of Empire: Decolonization and Europe's Imperial States, 1918–1975*, London: Bloomsbury, 2008, pp. 189–190.
66. TNA FO 959/15 Hanoi – Fate of Indians 1948: Telegram British Consul Saigon to New Delhi 29 January 1947, and telegram Consul General Hanoi to Consul Saigon 28 January 1947; http://www.gaumontpathearchives.com/index.php?urlaction=doc&id_doc=228192&rang=7. I am grateful to Michael de Gregorio for bringing this clip to my attention.

that broke out in Vinh in Central Vietnam on 16 December 1946 and who were prevented by the Viet Minh from leaving.[67]

British diplomatic representatives and newly-placed Indian authorities continued to grapple through the late 1940s with the problem of some one hundred Indians held by the Viet Minh. Negotiations with the Viet Minh over the welfare and release of Indian hostages were carried out through the British Consul in Hanoi. He initially represented the Interim Government of India; later, he acted on behalf of the newly independent states of India and Pakistan, neither of whom had as yet established diplomatic offices in Hanoi. Each batch of 'Indian' prisoners released through this channel, however, proved to include a number of French Indians. Indians from the French possessions (the records do not differentiate French citizens from French subjects) were not under the protection of Britain, India's interim government, or the newly independent nations of the subcontinent. Yet of the first group of Indian prisoners taken during the siege of Hanoi's old quarter in December 1946 and freed in late February of the following year, five of the thirteen released were 'French Indians'. All of the returnees were 'destitute and urgently [in need of] warm clothing'. The British Consul had been urging French social services to provide clothing, and was concerned that the 'situation both at Saigon and Hanoi [was] acute and likely to worsen as more and more Indians are returned'. In view of this he requested the Government of India 'to send by R.A.F. aircraft 100 half 200 battledresses'. Indian French citizens had donned the longhis of Muslim merchants to protect themselves from Japanese internment following the coup of March 1945. In the winter of 1947, with questions of national or imperial belonging for the moment suspended, French Indians returning from behind Viet Minh lines wore British battledress to keep out the cold. No parallel papers could be found documenting French efforts to attend to the welfare of French Indians released by the Viet Minh. As the wider political map transformed and senses of belong-

---

67. TNA FO959/15 Hanoi – Fate of Indians 1948: Telegram British Consul Hanoi to British Consul Saigon 16 February 1947; TNA WO203/6217 Indians in Siam and French Indochina, 4 Mar 1946–2 May 1946: 'Report on the condition of Indians in French Indochina (Secret)' by M.S. Aney, January 1946; BL IOR/L/PJ/7/13926 Arrival at Hanoi of a party of Indians released by the Viet Minh authorities at Vinh May-July 1948.

ing shifted, France appears to have left this task to the British Consul, Hanoi's acting representative for the new states of India and Pakistan.[68]

The following year the British Consul once again received Indochinese Indians handed over by the Viet Minh, this time on behalf of the independent states of India and Pakistan. Once again, the status of those released did not always bear a relationship to the parties acting as their protectors. The released group proved again to include Indians from the French possessions. Here, the released captives conveyed reports of one Indian French citizen who was not content, even at the cost of remaining in Viet Minh custody, to be counted among the newly or potentially decolonised.

In May 1948, British Consul Arthur Trevor-Wilson set out for the small town of Thường Tín, 19 kilometres south of Hanoi. He was following advice transmitted from the Viet Minh to the Indian government that a group of Indians held at Vinh for nearly a year and a half were due to be released. The Indians had arrived there under Viet Minh escort, at the end of a journey by sampan and on foot along the waterways of Central Vietnam. They had travelled for over three weeks, covering a distance of some 300 kilometres. In the late afternoon of 11 May, Trevor-Wilson waited at the edge of a paddy field, a Viet Minh-controlled village visible in the distance, for the group of Indians to emerge:

> About three quarters of an hour later we saw, through a pair of field glasses, the Indians coming out of the village and crossing the rice fields. They took about three quarters of an hour to cross the fields and we met them on the road at 6.30 pm and practically at this very moment a storm which had been rolling about the neighbourhood broke overheard and it poured with rain. Coolies were carrying the small quantities of luggage. One very touching sight was a coolie carrying in the two small baskets in the end of his bamboo stick a little boy and a little girl. When I said hello to the small boy he immediately began to cry, as Oriental children often do at the sight of a European! ... The leader of the group was carrying the flag of Pakistan, and many tears were seen as the Indians met.[69]

---

68. AMAE OCEANIE 1944–1955 INDE 109 Hindous en France Possessions Françaises, INDOCHINE 1 avril 1950–31 mai 1951: AFP Service Outre Mer 10 mai 1947 'Une Déclaration du Conseil britannique Trevor-Wilson au sujet de l'Entrevue du Pont des Rapides'; ANOM FM 376 Carton 252 Indochine Races 1885–1954: AFP 1947 SGN; TNA FO 959/15 Hanoi fate of Indians 1947: Telegram British Consul Saigon to Delhi, 3 March 1947.
69. BL IOR/L/PJ/7/13926 Arrival at Hanoi of a party of Indians released by the Viet Minh authorities at Vinh May-July 1948: Report from British Consulate Hanoi, 13 May 1948.

The returnees, according to a list compiled thereafter, were merchants, shop assistants, or salesmen. Save for one Surati, they were all Tamil Muslims. Seven people in the group were listed as 'French'; the seven were all Muslims, and merchants, suggesting they were most probably French subjects. The group included six women, four of whom were Vietnamese. In all cases the women were merchants' wives. The children carried out in baskets on a bamboo pole were among a total of eleven children in the group, most of whom were probably Indo-Vietnamese. Finally, the group included a Swiss man who had been the director of a factory at Vinh and was released at the same time.

A statement given by the leaders of the group – the chief and co-chief of Vinh's Muslim congregation – records that in December 1946 approximately sixty Frenchmen (military and civilian) and their families had been taken prisoner at Vinh. Among this group was 'an Indian civilian, CINAMOUR, who refused to leave the French'. The Swiss man released referred to him as 'Mr Sinamour, a French Indian employed at the delegation, [who] refused to be liberated by the Viet Minh'. His name and employment both suggest he was an Indian French citizen. His insistence that he remain with the French detainees indicates that he held fast to his identity as a Frenchman. He was not willing to be thrown into a group identified by the Viet Minh as participants in an anti-colonial freedom struggle, even if it might secure his release from Viet Minh detention.

Viet Minh motives for holding the Indians at Vinh appear to stem from the idea that local Indians sympathised with the nationalist movement in their own country, and would support the Vietnamese cause and draw attention to it within the region and internationally. The Indian residents detained at Vinh 'had been advised that they had nothing to fear' and had been asked to remain and carry on business as usual. According to the Swiss businessman, the Viet Minh themselves were among the merchants' customers at Vinh: 'For the winter, the Viet Minh bought cloth from the Indian merchants to dress the French prisoners.' The merchants 'continued to trade until their stocks ran out', at which point they requested to be released.

Viet Minh efforts to garner support from their Indian guests were not entirely successful, nor were the messages they attempted to transmit always well received. The Vinh returnees claimed that during their sampan journey north they had a nine-day stop in the town of Phủ Lý where they were 'obliged' to listen to 'an intense propaganda asking us to help the Vietnamese so that they are able to gain their independence just as India has'. They were not won over either by Viet Minh demands to relinquish any valuables or currency in excess of 500 piastres before leaving Phủ Lý. Neither Viet Minh cadres nor Indian merchants were as yet fully imagining life outside of the colonial capitalist structure.[70]

Indians were of value behind Viet Minh lines because of their potency as another colonised people poised for self-rule. Viet Minh reports on the welfare of Indians behind their lines could acknowledge that they sat under two different colonial umbrellas ('all Indians in [Viet Minh] hands whether British or French are free and well') but they operated under the premise that all Indians sought or should seek freedom from colonial rule, and could thus potentially support the Viet Minh cause.[71] They detained local Indians as 'Indians', and returned them as 'Indians', regardless of which imprint of imperial belonging they bore. Sinamour felt strongly enough as a French citizen to correct this assumption. Other Indians from the French possessions who were held by the Viet Minh were probably genuine supporters of India's independence, and may have assumed as many did by then that French India's merger was already a *fait accompli*. Still others may have feared that displaying an affinity which did not accord with Viet Minh expectations might dash any hopes of their release. Antoine Ratinassamy's case lies in the ambiguous territory between these positions. As for the Tamil Muslims released from Vinh and marching across the paddy fields carrying the Pakistani flag, we simply do not know if they chose to proudly identify themselves with the new Muslim state formed with India's Partition, or if they were instructed by their Viet Minh hosts to perform a gesture which would resonate with anti-colonial liberation movements internationally.

Viet Minh efforts to forge a relationship with the newly independent Indian state are evident in a letter from Ho Chi Minh's government to

---

70. All references to the Indian detainees at Vinh are from BL IOR/L/PJ/7/13926 Arrival at Hanoi of a party of Indians released by the Viet Minh authorities at Vinh May-July 1948: Report of information from Abdul Mazid, *chef de congrégation* (Vinh) and Abdul Rahine, *co-chef de congrégation* and their internment and stay at Vinh from 19 December 1946 to 17 April 1948, and in the same file, Declaration of M. Regamey (Swiss) Technical Director of SIFA at Vinh.
71. TNA FO 959/15 Hanoi fate of Indians 1947: Telegram British Consul Hanoi to British Consul Saigon, 16 February 1947.

the independent Indian government notifying it of the imminent arrival of the Vinh detainees at Thường Tín:

> We always respect [sic] that good relations between the two populations Vietnamese and Indian will gradually be closer in the only aim of help in order to fight against the common enemy...Good friendship Vietnam and Indian Forever, Union and independence of Viet-Nam forever, President Ho Chi Minh forever.[72]

The language of this letter echoes the tenor of Nehru's emerging foreign policy. Nehru had already voiced his objections to the presence of the 20th Indian Division in South Vietnam in September 1945. As Interim Prime Minister, his first actions in relation to France were to issue a complaint to French Overseas Minister Marius Moutet over French actions in Hanoi in December 1946, and to voice his support for Vietnamese independence. In early January of 1947, he expressed to the Indian press the same sentiments. Indochina was directly at issue again in India later that month. Nehru blocked the renewal of an Anglo-French agreement, originally signed in 1945, which allowed French military aircraft to fly over Indian airspace. This was a further statement of his strong opposition to French aggression against the Vietnamese.[73]

Yet Nehru later backed down on the issue of French military flyovers and agreed to renew the Anglo-French agreement. Historian Claude Arpi has read this reversal in the context of Indian interest, in the lead-up to independence, in negotiating the merger of French India with the Union. Nehru first raised the possibility with his French counterparts, in April 1947, of the return of the French *loges*.[74] Indochina now became the currency for India in negotiations with France. The following month, in May 1947, Nehru finally persuaded the French government to lift controls on money transfers from Indochina to India. French authorities had maintained restrictions on transfers of funds in order

---

72. BL IOR/L/PJ/7/13926 Arrival at Hanoi of a party of Indians released by the Viet Minh authorities at Vinh May-July 1948: Committee of resistance and Administration in Hanoi to Indian Government Consul Hanoi, 7 May 1948.
73. See Claude Arpi, *La Politique Française de Nehru, la fin des comptoirs français en Inde (1947–1954)*, Auroville: Collection des Pavillons, 2002, pp. 33–36.
74. The *loges* were twelve miniscule trading posts on the sites of former factories strung along the coastline and still nominally in French hands. A hotbed of smuggling (and 'of no use to France' in the words of their own French Governor) they covered an area collectively of only 4 sq km and were inhabited by just 2,000 people. Arpi, *La Politique Française de Nehru*, pp. 36–37.

to stabilise the Indochinese piastre, and Indochina's resident Indians had been lobbying to have them lifted since the end of the war. French correspondence indicates that currency controls were finally lifted not only to improve economic relations with India, but because they were 'likely favourably to dispose the Government of Delhi with regard to various political problems that may arise between France and India, such as the maintenance of our Establishments'.[75] Indochina and French India would remain closely intertwined subjects of Franco-Indian diplomacy right through to the recognition of Vietnam's independence at the Geneva conference in 1954.

THE LAST FRENCH DECADE: 1945–1954

Indian French citizens' firm belief in themselves as devoted citizens of France was extended into wider allegiances with other overseas Indians during the tense years of the Depression. Their political allegiances were tested during the Second World War, but more fluid 'Indian' identities were also put to good use. In the period post-Second World War, northern Vietnam experienced the greater share of open conflict, in the course of which old colonial identities were reshaped to fit into new national frameworks. Further south, while an equally uncertain political situation prevailed and there was instability in the countryside, Saigon and Phnom Penh remained relatively calm and even prospered. In this climate, Indian French citizens reasserted themselves as French citizens and colonial *Indochinois* loyal to France. At the same time, they established stronger ties with Pondicherry, and slowly began to leave Indochina. Coupled with these scattered but steady departures, French Indians now reasserted their citizenship in ways which suggested that the status of a colonial citizen was an increasingly precarious one.

Once shipping lines had restored their routes with Pondicherry and Karikal, many French Indians took a much-delayed long leave to visit relatives and friends whom they had not seen for at least five years. They returned restored, lending the impression that this was a community ready to resume where it had left off circa 1939. French Indians who were children or adolescents at the end of the war recall their relief at having the terror of aerial bombardments behind them, and their pleasure at returning to a

---

75. AMAE ASIE OCEANIE 1944–1945 INDE 109, 'Hindous en France Possessions françaises, Indochine 1 avril 1950–31 mai 1951 E.67.2': Note Direction Asie-Oceanie, 10 May 1947 ; see also Arpi, *La Politique Française de Nehru*, pp. 33–36.

steady routine at the French primary schools and *lycées* of Saigon, Hanoi, or Phnom Penh.[76] The Paris-based Foreign Missionary Society (*Missions Étrangères*) despatched to Saigon Father Bulliard, a Tamil-speaking priest, further fuelling the impression of a French Indian community settling and expanding in Indochina. 'The presence of a Tamil-speaking priest' in Saigon, the Mission reasoned, was 'desirable for the 2,000 Catholic French of India.' Father Bulliard was a retired missionary who had spent his career in South India; he delivered his first sermon, in Tamil, at Saigon Cathedral on New Year's Day 1951.[77]

Even as some French Indians returned to Indochina, however, others left for good. These departures were not as yet urgent reactions to the political situation in Indochina. Nevertheless, once circumstances permitted, some French Indians now took the opportunity to leave. Thus a civil servant in Cambodia whose contract expired in 1953 chose not to renew it but to return to Pondicherry; Saigon's only practising Indian lawyer, ailing with tuberculosis, hastened to return to India with his wife and family; a Justice of the Peace of Indian origin who had spent his working life in Indochina did not now press for a transfer within Indochina, but accepted a West African posting, while another left for the Tribunal at Tananarive.[78]

Saigon's Franco-Tamil newspapers of the 1920s and 1930s had long since folded. But Indian French citizens did not wait long after the war's end to find another suitable publication through which to express their aspirations and defend their interests. This newspaper, the *Trait d'Union*, was produced in Pondicherry rather than Saigon; it began publishing news from Saigon in June of 1946. Instead of the columns reporting news from French India in Saigon's pre-war Franco-Tamil publications, this Pondicherry-based monthly carried regular news of Indochina, appearing under the headings 'Indochina Reportage', 'News from Saigon', or 'News from Indochina'. It carried frequent reports from the Saigon-based *Amicale des Français de l'Inde*.[79]

76. Interview with Claude Marius, Pondicherry, January 2002; Interview with Mrs. Amélie Marius Le Prince, Pondicherry, November 2004.
77. http://archives.mepasie.org/notices/notices-biographiques/bulliard; 'Le Rev. Père Bulliard', *Trait d'Union*, Jan 1951.
78. Interviews with descendants in Pondicherry, November 2004 and September 2011; 'Nos compatriots en Indochine', *Trait d'Union*, Jan 1951.
79. The *Trait d'Union* first appeared in Pondicherry in November 1944 under the title *Jeunesse de l'Empire Français*. *Trait d'Union* is a pun on the word 'hyphen' (as between India and France)

Like Saigon's Franco-Tamil newspapers, the *Trait d'Union* was aimed at a readership which included both Indians who had become French citizens through renunciation, and *créoles*. The Saigon-based Yves Perrier, also active in the *Société mutuelle des créoles*, was a frequent contributor. In contrast to the *Indochine-Inde* which preceded it the *Trait d'Union* maintained a narrow focus in its reports from Indochina on issues of concern to Indian French citizens. It was firmly loyal to France. French citizenship had just been extended, through the *Loi Lamine Guèye*, to all subjects of the French Empire just a month before the *Trait d'Union* appeared. The matter was largely ignored by the publication. Instead, it emphasised the special history of renunciation in French India, and of renouncers' long and loyal association with France. It is significant they chose to publish their concerns in a Pondicherry-based newspaper. Its readership was limited to Indian French citizens in Saigon and Pondicherry. Their interests no longer stretched in Saigon to include those of other overseas Indians, Vietnamese, Chinese, or metropolitan French resident in the city, in the same way they had before the war. Their 'public sphere' had contracted to French India, and French Indians in Saigon acted as overseas correspondents. The cosmopolitan moment of the 1920s and 1930s, it appeared, had evaporated.

The increased traffic between Indochina and Pondicherry, both the restorative post-war visits and the more permanent returns of those who had barely known French India, brought tensions and contradictions. These were aggravated by the economic advantage that returning *Indochinois* were able to gain after the war. The lifting of currency controls coupled with the plummeting value of the Indian rupee made possible handsome profits for those returning with Indochinese piastres.[80]

Sharp criticism was expressed in the pages of the *Trait d'Union* of the braggarts returning from Indochina claiming that everything was bigger and better there. Humour was used to soften the blows aimed at those who went 'a little too far in considering India to be backward'.[81] One article relates the comical story of Mr. 'Altap', recently returned from Indochina. Altap is depicted as the Indochina prototype: the boy who

---

and 'mark of the Union', referring to the *Union Française*. The *Trait d'Union* continues to be published today: some of its longest-standing correspondents grew up in Indochina.
80. Georges Guénée, 'La Crise Monétaire', *Trait d'Union*, Dec 1952.
81. 'Le coin des cancans', *Trait d'Union*, Oct 1952.

failed his *bac* (*baccalauréat*, French secondary school qualification) and was packed off to Indochina in a last-ditch attempt to make something of him. Returning to Pondicherry, he goes on and on to his friend Kirouvin about how marvellously well he had fared in Indochina:

> I was named conservator of Forests and you can't imagine how well I have done. I bought six houses, banked some ten million piastres, and had three cars at my disposal. It's not like here. You are all poor sods at 80 rupees a month, you live in narrow houses, you eat very ordinary meals with your hands. You have to see it my friend … you have to see it in Indochina, it's much bigger!

Altap gets his come-uppance when he is bitten by a crab. Kirouvin responds calmly, 'It was perhaps not a crab but the fleas we have here. They are much bigger than their relatives in Indochina.' 'Altap', the article closes, 'understood the lesson.'[82]

Sentiment-laden nostalgia for Indochina can be found in the same pages. 'Saigon, Pearl of the Orient, city of my childhood,' intoned one memoir, 'you are all my life until the age of sixteen.' The author cannot have been yet eighteen when he wrote these words in 1946, but he already felt the finality of his journey from Saigon. The 'horrors of Japanese occupation [and] the Anglo-American aerial bombardments' had made him no less nostalgic for, 'the old house of my childhood, the *lycée* where I closed the cycle of my studies, the teachers who made me what I am'.[83] If the Indian French citizens no longer actively involved themselves in Saigon's print culture, documents such as this read as telling signs that they felt their future in Indochina, and indeed the very future of Indochina, to be in doubt.

The frenzied distribution of Cambodian royal honours by Saigon-based Indian French citizens can be read as another effort to indulge in Indochina's excesses in the face of instability. Between February 1951 and July 1952, more than twenty-two medals were pinned on the chests of members of the *Amicale des Français de l'Inde*, their supporters, and officials they sought to influence, all in the name of the King of Cambodia. At numerous banquets, lunches, and *vin d'honneur* hosted by the association, ceremonies to present the medals were accompanied by speeches and toasted with champagne. To close the 1951 annual banquet of the

---

82. Djinak, 'Un bluffeur', *Trait d'Union*, May 1948.
83. R. Antoine, 'Souvenirs', *Trait d'Union*, Nov 1946.

Amicale, 'after the champagne flutes were filled', medals were awarded in the name of his Majesty Norodom Sihanouk, King of Cambodia, to two prominent members of the association. The medals were presented by an 'Honorary Mandarin' of the Royal Court of Phnom Penh, who 'formulated the sacramental words' as he did so. In October 1951, while on leave in Pondicherry, the *Amicale's* President decorated various local personalities on behalf of Sihanouk during a *vin d'honneur* at the Pondicherry Municipality. The Honorary Mandarin and his family were treated to dinner at a Cholon restaurant prior to their departure to France on long leave in March of 1952. 'Over champagne', the President thanked the Honorary Mandarin 'for numerous services that he has rendered to his compatriots and more recently still the numerous decorations he has obtained for the meriting members of the AFI'. Thereafter, the President was made an 'Officer of the Royal Order of Sahamétrai', and medals were presented to four other *Amicale* members. Finally, in June of 1952, the *Amicale* held a lunch in honour of Mr. Vianes, Director of the Indochina Exchange Office. The President thanked Mr. Vianes for his help in re-establishing the post-war flow of remittances from Indochina to India. He continued: 'It was in the spirit of recognition for the services rendered to our community that I endeavoured especially to put your name forward to the Royal Council of Cambodia, for an important distinction that you have just been accorded.' The *Amicale* President then announced, 'In the name of His Majesty Norodom Sihanouk, King of Cambodia, and in virtue of the powers conferred upon me, [I] declare you an Officer of the Royal Order of Sahamétrai.'[84]

The man who obtained the medals on behalf of the *Amicale* was a Phnom Penh-based property manager of Pondicherry origin, and a French citizen. He had become friendly with Prince Monniridh, Sihanouk's brother, through a common love of football, and through him was introduced to the Royal Court. He had then been favoured with the title of 'Honorary Mandarin'.[85]

The distribution of medals to members of the *Amicale des Français de l'Inde* came to a stop when the Cambodian monarch objected that his medals were flowing too freely. Enthusiasm among *Amicale* members for

---

84. J.A. 'Nouvelles de Saigon', *Trait d'Union*, March 1951; J.A. 'Le Président de l'Amicale des Français de l'Inde', *Trait d'Union*, Oct 1951; J.A. 'Nouvelles de Saigon', *Trait d'Union*, April 1952; Julien Adicéam, 'Nouvelles de Saigon', *Trait d'Union*, June 1952.

85. Interview with a family member, October 2004.

distributing honours, however, did not end as abruptly. With Cambodian medals no longer accessible, the *Amicale* devised its own award, the 'Medal of Recognition' (*Médaille de Reconnaissance*). At a December 1953 reception at Saigon's Continental Hotel, the new medal was pinned on the chests of a number of dignitaries in Indochina, including the Commissioner of the Republic. The *Trait d'Union* noted once again that the champagne 'flowed freely'.[86]

In the near-decade between 1945 and the Vietnamese victory at Dien Bien Phu, the lives of Indochina's Indian French citizens apparently returned to normal. Despite the departure of some members of the community, their settlement in Indochina appeared to become more ingrained and they displayed a renewed confidence. The latter was nowhere more evident than in the *Amicale*'s eager distribution of Cambodian royal honours. Yet the situation beneath these appearances was deeply unsettled. The end of the Second World War did not signal peace, but the start of an even more violent anti-colonial struggle in Indochina, one in which the future of French India was profoundly implicated. Medal-giving among the French of India, as much as it signalled confidence, was also a vain assertion of colonial citizenship and colonial belonging in an Empire with an uncertain future.

Other roads from Dien Bien Phu

The French presence in Indochina effectively came to an end when Viet Minh troops besieged and defeated French forces following a prolonged siege at Dien Bien Phu in the northern mountains (13 March–7 May 1954). When Viet Minh troops paraded through Hanoi to celebrate their triumph, the city's Indian merchants greeted them with the flags of the Democratic Republic of Vietnam and the Indian Union flying side-by-side outside their shops. In one sense the gesture served as a show of solidarity, as recognition of the Vietnamese achievement as a shared victory in wider global processes of decolonisation. Viet Minh photographers recording the event were eager to capture the air of internationalism which the Indian flags lent to the scene.[87] In another sense the two flags, individually signalling the end of French Indochina and

---

86. 'Le vin d'honneur de l'AFI', *Trait d'Union*, Dec 1953.
87. Ủy Ban Nhân Dân Thành Phố Hà Nội [Hanoi People's Committee], *Kỷ Niệm 50 Năm Giải Phóng Thủ đô: Hà Nội Ngày Tiếp Quản.* [Souvenir of 50 Years of Freedom: The Day Hanoi Welcomed the Army], Hanoi: Xưa và Nay Publishers, 2004.

Plate 18: Vietnamese army (with Trần Duy Hưng, chairman of Hanoi Administrative Committee, standing) parading through Hanoi following their victory at Dien Bien Phu. The Indian national flag waves from a merchant's shop in the background. Photograph by Phan Xuân Thúy, 1954. Courtesy of Vietnam Historical Association.

British India respectively, together announced the dissolution of French India.

The French defeat at Dien Bien Phu in May of 1954 was a closely-watched event in a global drama of decolonisation, and an important marker in individual Vietnamese accounts of their own lives.[88] For Indians from the French possessions residing in Indochina, the significance of these events was no less weighty, both for the ways in which the fate of French India was to become further entangled in the final negotiations to end French rule in Indochina, and for the turns their personal lives would take.

The merger of the French possessions with independent India had begun prior to the official British handover of 1947, with the return of the French *loges*. Yet it was to take fifteen years, until 1962, before France formally relinquished all claims to its territories on the Indian subcontinent. In the long years of negotiation over French India's merger, the governments of France and India both promised, initially, to respect the principle of public consultation on the matter; both governments later reneged on this promise. Each government made full use, too, of

---

88. Bayly, *Asian Voices*, pp. 188–189.

the patchwork geography of the French Establishments to gain political leverage.

Chandernagore was the sole territory to benefit from the 1948 agreement on the principle of referendum, voting in June 1949 to join India. The merger of the remaining French Establishments (Pondicherry, Karikal, Yanaon, and Mahé) did not come about through public consultation. The blame falls in part on governments who chose to force public opinion to their side by making use of the fragmented nature of French territory and its division into isolated pockets. In a failed attempt to apply pressure on France, India ended its Customs Union with the French territories in April 1949. Pondicherry then entered a 'golden age of smuggling'. French India did little to control the illicit transfers across its permeable borders; its local (anti-merger) politicians, it was rumoured, were gaining both in popularity and personal wealth from the huge traffic of gold and diamonds through Pondicherry. The unchecked smuggling, coupled with violence against pro-merger parties, led the Indian government in October 1952 to abandon its agreement to a referendum and to insist instead on the direct transfer of the remaining French territories. The Government of India further resolved to control smuggling, and from late 1952 imposed a series of economic blockades. It sealed its frontiers with the French Establishments with barbed wire, periodically stopped supplying the electricity upon which the French Indian population depended, and introduced a permit system which could arbitrarily prevent French officials, such as municipal policemen, from reaching those French communes which lay surrounded by Indian territory.[89]

French India's political parties continued to practise a factional and opportunist politics largely unchanged from Chanemougan's time. An elected representative of the industrial working class nonetheless appeared for the first time in this period. V. Subbiah was a former labour leader at Pondicherry's Savana textile works and a candidate for the National Democratic Front (*Front Nationale Démocratique*), French India's main post-war political party. He secured the support

---

89. On this period see Annoussamy David, 'The Merger of French India', *Revue Historique de Pondichéry*, 21, 2004, 13–30, pp. 16–19; Miles, *Imperial Burdens*, p. 161; For the politics surrounding the Customs Union and smuggling in Pondicherry, see Akhila Yechury, 'Empire, Nation, and the French Settlements in India, c. 1930–1954', unpublished PhD thesis, 2012, University of Cambridge, esp. Chapter 3, and pp. 144–145.

of Pondicherry's industrial work force to win a seat in January 1947 on Pondicherry's *Conseil de la République*. Opposed to both French and British colonialism, he also openly voiced his support for the Viet Minh. Concerns over Subbiah's communist learnings led two political moderates with the National Democratic Front, the Pondicherry Deputy Lambert Saravane and the long-standing local politician Édouard Goubert, to leave the party in July 1947. The party they formed, the *Parti Socialiste de l'Inde Française* (PSIF), rapidly became the main pro-French political party in Pondicherry. Yet by early 1954 rumours circulated that the PSIF used hired thugs to attack pro-mergerists, and as smuggling became more controlled and less lucrative, the party lost the support of powerful business interests. Saravane and Goubert went their separate ways, both now forming parties which fully supported French India's liberation. Goubert's 'French Indian Liberation Congress' as well as Subbiah's communists were among the 'vigilante' groups who liberated isolated communes of Pondicherry and Mahé and areas of Yanaon in the spring of 1954.[90]

India's rigid customs cordon had made the remaining French territories virtually inoperable by early 1954. France pushed forward its decision to accept French India's merger following the defeat at Dien Bien Phu in May of that year. Despite French Indians' strong links with Indochina, the only justification for France to keep its Coromandel Coast ports was for their value as strategic supply stations en route to Southeast Asia. With Indochina gone, French India could not last much longer. French India's fate was sealed in the course of negotiations over Indochina at the Geneva Conference. India's unofficial presence at the talks secured a 'deal between Mendès France and Nehru'; the French President accepted India's assistance as an intermediary in negotiations with Ho Chi Minh's government in return for the cession of French India. For its labours, India also earned itself a lead role on the International Commission of Supervision and Control, set up at Geneva to oversee the border between North and South Vietnam. In July of 1954, as the Geneva talks came to a close, France agreed in principle to transfer administrative powers in its remaining territories on the subcontinent to the Republic of India. The elected representatives of the French pos-

---

90. Miles, *Imperial Burdens*, pp. 60–62; Weber, *Pondichéry*, p. 361; David, 'The Merger of French India', pp. 19–20.

sessions met in October 1954 in the Pondicherry commune of Kijéour to decide, without a popular referendum, on the issue of merger. They voted 170 to 8 to join the Indian Union. Their ballots were cast in a shed constructed expressly for the purpose. It straddled the French-Indian border and was intended to allow those voting for merger to move quickly to the safety of Indian territory should they come under attack for their anti-French vote. The *de facto* agreement took effect from 1 November 1954; a Treaty of Cession which handed sovereignty of the remaining French territories of Pondicherry, Karikal, Mahé, and Yanaon to India was signed in 1956.[91]

Indochina's Indian French citizens remained distanced from the intricacies of local anti-merger and liberation politics in Pondicherry up to 1954. Symphorien Lami of Saigon's *Amicale des Français de l'Inde* criticised Pondicherry's politicians, and declared his own association loyal to France and French India, but he did so in ways which were oddly (or perhaps characteristically) extraterritorial. Lami wrote a letter in November 1951 to protest against what he called Lambert Saravane's 'undemocratic action'; Saravane had just proposed to dispense with the process of referendum to decide on the merger of the remaining Union territories. Lami's article was published not in the French Indian press, but in the Paris-based *République Française*. Later, in April 1952, the *Trait d'Union* published an exchange of letters between Lami and Mr. Letourneau, High Commissioner for France in Indochina. Lami expressed the 'unflagging loyalty' of Indian French citizens and declared that the *Amicale's* 'prime goal' was 'to bring about the union of all our compatriots in Indochina, with a view to putting our full support behind the maintenance of the French Establishments in India within the French Union'. Yet the underlying purpose of Lami's letter was to maintain the *Amicale's* position in Indochina. With Marshal Lattre de Tassigny's recent death, the association had lost its Honorary President. Lami's brief eulogy to the Marshal ('our noble benefactor … who rose up in the midst of recriminations from the Indian Union, a champion of our freedoms') places the Indochina conflict firmly within the context of the tensions of French decolonisation stretched across the Indian

---

91. On this period see Weber, *Pondichéry*, p. 395; Miles, *Imperial Burdens*, pp. 66–67, 77; David, 'The Merger of French India', p. 20; D.R. SarDesai, *Indian Foreign Policy in Cambodia, Laos and Vietnam, 1947–1964*, Berkeley: University of California Press, 1968, p. 47; Arpi, *La Politique Française de Nehru*, p. 85.

Ocean. Lami's proposal to Letourneau to replace Lattre de Tassigny's position at the *Amicale* was duly accepted.[92]

In the period which followed the *de jure* agreement of late 1954, and as the terms for the merger were being shaped, a number of political parties and interest groups formed which were intent on protecting the interests of the original renouncers and their descendants. The 'French of India' or the 'renouncers' were now beginning to refer to themselves as 'Indo-French', 'Franco-Indian', 'Franco-Pondicherrian' (*Franco-Pondichérien*) or simply 'Pondicherrian' (*Pondichérien*) to distinguish themselves from Indians from the French possessions who did not have the same distinct history of citizenship. These new advocacy groups sought to retain their connections to France's institutions and its culture, to find a place for themselves in the new India and the new Southeast Asia, and to maintain their mobility. Arthur Annasse's group, the *Patriotes de l'Inde Française*, insisted upon dual nationality for Franco-Indians, respect for their French culture, and the maintenance of their social and salary advantages.[93] Another group, the 'Representatives of Pondicherrian Interests', published a memorandum dated March 1956. In it they argued that a sector of Pondicherry's population had special interests which required protection:

> There exists in the State of Pondicherry...an intellectual elite...that makes up the core of a population imbued with a psychology and a personality somewhat different from its homologue in the Indian Union. [This group] requests that its life and interests regulated by the [French] Civil Code for two centuries are not overturned from one day to the next. It requests the continuation of rights acquired over a long period, so that the transition from one regime to another takes place without shocks and according to rational conditions.[94]

The group's specific requests included the ability to choose their preferred nationality (French or Indian) during the period of transition; dual nationality on request; no restrictions on travel between India and France; and simplified and well-defined regulations for personal and commercial transfers of funds between the two countries. The group

---

92. ANOM RST 04217 Renseignements sur l'association des indiens étrangers en Indochine et sur les commerçants indiens: Protestation des Français de l'Inde résident en Indochine', *République Française*, Nov 1950; J.A. 'Nouvelles de Saigon', *Trait d'Union*, 8 April 1952.

93. Weber, *Pondichéry*, p. 397; Annasse, *Les Comptoirs français de l'Inde*, p. 167.

94. École Française d'Extrême Orient (EFEO), Pondicherry Branch, Emmanuel Adicéam Papers: 'Memorandum', 26 March 1956.

also voiced concerns related to the recognition and maintenance of French language, culture, and education. These ranged from the general, that Pondicherry should remain (in Nehru's own words) 'a window on France', to very specific requests aimed at securing a future for a French-trained elite who had served France overseas. They requested that French should remain the official language in the former French territories, at least until such time as India declared a national language. They asked for a system of equivalence for French qualifications, to allow Franco-Indians trained in the liberal professions to practise unhindered in independent India. Finally, pointing most clearly to Indochina-based interests, they insisted that a French representative in India be enabled to pay the pensions of those Pondicherrians who had served France overseas. Of the fourteen signatories to this document, five are recognisable as *Indochinois* who had retired to Pondicherry.[95]

The Treaty of Cession, France's agreement on the conditions to cede sovereignty to India, was signed in May of 1956. The series of articles in the treaty which most clearly addressed the circumstances of Indian French citizens overseas, those defining the legal status of French Indians following the handover to Indian sovereignty, proved to be the most controversial. Under the 'Option', as it came to be known, people originating in the French Territories in India immediately became Indian nationals if they were present in India when the Treaty of Cession entered into force (*de jure* transfer, on 16 August 1962). This category of individuals had the option to retain French nationality, however, as long as they formally registered their desire to do so within six months of the transfer (that is, before 16 February 1963). For French Indians who were outside India at the time of the handover, the rules were reversed. They automatically retained French nationality; in order to become Indian nationals they had to make a formal declaration to an Indian consular office, before the end of the same six-month grace period. Those who retained French nationality nonetheless had the right to remain on Indian soil, with the same rights and obligations as Indians citizens as far

---

95. The signatories included Dr. Tirouvanziam, 'President of the General Federation of Retirees of France Overseas', L. Nadin, General Treasurer of the same society, Firmin Paul, 'President of Retired Servicemen of French India', Mathias Clairon, President of the Association of French Free Forces, and Marius Clairon, 'Honorary Inspector of Customs and Revenue of Indochina'. EFEO Pondicherry Branch, Emmanuel Adicéam Papers: 'Memorandum', 26 March 1956; See also Miles, *Imperial Burdens*, p. 69.

as taxation, commercial activities, and public services were concerned. They did not, however, have the same political rights as Indian citizens.[96] Other requests put forward by Franco-Indian overseas interests which found their way into the Treaty of Cession included recognition for those in the liberal professions, and the payment of pensions in India to former employees of the French government.

The 'Option' has been criticised for being poorly managed, indeed chaotic in its implementation. Stories continue to circulate in Pondicherry about people who were unaware, until it was too late, that they were required to state their preference at the French Consulate or an Indian consulate overseas. Some critics object that the 'Option' placed too much emphasis on the French character of the former territories, thus permitting many people in French India who did not speak fluent French to opt for French nationality. Others contend that it failed to make a sharp distinction between those who had opted to be governed by the French Civil Code, that is those who had renounced, and those who had not. It made French citizens in some cases of people who had had very little attachment to France, and in other cases left out individuals whose families had for several generations lived as French citizens and considered themselves to be fully assimilated to France. Those who were 'caught out' by the Option and failed to register in time included renouncers who had recently left Indochina for good and were trying to reorient themselves back in Pondicherry, a 'home' many of them had barely if ever known before. Some of these people automatically became Indian against their will. On the other hand, many Indian merchants stayed on, while they could still continue to do business, in the independent territories of the former Indochina. Most were non-renouncers, and did not have close attachments to France. Yet unaware of actions they could have taken to become Indian nationals, they automatically became French on the final day in February 1963. Annasse maintains that many French citizens, due to the prevailing upheavals, 'were prevented from making their declaration within the prescribed time'. Thus, 'against their will and to their eternal regret, they automatically became nationals and citizens of the Indian Union'. He contrasts in bitter terms the solemn and enduring character of renunciation under the terms of the decree of 21 September 1881, its

---

96. Miles, *Imperial Burdens*, pp. 255–256; EFEO Pondicherry, Emmanuel Adicéam papers, 'Confidential notes: Personal Status of the natives of French India'.

'definitive and irrevocable' nature not only for the renouncers themselves, 'but for all their descendants', and the way this faculty 'was so lightly dismissed (*bafoué*) in 1963'.[97]

Too much emphasis can be placed though on the argument that French India's citizenship 'Option' was mis-managed for those who wished to retain French nationality. The fact remains that there were also Pondicherrians who chose to become Indian nationals; the large income gap between those who chose French nationality and those who declined it may have, understandably, given rise to later regrets. Moreover, mismanagement does not discount the way renouncers who chose to 'opt' for French citizenship were able to retain a characteristically mobile form of citizenship even as they were obliged to leave Indochina, and how they gained special privileges within independent India.

Indian French citizens old enough to remember the events of 1954 recall the defeat at Dien Bien Phu as an abrupt end. In the north it precipitated a rapid departure. 'After Dien Bien Phu, in March, April, the Viet Minh gave us 48 hours to leave, 48 hours for all French to leave', the son of an Indian bureaucrat stationed at Hanoi later recalled. 'We left immediately because the Vietnamese knew my father was in the French police force…we left our goods for the Vietnamese to take care of…we left everything with the servants.'[98] The first journey for Indians, as for others closely connected to France, was south to Saigon, from where the departure was slower and more staggered.

Many of those who had long served in the French administrations of Indochina now embarked upon new circuits which included an initial sojourn in Pondicherry or Karikal. These places were themselves in the process of negotiating a merger with independent India. Franco-Pondicherrians speak of the unfamiliarity of 'home', of extended family dwellings and shared sleeping quarters which were a few steps down in their eyes from the modern habitations they knew in Indochina. They speak of different rules of decorum for interactions across gender and caste lines. Those who were not yet of an age to retire generally stayed a brief period before embarking on further circuits of expatriation. Some French Indian functionaries went to serve in France's remaining

---

97. On the 'Option', see Yechury, 'Empire, Nation, and the French Settlements in India', p. 169; David, *The Merger of French India*, p. 22; quotes from Annasse, *Les comptoirs français dans l'Inde*, p. 231.

98. Interview with Mr. Antoine André, Reddiar Palayam, Pondicherry, August 2004.

overseas territories. One man, who served as an air traffic controller in Madagascar, claimed that Franco-Indians sought out places with climates similar to that they had known in Indochina. France's overseas departments, notably Réunion, became more permanently settled with Pondicherrians. The subsequent decolonisation of France's remaining overseas territories put an end to colonial service. More and more Indians with Indochinese pasts followed a path to France. There they were reassigned to posts in the metropolitan administrations; they became some of the earliest occupants of Paris's post-war suburbs. They did not all settle, though, but often sought to leave again. French technical cooperation with its former colonies allowed Pondicherrians with technical or professional skills a smooth transition from colonial service to the era of post-colonial development. Several magistrates in the law courts of Africa's newly independent capitals were Indians who had worked previously in Indochina. In this way too, Pondicherrians doubled-backed on the independent states of Indochina, serving as teachers and technical experts in Phnom Penh, Saigon, or Vientiane right up until 1975. New intermediary roles were created for older diasporas in the post-colonial age in a number of interesting ways. Lurdusammy was employed as a liaison between the French and American armies in Laos in the mid-1960s. Other Indian French citizens returned to Indochina as employees of the Indian-led Committee for Supervision and Control. One strategic aim was to work one's way up through the administration to 'category C' of the Foreign Affairs department, thus accessing employment in France's embassies and consulates overseas.[99]

Indian French citizens fought at Dien Bien Phu, and some lost their lives there, but their numbers are difficult to establish. After the French Army was decommissioned in Indochina (1955–1956), Indian soldiers went on to fight in France's other wars of decolonisation. Among them was Symphorien Lami's son, injured in Algeria in 1958. The Indochinese decommissioning also brought Indians and Indo-Vietnamese to France, particularly to the garrison towns in the south of France (Fréjus, Castres, Nîmes).[100]

99. Discussions and interviews in Pondicherry and Paris, 2004 and 2012; Sébastia, 'Les Pondichériens de l'Ile de France', p. 38; Claude Marius, 'La migration des Pondichériens vers l'Indochine (suite et fin)', *Revue Historique de Pondichéry*, vol. 23, 2009, pp. 3–37, 32–33.

100. Interview with Mr. Antoine André, Reddiar Palayam, Pondicherry, August 2004; 'Un Français de l'Inde au Viet Nam, cité à l'ordre du jour sur le front d'Algérie', *Trait d'Union*, February 1958; Sébastia, 'Les Pondichérens de l'Ile de France', p. 7.

While those who wished to continue their employment in the French civil service left Indochina in the wake of the French defeat there, the departure of French Indians who were employed in the private sector or self-employed was less swift. Indian merchants did not immediately depart from communist-held North Vietnam in 1954. But by 1956, for commercial reasons, they went south and west, to South Vietnam, to Cambodia, or to Laos. Indian businessmen continued to operate in these new independent states into the 1970s, and through the American war. Indian French citizens employed outside the colonial administration – de Condappa, Léon Prouchandy, the Sinnas family – stayed on too. The continued presence of French commercial interests in South Vietnam, as in Laos and Cambodia, meant that French Indians employed as clerks or accountants in these companies did not lose their livelihoods. In turn, some French institutions in the non-communist parts of Indochina continued to function after 1954. In 1957, Symphorien Lami was still working as a school supervisor at the *Lycée Chasseloup Laubat* in Saigon. A further reason for not leaving was to regulate questions of family property. Thus a French Indian teaching in schools in Dalat and Phnom Penh in the 1950s and early 1960s also managed family properties which his father had left behind on his return to Pondicherry in the later 1940s. Other Franco-Indians who stayed on acted as *mandataires* over properties of those who left.[101]

Indian departures from Indochina were also complicated by mixed marriages and mixed unions. French Indians with Indochinese wives and children, many of whom were former soldiers, were too entrenched in local life and local culture, or in some cases simply too poor, to be able to pack up and leave. It was primarily members of this group who eventually reached France through the *service des rapatriés d'Indochine*. This agency was charged with receiving and resettling French citizens from Indochina who had no relatives in France. Reception centres established in several locations in France received a first wave of 'returnees' from 1955. In this first wave were many Eurasians who had no previous experience of France. Many of Vietnam's remaining Franco-Indians (or Franco-Indo-Vietnamese) shifted to Laos or Cambodia – where the situation was not yet quite as unstable and less tense for people with French connections – before eventually making use of their citizen-

---

101. Interviews with descendants, Pondicherry and Paris, 2002, 2004.

ship to go to France. With the escalation of American involvement in Indochina, they too made use of the *service des rapatriés d'Indochine*. At Noyant-sur-Allié, the main centre to receive this wave of returnees, over 200 of the 2,000 *rapatriés* were Indian and Indo-Vietnamese. Like many of the Eurasians who preceded them, they too had little or no experience of the Metropole.[102]

Conclusion

In the experiences of Indian French citizens negotiating Vichy rule, Japanese occupation, and Subash Chandra Bose's brand of nationalism in Second World War Indochina, there is a palpable sense of disrupted patterns of imperial belonging. Incidents of migrant Indians shot, under siege, captured, or freed by the Viet Minh, and even French Indians bragging in Pondicherry about the grandeur of Indochina or pinning themselves with medals in Saigon, are all equally revealing of this great upheaval of belonging. The ambiguities of nationality, citizenship, and belonging could be played to advantage, by Indian functionaries donning Muslim longhis to save themselves from Japanese arrest as much as by French diplomats querying the 'Indian' or 'Pakistani' identities of victims of atrocity to delay a large pay-out. Precise definitions of legal status and national belonging could become blurred, such as when mixed groups of 'Indians' (French, British, and potentially Indian or Pakistani) were released by the Viet Minh into British Consular hands urgently requiring clothing – any clothing, even British battledress. Either way, old empires could no longer relate in their accustomed ways to the subjects or citizens with whom they had been associated.

The French Indians of Hanoi gathered in 1939 with their other Indian compatriots to admire Jawaharlal Nehru as an emerging national leader who extended his support to Indian communities overseas. The next time Nehru was photographed in Hanoi was in October of 1954, seated next to Ho Chi Minh. By this time, the former was Prime Minister of an independent India, and the latter was President of the Democratic Republic of Vietnam. In the years in between, Indochina's French Indians were doubly caught out as hopes for independence came to face the realities of foreign policy. Nehru's support for anti-colonial movements on the international

---

102. Pierre-Jean Simon, *Rapatriés d'Indochine*, p. 214; Interview with Michel Audemar, Pondicherry, November 2004.

stage did not allow him to maintain an ongoing commitment to Indians overseas, whose interests were frequently at odds with those nationalist movements. And his involvement in negotiations over the French departure from Indochina was intended as much to hasten the transfer of France's remaining territories on the subcontinent to Indian sovereignty as it was to support a Vietnamese nationalist cause.

Although the Viet Minh put forward an internationalist ideology at the height of their struggle for freedom, at independence this gave way to a nationalist vision which was both politically and ethnically more narrow. Yet it was their French citizenship, finally, which drove the French of India out of North Vietnam, and would guide their final departure from the other former territories of French Indochina. Unlike Southeast Asia's other colonial diasporas, the Indian French citizens were not forced to choose between settling or returning. Rather, they used their claims to French citizenship to retain their mobility and to create a rare example of a post-colonial identity not rooted in ethnic or territorial belonging.

AFTERWORD

What has been gained then, by studying the Indian French citizens of Indochina? How can the study of inter-colonial connections contribute to a fuller understanding of the colonial encounter? What do the 'renouncers', the Indian French citizens of Indochina, have to contribute to the study of citizenship within the French Empire, or beyond it to post-colonial contexts?

Histories produced in the immediate post-colonial decades were driven by a desire rightly to condemn the injustice and oppression of colonial occupations. But many of these same histories constructed seemingly 'natural' boundaries around the newly independent nations and their peoples by producing historical narratives which placed the new nation at the centre. Histories of colonialism until recently were reluctant to recognise relationships beyond that of the coloniser and the colonised, or to acknowledge colonial-era connections other than those between the Metropole and the colony. For precisely these reasons, the lives and experiences of French Indian migrants to Indochina have up to now been little studied. Yet when the connections between French India and French Indochina are re-established, and the relationships they produced re-assessed, Indian migrants – from French and British Empires alike – no longer appear as a minor footnote in Indochina's colonial history.

Indochina played a more significant role than has previously been acknowledged in the story of late French colonialism in India; the French of India made their mark in turn on the territories of French Indochina, and in particular on the history of Cochinchina, now within the southern part of Vietnam. The French conquest of Indochina revived the flagging fortunes of French India's Coromandel ports. Yet if it gave them new strategic importance, it did still more for French Indians themselves. The French presence in the Indochinese peninsula provided new sources of employment for ambitious, French-trained Indians. Their ambitions were further fulfilled once they managed to secure recognition in Cochinchina as full French citizens, allowing them to live a privileged existence relative to Indochina's mass of local colonial subjects and *protégés*.

Along with an Indian expatriate population of more diverse origins, Indian French citizens played a meaningful part in shaping colonial society and politics in the Indochinese peninsula. The everyday dynamics of colonial rule in Indochina were complex; French authority was channelled in its quotidian forms through a wider variety of actors. The peoples of Indochina experienced colonialism in their daily lives in part through the Indian French citizens who policed Indochina's municipalities and manned its bureaucracies, and through the Tamil tax farmers stationed in the market and at the ferry crossings of the Mekong Delta. Dissent too was triggered not by French actions alone, but by the presence and privileges of colonial intermediaries. Southern Vietnamese reformers of the 1920s fashioned their calls for change in ways intimately tied to Indian French citizens' exercise of their citizenship rights in Cochinchina.

In their diversity, colonial actors in turn expressed their wills, made claims, and engaged with one another in their own right. Even as they put forward vocal claims to their rights as Frenchmen, Indian French citizens interacted in Saigon with other Tamil migrants in ways out of keeping with scholarly notions of tightly-knit diasporic merchant networks. In interwar Saigon they participated across ethnic lines in modernist and cosmopolitan social and political debates. They incorporated and re-deployed the European racial thinking of the time, a strategy which they shared with their urban Vietnamese detractors, and which suggests broader ways in which racial ideas came to sustain colonial societies. Vietnamese moderates in the 1920s may have debated with French Indians in terms which were fraught with tension and disagreement. Yet the intellectual interests of the interwar years were shared ones. The migrants' religious practices were absorbed and adopted locally, and inter-ethnic marriages and families were formed.

This is far from the picture of a plural society where ethnic groups met only in the context of economic exchange. Saigon might not have displayed quite the inter-ethnic dynamism of Singapore, Penang, or Rangoon. Yet if we invest greater interest in how Asian migrants may have been involved in Saigon's public discussions of the 1920s and 1930s, interwar Saigon may well begin to appear as a centre not just of economic life but of inter-Asian intellectual and cultural exchange, as a cosmopolitan port city which could hold its own in Southeast Asia.[1]

In the modern age, membership within a nation-state has come to be the most powerful form of belonging, so powerful that it appears to be natural and self-evident. We tend to think that the ideas that created and sustained nations were produced, and are re-produced, within the boundaries of these nations, by their states and their 'nationals'. In early twentieth century Southeast Asia though, migrants played an active role in shaping senses of belonging in response to the tensions and upheavals beginning in the interwar years. The ways in which these emerging identities then fed into claims to citizenship within newly independent nations are processes which are still not adequately understood. Indian French citizens' eager 'profile-raising' in interwar Saigon, their use of much older histories of Indian migration to justify their presence, their clothes-swapping of the war years, their rejection of Viet Minh definitions of who they ought be in an era of decolonisation, and even their involvement in negotiating the 'Option' for post-merger French India, all suggest fruitful avenues through which the role of Asian migrants in shaping post-colonial identities in Southeast Asia might be further explored.

The Indian presence in colonial Indochina – and here I refer to the presence of migrants from both British and French-ruled India – invites a number of conclusions. Undue emphasis in post-colonial histories on the relationship between the coloniser and the colonised has detracted from the study of the relations sustained with other actors in society. Inter-Asian relationships were crucial in shaping the colonial encounter. The creation of separate legal categories for different peoples acted in itself as a source of dissension and rivalry, and inter-Asian debates provided some of the senses of belonging from which modern post-colonial citizenships and international relationships across new nation-states were later formed.

Very similar conclusions are arrived at by another scholar of inter-Asian connections, Christopher Goscha, in his study of relations between

---

1. Aside from the Indian press debates examined here, Goscha's study of the Sino-Vietnamese debates of 1919–1923 is a bold step in this direction. See Goscha, 'Widening the Colonial Encounter'. On the colonial port cities of Southeast Asia and cosmopolitanism, see especially Harper, 'Globalism and the Pursuit of Authenticity', and Su Lin Lewis, *Cities in Motion: Urban Life and Cosmopolitanism in Southeast Asia 1920–1940*, Cambridge: Cambridge University Press, 2015.

Indochina's Vietnamese, Lao, Cambodian, and Chinese populations.² In the debates that Goscha examines, Lao, Cambodian, and Vietnamese people all expressed frustration at what they saw as unwanted 'foreign' incursions into spaces they regarded as their own rightful territories within the larger space of the Indochinese Union. Each of these ethnic groups opposed special privileges for immigrants. The Lao and Cambodians in opposition to Vietnamese immigrants, and the Vietnamese in response to the migrant Chinese, all demanded greater control over immigration into their *pays* or territory within the French whole. Each group insisted that incomers should be equal to locals, absorbed into the local administration, subject to the same regulations, and with the same subject or *protégé* status.³

The lively debates which engaged Indian French citizens in Cochinchina were also over who belonged and who didn't. Crucially though, they made their arguments with reference to a different sense of belonging. Rather than struggles to secure the 'equal' subjugation of immigrants within Indochina's internal boundaries, contests over French Indian status in Cochinchina were about securing the rights and privileges of French citizenship. Aside then, from what it reveals about the importance of inter-colonial and inter-Asian relationships in shaping colonial encounters, the other value of this work lies in what it tells us, through the peculiar clash of citizenship regimes which took place in Cochinchina, about citizenship in the French Empire.

In the 1960s and 1970s, social scientists treated citizenship largely as a theoretical concept, and most historians understood France's extension of citizenship rights to the peoples it colonised as a transfer of policy from Metropole to overseas possessions. These theoretical reflec-

---

2. Goscha, 'Widening the Colonial Encounter'; also Goscha, *Going Indochinese*.
3. Vietnamese at the receiving end of Lao and Cambodian complaints requested for their part the introduction of an 'imperial citizenship' for Indochina. This 'citizenship', they hoped, would allow them to travel within the Union unhindered by Lao or Cambodian administrative regulations. Although the Constitutionalist Bùi Quang Chiêu was an avid supporter of the movement to promote 'Indochina citizenship', this was a demand for special administrative and immigration rights within the Indochinese Union, and separate from his requests for greater access for Cochinchina's commercial and intellectual elite to the political and civil rights of *French* citizenship. Indochina's Vichy government raised the possibility of a similar Indochinese 'imperial citizenship' during World War Two. Again, this was not a plan to extend the rights of French citizens; rather it consisted of a number of social rights extended to subjects and *protégés* of Indochina within Vichy's contradictory programme of federalism and indigenous 'National Revolutions'. Both types of 'Indochinese citizenship' bear similarities with the British 'imperial citizenship' I discuss at the end of this chapter. On 1920s and 1930s discussion of 'Indochinese citizenship', see Goscha, '*Going Indochinese*'; on its war-time Vichy equivalent, see Anne Raffin, 'The Integration of Difference in French Indochina during World War II: Organizations and Ideology concerning Youth', *Theory and Society*, 31, 3, 2002, 365–390.

tions have become displaced by the work of scholars who study more closely how French citizenship was made within specific colonial contexts. Such studies provide valuable insights into factors at local levels which assisted or prevented colonised peoples from gaining the rights of citizens. Citizenship in France's overseas possessions, these studies show, rarely if ever matched up to France's republican ideals.

Yet when France's colonised people became citizens, they did so through processes which were astonishingly varied. Citizenship regimes were shaped under specific local conditions, and at different stages within the life of the French Empire. The conclusions drawn depend upon the kind of citizenship regime and the period studied. Some regimes may be referred to in order to reinforce the idea that France extended the rights of citizens to its colonies free of racial considerations; studying other avenues to citizenship, such as that put in place for the mixed-race children of France's overseas empire, prompts the conclusion that the very notion of French nationality was founded in race.[4] Some periods in France's history of colony citizenship can be used to demonstrate that the state embraced colonial citizenship, while others show that every obstruction was put in the way to prevent colonised people from becoming citizens. French citizenship in colonial contexts was all of these things, and more, at different times and in different places. The complexities of this history have made it difficult to produce an overall picture of citizenship which might account for its many contradictions at the level of the French Empire as a whole.

The case of renouncers in Indochina may well be unique. It may be a rare instance in the history of the French Empire that a substantive flow of migrants from one of France's old colonies moved to a new one; that they became involved there in embattled discussions about their rights as citizens in a new context where a colonial social order was being introduced which favoured racial separation over legal assimilation; and that by securing their citizenship as a legal right they contributed to a distinctive form of colonial society, and a distinctive reformist politics, in their host country. It certainly offers a valuable opportunity to expand an otherwise still limited view of French citizenship and how it reached across the diverse conditions within the Empire and across time.

By showing how renouncers in the French Indian context were able to have a remarkable measure of influence over the terms on which they

---

4. Saada, *Les Enfants de la Colonie*.

could accede to citizenship, this work has highlighted the importance in the old colonies – particularly the enclave colonies – of the ideas and actions of indigenous people in shaping citizenships. In the old colonies, colonised people had a say in *how* they were going to become citizens and on what terms. The *originaires* of Senegal did so by rejecting France's offer of the Civil Code, while in Pondicherry some colonised people actively 'renounced' their customary codes. From later citizenship regimes based on naturalisation – which are more familiar from a twenty-first century perspective – the assumption is made that citizens' rights were always very difficult for colonised peoples to obtain. In the islands and enclaves of the old empire, this was simply not the case. To acknowledge that colonial citizenship was more readily obtained in the 'old colonies', a pattern established prior to France's extension of its empire from the mid-nineteenth century, is to begin to form a very different picture, overall, of the role citizenship played within the French Empire.

This kind of local agency, the way colonised people in the old colonies managed to have a say about the terms upon which their citizenship was extended, is distinct from the leverage gained once they had become citizens. The latter form is another equally important kind of indigenous agency pertaining to citizenship in colonial contexts. Frederick Cooper speaks of this kind of leverage in his recent work on French citizenship in late colonial Africa. Studying citizenship in French colonial contexts is important, he argues, because it shows not just how people were subjugated by colonial rule, but how they could have a say within the system. Citizenship gave people in the French colonies, those who could obtain it, 'the right to have rights, the right to make claims'. It created, in Cooper's words, 'cracks in the system' which colonial citizens could pry open to gain a better position within colonial systems. Cooper emphasises that these 'cracks' were wrenched open by people working *within* colonial systems rather than against them. Studying citizenship thus allows us to focus serious attention on people often dismissed as 'collaborators' in national histories; it reveals them as complex agents with agendas of their own, who tested and troubled the system even though they may not have done so in ways which were 'anti-colonial'.[5]

But the 'cracks' created by the possibility of citizenship within French colonialism should not detract from the great fissure scarring the land-

---

5. Cooper, *Citizenship between Nation and Empire*, p. 8.

scape of the French Empire as a whole, and dividing the ways in which the rights of citizens were made and exercised in the old colonies from the restrictions imposed on citizenship in the new. French Indians did not just cross the 'black water' to reach Cochinchina; they crossed a great citizenship divide. Their passage has obliged us to recognise and consider both sides of this divide. Indeed it has been the troubled encounter of two citizenship regimes across the great divide which produced the conflicts and contradictions at the heart of this story.

I have used the metaphor of a landscape to describe the range of citizenship regimes, the different terms upon which colonised people in different locations were able to accede to the rights of citizens across the Empire. To convey the political opportunities provided and constraints encountered by extending citizenship to the French Empire, a monetary metaphor is more appropriate. The moral imperative for extending citizenship overseas may have originated in republican ideas of the Rights of Man, but the logic of actually implementing such principles in the colonies turned on the question of whether political structures which were unequal, or indeed dependent upon subjugation, could bear the (political) cost of large numbers of people enjoying citizens' rights.

In his study of post-war federalism and subsequent decolonisation in French Africa, Frederick Cooper uses just such a monetary logic when he asks whether France at the end of empire could 'afford' equality. He does so in the context of the moment in France's history of citizenship which pushed this logic to its absolute limit, following the blanket extension of citizenship to all peoples within the French overseas possessions under the 1946 Lamine Guèye Law. The story he tells is of new citizens in the African states of the French Union in the 1940s and 1950s, who made powerful claims to labour rights, wages, and civil rights on a par with those obtainable in metropolitan France. Faced with the sheer cost, in workers' wages and benefits, and in the social protections of the post-war era – in short the cost of equality on this scale – France began to accelerate the transfer of fiscal responsibility to the West African states themselves. In so doing it created a momentum for self-government which led finally to the collapse of the Union.[6] In reply to Cooper's ques-

---

6. Cooper, *Citizenship between Nation and Empire*; also Rogers Brubaker and Frederick Cooper, 'Our Strike': Equality, Anticolonial Politics, and the French West African Railway Strike of 1947–48,' *Journal of African History*, 37, 1996, 81–118.

tion, these events demonstrated that France patently could not afford to extend citizenship on so large a scale within a structure which, albeit now re-christened a 'French Union', remained imperial.

The case of Indian renouncers in French Indochina has invited us to consider closely more than one means by which citizenship was extended, and to reach further back into France's post-Revolutionary history of citizenship. In doing so, we find that the extension to the overseas possessions of equal political and civil rights was always costly to the smooth operation of colonial projects, and France was continually making calculations about the political cost to empire of this kind of equality. Citizenship regimes were more open and generous among the modest, contained populations of the islands and enclaves that made up the French Empire in the early nineteenth century. There was an official willingness to see citizens' rights extend broadly through these populations, and even a willingness, in the enclave colonies, to concede to 'native' innovations in the terms on which people could accede to such rights. Within these systems, it appears that the French Empire could 'afford' citizenship. But it could only do so, even on this limited scale, by devaluing the 'currency' of colonial citizenship at the ballot box. Separate electoral lists, described in this book for Pondicherry, curtailed the power of the indigenous electorate to override the votes of the otherwise inconsequential electorate of metropolitan origin in the colonies. Even with these checks in place, colonial citizens always threatened to use their rights in ways that reached beyond French colonial designs. The election of Chanemougan as Mayor of Pondicherry is a reminder of this; one reason Pondicherry authorities agreed to legally recognise renunciation, we must recall, was because they hoped it would create a body of citizens who could vote in the European list to counterbalance the votes of Chanemougan's casteist, 'anti-French' supporters.

Once France began to claim larger territories overseas, the idea that political or civil rights could be widely extended to much larger populations while still allowing France to retain political control in these territories simply did not hold up.[7] France recognised that it clearly could not afford colonial citizenship on that scale; with the renewal

---

7. Algeria warrants further study to elucidate where its very uneven system – one rule for Jews, another for Muslims, and incorporating 'renunciation', naturalisation, and blanket citizenship – fits in. It is arguably a transitional case, as I claim in Chapter Two, which marks the point of changeover, or the 'citizenship divide'.

of republicanism under the Third Republic, citizenship was extended to Cochinchina, but with a new control placed on it. The process of naturalisation – citizenship through the state's careful selection of suitable citizens – permitted republican principles to be extended to the colonies, but it allowed colonial authorities to control the number of new citizens produced. Electoral lists were no longer needed; the native electorate was controlled before it reached the ballot box. Thus at different periods in France's post-Revolutionary history, even in an earlier age when the moral principle of extending citizenship was embraced, political calculations were continually made about whether France could afford equality.

The introduction of naturalisation was not just a change in the way citizenship was accorded, but part of a more fundamental change in how French imperialists sought to manage the colonial order in a larger territorial empire, through racial separation and hierarchy. As this new order began to be formalised in the 1880s, and when the naturalisation decree for Cochinchina was put into place, it brought the citizenship regime of French Indians into conflict with the new racialised order. One common way of framing French colonial citizenship within the wider history of empires and their management of indigenous social orders is to claim that Imperial France offered an alternative to the rigid social and racial hierarchies characteristic of colonial societies in the age of high imperialism. But in late nineteenth-century Cochinchina the framework of a racialised social structure was being put in place through practical measures such as regulations governing concubinage, a decree on naturalisation, and petty instructions to channel colonial benefits away from 'Asian' employees. In French Indian debates with the colonial administration, their defence of their legal rights as citizens came up continuously against objections grounded in race science. Citizenship was not an alternative to racial hierarchy in Cochinchina; racial discourse and the language of rights and citizenship were embedded in the same debate, with one logic used to attack and undermine the other. This suggests that, for a wider understanding of the relationship between race and citizenship, to reach beyond the judgement of whether or not France was colour-blind in its colonies we need to identify the specific points at which the language of race was used to support or to challenge claims to citizenship.

AFTERWORD

The story of French India's renouncers in Indochina may be an unusual one in the history of the French Empire, but it is unlikely that there were no other such embattled inter-colonial debates over citizenship within the French Empire. With so many people on the move across Europe's empires from the latter half of the nineteenth century, France's localised forms of 'old' colonial citizenships could surely not have remained contained within local contexts. Citizenship could not continue to be so locally defined – indeed so ill-defined – when areas beyond the islands and enclaves where these rights applied had become so much more accessible.

A key question is not just about the nature of these different kinds of citizenship but about what happened to them when they 'moved'. One answer, discussed above, was that colonial migrants had their rights challenged by authorities using racial thinking. Another, as the renouncers discovered, was that if migration called rights into question the migration itself was empowering with respect to securing rights. The renouncers of French India found when they moved with their vague electoral and civil rights to another French colony that their claims to citizenship and their claims as citizens became more powerful at the level of empire than within their 'home' colony. When they arrived in Cochinchina, the law applicable to them did not explicitly state that they *were* citizens, but that they were *like* citizens, and it was silent on whether they could exercise their rights outside of French India. Raising the question in Saigon rather than Pondicherry, the renouncers transformed the issue from a colonial one into an imperial one. By appealing to republicans in France, to the parliamentary representatives they were already empowered to elect from India, and to legal experts in France, they were able to prompt a principled, republican answer to the question of whether they were really French citizens. The answer which came back from the Supreme Court was 'yes'. It was an answer suited to how the Third Republic wished to see itself and its overseas empire in the 1880s. It was patently not an answer which pleased the Cochinchinese administration, which was beginning to justify its privileges using racial criteria while straining to pay for them from the local budget and tax base. Legal rights won out in the French courts against the 'racial code'. Even though administrators continued to use racial logic and race science to undermine the rights of Indian French citizens, these citizens could use their political rights to defend themselves. And they could rely on the willing assistance of 'republican' local and parliamentary politicians, however self-serving some of these men might have been. Renouncers' citizenship was fuller, or stronger, in Cochinchina than it was in French India. It was a citizenship which was applicable throughout the Empire and put them on a par with a European electorate rather than on a farcical 'native' electoral list. It was, in short, a universal imperial citizenship.[8]

The possibility of citizenship for colonised peoples was an important feature of the French Empire, which made it distinct from other European colonial empires. Yet colonial citizenship across the space and lifespan of the French Empire was a peculiar and contradictory phenomenon as well as a powerful one. French India and French Indochina were brought into contact to the mutual benefit of colonial capitalism and colonial state-building in both places. Yet this contact also gave rise to an embattled relationship over citizenship, which contributed to a distinctive Indochinese colonial society and politics. The power of a few hundred Indian French citizens to dominate European elections in a colony of three million indigenous people, to hold positions of relative power within the colonial structure, and to unsettle a social order

---

8. The knowledge that imperial citizenship was more powerful than colonial citizenship was not restricted to the French Empire. One of the most significant examples of a movement for 'imperial citizenship' came from within the British Empire, and was Indian-driven. The 'Imperial Indian Citizenship Association', formed in Bombay in 1914, began as a body to protect the rights of Indians residing in parts of the British Empire outside India. It was later at the forefront of a politics aimed at improving Indian status within the Empire. The Association defined 'citizenship' as a shared loyalty to the British sovereign and Empire. It protested against immigration restrictions imposed by the White Dominions and claimed that as loyal 'citizens of Empire' Indians had a right to equal treatment, equal status, and free movement within it. British 'imperial citizenship' was based on loyalty within empire; it was not the stronger political stuff of the French Revolution. Indian claimants to 'imperial citizenship' nonetheless addressed their claims at the level of Empire as a stage for making claims *within the system* rather than at the lower and less influential level of individual colonies. But here too inter-colonial migrants were at the forefront, pushing 'citizenship' claims up to imperial level. Claims of the colonised to belonging or entitlement at the imperial level were distinct types of claims produced in and enabled by the age of mobility, when colonised peoples began from the late nineteenth century to move across empires with an intensity previously unprecedented. On 'imperial citizenship' in the British Empire see Hugh Tinker, *Separate and Unequal: India and the Indians in the British Commonwealth 1920–1950*, London: C. Hurst, 1976, esp. Chapters 2 and 10; Daniel Gorman, *Imperial Citizenship: Empire and the Question of Belonging*, Manchester: Manchester University Press, 2006; Sukyana Banerjee, *Becoming Imperial Citizens: Indians in the Late Victorian Empire*, Durham: Duke University Press, 2010. See also Keiko Karatini, *Defining British Citizenship: Empire, Commonwealth and Modern Britain*, London: Frank Cass, 2003; Niraja Gopal Jayal, *Citizenship and its Discontents: an Indian History*, Cambridge, Mass.: Harvard University Press, 2013.

newly striving to be based on racial separation, are all reasons why the small number of Indian French citizens mattered in Indochina, and need to be taken seriously as part of Indochina's social and political history. They need to be taken seriously too for the ways in which, as migrants, they helped to shape new senses of belonging and a unique form of post-colonial identity for themselves, as the sun set on France's Empire in Asia. They were mobile citizens in several senses. They arrived in Cochinchina with the rights of citizens; their citizenship was challenged and reshaped as a result of their movement; as colonial intermediaries they enjoyed the privileges of citizenship outside their own colony; and as migrants in a modern age of mobility they forged new notions of 'citizenship'. And today their descendants remain some of the most mobile of French citizens.

APPENDIX

TEXT OF THE 'DECREE RELATIVE TO PERSONAL STATUS', 21 SEPTEMBER 1881

DECREE

Relative to personal status
Mont-Sous-Vaudrey, 21 September 1881
THE PRESIDENT OF THE FRENCH REPUBLIC,
At the proposal of the Minister of the Navy and Colonies, and the Guardian of Seals, Minister of Justice,

Decrees:

ARTICLE 1: In the French Establishments in India, natives of both sexes and all castes and religions, who have reached the legal age of twenty-one years, may renounce [*renoncer*] their personal status in the forms and under the conditions determined below. By the fact of this renunciation, which is definitive and irrevocable, they are governed as well as their wives and their under-age children by the civil and political laws applicable to French people in the colony.

ARTICLE 2: Natives who are aged less than twenty-one years may renounce their personal status with the aid of those persons whose consent is required to validate marriage.

When the renunciation takes place at the moment of marriage, it may be confirmed in the act of the marriage ceremony.

ARTICLE 3: Natives who are aged less than twenty-one years who are married may undergo renunciation in the form prescribed for those who have reached legal age.

ARTICLE 4: The renunciation of personal status, when it is not confirmed as part of the marriage ceremony, as stated in Article 2, will be received by the Office of the Civil Registry [*état civil*] on a special register established for this purpose, and kept in conformity with Article 40 of the Civil Code modified by the decree of 24 April 1880. It may equally be made in front of a Justice of the Peace assisted by his Registrar [*greffier*] and two witnesses, or in front of a notary.

In the two latter cases, a copy of the verbal transcript [*procès-verbal*], or of the notarised act, will be immediately transmitted to the cognizant officer of the Civil Register who will make an entry in the register.

ARTICLE 5: Within fifteen days of the renunciation or of its transcription, it shall be made public by an entry, for which no fee shall be charged, in the colony's Official Gazette [*Moniteur Officiel*].

ARTICLE 6: Natives who renounce their personal status shall indicate in the act of renunciation a surname [*le nom patronymique*] that they intend to adopt for themselves and their descendants.

ARTICLE 7: Anyone may obtain extracts of acts of renunciation through the keepers of the registrar dedicated to such acts. These extracts will be delivered in conformity with the registers and legalised by the President of the Court of First Instance [*tribunal de première instance*] or by the judge replacing him, and are authentic unless proved to be false.

ARTICLE 8: Officers of the Civil Registry will charge no more than thirty *centîmes* for each copy of a Certificate of Renunciation of Personal Status, as for a copy of a birth or death certificate or for a marriage certificate. No fee is chargeable for the execution of these acts or their transcription into the registers.

ARTICLE 9: Renunciations made prior to the promulgation of the present decree in front of registrars, notaries, or scribes [*tabellions*], must be transcribed on the special register by the relevant parties or by the State Prosecutor. Renouncers may renew their renunciation in order to benefit from Article 6 and to secure the provisions of Article 1 and those that follow.

ARTICLE 10: Renunciation may not take place under any general rule of law or in any forms other than those provided for in the present decree.

ARTICLE 11: The Minister of the Navy and Colonies, and the Guardian of Seals, Minister of Justice, are charged, each in the area which concerns him, with the execution of the present decree which will be inserted in the Bulletin of the Laws [*bulletin des lois*] and the *Official Naval Bulletin* [*Bulletin officiel de la marine*].

    Declared at Mont-Sous-Vaudrey, 21 September 1881.
    Jules GRÉVY
    By the President of the Republic

The Minister of the Navy and Colonies,
G. CLOUÉ
The Guardian of Seals, Minister of Justice,
JULES CAZOT

(from the *Annuaire des Établissements français dans l'Inde pour 1881*, pp. 472–473. My translation from the French original.)

BIBLIOGRAPHY

SERIAL RUNS

Les adresses de l'annuaire de l'Indochine

Annuaire des Établissements français dans l'Inde

Annuaire de la Cochinchine Française

Annuaire Générale de l'Indochine

Annuaire Statistique de l'Indochine

Courrier de Saigon

Echo Annamite

Indochine-Inde

Journal d'Outre Mer

Journal Officiel des Établissements Français dans l'Inde

Le Monde Colonial Illustré

Lục Tỉnh Tân Văn

Moniteur Officiel des Établissements Français dans l'Inde

Réveil Saigonnais

Le Trait d'Union

La Tribune Indigène

La Tribune Indochinoise

Saigon-Dimanche

BOOKS AND ARTICLES

Abdoule-Carime, Nasir, 'Les communautés indiennes en Indochine', Association d'échanges et de Formation pour les Études Khmères, http://aefek.free.fr/iso—album/vidy.pdf, 2003 [last accessed March 2015].

Adas, Michael, *The Burma Delta: Economic development and Social Change on an Asian Rice Frontier, 1812–1941*, Madison: University of Wisconsin Press, 1974.

Affonço, Denise, *To the End of Hell: One woman's struggle to survive the Khmer Rouge*, London: Reportage Press, 2009.

Aiyar, Sana, 'Anticolonial Homelands across the Indian Ocean: The Politics of the Indian Diaspora in Kenya, ca. 1930–1950', *The American Historical Review*, 116, 4, 2011, 987–1013.

Aldrich, Robert, *Greater France: A History of French Overseas Expansion*, Basingstoke: Palgrave, 1996.

———, 'France's Colonial Island: Corsica and the Empire', in Gemma M. Betros (ed.), *French History and Civilisation: Papers from the George Rude Seminar*, 3, 2009, 112–125.

Amrith, Sunil S., 'Tamil diasporas across the Bay of Bengal', *The American Historical Review*, 114, 3, 2009, 547–572.

———, *Migration and Diaspora in Modern Asia*, Cambridge: Cambridge University Press, 2011.

Andrew, C.M. and A.S. Kanya-Forstner, 'The French "Colonial Party": its Composition, Aims and Influence, 1885–1914', *The Historical Journal*, 14, 1, 1971, 99–128.

———, 'The Groupe Colonial in the French Chamber of Deputies, 1892–1932', *The Historical Journal*, 14, 4, 1974, 837–866.

Annasse, Arthur, *Les comptoirs français dans l'Inde (trois siècles de présence française)*, Paris: La Pensée Universelle, 1975.

Anon, 'Mẹ Maria Lệnh Cho Ta Dùng Phương Pháp Cứu Rỗi Là Lần Hạt Mân Côi', http://www.dongcong.net/MeMaria/ThangManCoi/12.htm [last accessed March 2015].

Anthony, Francis Cyril (ed.), *Gazeteer of India: Union Territory of Pondicherry Vol I*, Pondicherry: Administration of the Union Territory of Pondicherry Press, 1982.

Appavou, T.P., *Absurde renonciation des Indous chrétiens*, Saigon: Imprimerie Aug. Boch, 1890.

Arendt, Hannah, 'Why the Cremieux Law was abrogated', in Hannah Arendt, *The Jewish Writings*, New York: Random House, 2007 [1943], 244–253.

Arpi, Claude, *La Politique Française de Nehru, la fin des comptoirs français en Inde (1947–1954)*, Auroville: Collection des Pavillons, 2002.

Arsan, Andrew, Su Lin Lewis, and Anne-Isabelle Richard, 'Editorial – the roots of global civil society and the interwar moment', *Journal of Global History*, 7, 2, 2012, 157–165.

Baker, C.J., 'Economic Reorganization and the Slump in South and Southeast Asia', *Comparative Studies in Society and History*, 23, 3, 1981, 325–349.

Baker, C.J. and D.A. Washbrook, *South India: Political Institutions and Political*

Change, 1880–1940, Meerut: Macmillan of India, 1975.

Banerjee, Sukyana, *Becoming Imperial Citizens: Indians in the Late Victorian Empire*, Durham: Duke University Press, 2010.

Barrett, Tracy, *The Chinese Diaspora in South-East Asia: The Overseas Chinese in Indochina*, London: I.B. Tauris, 2013.

Bayly, C.A., *The Birth of the Modern World 1780–1914*, Oxford: Blackwell, 2004.

Bayly, Christopher and Tim Harper, *Forgotten Armies, The Fall of British India, 1941–1945*, Cambridge, Mass: Belknap Press of Harvard University Press, 2004.

———, *Forgotten Wars: The End of Britain's Asian Empire*, London: Penguin, 2008

Bayly, Susan, *Caste, Society and Politics in India from the Eighteenth Century to the Modern Age*, Cambridge: Cambridge University Press, 2001.

———, 'Imagining "Greater India": French and Indian Visions of Colonialism in the Indic Mode', *Modern Asian Studies*, 38, 3, 2004, 703–744.

———, *Asian Voices in a Postcolonial Age, Vietnam, India and Beyond*, Cambridge: Cambridge University Press, 2007.

Benda, Harry J., 'The Structure of Southeast Asian History: Some Preliminary Observations', *Journal of Southeast Asian History*, 3, 1, 1962, 106–138.

Betts, Raymond, *Assimilation and Association in French Colonial Theory: 1890–1914*, Lincoln: University of Nebraska, 2005 [1962].

Boittin, Jennifer Anne, Christina Firpo, and Emily Musil Church, 'Hierarchies of Race and Gender in the French Colonial Empire, 1914–1946', *Historical Reflections*, 37, 1, 2011, 60–90.

Bose, Sugata, *A Hundred Horizons: The Indian Ocean in the Age of Global Empire*, Cambridge, Mass.: Harvard University Press, 2006.

———, *His Majesty's Opponent: Subhas Chandra Bose and India's Struggle Against Empire*, New Delhi: Allen Lane, 2011.

Bose, Sugata, and Ayesha Jalal, *Modern South Asia: History, Culture, Political Economy*, London and New York: Routledge, 1998.

Bose, Sugata and Kris Manjapra (eds), *Cosmopolitan Thought Zones: South Asia and the Global Circulation of Ideas*, London: Palgrave Macmillan, 2010.

Bouinais, A. and A. Paulus, *L'Indo-Chine Française contemporaine*, Paris: Challamel Ainé, 1885.

Brébion, Antoine, *Dictionnaire de Bio-Biographie Générale de l'Indochine Française*, Paris: Société d'Éditions Géographiques Maritimes et Coloniales, 1935.

Brett, Michael, 'Legislating for Inequality in Algeria: The *Senatus-Consulte* of 14 July 1865', *Bulletin of the School of Oriental and African Studies, University of London*, 51, 3, 1988, 440–461.

Brocheux, Pierre, 'Note Sur Gilbert Chiêu (1867–1919), Citoyen Français et Patriote Vietnamien', *Approches Asie*, 11, 1991, 72–81.

———, *The Mekong Delta: Ecology, Economy and Revolution, 1860–1960*, Madison: University of Wisconsin-Madison Centre for Southeast Asian Studies, 1995.

———, and Daniel Hémery, *Indochina: An Ambiguous Colonization, 1858–1954*, Berkeley: University of California Press, 2009.

Brown, Ian, *Burma's Economy in the Twentieth Century*, Cambridge: Cambridge University Press, 2013.

Brown, Rajaswary Ampalavanar, *Capital and Entrepreneurship in Southeast Asia*, Basingstoke: Macmillan, 1994.

Brubaker, Rogers, *Citizenship and Nationhood in France and Germany*, Cambridge, Mass.: Harvard University Press, 1992.

Brubaker, Rogers, and Frederick Cooper, '"Our Strike": Equality, Anticolonial Politics, and the French West African Railway Strike of 1947–48', *Journal of African History*, 37, 1996, 81–118.

Brun, Christelle, 'Chettys, prêteurs d'argent indiens et l'économie indochinoise (1880–1940)', unpublished DEA thesis, Université Aix-Marseille, 2003.

Bùi Thị Ngọc Trang, *Lăng Tả Quân Lê Văn Duyệt* [The Mausoleum of General Lê Văn Duyệt], HCM City: Nhà Xuất Bản Tổng Hợp, 2004.

Burbank, Jane and Frederick Cooper, *Empires in World History: Power and the Politics of Difference*, Princeton and Oxford: Princeton University Press, 2010.

Butcher, John and Howard Dick (eds), *The Rise and Fall of Revenue Farming*, Basingstoke: St Martin's Press, 1993.

Camilli, Bertrand, *La représentation des indigènes en Indochine*, Toulouse: Imprimerie J. Fournier, 1914.

Carter, Marina, 'Mauritius' and 'The Mascarenes, Seychelles and Chagos Islands', in Brij V. Lal (ed.), *Encyclopedia of the Indian Diaspora*, Singapore: Éditions Didier Millet, 2003, 263–275.

Chanda, Nayan, 'Indians in Indochina', in K.S. Sandhu and A. Mani (eds), *Indian Communities in Southeast Asia*, Singapore: Times Academic Press, ISEAS, 1993, 31–45.

Clairon, M., *La renonciation au statut personnel dans l'Inde Française*, Montpellier: Causse, Graille et Castelnau, 1926.

Clammer, John, 'French Studies on the Chinese in Indochina: A Bibliographical Survey', *Journal of South East Asian Studies*, 12, 1, 1981, 15–26.

Clarke, Colin, Ceri Peach, and Steven Vertovec, 'Introduction: themes in the study of the South Asian diaspora', in Clarke, Peach and Vertovec (eds), *South Asians Overseas, Migration and Ethnicity*, Cambridge: Cambridge University Press, 1990.

Coedès, G., *Les États hindouisés d'Indochine et d'Indonésie*, Paris: de Boccard, 1989 [1948].

Cohn, Bernard S., *Colonialism and its Forms of Knowledge: The British in India*, Princeton: Princeton University Press, 1996.

Conklin, Alice, *A Mission to Civilise: The Republican Idea of Empire in France and West Africa, 1895–1930*, Stanford: Stanford University Press, 1997.

Cooke, Nola and Li Tana (eds), *Water Frontier: Commerce and the Chinese in the Lower Mekong Region, 1750–1880*, Lanham: Rowman and Littlefield, 2004.

Cooper, Frederick, *Colonialism in Question: Theory, Knowledge, History*, Berkeley: University of California Press, 2005.

———, 'Possibility and Constraint: African Independence in Historical Perspective', *Journal of African History*, 49, 2009, 167–196.

———, *Citizenship between Nation and Empire: Remaking France and West Africa, 1945–1960*, Princeton: Princeton University Press, 2014.

Cribb, Robert and Li Narangoa, 'Orphans of Empire: Divided Peoples, Dilemmas of Identity, and Old Imperial Borders in East and Southeast Asia', *Comparative Studies in Society and History*, 2004, 46, 1, 164–187.

Dareste, Pierre, G. Appert and Maxime Legendre, *Recueil de législation et jurisprudence coloniale*, Paris: A. Challamel, 1903 and 1911 editions.

David, Annoussamy, 'The Merger of French India', *Revue Historique de Pondichéry*, 21, 2004, 13–30.

de Feyssal, P., *L'Endettement agraire en Cochinchine: Rapport d'ensemble au gouverneur général de l'Indochine*, Hanoi: Impr. d'Extrême-Orient, 1933.

Delval, Raymond, *Musulmans français d'origine indienne*, Paris: Centre des Hautes Études sur l'Afrique et l'Asie Modernes, 1987.

Deming Lewis, Martin, 'One Hundred Million Frenchmen: The Assimilation Theory in French Colonial Policy', *Comparative Studies in Society and History*, 4, 1962, 129–153.

Deschamps, Damien, 'Une citoyenneté différée: cens civique et assimilation des indigènes dans les Établissements français de l'Inde', *Revue française de science politique*, 47, 1, 1997, 49–69.

Dessama, Evariste, *Tribulations de l'Inde Française*, Saigon: France Asie, 1950.

Devillers, Philippe, *Histoire du Vietnam de 1940 à 1952*, Paris: Éditions du Seuil, 1952.

Diouf, Mamadou, 'The French Colonial Policy of Assimilation and the Civility of the *originaires* of the Four Communes (Senegal): A Nineteenth Century Globalisation Project', *Development and Change*, 29, 1998, 671–696.

Dirks, Nicholas B., *Castes of Mind, Colonialism and the Making of Modern India*, Delhi: Permanent Black, 2003.

Dumont, Louis, *Homo Hierarchicus. The Caste System and its Implications*, Chicago: University of Chicago Press, 1976.

Dutton, Paul, *Origins of the French Welfare State: The Struggle for Social Reform in France, 1914–1947*, Cambridge: Cambridge University Press, 2002.

Edwards, Penny, 'Womanizing Indochina: Fiction, Nation and Cohabitation in Colonial Cambodia, 1890–1930', in Julia Clancy-Smith and Frances Gouda (eds), *Domesticating the Empire: Race, Gender and Family Life in French and Dutch Colonialism*, Charlottesville, Viriginia: University Press of Virginia, 1998, 108–130.

Englebert, Thomas, 'The Khmer in Southern Vietnam – Cambodians or Vietnamese?', in Ingrid Wessel (ed.), *Nationalism and Ethnicity in Southeast Asia*, Münster/Hamburg: LIT, 1993, 155–196.

Esquer, A., *Essai sur les Castes dans l'Inde*, Pondicherry: A. Saligny, 1870.

Falzon, Mark-Anthony, *The Sindhi Diaspora 1860–2000*, New Delhi: Oxford University Press, 2005.

Firpo, Christina, 'Crises of Whiteness and Empire in Colonial Indochina: The Removal of Abandoned Eurasian Children from the Vietnamese Milieu, 1856–1954', *Journal of Social History*, 43, 3, 2010, 587–613.

Freedman, Maurice 'The Growth of a Plural Society in Malaya', *Pacific Affairs*, 33, 2, 1960, 158–168.

Furnivall, J.S., *Colonial Policy and Practice: A Comparative Study of Burma and Netherlands India*, New York: New York University Press, 1956.

Gilbert, Marc Jason, 'Persuading the Enemy', in Wynn Wilcox (ed.), *Vietnam and the West, New Approaches*, Ithaca: Cornell Southeast Asia Program Publications, 2010, 107–142.

Girault, Arthur, *Principes de colonisation et de législation coloniale. Volume II: Généralités – Notions Historiques*, Paris: Recueil-Sirey, 1927.

Gorman, Daniel, *Imperial Citizenship: Empire and the Question of Belonging*, Manchester: Manchester University Press, 2006.

Goscha, Christopher E., 'Widening the Colonial Encounter: Asian Connections inside French Indochina during the Interwar Period', *Modern Asian Studies*, 43, 5, 2009, 1189–1228.

———, *Historical Dictionary of the Indochina War 1945–1954, An International and Interdisciplinary Approach*, Copenhagen: NIAS Press, 2011.

———, *Going Indochinese: Contesting Concepts of Space and Place in French Indochina*, Copenhagen: NIAS Press, 2012.

Gouvernment des Établissements français dans l'Inde, *Livre Jaune de l'Inde Française: Recueil des correspondences échangées avec la France, l'Indochine et l'Inde Britannique pendant la période du 24 mai 1940 au 1er octobre 1940*, Pondicherry: Imprimerie du Gouvernment, 1940.

Government of India, *The Imperial Gazeteer of India, Volume XXVI, Atlas*, Oxford: Clarendon Press, 1931.

Guha, Sumit, 'The Politics of Identity and Enumeration in India, c. 1600–1990', *Comparative Studies in Society and History*, 20, 2003, 148–167.

Gupta, N., 'The Citizens of French India: the Issue of Cultural Identity in Pondicherry in the XIXth Century', *Association historique internationale de l'Océan Indien, Les relations historiques et culturelles entre la France et l'Inde XVIIe-XXe siècles, Actes de conférence internationales France-Inde*, 21–28 juillet 1986, 161–173.

Ha, Marie-Paule, 'French Women and the Empire', in Kathryn Robson and Jennifer Lee (eds), *France and 'Indochina', Cultural Representations*, London: Lexington Books, 2005.

Harper, T.N., 'Globalism and the Pursuit of Authenticity: The Making of a Diasporic Public Sphere in Singapore', *Sojourn: Journal of Social Issues in Southeast Asia*, 12, 2, 1997, 261–292.

Harper, Tim and Sunil S. Amrith, 'Sites of Asian Interaction: An Introduction', in Harper, Tim and Sunil S. Amrith (eds), 'Sites of Asian Interaction', *Modern Asian Studies* Special Issue, 46, 2, 2012.

Herchenroder, Philippe, *Étude sur le statut juridique des indigènes chrétiens*, Paris: Domat Montchrestien, 1935.

Ho, Engseng, *The Graves of Tarim, Genealogy and Mobility Across the Indian Ocean*, Berkeley: University of California Press, 2006.

Hofmeyr, Isabel, Preben Kaarsholm and Bodil Folke Frederiksen (eds), 'Print cultures, Nationalism, and Publics of the Indian Ocean', *Africa* Special Issue 1, 81, 2011.

Hooker, M.B., *Legal Pluralism. An Introduction to Colonial and Neo-Colonial Laws*, Oxford: Clarendon Press, 1975.

Huard, P. 'Chinois, Japonais et Hindous en Indochine', *Bulletin économique de l'Indochine*, 3, 1939, 467–486.

Huỳnh Văn Út, 'Cộng đồng người Ấn ở TP. Hồ Chí Minh - cầu nối cho mối quan hệ Việt Nam - Ấn Độ' [The Indian Community in Ho Chi Minh City – a bridge for relations between Vietnam and India], unpublished thesis, Ho Chi Minh City Open University, 2011.

Idowu, H. Oludare, 'Assimilation in 19th Century Senegal', *Cahiers d'Études Africaines*, 9, 34, 1969, 194–218.

Irschick, Eugene F., *Politics and Social Conflict in South India. The Non-Brahman Movement and Tamil Separatism, 1916–1929*, Berkeley: University of California Press, 1969.

Jain, Ravindra K., *Indian Communities Abroad: Themes and Literature*, New Delhi: Manohar, 1993.

James, C.L.R., *The Black Jacobins: Toussaint l'Ouverture and the San Domingo Revolution*, Tiptree, Essex: Allison and Busby, 1989 [1938].

Jennings, Eric, *Vichy in the Tropics: Pétain's Nationalist Revolution in Madagascar, Guadaloupe and Indochina, 1940–1944*, Stanford: Stanford University Press, 2001.

Jayal, Niraja Gopal, *Citizenship and its Discontents: an Indian History*, Cambridge, Mass.: Harvard University Press, 2013.

Karatini, Keiko, *Defining British Citizenship: Empire, Commonwealth and Modern Britain*, London: Frank Cass, 2003.

Kelly, John D., 'Fear of Culture: British Regulation of Indian Marriage in Post-Indenture Fiji', *Ethnohistory*, 35, 4, 1989, 372–391.

Lambert, Michael C. 'From Citizenship to Negritude: "Making a Difference" in Elite Ideologies of Colonized Francophone West Africa', *Comparative Studies in Society and History*, 35, 2, 1993, 239–262.

Larcher, Agathe, 'La voie étroite des réformes coloniales et la "collaboration franco-annamite" (1917–1928)', *Revue française d'histoire d'outre mer*, 82, 309, 1995, 387–420.

———, and Kareem James Abu-Zeid, 'Bùi Quang Chiêu in Calcutta (1928): The Broken Mirror of Vietnamese and Indian Nationalism', *Journal of Vietnamese Studies*, 9, 4, 2014, 67–114.

Leconte, Nadia, 'La migration des Pondichériens et des Karikalais en Indochine ou le combat des Indiens-renonçants en Cochinchine pour la reconnaissance de leur statut (1865–1954)', unpublished DEA thesis, Université de Haute-Bretagne, 2001.

Leonardi, Ch., 'L'Usure en Cochinchine', *Extrême-Asie*, May 1926, 226–231.

Lewis, Su Lin. *Cities in Motion: Urban Life and Cosmopolitanism in Southeast Asia 1920–1940*, Cambridge: Cambridge University Press, 2015.

Malleret, L., 'Cochinchine, terre inconnue', *Bulletin de la Societé des Études Indochinoises*, 18, 3, 1943, 9–26.

———, *L'Archéologie du delta du Mékong*, Paris: École Française d'Extrême Orient, 1959.

Mandal, Sumit, 'Popular Sites of Prayer, Transoceanic Migration, and Cultural Diversity: Exploring the significance of keramat in Southeast Asia', *Modern Asian Studies*, 46, 2, 2012, 355–372.

Marius, Claude, 'Les Pondichériens dans l'administration coloniale de l'Indochine', in J. Weber (ed.), *Les relations entre la France et l'Inde de 1673 à nos jours*, Paris: Les Indes Savantes, 2002, 391–398.

———, 'La Migration des Pondichériens vers l'Indochine', *Revue Historique de Pondichéry*, 22, 2007, 103–106.

———, 'La Migration des Pondichériens vers l'Indochine (suite et fin)', *Revue Historique de Pondichéry*, 23, 2009, 3–38.

Markovits, Claude, 'Indian Merchant Networks outside India in the Nineteenth and Twentieth Centuries: A Preliminary Survey', *Modern Asian Studies*, 33, 4, 1999, 883–991.

———, *The Global World of Indian Merchants 1750–1947, Traders of Sind from Bukhara to Panama*, Cambridge: Cambridge University Press, 2000.

Marquet, Jean, *Les Cinq Fleurs, l'Indochine expliquée*, Hanoi: Directeur de l'instruction publique, 1928.

Marr, David, *Vietnamese Anti-Colonialism, 1885–1925*, Berkeley: University of California, 1971.

———, *Vietnamese Tradition on Trial, 1920–1945*, Berkeley: University of California Press, 1981.

———, *Vietnam 1945: The Quest for Power*, Berkeley: University of California Press, 1995.

Marsot, Alain G., *The Chinese Community in Vietnam under the French*, Lewiston, N.Y.: Edwin Mellen Press, 1993.

Mathieu, E., *Les Prêts Usuaires et le Crédit Agricole en Cochinchine*, Paris: Recueil Sirey, 1912.

McHale, Shawn Frederick, *Print and Power: Confucianism, Communism, and Buddhism in the Making of Modern Vietnam*, Honolulu: University of Hawai'i Press, 2004.

———, 'Ethnicity, Violence, and Khmer-Vietnamese Relations: The Significance of the Lower Mekong Delta, 1757–1954', *The Journal of Asian Studies*, 72, 2, 2013, 367–390.

McKeown, Adam, 'Global Migration, 1846–1940,' *Journal of World History*, 15, 2, 2004, 155–189.

Metcalf, Thomas R., *Imperial Connections: India in the Indian Ocean Arena, 1860–1920*, Berkeley: University of California Press, 2007.

Michalon, Paul, 'Des Indes françaises aux Indiens français ou Comment peut-on être Franco-Pondichérien?', unpublished DEA thesis, Université Aix-Marseille, 1990.

Michel, Pierre, 'Les Mystifications Épistolaire d'Octave Mirabeau', University of Angers 1990, 1–6, pp. 3–4. http://mirbeau.asso.fr/darticlesfrancais/PM-Les%20mystifications%20epist.pdf [last accessed February 2015].

Miles, William F.S., *Imperial Burdens: Countercolonialism in Former French India*, Boulder: Lynne Rienner, 1995.

Mohan, Jyoti, 'British and French Ethnographies of India: Dubois and his English Commentators', *French Colonial History*, 2004, 5, 1, 229–246.

More, J.B.P., 'The Marakkayar Muslims of Karikal, South India', *Journal of Islamic Studies*, 2, 1, 1991, 25–44.

———, 'Indians in French Indochina', in K.S. Mathew (ed.), *French in India and Indian Nationalism (1700 A.D.–1963 A.D)*, Delhi: B.R. Publishing Corporation, 1999, 447–460.

———, 'Pathan and Tamil Muslim Migrants in French Indochina', *Pondicherry University Journal of Social Sciences and Humanities*, 1, 1 and 2, 2000, 113–128.

———, 'Léon Prouchandy, Réformateur Social de Pondichéry en Indochine Française, 1930–1939', *La Lettre du CIDIF*, 39, 2009, 75–88.

———, *Indian Steamship Ventures, 1836–1910: Darmananden Prouchandy of Pondicherry, First Steam Navigator from South India, 1891–1900*, Pondicherry: Léon Prouchandy Memorial Sangam, 2013.

Morice, A., *People and Wildlife in and around Saigon, 1872–1873*, Bangkok: White Lotus, 1997 [1875].

Morris, H.S., 'The Plural Society', *Man*, 57, 1957, 124–125.

Muller, Gregor, *Colonial Cambodia's 'Bad Frenchmen': The rise of French rule and the life of Thomas Caraman, 1840–1887*, London: Routledge, 2006.

Murray, Martin, *The Development of Capitalism in Colonial Indochina (1870–1940)*, Berkeley: University of California Press, 1980.

Muthiah, S., Meenakshi Meyappan, and Visalakshi Ramaswamy, *The Chettiar Heritage*, Chennai: Madras Editorial Services, 2002.

Nasution, Khoo Salma, *The Chulia in Penang: Place Making and Patronage around the Kapitan Kling Mosque, 1786–1957*, Penang: Areca Books, 2014.

Ner, Marcel, *Les musulmans de l'Indochine française*, Hanoi: Bulletin de l'École Française d'Extrême-Orient, 1941.

Newbigin, Eleanor, 'The codification of personal law and secular citizenship; revisiting the history of law reform in late colonial India', *Indian Economic and Social History Review*, 2009, 46, 83–114.

Ngô Vĩnh Long, *Before the Revolution: The Vietnamese Peasants Under the French*, New York: Columbia University Press, 1991 [1973].

Nguyễn Mạnh Cường and Nguyễn Minh Ngọc, *Người Chăm (Những Nghiên Cứu Bước Đầu)* [The Cham (Initial Studies)], Hanoi: Nhà Xuất Bản Khoa Học Xã Hội, 2003.

Nguyễn Phương Thảo, 'Văn hón dân gian miền Nam Việt Nam' [The Culture of Worship in the South of Vietnam], [no publisher or place of publication given], 1997.

Omissi, David, *The Sepoy and the Raj: The Indian Army, 1860–1940*, Basingstoke: Macmillan, 1994.

Osborne, Milton E., *The French Presence in Cochinchina and Cambodia*, Bangkok: White Lotus Press, 1997 [1969].

Pairaudeau, Natasha, 'Indo-china: Vietnam, Laos and Cambodia', in Brij V. Lal (ed.), *The Encyclopedia of the Indian Diaspora*, Singapore: Éditions Didier Millet, 2006, 200–203.

———, 'Via l'Indochine: trajectoires coloniales de l'immigration sud-indienne', *Hommes et Migrations*, 1268–1269, 2007, 24–33.

———, 'Vietnamese Engagement with Tamil Migrants in Colonial Cochinchina,' in *Journal of Vietnamese Studies*, 5, 3, 2010, 1–71.

———, and Chi Pham Phuong, 'The Indian Dimension', at http://www.endofempire.asia/0924.2-indochinas-indian-dimension/.

Peabody, Sue and Tyler Stovall, 'Introduction: Race, France, Histories', in Sue Peabody and Tyler Stovall, (eds), *The Color of Liberty: Histories of Race in France*, Durham and London: Duke University Press, 2003.

Pelley, Patricia M., *Postcolonial Vietnam: new histories of the national past*, Durham NC: Duke University Press, 2002.

Peters, Erica J., 'Resistance, Rivalries and Restaurants: Vietnamese Workers in Interwar France', *Journal of Vietnamese Studies*, 2, 1, 2007, 109–143.

———, *Appetites and Aspirations in Vietnam: Food and Drink in the Long Nineteenth Century*, Lanham: Rowman and Littlefield, 2012.

Peycam, Philippe M.F., *The Birth of Vietnamese Political Journalism: Saigon, 1916–1930*, New York: Columbia University Press, 2012.

Phạm Phương Chi, 'The Rise and the Fall of Rabindranath Tagore in Vietnam', unpublished MA thesis, University of California at Riverside, 2012.

———, 'Who killed Ganesh Sang: Nationalism and Survival of the Indian Diaspora in Vietnam', unpublished PhD thesis, University of California at Riverside, 2015.

Phan Thị Hồng Xuân, 'Cộng Đồng Người Ấn ở Thành Phố Hồ Chí Minh – Cầu Nối cho Mối Quan Hệ Hữu Nghị Giữa Việt Nam và Ấn Độ Trong Giai Đoạn Hiện Nay' ['The Indian Community in Ho Chi Minh City – a bridge for ties between Vietnam and India in the current period'], *Khoa Học, Journal of Science*, 3, 31, 2013, 87–95.

Phan Trung Nghĩa, *Công tử Bạc Liêu Sự thật và giai thoại* [*Bạc Liêu Playboy, Truth and Myth*], Ho Chi Minh City: Youth Publishing House, 2006.

Pretini, Jean-Louis, 'Saigon-Cyrnos', in Philippe Franchini (ed.), *Saigon 1925–1945: De la 'Belle Colonie' à l'éclosion révolutionnaire ou la fin des dieux blancs*, Paris: Éditions Autrement, 1992, 92–103.

Price, Roger, *A Concise History of France*, Cambridge: Cambridge University Press, 1993.

Raffin, Anne, 'The Integration of Difference in French Indochina during World War II: Organizations and Ideology concerning Youth', *Theory and Society*, 31, 3, 2002, 365–390.

———, *Youth Mobilization in Vichy Indochina and Its Legacies: 1940 to 1970*, New York: Lexington Books, 2005.

Reddi, V.M., 'Indians in the Indochina States and their Problems', in I.J. Bahadur Singh (ed.), *Indians in South East Asia*, New Delhi: Sterling Publishers Private Ltd, 1982, 155–158.

Robequain, Charles, *The Economic Development of Viet-Nam and Indo-China*, London: Oxford University Press, 1944.

Rosanvallon, Pierre, *Le sacré du citoyen: le suffrage universel en France*, Paris: Gallimard, 1992.

Ross Barnett, Marguerite, *The Politics of Cultural Nationalism in South India*, Princeton: Princeton University Press, 1976.

Rudner, David, 'Banker's Trust and the Culture of Banking among the Nattukottai Chettiars of Colonial South India', *Modern Asian Studies*, 23, 3, 1989, 417–458.

———, *Caste and Capitalism in Colonial India, the Nattukottai Chettiars*, Berkeley: University of California Press, 1994.

Saada, Emmanuelle, 'Citoyens et sujets de l'Empire Français: Les usages du droit dans la situation coloniale', *Genèses*, 53, 2003, 4–24.

———, *Les enfants de la colonie: les métis de l'Empire français entre sujétion et citoyenneté*, Paris: La Découverte, 2007.

Salesa, Damon, 'Race', in Philippa Levine and John Marriott (eds), *The Ashgate Research Companion to Modern Imperial History*, Farnham: Ashgate, 2012, 429–448.

Salmon, Claudine, 'The Contribution of the Chinese to the Development of Southeast Asia: A New Appraisal', in *Journal of South East Asian Studies*, 12, 1, 1981, 260–275.

Samson, Jane, *Race and Empire*, Harlow: Pearson, 2005.

SarDesai, D.R., *Indian Foreign Policy in Cambodia, Laos and Vietnam, 1947–1964*, Berkeley: University of California Press, 1968.

Schneider, William, 'Towards the Improvement of the Human Race: the History of Eugenics in France', *Journal of Modern History*, 54, 1982, 269–291.

Schreier, Joshua, *Arabs of the Jewish Faith: The Civilising Mission in Colonial Algeria*, New Brunswick: Rutgers University Press, 2010.

Seal, Anil, 'Imperialism and Nationalism in India', *Modern Asian Studies*, 7, 3, 1973, 321–347.

Sébastia, Brigitte, 'Les Pondichériens de l'Ile de France. Étude des pratiques sociales et religieuses', unpublished DEA thesis, Université Toulouse, 1999.

Simon, Pierre-Jean, *Rapatriés d'Indochine: Un village franco-indochinois en Bourbonnais*, Paris: Éditions l'Harmattan, 1981.

Smith, R.B., 'Bui Quang Chieu and the Constitutionalist Party in French Cochinchina, 1917–1930', *Modern Asian Studies*, 3, 2, 1969, 131–150.

———, *Vietnam and the West*, Ithaca, New York: Cornell University Press, 1971.

———, 'The Development of Opposition to French Rule in Southern Vietnam 1880–1940', *Past and Present*, 54, 1972, 94–129.

Sơn Nam, *Phong Trào Duy Tân ở Bắc Trung Nam, Miền Nam Đầu Thế Kỷ XX - Thiên Địa Hội và Cuộc Minh Tân* [The Duy Tân movement in the North, Centre and South and The South in the Twentieth Century; The Heaven and Earth Society and The Minh Tân Organisation], Ho Chi Minh City: Nhà Xuất Bản Trẻ, 2003, [originally two volumes, 1975 and 1971 respectively].

———, *Đất Gia Định - Bến Nghé Xưa và Người Sài Gòn* [Gia Định Soil; Old Bến Nghé; People of Saigon], Ho Chi Minh City: Nhà Xuất Bản Trẻ, 2004 [three volumes first published respectively 1984, 1992 and 1992].

Stokhof, M., 'Javanese in Hồ Chí Minh City today: an Aftermath of Coolie Migration in French Colonial Vietnam', unpublished Master's thesis, University of Amsterdam, 2002.

Stoler, Ann Laura, *Carnal Knowledge and Imperial Power: Race and the Intimate in Colonial Rule*, Berkeley: University of California Press, 2002.

Suignard, Jean, *Les Services Civils de l'Indochine*, Paris: Larose, 1931.

Sundararajan, Saroja, *Glimpses of the History of Karaikkal*, Madras: Lalitha Publications, 1984.

Tai, Hue-Tam Ho, 'The Politics of Compromise: The Constitutionalist Party and the Electoral Reforms of 1922 in French Cochinchina', *Modern Asian Studies*, 18, 3, 1984, 371–391.

———, *Radicalism and the Origins of the Vietnamese Revolution*, Cambridge, Mass.: Harvard University Press, 1992.

Tamby, Pourouchotan, *British raj et swaraj*, Pondicherry: L. Sinnaya Press, 1918.

Tana, Li, 'Vietnam', in Lynn Pan, (ed.), *Encyclopedia of the Chinese Overseas*, Richmond: Curzon Press, 1999.

Taylor, Philip, *Goddess on the Rise: Pilgrimage and Popular Religion in Vietnam*, Honolulu: University of *Hawai'i Press*, 2004.

———, *Cham Muslims of the Mekong Delta: Place and Mobility in the Cosmopolitan Periphery*, Singapore: NUS Press, 2007.

Thomas, Martin, with Bob Moore and L.J. Butler, *Crises of Empire: Decolonization and Europe's Imperial States, 1918–1975*, London: Bloomsbury, 2008.

Thompson, Virginia, *French Indo-China*, London: George Allen and Unwin, 1937.

Thurston, E., *Castes and Tribes of South India*, Madras: Government Press, 1909.

Tinker, Hugh, *Separate and Unequal: India and the Indians in the British Commonwealth 1920–1950*, London: C. Hurst, 1976.

———, 'Between Africa, Asia and Europe: Mauritius: Cultural Marginalism and Political Control', *African Affairs*, 76, 304, 1977, 321–337.

Tran Tu Binh, *Red Earth: A Vietnamese Memoir of Life on a Colonial Rubber Plantation*, Athens, Ohio: Ohio University Press, 1985.

Truong Buu Lam (ed.), *Colonialism Experienced:, Vietnamese Writings on Colonialism 1900–1931*, Ann Arbor: University of Michigan Press, 2003.

Ủy Ban Nhân Dân Thành Phố Hà Nội [Hanoi People's Committee], *Kỷ Niệm 50 Năm Giải Phóng Thủ đô: Hà Nội Ngày Tiếp Quản* [Souvenir of 50 Years of Freedom: The Day Hanoi Welcomed the Army], Hanoi: Xưa và Nay Publishers, 2004.

Valmaire, M., *Rapport sur l'enseignement dans l'Inde Française du XVIIIe siècle à nos jours*, Pondicherry: Imprimerie moderne de Pondichéry, 1922.

Vann, Michael, 'The Good, the Bad and the Ugly: Variation and Difference in French Colonial Racism', in Sue Peabody and Tyler Stovall (eds), *The Color of Liberty: Histories of Race in France*, Durham: Duke University Press, 2003.

Vassal, Gabrielle M., *Three Years in Vietnam (1907–1910)*, Bangkok: White Lotus, 1999 [1910].

Vidy, G., 'La communauté indienne en Indochine', *Sud-Est*, 6, 1949, 1–8.

Vimeux, *De l'immigration en Cochinchine et les taxes spéciales aux immigrants asiatiques*, Paris: Challamel Ainé, 1875.

Vinson, Julien, 'Les musulmans du sud de l'Inde', *Revue du Monde Musulman*, 2, 1907, 199–204.

Vương Hồng Sến, *Sai Gon Năm Xưa* [Saigon in the Past], Ho Chi Minh City: Nhà Xuất Bản Thành Phố Hồ Chí Minh, 2003 [1960].

Walzer, Michael, 'Citizenship', in Terence Ball, James Farr, and Russell L. Hanson (eds), *Political innovation and conceptual change*, Cambridge: Cambridge University Press, 1995, 211–219.

Weber, Jacques, 'Accumulation et assimilation dans les Établissements de l'Inde la caste et les valeurs de l'occident', conference proceedings, CRASOM XXXVIII, 2–3 February 1978.

———, *Pondichéry et les comptoirs de l'Inde après Dupleix: La démocratie au pays des castes*, Paris: Denoel, 1996.

Winnacker, Rudolph A., 'Élections in Algeria and the French Colonies Under the Third Republic', *American Political Science Review*, 32, 1938, 261–277.

Yechury, Akhila, 'Empire, Nation, and the French Settlements in India, c. 1930–1954', unpublished PhD thesis, University of Cambridge, 2012.

Zinoman, Peter, *The Colonial Bastille: A History of Imprisonment in Vietnam, 1862–1940*, Berkeley: University of California Press, 2001.

———, 'Vũ Trọng Phụng's *Dumb Luck* and the nature of Vietnamese Modernism', introduction to Vũ Trọng Phụng, *Dumb Luck*, Ann Arbor: University of Michigan Press, 2002.

INDEX

bold = extended discussion; n = footnote; * = plate; t = table

11th Colonial Infantry Regiment (*régiment d'infanterie coloniale* or R.I.C.) 86, 292
20th Indian Division, of Indian Army **289–291**, 303

Abraham, S. 240, 253
accountants 71, 83, 165, 260
acculturation 17–18
Adicéam, C. G. 158n, **160–4**, 168, 177
advertisements/advertising 101, **215**, **243***, **244***
Africa 318, 327, 328
Africans in Indochina 215
agency, of colonised peoples 18–19, 43, 327
air raids 285, 304, 307
Algeria **38–9**, 43, 120, 151, 241, 318
All-India Association for Indochina (proposed, 1929) 270
Alsace-Lorraine 21
Amicale des Français de l'Inde 235, 239, 282, 305, **307–9**, **313–14**
Aney, M. S. 287, 292
Angkor 247, 248, 250, 252, 262
Annam (protectorate of) 3, 12, 72, 145, 186, 192, **219**, 222, 293
Annamalaichetty (banker) 270–1
'Annamite' 65, 101, 115, 126, 138, 139, 151, 155, 158, **159–60**, 162, 164, 168, 176–7, 182, 189, 194, 205, 208, 210, 218, 219, 225, 227–8, 245–6, 254, 264–5, 270, 292, 295, 298
law **63**. See also personal status

naturalisation decree (Cochinchina, 1881) 34, 39–40, **58–60**, 69
see also Vietnamese people
Annasse, A. 29, 280, **281–2**, 314, **316–17**, 339
anti-colonialism
Indian 301–2, 320–1
transnational 26–7
versus reform within imperial systems 22, 327
Vietnamese 9, 22, 192, 200, 209, 229, 231, 263, 272
Appapoulé, *Monsieur* 96, 109, 222, **267***
Appassamy, S. 88, 98, 103–5, 108
Arabs 151, 221
archaeology 245, **247–9**, 252
Arpi, C. **303–4**, 339
'Asian' agents and cadres 353. See employment status
assimilation 34–5, 37, **39–40**, **42–3**, 50, 58–9, 63–4, 69, 120, 162, 164, 171, 185, 193, 238
Association of Indians in Indochina (Hanoi) 286, 287
associational life **233–43**
Atmaram (Indian merchant) 295–6. See also Palace of Silks Affair
Avadiayappachettiar (aviator) 245
Aymonier, E. (archaeologist) 249
Azad Hind (Free India) 287
Aziz, J. M. Abdul (Ishmael Brothers) 288

Bà Đen ('Black Lady'; deity) 220–1
Bà Rịa 90t, 109, 114

353

Bạc Liêu 90t, 98, 109
baccalauréat 55, 307
bailiffs 76, 84, 97, 170
Bangkok 282, 283, 287, 293, 294
Bank of Indochina (*Banque de l'Indochine*) 110, **268**
bankers **93–8**, **267***, **268**
bankruptcy 92, **96–7**
banks and banking 12, 67, 68, 83, 96, 109, 110, 117, 195, 270
Bava Bilal (Muslim 'saint') **221**
Bawean (people) 198
Bầy and *Bầy Chà* **198**, 199–200
Bayly, C. 25
Bayly, S. 14n, 247
Belland (Police Commissioner) **177–9**
belonging 9, 32, 161, 163, 202, 249, 263, 270–2, 274, 294, 299, 302, 309, 320–1, 324, 343
Belvindrassamy, J. 178
'Bengalis' 68
Bhoras 68
Biên Hoà province 90t, 213
'black water' (*kala pani*) 80
Blanchy, P. 139, 142
Blancsubé, M. J. **123–4**, 128, 131, 132
Bombay 68
'Bombay' traders 285, 286, 293, 294. *See also* traders
Bonaparte, N. 262
Bonhoure, L. A. 182
Bonvin, L. **276–7**
Bose, Sugata, **21**, 22
Bose, Subash Chandra, 9, 275, 279, 284, **286–9**, 320
'boundaries of rule' **154–7**
bourgeoisie 12–13, 72, 201, 212, 233
Brébion, A. 123–4, 128, 131
brevet élémentaire 78
British-ruled India 6, 10, 13, 21, 37, 79, 177, 238–9, 241, 248–9, 273, 276, 310, 322, 324
    comparisons with French rule **13–15**, 143, **209–12**, 238, **256–7**

'British Indians' 11, 15, 52, **64–6**, 68, 90, 127, 264, 265, 283
    classified as 'Foreign Asians' (*asiatiques étrangers*) in Cochinchina 63, 65
Brocheux, P. 16n, 28n, 197, 213, 222, 341
Bronze Medal for Mutuality 236, **237***
Buddha and Buddhism 197, 233
Bùi Quang Chiêu **203–4**, **209–11**, 253, 269, 325n
Bulliard, Fr. 305
bullock carts (*chariots*) 99, **100***, 104
Bureau de l'Enregistrement, des Domaines et du Timbre 76, 91
Burma 12, 13, 23, 73, 284, 287
businessmen, 88, 98, 175, 196, 201, 229, 270, 288

cà ri Ấn Độ (Indian curry) 31
Cadarsah (non-renouncer) 138
cafés and *buvettes* **110–11**
Calcutta 211
Cambodia 3, 109, **132–3**, 145, 305, 307, 319
Cambodia–France Treaty (1884) 132
Cambodians 15, 29, 63, 162, 202, 325. *See also* Khmers
Candassamy (banker) **96–7**
Cannoussamy, V. **45–6**, 54, 76
Cantho 90t, 203, 213, 221
Cape Town 57
capitalism 332, 347, 350
Cap-St-Jacques (Vũng Tàu) 108, 145
Carabelli, R. (Mayor of Saigon) **128–37**
carriages 99, 179
carters 213
caste 5, 6, 13, 14, **41–3**, 44, 47–8, **49–51**, **53–5**, 67–8, 72–3, **78–80**, 82–3, 94, 96, **101–2**, 108, **223**, 250, **255–63**, 317, 329
'caste and creed' 37, 40, 269, 270, 335
Catholics 4, 6, 14, 40, **41–2**, 46, 47, **48**, 49, **51–2**, 53, 80, 103, 140, 222, 223, 256, 270, 305
    and caste in French India **42–3, 49**

INDEX

tendency to renounce 4, 6, **42–43**, 46, 47, 51–52, 270
see also renunciation (of personal status)
Catinat Street (Saigon) 91, 92, 93, 111, 217, 250
Cédile, General J. 291
cemeteries **48**, 49, 221
census-taking 11, 13, 24, 53n, 61, 62
Chà and Chà Và **197–8**, 199, 200, 215, 216, 226
Cham people 4, 31, 63, 89, 92, 121, 221, 248–9, 252
Champa Kingdom 249
Chandernagore 1, 49, 141, 311
Chanemougan (Mayor of Pondicherry, 1880–1908) **41–2**, 45, **53–4**, **238**, 311, 329
Châu Đốc 89, 90t, 109, **114–15**
Chệc (or Chệt) 198
Chettiars xi, 12, 71, 74, 84, 87, 92, 110, 191–2, 195, 201, **215–16**, 219, 221–2, **223**, 230, 250, 254, 264–5, **269–71**, 272, 287–8
  banking enquiry, Cochinchina (1937) 96, 109
  defence of in Franco-Tamil press **267–9**
  see also Chetty; moneylenders; Nattukottai Chettiars
Chettinad (South India) 67
Chetty **67–8**, **95***
Chiang Kai-shek (Jiang Jieshi) 295
Chiếu Trần Chánh, G. 216, 226, 229
  journalism and politics of **195–201**
children 43, 60, 64, 74, 80, 82, 85, 154, 209, **214–15**, 227–8, 233, 238, 244, 256, 300–1, 304, 319, 326. *See also* family, intermarriage, marriage, mixed unions
China 20, 32
Chinese
  boycott (1919) 200
  community 3, 12, **15–17**, 30, 63, **65–6**, 67, 105–6, 139, 162, 164, 177, 196, **197–9**, 217, 222, 225, 229, 245, 325

Cholon 3, 65, 66, 88–9, 90t, 96, 101, 103–7, 108, 110, 115, 121, 123, 242, 263, 308
Chợ Quán (hospital) 171
'Chulia' 68n
Chungking (Chongqing) 273
citizenship **4–11**, 14, 124–5, 129–30, 138–9, 143, 152, 196, 201–2, 205, 207–8, **227–9**, 272, 274, 285, 304, **315–316**, **322–33**
  colonial **17–27**, 29, **32–3**, **35–40**, 46, 54, 60, 69, **153–90**, 297–8, 309
  imperial 325, 331–32
  and indigenous agency 18–19, 43, 327
  in 'old' versus 'new' French colonies 120–3
  regimes (French Empire) **17–20**, **326–30**
  as subject of study 17–20, **327–8**
  see also naturalisation; renunciation (of personal status)
Civil Code (*Code Civil*). *See* French Civil Code
civil practices **6–7**
civil status 53, **120–1**, 125, 184, 328, 329, 331
civil servants 13, 61, 201, 206, 245, 305. *See also* functionaries
civilising missions 208, 229, 248–49
Clairon, M. 29, 55, 140, 315n, clans **223**, 258
clerks 83, 185, 319
clerks of court (*commis-greffier, greffier-notaire*) 76–7
climate 156–9, 161, 171, 176, 189, 194
climatology 24
Cloche Fêlée ('Cracked Bell') 203–4, **207–8**
cloth trade and traders 89*, 91–3, 98, 124, 218, 226, 227, 264, 298, 301. *See also* Palace of Silks Affair
clothing (as marker of identity) 249, 273, **285–6**, 320. *See also* 'Clothing Crusade'
'Clothing Crusade' (1933) **265–7**, **267***
coaches (*voitures*) 99

355

Cochinchina 2–3, 7–9, 4–5, 11, 12, 15–17, 21–3, 46, 50, 53–4, 69, 74, 79, 83–5, 96, 106, 109, 153–90, 192–3, 195, 197, 199–202, 205–8, 212, 222, 325, 328, 330–3
   Colonial Council 124, 134, **142–3**, 147–8, 163, 204
   contractual rights of Indians in administration **153–190**
   Indian vote in **119–52**
collaboration and collaborators 30, 121, 209, 228, 275, 281, 327
Coedès, G. **248**, 342
Collège Calvé 54
Colombo 57
colonial
   citizenship. *See* citizenship, colonial
   examinations (*concours coloniaux*) **79–80**, 82
   expertise **21–2**
   intermediaries **74–84**
   society **23–7**, 32, 132, 178, 193, 232, 326
Colonial Council. *See* Cochinchina
colonies, 'old' versus 'new' **18–20**, 35, 59, 69, 155, 331, **326–7**
'colour-blindness' 17, 25, 193, 194, 330
Committee for Supervision and Control, 318
communism 9, 30, 195, 212, 219, 312
Compagnie des Messageries Fluviales **114–16**
comptoirs (coastal trading posts) **1**, 22, 28, 49, 74, 234, 238
concubinage. *See* mixed unions
'congregations' (French *congrégation*, Vietnamese *bang*) **16**, **65**, 127
Conklin, A. 19
'consistories' 38
Constans, J. **128**
Constitutionalists 192, 231, 234, 272
   attitudes towards British India **211–2**
   and the 'Indian question' in Cochinchina **201–12**
   see also Vietnamese reformers
contract labour 12, 20, 72

contractors to government 104, 114. *See also* tax farming
Cooper, F. 27, **327–9**
Corsica and Corsicans 21, 61, 71, 75–7, 83–4, 130, 207
corvée 213
cosmopolitanism 8, 24, **232–3**, 306, 323–4
Courrier de Saigon 129
créoles **10–11**, 56, 62, 71, 76, 86n, 88, 123, **132–3**, 157, 159, 306
Của, P. *See* Huỳnh Tịnh (Paulus)
Của culture 59, 66–7, 72–3, 153, 160, 170, 176, 185–6, 221, 241, 243, 248, 251, 253, 262, 314–15, 319
currency controls **303–4**, 306
customs (and excise) 76, 84, 117, 203

Đại Nam 2
Dalat 319
Danang 2
Danel, H. 144
Darles, *Monsieur* **254–5**
de Condappa, X. 88, 105, **108**, 110, 239, 245, **255–6**, 319
de Gaulle, General C. **276–8**, 281
de Lachevrotière, H. **148**, 150, 238
de Lattre de Tassigny, Marshal J. 313
debt and loan foreclosure 64, 87, 106, 192, 216, 219, 268
'Declaration of the Rights of Man and the Citizen' (1789) 35, 328
decolonisation 33, 276, 300, 309–10, 313–14, 318, 324
Decoux, Admiral J. 279, **281–5**, 287, 288
Deloncle, F. 96n, **143–4**, **167–75**, 182, 238
Deming Lewis, M. 39
diamonds 91, 311
diaspora. *See* migrants, migration
Dien Bien Phu (1954) 272, 274, 275
Djiring province (Annam) 145
Doumer, P. **139**, **142–3**, 145, 195
Douressamy-Naiker (Saigon municipal councillor) 123, 242

INDEX

dress 59, 81, 95, 161, **265–7**, **267***, 273, 279, 293, 299, 320, 324
Dương Văn Giáo (Vietnamese reformer) 253
Duranton (Saigon Mayor) **174–80, 183–4**
Dutch East Indies 73
Duy Tân movement 196, 197

East Asian Co-Prosperity Sphere 284
Echo Annamite 203, **204–6**, 208, 217
economic crisis (1930s). *See* Great Depression
education **4–5**, **54–6**, 60, 72, 82, 207, 315
educational attainment **78–9**, 153, 167, 169–72, 184–7, 194, 201–2, 210, 212, 231, 233, 258, 261–2, 307
'*electeurs*' versus '*citoyens*' 5
elections 121, **128–38**, 187, 206, 211, 240, 242, 258, 332. *See also* Cochinchina: Indian vote in
electoral
  colleges 45, 119, 122, 123, 152, 207–8, 210
  franchise 5, 7, 36, 38, **41–2**, 202, 212
  lists **122**, 211, 242
  politics 33, **179–80**
  registers **125–31**, 134, 139–42, 329, 330, 332
  rights 8, 17, 22, 53, 60, 63, 68, 155, 157, 167, 170, 182, 190, 201, 246, 279, 331–2
  venality 132, **140–3**, **149**, 207, 242
electricity 105, 311
elites 6, 33, 38, **54–5**, 82, 121, 172, 189, 192–5, 201–4, 208–12, 216, 223, 229, 279, 314, 315
employment **12–14**, 147, 231, 258
  of Indian communities in Indochina **71–118**
  in Indochinese administrations 153–190
  shortage of posts in French India 55–6
employment status **153–190**
  'Asian cadre' 186, 280, 281, 282

'European' status and terms 75, **157–66**, 168
'Indian cadre' 173, 187
'native' terms 78, 166–72, 184–9
'special cadres' 78, 180, 187–8
'special superior cadres' 173, 178, 180, 183, 188
'enclave colonies' 5, 36–9, 327, 329
entrepreneurs 12, 88, 98, **102–3**, 105, 108, 142, 156, 236, 245
equality 5–7, 19, 22, 25, 32, 34, 36–7, 42, 43, 49–51, 120, 141–2, 185, 193, 212, 328–30. *See also* republican principles
equality before law 36, 175, 188
état civil 40, 47
ethnicity 13, 18, 31, 72, 73, 202, 272, 275, 321, 325
ethnography (colonial) **13–14**
Eurasians 10, 154, 319, 320
'European and assimilated' (category) 61, 62
European prestige 154, 155
European privileges 153, 156, 162, 167, 170, 173

family 37, 40, 51, 80, 154, 157, 228, 241, 278, 281, 286, 304, 317
Ferry, J. 143
ferry tax 103, 104, 199, 213, 323
Filipinos. *See Tagals* films **244***
financial services (Muslim) **91–3**
firms (French) **83**
footwear **42**, 49
'Foreign Asians' (legal status) 97
Foreign Missionary Society (*Missions Étrangères*) 305
forestry 107, 307
Français de l'Inde ('French of India') 10, 242–3, 245 263, 271
France 10, 29, 55, 197, 243, 246, 249, 263, 319, 328
  capitulation to Nazis 275, 276
  Chamber of Deputies 143, 185
  Colonial Administrative Tribunal

(*Comité Consultatif des Contentieux*) **182**
Foreign Affairs department (category C) 318
Indian foreign policy **303**
Justice Minister 174, 336–7
'military genius' 57–8
Minister of (Navy and) Colonies **46**, 139, **158–60**, 161–2, **163–4**, 166, 174, 175, **181–4**, 186, 219, 282–3, 287–8, 336–7
Parliament 60, 120–1, 123, 130, 143, 153, 182, 206, 207
post-war constitution 297
'right of conquest' 247
Second Republic 38
Senate 123, 129, 182, 206
Supreme Court 8, **40–1**, 126, **127–30**, **138–40**, 167, **174**, 331
Third Republic 7, 19, 39, 58, 120, 330, 331
see also Metropole
Franco-Indians 314, 318, 319
Franco-Indo-Vietnamese 319
Franco-Pondicherrians (*Franco-Pondichériens*) 30, 314, 317
'Franco-Vietnamese collaboration' (Sarraut) **202–3**, 231
Free French/Gaullists 275, **276–8**, 279, 282–3
French Antilles 10, 21, 62, 71
French citizenship 241, 257, 271–2, 275–6, 297, 302, 319–21, 325–6
advantages in Cochinchina **60–3**
blanket extension (1946) 306. *See also* Loi Lamine Guèye
'status naturalisation' (*naturalisation dans le statut*) 37, 39, 130, 297
see also citizenship; French Indians; personal law/personal status; renunciation (of personal status)
French Civil Code **5–6**, 8, **36–41**, 43, 45–6, 49, **51–2**, 59, 223, 314, 316, 327, 336
French East India Company 2
French Empire 4, 7, 10, 16–17, 20–1, 27, 45–6, 68, 120, 152, 156, 184, 193, 232, 273, 276, 278, 282, 306, 322, 325, **325–33**
replaced by 'French Union' (1946) 297–8
French Establishments in India 1, 5, 37, 42–3, 53, 56, 58–9, 63, 68, 84, 311, **335–7**
decree (1819) 41
elections **121–2**
see also French India
French 'genius' **252**
French Guyana 35
French India 7–11, 19–22, 28–9, 36, 38, 45, 54, 69, 119, 120, 238–9, 241, 273–4, 322, 331–2
dissolution 310
end of Customs Union with India (1949) 311
Gaullism 9
loss of Indochina (impact) 312
merger with Republic of India (completed 1962) 9, 276, 302, 303, **310–17**, 321, 324
population (religious composition) 47–8n
universal franchise 14
'French of India'. *See Français de l'Inde*
French Indian Liberation Congress 312
French Indians **3–4**, 5, **7–8**, 14–15, **16–17**, 22, 31–3, 38, 62, 68, 301
impact of decolonisation **9–10**
internal disagreements, Cochinchina **254–63**
mortality (in Cochinchina) 171
numbers 4
see also Indian French citizens
French Justice Service 98
French language 56, 59, 71, 74–5, 78, 85, 91, 97, 122, 203, 315, 316, 337. *See also* language
French law 63–4, 84, 189, 227–8, 235
French Resistance 281
French Revolution 5, 17, 35, 40, 120, 151, 278, 332n
French subjects 235, 261, 299
Indian versus Cochinchinese 63
see also Indian French subjects

INDEX

French Union (1946–) 298, 313, 328–9
French West Africa 297, 298, 305, 328
friendly societies (*amicales*) 234
Funan 248
functionaries 96–7, 142, 143, 160, 167, 208, 217, 246, 261, 273, 280, 282, 285–6, 317–18, 320
   Indian **81***
   lower-ranking ('*petits fonctionnaires*') 78, 95, 149, 158, 170, 172, 187, 240
   see also public administration
Furnivall, J. S. 23, **73**

G. M. Said (Pondicherry firm) 91
Gaebelé, H. 206
Gandhi, M. K. 210, 217, 284, 289
gas lighting 105
Gauche démocratique 143
Gauche radicale 145
Gauche républicaine démocratique 145
Geneva Conference (1954) 312
gens de couleur 35
Gia Định 89, 90t, 109, 137
Gia Long, Emperor 221
Gilbert, M. J. 291
Girault, A. 155, 174, 343
Gò Vấp province 109, 292
Goscha, C. E. 30n, **202**, 291n, **324–5**, 344
Goubert, É. **312**
government tenders **103–5**
Gracey, General D. **290–1**
Great Depression (1930s) 9, 26, 51, 78, 94, 96–7, 106, 109, 145, 149, 184, 187, 192, 212, 215–16, 219, 231, 235, 258, 260, 262–4, 267, 269, 272, 274–5, 304. *See also* inter-war years
'Greater India' 9, 221, 234, **247–54**, 262, 340
Groupe colonial 143
Guadeloupe 35, 241, 345
Gurkhas 13

Hà Tiên **114–16**

Haiphong 3, 57, 66, 74
Hanoi 3, 57, 66, 74, 79, 81*, 90–1, 107, 144, 163, 194, 202, 209, 214, 227, 233, 285, 303, 305, 309, 317
   '36 streets' (Franco–VM fighting, 1947) **298–9**
   Ba Dinh Square 290
   battle for 295
   British Consul **299–300**
   École Française d'Extrême Orient 252
   Indian community (1939) **273–4**, 274*, 292, 320
   Lycée Albert Sarraut 293
   Registration Bureau 228
   rue Paul Bert 295
Hanoi Administrative Committee 309n
Hébrard, J. **129**
Hindoue Tamoule Djana Sangam (1936–) 270
Hindu law 40–1, 64–5
Hindus 41, 47–8, 51–2, 64–65, **67–8**, 80, 83, 93, 96, 101–3, 108–9, 117, 140, 207, 218–9, **220–1**, 223, 250, 256, 265, 270, 272
historiography 197, **322**
   of citizenship 17–20, 35–40, 325–332
   of migration 20–24, 26, 73–4, 331
   national frameworks **27–9**
   of race and empire 23, 24–5, 154–7, 193–5, 323, 326, 330
   'transnational turn' **30–2**
Hitler, A. 289
Ho Chi Minh 290, 302–3, 312, 320
Ho Chi Minh City 31–2
   Bà Chiểu market 222
horses 178–9
hospitals 60, 101, 114, 168, 171, 261
Hue 174, 227
Hue incident (1937) **219**
Hugo, V. 262
Hui Bon Hoa (landowner) 107
Huỳnh Tịnh (Paulus) Của 181, 190
hygiene 101, 176, 177, 233, 244

immigration 148, 325

imperial citizenship 325n, 331, 332
Imprimerie R. Vernier 240
imprisonment 60, 64, 84, 213, 255, **288**, 352. *See also* prisoners
India 20, 32
  independence from Britain 9
  map of French Establishments **xviii**
  Partition (1947) 296, 302
'Indian' (terminology) 73
'Indian cadre' **173**, 187
Indian French citizens **4, 8–10**, 12, 20–**1**, 23–4, 29, 141, 276, 288, 294, 298–300, 313, 324–5, 331
  allegiances with other overseas Indians (1930s) 304
  colonial citizenship and contractual privileges 32–3, **153–90**
  departures from Indochina 304, 305, **306–7**, 309, **316–20**
  employment in Indochina **32, 71–118**
  importance as subject of study **332–3**
  interactions with peoples of French Indochina 33, **191–230**
  legal rights in Cochinchina **60–3**
  loss of lives at Dien Bien Phu 318
  'pioneers' of French colonialism **246–7**
  stayers-on (post-1954) **319**
  voters ('venality') 132, 140, **149**, 207, 242
  see also renouncers
Indian French subjects 52, **64–6**, 68, 250. *See also* French subjects; non-renouncers
Indian Independence League (IIL) **286–9**, 290, 296
Indian National Army (INA) 279, **286–9**, 290, 291
Indian National Congress 210, 211, 273
Indian Ocean **21**, 26, 176, 233, 313–14
'Indian proletariat' 261
Indian public profile (interwar Indochina) 33, **231–72**, 324
'Indian shops' **88–93**
Indian Union 309, 313, 314, 316
Indian vote (Cochinchina) **32–3**, **119–52**

'indigenous personal law' **40–1**, 42
indenture. *See* contract labour
Indo-French 57, 71, 82, 232, 234, 250, 263, 314
Indo-French *créoles* **10–11**
Indo-Vietnamese 29, 30, 31, 74, 198, 221, 301
Indochina/French Indochina **xx,** 2, 3, 9–11, 15–16, 19, 22, 24, 29, 309, **310**, 322, 332
  employment **32, 71–118**
  Indian migration (distinguishing features) **12–13**
  Japanese coup (March 1945) 275, **285–6**, 299
  Japanese occupation (1940–5) **278–89**
  renunciation and migration (links) **53–8**
  'second metropole' 8
  Vichyite 9, **276–86**, 320, 325n, 345
Indochina Exchange Office 308
Indochina Wars
  First (1946–54) 274, 294, 295, 298
  Second ('Vietnam', 1964–75) 319
Indochine-Inde (newspaper, 1936–7) 78, 108–9, **218**, 237, 243, **243–4***, 270, 306
Indochinese Association of Nattukottai Chettiars (1931–) 96, 97, **269–70**
Indochinese Union 3, 325
Indōṣin-Indiyā (1939–41) 237
inheritance 40, 51, 109
intellectuals 227, **251–2**, 314, 323–4
inter-Asian connections **324–5**
inter-colonial connections 2–3, 220–3, 330–2
intermarriage **222–7**
  and 'boundaries of rule' **154–5**
  see also créoles; Indo-Vietnamese; marriage; *métis*; mixed unions
internal security service (*Service de la Sûreté*) 66, 78, 91, **108–9**, 211–12, 219, 257–9
International Commission of Supervision and Control 312

INDEX

interpreters 97, 146, 186
interwar years **8–9**, 13, 16, 24, 25, 49, 76, 101, 103, **106–8**, 113, 118, 146, 184, 190, 192, 214, 221, 231–5, 243, 247, 306, **323–4**. *See also* Great Depression
Ishmael, J.M.M. 106
Islam 5, 51, 89
Islamic law 37, 40, 64–5, 224

J.M.M. Ishmael Frères (firm) 91, 97n, **106–7**, 110, 288
Japan 9, 196
    advance into southern Indochina (July 1941) 283
    pan-Asianism **283–9**
    surrender (1945) 289, 291, 295
Japanese occupation 274, 307, 320
Japanese people 62, 157, 164, 266
Java 198, 289, 290
Jennings, E. 282, 345
jewellers 98
Jews **38–9**, 151, **278–9**
journalism 196, 233, 239
journalists 88, 192, 195, 216, 240
judicial service (Cochinchina) 184, 186. *See also* magistrates
juges suppléants 77
justice system (colonial) **76–7, 84**

Kampot 116
Kampung Thom (Cambodia) 107
Karikal **1–2**, 5, 11, 45, 47–9, 54, 56, 66, 84–5, 99, 125, 165, 227, 277, 304, 311, 313, 317
Katthéappathévar 108–9, 270
Kempeitai 286
keramat 221
Kewelram Affair (1946). *See* Palace of Silks Affair
Khmers 4, 121, 220–1. *See also* Cambodians
kinship (inter-racial) **222–9**
kitangi 96

Koothanallur 66, 91
Kratie (Cambodia) 57
Krull, G. 292
Kuomintang (Guomindang) 295
Ky, Pétrus 181–2

L'Impartiale (newspaper) 148
L'Inde Illustrée (magazine, 1933–4) 237, 265, 266, **267***
La Dépêche (newspaper) 148
La Lutte (newspaper), 219
La Vang (pilgrimage site) 222
labour 12, 72, 328
Lami, S. 236, **237***, **313–14**, 318, 319
land 216, **268**
    urban and rural investments **106–10**
landed 'aristocracy' 41
landowners 88, 94, 96, 106, 191, **195**, 196, 201, 203, **216**, 261
language 72, 73, 78, 82, 117, 176, 179, 214, 237, 241, 248, 294, 305. *See also* French language
Lannes, G. 169
Lao people 15, 29, 202, 325
Laos 3, 145, 318, 319
Laurans (lawyer) 123n, 126, **129–34**, 242n
law 153, 157, 166, 189
    courts 6, 97
    of *indigénat* 213
    profession 78, **86–7**, 88, 105, 240
lawyers 87, 97–8, 126, 130, 160, 168, 173, 180, 254, 270, 297, 305
Lê Văn Duyệt, General (mausoleum) **221–2**
League of Human Rights 61, 181
leave 60, 168, 171, 176, 186, 194, 223, 255, 261, 277, 281, 304, 308
Lebbais (Tamil Muslim group) 66–7
Leconte, N. 31n, 178, 345
legal clerks 71, 84, 86–7, 97, 105, 236
legal status 73, 155, 163, 166, 294, 315
    in India and Indochina **32, 34–70**
Legion of Honour 145, 148, 288n
Leiden University 248

Letourneau, J. **313–14**
Lévi, D. 297
Lévi, S. **249–50**, 251
licensing fee (*patente*) 98
lighthouse guards 71, 77, 78, 84, 136, **165**, 170, 186
livestock **99–103**, 104–5, 108–9, 117
loges **303**, 310
Loi Lamine Guèye (1946) **297–8**, 306, 328
loincloths (*vershti*) 95
London 281
Long, M. 204
Long Xuyên 90t, 109
loyalty 5, 13, 27, 36, 65, 141, 167–8, 170, 205, 243, 246, 249, 252, 256–7, 263, 282, 289, 306, 313
Lục Tỉnh Tân Văn (News of Six Provinces) **197–200**, 215, 217, 226ß
Luxembourg 116
lycées 2, 4, 55, 305, 307

Madagascar 13n, 176, 345, 318
Madras 66
magasiniers 2, 85
magistrates 45, 54, 84, 86, **87***, 109, 126, 132, 138, 150, 305, 318
Mahé 1, 49, 311, 313
malabar carriages 99, 137, 190
'Malabars' (people) iv, xii–xiii, 99, 116, 124, 133, 136–7, 146, 151–2, 226, 228
Malaya/Malay States 12, 13, 68n
Malays 155, 157, 162, 164, 198, 221
Marakkayar/Marécar (Tamil Muslim group) 12, 66–7, 347
Mariamman (goddess) 218, **220–1**
Mariapragassam, A. **227–8**
Mariapragassam, P. L. (Nguyen Dinh Luy) **227–9**
Marius, C. 346
Marius, E. 78, **260**
Marius, F. (*né* Dourressamy) 165
Marius Le Prince, André **280–1**
market tax **103–4**, 105, 199, 212, 213, 214
market vendors 119, 214, 224

'marketplace' 23, 74
Marquis, É. 8, **88**, **206–7**, 236, **239–40**, 241–2, **246**, **251–2**, **256–7**
marriage **40–1**, **51–2**, 64, 80–1, 86, **222–7**, 319, 323, 335–6
Marseille 239
'martial races' 13, 14, 79, 177
Martinique 35, 241
Mascarenes 21, 62, 71
Maspéro, G. 203
Matsumoto, S. 284–5
Mauritius 40
Mayavaram 66
Médaille de Reconnaissance 309
medals 77–8, 236, **237***, **307–9**, 320
medic (*agent sanitaire*) 88
medical profession 86, **87–8**, 105, 239
Mekong Delta 3, 4, 16, 30, 79, 85, 89, 93, 94, 104, 113, 195, 198, 213, 216, 221, 248, 269, 323, 341, 347, 351
Mendès-France, P. 312
merchants 11, 12, 15, 20, **26**, 68, 71, 74, **88–93 (89*)**, **98**, 104, 112–13, 116, **117**, 124, 132, 142, 214, 217, **224–6**, 264, 273, 285, 292–3, 295, 298–9, 301–2, 309, 316, 323
Metcalf, T. **21**, 22
métis 61–2, **155**, **164**, 228, 350
Metropole 17–18, 20, 27, 30, 35, 36, 45, 61, 69, 121, 138, 141, 149, 153, 204, 208, 322, 325
 'second metropoles' 8, 10
 see also France
Michalon, P. 46–7
migrants
 to Indochina 10–13
 status in Cochinchina 60–70
migration **20–7**, 73, 202, 331
 Chinese and Indian compared (Indochina) 15–17
 internal to Indochina 30n, 202, 324–5
 links to renunciation **53–8**
 to Southeast Asia 10–15, 20–3
 global 'age of mobility' (from late 19th century) **20**, **333**
 see also historiography of migration

INDEX

military service **56–8**, 62, 137, 175, 205, 215, 224, 280, 285, **318**. *See also* soldiers
milk and milkmen 5, 48, **100–3**, 104, 108–11, 113–14, 117, **215**, 216
Mille, P. **151–2**
Minh Hương 63, 63n
Minh Tân (New Light) movement **195–201**, 216
mise en valeur 156
missing persons 294, 298
mission civilisatrice 208, 229, 247, 249
mission schools (Pondicherry) 5
mixed unions 154, 155, **223–227**, 330
mobile citizens 10, 27, **32–3**, 317, 321, **322–33**
modernism 8, 24, 25, **191–2**, 196, 243, 244, 273, 323
Moïs 63, 63n
moneylenders 64, 67, 91–3, **94**, 96, 109, 212. *See also* Nattukottai Chettiars; Chettiars; Chettys
Monin, P. 146–7, 211
Moniteur Officiel (later *Journal Officiel*) of French India 47, 277, 336
Monivong, King 145
Monniridh, Prince 308
Montpellier 88
mooring tax 103, 104, 212, 213
moral values 7, 45–6, 54, 59, 178, 188, 208, 251, 252, 268, 278
Morice, Dr. A. 99
mosques 12n, 31, 91n, 92n, 214, 271n, 348
Mouhamed Haniff 91
Mountbatten, Admiral Lord 290
Moutet, M. 303
Mouttayah, Mr. (lawyer) 97–8
municipal decrees 180–1, 182
municipalities 74, 126, 323
murder **226–7**, 295, 298
Muslims 5, **38–9**, 47–8, 51, 54, **66–7**, 71, 101, 109–10, 140, 198, 214, 230, 250, 256, 264–5, 273, 299, 320
Indian (in France) 29

South Indian 74, 116, **117**, **223–4**
Tamil **66**, **88–93** (89*), **98**, 104, **221**, 270–2, 301–2
mutual associations 234, **235**, 240
Mutualité Hindoue 254, **258–9**, 260
merger (1934) with *Mutuelle des Indo-Français* 235, **261**
Mutuelle Hindoue de la Cochinchine **261–2**, **282–3**
Mutuelle des Indo-Français Employés de Commerce et d'Industrie (1931–) 236, **259–61**
merger (1934) with *Mutualité Hindoue* 235, **261**
Mỹ Tho 54, 76, 90t, 109, 196, 282

Nadin, L. 236, **237***
Nag, K. 211, **251–3**
Nagalingapoullé (entrepreneur) 108
Naidoos (caste) 78
Napoleon III 120
nation-states 274, 276, 324
National Democratic Front (*Front Nationale Démocratique*) **311–12**
nationalism 24, 26–7, 195, 197, 210–11, 239, 257, 261, **274–6**, 279, 284, 289–90, 294–5, 301, 320–1
'native' employment status 78, 166–72, **184–9**
'natives' 40, 46, 75, 155
suffrage ('old' versus 'new' colonies) **120–3**
Nattukottai Chettiars **67**, 74, **93–8**, 109, **117**, **223**
as landowners **106**
legal status 97
see also Chettiars
naturalisation 7–8, 29, 32, 52, 62, 96, 116, 121, 138, 141, 155, 166, 174, 182, 185, 193, 201–2, 205–6, 210, 228–9, 327, 330. *See also* citizenship; French citizenship
naturalisation decree (Cochinchina, 1881) 34, 39–40, **58–60**, 69, 155, 158, 330
Nazis 275, 276, 289

363

Nehru, J. **273**, 289–90, 292, **303**, 312, 315, **320–1**
Nellitope (village) **48**
Nestlé 101
networks 12, 67, 68, 71–2, 73, 77, 79, 85, 91, 92, 104, 108–9, 117, 118, 217, 292–3, 323, 346
newspapers 81, 83, 104, 146, **148**, 170, 181–2, 187, **196–201**, **188**, **203–11**, **216–19**, 232, **233–43**, 253, 303, 305
Nghệ An province 293
Nguyễn An Ninh 203–4, **207**, 208, 210, 211–12
  'question indienne' **201–12**
Nguyen Dinh Luy (P. L. Mariapragassam) **227–9**
Nguyễn dynasty 2, 3, 65
Nguyễn Phan Long 203, **206–7**
Nice 61
night-watchmen 68
Nîmes 318
Nông Cổ Mín Đàm (*Discussions on Commerce and Agriculture*) 196, 197, 200
non-renouncers (*non-renonçants*) 6, 11, 63, 83, 96, 119, 121–2, 125–7, 129–30, 137–9, 152, 316. *See also* renouncers
Norodom, King 132
North Africans 215
North Vietnam (DRV) 290, 309, 312, 319–21
Noyant-sur-Allié 320

Oc Eo (Mekong Delta) 248
officier de santé (Pondicherry) 87, 105
Ohier, Admiral 75–6
oil presses and oil pressers 102, **112***, 113
Opinion (newspaper) 238
'Option' (1956) **315–17**, 324
originaires (Senegal) 37, 39, 327
Outrey, E. 83, 143, **144–50**, 151*, 170n, 183, **185–7**, **207**, 208n, 212n, **240**, 241–2, 258

Pajaniappatevane (Pajaniappathévar) **102–3**, 108, 109
Pakistan 296–7, 299, 300, 302, 320
Palace of Silks Affair (1946) **295–7**, 298
Pallis (caste) 102
pan-Asianism 9, 234, 247, 251, 275, 278–9, **283–9**
Pardon, N. **124–8**
pariah 5, **42**, 47–8, **49–50**, **54–5**, 72, 78, 207, 210, 258, 262
Paris 29, 35, 126, 143, 160, 172, 182, 209, 305, 313, 318
  École Coloniale 203
Pâris, P. 144
Paris Match 289
Parsis 68, 250
Parti Français (Pondicherry) 238
Parti Socialiste de l'Inde Française (PSIF) 312
Patel, V. 290
paternity 51, 62, 191
  false recognition of **227–8**
Pathans 68, 347
Patriotes de l'Inde Française 314
Pattanavan caste 102
Pattanis 67
peddlers 213
Penang 57, 323
pension funds affair (1881) **157–66**, 280
pensions 57, 134, 168, 171, 186, 261, 315
personal law/personal status 6, 8, 34, **37–40**, **41–9**, 54, 57, 58, 60, 63–4, 68, 75, 85, 121, 140, 155, 157, 162, 166
  Catholic 51–2
  Hindu 52, 64–5
  Muslim 64–5, 66, 91
  regulation in British and French India **6–7**, **64–5**
  see also 'caste and creed'; civil status; French Civil Code; 'indigenous personal law'; renunciation (of personal status); status naturalisation; 'usages and customs'
Pétain, Marshal P. **276–8**, **282–3**, 345
Peters, E. J. 215n, 348–9

INDEX

petit bourgeoisie 72
petit fonctionnaires. See functionaries
petitions 7, 157, **158–62**, 169, **174–5**, 178, 179, 185, 219–20
petrol stations 98
Phan Bội Châu 196, 209
Phan Chu Trinh 209
philanthropy 109, 233, 270
Phnom Penh 3, 48, 79, 82, 88, 101, 113–15, 145, 293, 304–5, 308, 318–19
  in World War II 285–6
photography **81**
Phủ Lý 302
Phước Tân village 213
piastre 168, 171
Picanon, É. (Lieutenant Governor of Cochinchina) 139
plantations 12, 72
'plural society' **23–4**, **73–4**, 105, 117, 272, 323, 343, 347
police and policemen 13, 50, 71, 77–8, 84, 98, 117, **136**, 142, 170, 186, 208, 260, 280, 285, 292–5, 311, 317, 323
  Indian policemen in Saigon **172–84**, 187–8, 234, 246
polygamy 38, 46, 224
Pondicherrians (*Pondichériens*) 29, 314, 315, 318
Pondichéry **1–3**, 5, 11, 14, 32, 34, 40, **41–2**, 45–50, 52, 54–7, 69, 76, 78–87 (81*), 97, 99, 101–2, 107, 114, 122–3, 125, 140–1, 143, 145, 159–61, 182, 185, 208, 211, 236–7, 239, 245, 254, 256–7, 273, 280, 284, 286, 288–9, 295, 304–7, 316, 319–20, 327, 329, 331
  Conseil de la République 312
  Gaullist (WW2) 275, **276–8**, 283
  smuggling 311–2
  maps xviii, **xix**
  transfer of sovereignty to India (1956) 27, 28, 313
  'little Saigon' (Reddiar Palayam) 48, 285
  lycée 2, 55
  Savana textile works 311
Villa Aroumé 110
Villa Ernest Outrey 150, **151***
Pondicherry Indians 7
Pondicherry Medical School 87
Pondicherry Municipality 308
port cities 3, 12, 81, 104, 324
porteurs de contraintes 76
Portuguese people 10, 111
postal services 5, 84, 99, 114, 115
postcards **89***, **95***, **100***, **112***, 113
postcolonialism 10, 32, 274–6, 318, 321–2, 324
postmen 71, 77–8, 146, **167–9**, 170, 172, **187–9**
postwar era (1945–) 9, 33, 287, **289–309**, 318, 328
Poulo Condore **77–8**, 88, 239
Pounnoutamby (later Pounnoutamby Laporte) **42–4**, **44***, 49, 52, **53–4**, 134, 144, 182n
poverty 94, 103, 319
pragmatism 19, 35, 50, 153, 184
presidential decree (1871) **63–4**, 162
prison guards 77, 78, 170
prisoners 104, 105, 291. *See also* imprisonment
private life 59, **154–6**
private sector 261, 280, 319
professions 83, **86–8**, 315–16
Progressive Society for Renounced *Valangamougattars* 50–1
propaganda 278, 279, 290–1, 302
protest 8, 16, 46, 71, 136, 144, 157–8, 165, 167, 172, 174–5, 182–3, 185, 187, 210, 217, 220, 234, 236, 261, 313, 332n
Prouchandy, Darmanaden (or Pierre) **111**, 117, 347
  steamboat ventures **113–16**
Prouchandy, L. 108, 265, 319, 347
Prouchandy, S. 108, 110
psychology 215, 314
public administration 3, 4, 8, 11, 13–14, 33, 41, 45, 53–4, 56, 61, **74–84**, 85, 86, 91, 94–5, 113,

365

116–17, 145, 156, 185, 192, 317, 319, 323
  admission of more Vietnamese (1925 reform) 187
  higher classes 186–7
  lower-level 'European' ranks 184, 186
  middle-level positions 184
  see also civil servants
public culture **232–3**
public sphere (instruments) **233–43**
publishers and publishing 88, 203, 236
Puducheri. *See* Pondicherry

Qing (Ch'ing) Empire 20
Quaintenne, R. **237–9**
Quaintenne, V. 237–8
quốc ngữ 197, 203

race and racism 17–18, 32–3, **63–4**, 132, 142, 146, 152–3, 156–7, 159, **162–3**, 176–8, 189, 191–2, **197–8**, 199–200, 208, 212, 215, 222, **224–9**, 230, 232–3, 253, 264, 272, **278–81**, 323, 326, 330–2
Rạch Giá 54, 89n, 90t, 196, 282
racial
  discourse 23, **24–5**
  hierarchy **193–5**
radical politics **209–10**
railways 77, 84, 132, 186, 281
Rangassamy-Naiker, C. 65, 110–11
Rangoon 323
Rassendren, L. 182
Ratinassamy, A. **292–4**, 302
Ratinassamy, L. **228–9**, **292–5**
Rawthers (Tamil Muslim group) 66–7
'recognition' (of paternity, *reconnaissance*) 227–8
Red Cross 277
Reddiar caste 83
Reddiar Palayam ('Little Saigon') **48**, 285
religion 13, 14, 65, 72, 73, 250, 270, 323
religious practices, syncretic **220–2**, 229
remittances 91, 277, 308
renouncers (*renonçants*) **6–8**, 22, 25, 26–7, 30, **43**, 44*, 60–1, 64, 66, 69–71, 124, 128, 140, 143–52, 211–12, 222–3, 228–9, 235–6, 238, 249–50, 270, 314, **326–7**, 329, 330–1, 331–2
  contractual privileges 32–3, **153–90**
  Hindu and Muslim 47–8, **51**
  see also citizenship; French citizenship; non-renouncers
rental income 94, 106–7, 108
renunciation (of personal status) 4, 29, **34–5**, 38, 122, 185, 228, 262–3, 306, 329
  versus *Annamite* naturalisation **58–60**
  Cochinchina versus Pondicherry **52–3**, 53t
  distinct from worldly renunciation **6**
  extent and appeal **46–53**
  influence of religion on **47–8, 51**
  local agency 43
  and migration (links) **53–8**
  see also citizenship; French citizenship; renouncers
renunciation decree (French India, 1881) 34, 39–40, 43, 45, **46**, 52, 58, 69, 75, 125, 157, 162, 183, 316–17
  full text **335–7**
renunciation movement 32, 34, **40–6**
Representatives of Pondicherrian Interests 314
republican principles 7, 17, 19, 39, 40, 50, 57, 134, 142, 145, 152–3, 174, 184, 193, 205–6, 212, 226–7, 279, 283, 326, 330–1, 342
République Française (newspaper) 313
restaurants 113, 243, 308
Réunion 35, 57, 62, 83, 207, 241, 318
Réveil Saigonnais (1907–29) 143, 146–7, 188, **206–7**, 217–18, 226–7, 236, **237–40**, 241–2, **249–50**, 251, 254, 263, 266–7
Viénot Street incident (1928) **264–5**
Réveil Social (renouncer-led society, 1907–) 50–1, 55
riba (interest) 92
rice 93, 106, 269, 285
ritual pollution 80
Robaitche Claive (surname) 58, 59

INDEX

Robequain, C. **61–2**, 105, 111, 349
Royal Order of Sahamétrai 308
rubber 12, 89
rubbish collection (tax farms) 104
Rudner, D. 97
rule of law **140**, 156, 184, 193
Russian Empire 20

Saada, E. 19 , 30n, 40, 62n, 155, 228n, 350
Saigon 2–3, 7–9, 14, 24–5, 29, 50, 52–3, 55, 57, 61, 65–6, 68, 71–2, 74, 79–82, 85–90, 97–9, 101, 103–14, 116, 119, 124, 145, 159–60, 163, 166–8, 186, 190, 196, 209, 211, 214, 221, 233, 238, 248, 272–3, 275, 288, 295, 298–9, 304–6, 317–20, 331
  20th Indian Division **289–94**, 303
  campaign to defend Indian policemen **172–84**, 187–8, 234, 246
  customs department 280
  expatriates (Tamil purveyors) **110–13**
  Indian visitors **263**, 269, **270–1**
  interwar years **323–4**
  Japanese 'harsh treatment' 284
  map (1928) **93***
  Mayoral election (1925) 147
  municipal council elections 121
  municipal elections (1919) 211
  postwar nostalgia **307**
  street names **92**
  Vichyite **276–8**
  visit by Tagore, actual (1929) 234, **253–4**; ~ projected (1924) **250–1**
  zones of South Indian Muslim enterprise **92**
Saigon, places and incidents in
  Adran street 111
  Amiral Roze Street Temple incident (1936) **218–19**, 220
  'Bombay boycott' (1925) **217**
  Catinat Street 91, 92, 93, 110, 217, 250
  Central Market 107
  City Hall 136
  Civil Tribunal 260
  Continental Hotel 309
  Court of Appeal 76–7
  Dakao quarter 226
  Go Vap suburb 292
  Lagrandière Street **113**
  Lycée Chasseloup Laubat 319
  Majestic Hotel (Bose speech) 289
  Ohier Street **95–6**, **98**, 108, 111
  rue d'Espagne 112
  rue Viénot incident (1928) **217–18**, **264**
  Vannier Street 92, 93
Saigon-Bangkok steamboat line 114
Saigon-Dimanche (1927–35) 86, 96, 108, 147, **149**, 188, 215, 218, 236–7, **240–3**, 245, **246**, 253, 255, 259, **267–9**, 270
  'Clothing Crusade' (1933) **265–7**
Saigon Indian Association (1943–) **286–7**
Saigon Municipality 123, 242, 259, 292. *See also* Duranton
Saigon Public Library 239
Saigon Tribunal 77
Saigon Vartamany (1928) 237
St. Domingue (Haiti) **35**
St. Denis (Réunion) 57
Saint Louis, sub-brigadier 173, **180–2**
Saint-Jacques, H. D. **109–10**, **150**
salaries 4, 60, 74, 87, 142, 157, 186, 194, 235, 261, 279, 314, 328
  'European' entitlements 75, 159, 168
  'colonial supplement' 79–80
Saravane, L. **312–13**
Sarraut, A. **185–6**, **202–3**, 231
Sayyids 67
schools (Franco-Tamil) 82
science 233, 252
Senatus-Consulte (1865) **38–9**
Senegal (Sénégal) 38, 43, 57, 152
  Quatre Communes 5, 36, 37
  originaires 37, 39, 327
sepoys (auxiliaries) 57
servants 42, 50, 72, 81, 91, 116, 215
service des rapatriés d'Indochine 319, 320
sesame press **112***

shipping lines 304
shop houses (*compartiments*) 106, 107, 108
shopkeepers 91, 192, 198, 217
shops **88–93**, 214, 301
Sihanouk, King Norodom **307–8**
Sikhs 13, 68
Sinamour (Cinamour), Mr. 301, 302
Sindhis 12, 68, 217, 295, 296
Singapore 323
Sinnas, E. L. **107–8**, 319
Sinnas, R. 107
Sinnaya, L. 87, 88, 211, 236, 351
slavery **35–6**, 38, 120
slaughterhouses (tax farms) 104
Smith, R. B. 204, **210–11**, 350
smuggling 1, **311–12**
Soai Rieng 109–10
Sóc Trăng 98, 168
Soccalingam, Ra. (banker) 68, 96, **143–4**, 144n, 182, 236, 238n
social class 13, 72, 172, 203, 212, 216, 244, 258, 261, 311
Social Darwinism 24
social inequality 256–7
social reform 25, 38, 43, 72, 196, 235, 238–239, **256–257**, 263, **265–267**
'social union' **254–8**
Socialist Republic of Vietnam 30
Société de Secours Mutuels des Indiens en Cochinchine 236
Société mutuelle des créoles 306
soldiers 13–14, 22, 71, 146, **226–7**, 231, 246. *See also* military service
Solidarité (mutual association) 236, 240, 246, 254, **255–7**
Sơn Nam 31n, 195, **197**, **199–200**, 213n, 226n, 350–1
South Vietnam (Republic of Vietnam) 30, 312, 319
Southeast Asia 9, **12**, 26, 67, 72, 73, 81, 103, 154, 221, **247–8**, 243–4, 250, 266, 273, **274–5**, 279, 283, 284,

286–7, 290, 312, 314, 321, **324**, 339–42, 346, 350
age of mass migration **20–1**
interwar cosmopolitanism **232–4**
'special cadre' 178, 180, 187–8
'special superior cadre' 173, 178, 180, 183, 188
spices 111, 112
sport 233, 234, 245, 308
state 17, 36, 156, 326, 332
'status naturalisation' (*naturalisation dans le statut*) 37, 39, 130, 297
statut personnel. See personal law/personal status
steamboats **113–16**
Subbiah, V. **311–12**
subsidies 15, **113–14**, 116
Sumatra 12
Sûreté. See internal security service
surnames **57–8**, 96, 98, 165, 336
Syndicat des Français de l'Inde 182, 234, 236

Tagals (Filipinos) **62**, 155, 164, **165–6**
Tagore, R. 211
   visit (actual) to Saigon (1929) 234, **253–4**
   visit (projected) to Saigon (1924) **250–1**
Tai, Hue-Tam Ho 141, 145, 201n, 237n, 351
tailors 92
Tamil schools (Saigon) 82
Tamil Hindus 67–8
Tamils 1, **11–12**, 14, 24, 70, 134, 177, 194, 198, 214–15, **222–7**, 230, 236, 243, 263, 323
single name 'norm' 43
Tamils: areas of employment in Indochina **32, 71–118**
   bankers **93–8**
   cafe owners and shopkeepers **110–13**
   'Indian shops' and Muslim enterprises **88–93**
   land ownership **106–10**

INDEX

livestock and transport **99–103**
military service **84–6**
milk and milkmen **100–3**, 215
professionals **86–8**
steamboats **113–16**
tax farms and tendering **103–5**
Tananarive 305
Tanjore district 66
Tavalacoupam 110
tax 15, 16, 26, 60, **65–6**, 71, 76, 84–5, 91, 125, 142, 156, 159–60, 163, 208, 316, 331
  farming **103–5**, 192, 198, 199, **212–14**, 216, 224, 323
  inspectors (*porteurs de contraintes*) 167, **169–72**
Tây đen 214–15
Tây Ninh 90t, 103
teachers 196, 201, 319
temples 31, 95–6, 106, 108, 219, **220–1**, 223, 250, 254, 267
tenants 94, 98, 195
Ternisien, H. 37n, 120n, **130–7**, 246n
textiles 117, 311. *See also* cloth trade and traders
Thái Nguyên prison revolt (1917) 254–5
Thaipusam chariot procession 267
Thanh Hóa province 293
theft 218, 219
Thompson, V. 140, 144n, 148, 149n, 150–1, 207n, 351
Thủ Dầu Một 145, 199
Thường Tín (town) 300, 303
Tirouvanziam, Dr. 88
Tonkin 3, 12, 48, 72, 91, 254–5
Tourane **224–6**
traders 2, 11, 12, 15, 66, 191, 195, 198, 216, 224
  (petty) 11, 68, 192
  see also 'Bombay' traders
Trait d'Union (Pondicherry newspaper) **305–9**, 313
Trần Duy Hưng **309***
transport 20, **99–103**, 104, 105, 117
Treaty of Cession (1956) 313, **315–17**

Treaty of Paris (1815) 56, 85
Trevor-Wilson, A. **300**
Tribune Indigène (newspaper, 1917–25) 67, 203, 204–5, 247
Tribune Indochinoise (1926–42) 203, 204
Trung Lập Báo (newspaper) 217
Tulukar caste 67
Turkey 273

Union Amicale Indo-Française 146
'untouchables' 6, 14, 49. *See also* pariahs
Uppalam 48
'usages and customs' 40, 52
usury 94, 215–16, **267–8**

Valangamougattar caste 48, **48n**, 50–1
Valmaire, M. **55–6**, 352
Vannia caste 48, 78, 102
Varenne, A. **187–8**, 205, 231, 240
Vassal, G. M. 99, 352
Vellala caste 14, **41–2**, **48–9**, 53, 78
verbal abuse **213–15**, 218, 219, 225
Vernier, R. R. 149, 236, **240–2**, **265–6**, **268–9**, 270
Vichy Government 275, 286, 288, 320, 345
  fall (1944) 284
  French Indian experiences of **278–83**
  slogan 278, 281
Vientiane 318
Viet Minh (1941–) 26–7, 195, 272, 275, **292–5**, **298–303**, **309**, 312, 317, 320–1, 324
  attack on French forces in Hanoi (1946) 295
  propaganda **290–1**
Vietnam 197
  modern state **27–8**
  independence (1945/1954–) 9, 118, 209, 272, 275–6, 289–90, 302–4
Vietnamese people 15, 29, 31, 121, 125, 141, 181, 202, 325
  attitude towards French naturalisation 182, **205**

369

constructions of racial hierarchy **193–5**
engagement with Indian migrants **33, 191–230**
political representation 203–4, **271–2**
see also 'Annamites'
Vietnamese reformers 8, 184, 192–3, 195, 212, 233, 247, 253, 275, 323. *See also* Constitutionalists
Vinh (Central Vietnam) 299, **300–2**, 303
Vinh incident (1928) **217–18**
Vĩnh Long 90t, 214
violence 192, 207, 212–13, **216–18, 226–7**, 264, 275, 285, 291, 294, **295**, 311, 312
Võ Văn Kiệt 214

Wavell, Lord 290
Weber, J. 46, **52**
West Indies 132, 133

Winnacker, R. A. 119–20n, 140–1, 352
'Wish List of Vietnamese People' (1925) **205–6**
women 36n, 43, 74, **80–2**, 86, 154, 157, 164, 179, 191, 194, 199, 209, 214–15, **217**, 219, **222–7**, 233, 237–8, 301, 305, 319
World War I 65, 108, 146, 184, 185, 201, 205, 231, 239, 271
World War II 4, 9, 26, 29, 118, 140, 272–3, **274–89**, 304, 320, 324. *See also* Indian Independence League; Indian National Army; Japan; Vichy Government
'writers' (*fonctionnaires*) 75–6

Xavier, J. 87, 97, 254

Yadaval caste 102
Yanaon 1, 311, 313
youth 244, 245, 279